Queering Straight Teachers

OMPLICATED

A Book Series of Curriculum Studies

William F. Pinar
General Editor

VOLUME 22

PETER LANG
New York • Washington, D.C./Baltimore • Bern
Frankfurt am Main • Berlin • Brussels • Vienna • Oxford

Queering Straight Teachers

Discourse and Identity
in Education

Edited by
Nelson M. Rodriguez & William F. Pinar

PETER LANG
New York • Washington, D.C./Baltimore • Bern
Frankfurt am Main • Berlin • Brussels • Vienna • Oxford

Library of Congress Cataloging-in-Publication Data

Queering straight teachers: discourse and identity in education /
edited by Nelson M. Rodriguez, William F. Pinar.
p. cm. — (Complicated conversation: a book series of curriculum studies; vol. 22)
Includes bibliographical references and index.
1. Homosexuality and education. 2. Sexual minorities—Education.
3. Sexual minorities—Identity. 4. Education—Social aspects.
5. Queer theory. I. Rodriguez, Nelson M. II. Pinar, William.
LC192.6.Q86 371.826'6—dc22 2006023014
ISBN 978-1-4331-0048-2 (hardcover)
ISBN 978-0-8204-8847-9 (paperback)
ISSN 1534-2816

Bibliographic information published by **Die Deutsche Bibliothek**.
Die Deutsche Bibliothek lists this publication in the "Deutsche
Nationalbibliografie"; detailed bibliographic data is available
on the Internet at http://dnb.ddb.de/.

Cover design by Joni Holst

The paper in this book meets the guidelines for permanence and durability
of the Committee on Production Guidelines for Book Longevity
of the Council of Library Resources.

Printed in the United States of America

TABLE OF CONTENTS

PREFACE
Just Queer It

Nelson M. Rodriguez

The 21st century in the United States has already witnessed much queer cultural production. From this perspective, popular culture has been "queered" in that queer content is becoming more mainstreamed, more available for consumption, indeed much more visible. In television, for example, the hit shows *Queer Eye for the Straight Guy*, *Queer as Folk*, *Will & Grace*, *The L Word*, *TransGeneration*, and Logo—a 24-hour, 7 days-a-week gay cable channel owned by Viacom's MTV Networks division—have queered the kinds of television programming to which the public now has access. In addition, the recent and highly publicized film *Brokeback Mountain* has queered mainstream cinema—again by making queer content a part of mainstream discourse—and arguably has served as a launching pad for future mainstream queer filmic productions.

Concurrently, at the legal level, and perhaps the most vivid and politically contentious example of contemporary queering, is the queering of heterosexual marriage in such countries as Canada, South Africa, Spain, Belgium, and the Netherlands—and in the United Kingdom, in the form of civil partnerships. In Israel, while same-sex marriage is not currently legal, the Supreme Court of Israel ordered the government on November 21, 2006, to recognize same-sex marriages performed abroad, and in the same month and year same-sex civil unions were legalized in Mexico City. In the United States, the Supreme Judicial Court of Massachusetts queered heterosexual marriage when it ruled in *Goodridge* that it was unconstitutional to allow only heterosexual couples to marry. Most recently, the New Jersey Supreme Court ruled on October 25, 2006, that same-sex couples have the same rights as heterosexual couples; thus, the Court has given the New Jersey Legislature until April 24, 2007, to restructure the state marriage laws to either include same-sex couples or to create a "parallel structure." On December 16, 2006, the New Jersey Legislature passed a bill establishing civil unions. Other states like

Vermont and Connecticut have adopted civil unions. All of these legal cases, in my view, and the political movements leading up to them, have contributed to a general queering of outlook on, and rethinking of, same-sex love, desire, and relationships. To put this another way: There's been a major queering of what cultural theorist Raymond Williams would call the general *structure of feeling* about "nonnormative" gender and sexual configurations, while at the same time a calling into question of heterosexuality's moral authority. Media scholar John Fiske (1994) refers to a structure of feeling as,

> what it feels like to be a member of a particular culture, or to live in a particular society at a particular time. It is a necessarily diffuse concept, because it stretches seamlessly from the realm of the subject to that of the social order. It encompasses the formal political processes and institutions of a society, its law courts, its workplaces, its military, its schools and churches, its health care system, as well as its more informal ones, such as the family and everyday social relations in the streets, stores, and workplaces. It includes the arts and culture industries, sports and entertainment, and, at the micro level, the ordinary ways of talking, thinking, doing, and believing. (pp. 8–9)

This queering of the structure of feeling has not emerged without the rise of intense political obstacles as well as major intellectual challenges. Indeed, on the one hand, there's been a feverish (and irrational) political right-wing backlash to, say, gay marriage. One only has to be reminded, for example, in the U.S. context of the large number of states that have successfully—even if temporarily—banned same-sex marriage by writing discrimination into their state constitutions. On the other hand, and perhaps more germane to the project here, new intellectual challenges have emerged which will require a critical and ongoing examination of the meanings and politics of, and problems with, the popularization of queering and, more specifically, in terms of queer(ing) heterosexuality or straight (teacher) identity, the complex and contradictory intersections between queerness and straightness—or, as Annette Schlichter (2004) puts it, "the paradoxical figure of the queer straight" (p. 545), a point to which I return in my own chapter contribution to this volume. Still, there has been a dramatic shift in, a queering of, the structure of what it feels like to live at this particular moment in history—both as a straight person and as a GLBTQ (gay, lesbian, bisexual, transgender, and queer) "Other." With so much queering going on, then, in culture and society, gay folks and heterosexuals now have much more exposure to a range of discourses on sexual and gender realities, epistemologies, and ways of being.

In academia, the "postmodern turn" in theorizing has significantly reshaped how the categories of gender and sexuality, among other identity categories, are analytically framed and understood, especially in relation to questions of power. Here, within a postmodern frame, gender and sexual identity are shown to be thoroughly socially constructed, internally unstable/ incoherent, and performative, thus queering normative conceptualizations of gender and sexuality as fixed, coherent, and stable. If the exclusionary heterosexist landscapes of culture (e.g., popular culture) and society (e.g., heterosexual marriage) have been forever challenged (and altered/queered) by the ushering in and institutionalization of queer discourse, then it might also be accurate to say that, in academia, Modernist narratives of gender and sexual identity categories have been indefinitely undermined and queered by post-modern theorizing.

I situate *Queering Straight Teachers: Discourse and Identity in Education* within a brief discussion of the queering goings-on in academia and, more generally, in culture and society in order to highlight the point that the very *idea* of queering straight teachers—that is, the very possibility of imagining the theoretical and practical contours of such a project—would probably not be possible to articulate and conceptualize if it weren't for the fact that such an idea draws its inspiration, indeed its very possibility as an intellectual and political project, from other available discourses already immersed in forms of contemporary queering. From this perspective, then, the overarching goal of *Queering Straight Teachers* is to draw from the insights of Queer Theory, as a form of postmodern theorizing around questions of (sexual) identity and power, in order to explore *the range of possibilities for what it might mean in theory and/or in practice to queer straight teachers*.

Given this overarching goal, several related essential questions emerge that link the essays in this volume: (1) What might heterosexuality and heterosexual (teacher) identity mean when "read through" the critical framework of Queer Theory? (2) What constitutes queer heterosexuality, queer heterosexual (teacher) identity, and is the very idea of queer heterosexuality an oxymoron? (3) Can queering heterosexual (teacher) identity be seen as an example of Queer Theory's desire to disrupt identity, or is such a theoretical move a way of reifying static identity? (4) What would heterosexual identity look like in light of Queer Theory's stress on multiplicity, fluidity, and instability in identity? (5) Following queer theorist Michel Foucault, what would constitute the political project of remaking the heterosexual (teacher) self as a "work of art" in ways that resist forms of imposed subjectivity?

In addition to drawing on Queer Theory's insights in order to think through the meanings, practices, and politics of queering straight teachers, the essays in this collection, because they articulate Queer Theory to a project focusing on questions of heterosexuality and heterosexual (teacher) identity, albeit in a critical fashion and in relation to the GLBTQ Other, implicitly challenge Queer Theory in three important ways: First, because Queer Theory is deployed as an "analytic resource" for critically reading heterosexuality and identity, *Queering Straight Teachers* necessarily challenges Queer Theory's primarily exclusive focus on sexualities and sexual identities other than the heterosexual (i.e., nonnormative sexualities). Also, by using Queer Theory to think through heterosexuality, both within the context of constructing a language of critique and a language of possibility, this volume challenges Queer Theory's often critiqued insider/outsider politics—that is, Queer (Theory) positions itself, even if unwittingly, as the "sexual outlaw" and conversely situates heterosexuality and heterosexual identity as hopelessly oppressive. Finally, because the collective project here of queering straight teachers takes place within a broader context of concerns for equity and social justice, Queer Theory is being pushed to constitute itself *as a social theory*—which is to say as a social rather than ludic form of postmodernism concerned with the reform of the social by way of offering a radical critique of hegemonic heterosexuality/identity.

Along with drawing from, while simultaneously critiquing, Queer Theory, *Queering Straight Teachers* makes use of, is indirectly situated within, and contributes to the burgeoning field of study known as Critical Heterosexual Studies. The latter field aims to seriously question traditional assumptions regarding heterosexuality as natural, normal, and universal. From this perspective, Critical Heterosexual Studies importantly explores the nature of the institution of heterosexuality in an attempt to destabilize "heteronormativity"—the historical, social, political, cultural, and economic dominance of institutionalized hegemonic heterosexuality. An important concept in Critical Heterosexual Studies is what Chrys Ingraham (2005), in her publication *Thinking Straight: The Power, the Promise, and the Paradox of Heterosexuality*, calls the *heterosexual imaginary*—defined as "that way of thinking that conceals the operation of heterosexuality in structuring gender and closes off any critical analysis of heterosexuality as an organizing institution" (p. 4). This uncritical practice of thinking straight is characterized, in part, as "thinking in terms of opposites and polarities when none exist and naturalizing social practices and beliefs rather than seeing them as social, political, and economic creations.... [To think straight is to] comply with the prevailing meanings and ideological messages that organize heterosexuality" (Ingraham, 2005, pp. 2–3). According to Ingraham, some examples of thinking straight include:

> Thinking straight is to confuse institutionalized heterosexuality with something that is naturally occurring.
>
> Thinking straight means believing that the world is only and has always been hetero-sexual—not historically or regionally variant or as a cultural invention.
>
> Thinking straight is embracing a sense of entitlement, social and economic, just by virtue of participating in married heterosexual life regardless of the ways that enti-tlement denies those who do not have access to equal opportunity and citizenship.
>
> One of my favorite examples of thinking straight is the notion that white weddings and diamond rings are heterosexual traditions and not just the effect of very success-ful marketing campaigns. (pp. 3–4)

Collectively, through the specific project of queering straight teachers, the essays here hope to contribute to a constellation of discourses that disrupt the heterosexual imaginary—discourses that function as "a hindrance, a stumbling-block, a point of resistance and a starting point for an opposing strategy" (Foucault, 1978, p. 101) in relation to hegemonic heterosexuality. In this way, *Queering Straight Teachers* aims to benefit from, as much as it hopes to contribute to, a set of "reverse" discourses on heterosexuality within the evolving field of Critical Heterosexual Studies and beyond.

Lastly, *Queering Straight Teachers* aims to make a contribution to the field of (teacher) education by enlarging the scope of how gender, sexuality, and sexual identity can be taken up with prospective teachers (and other students) within the context of a critique of heterosexuality and heterosexual (teacher) identity. Indeed, while much theoretical literature exists regarding the needs and concerns of GLBTQ students and teachers, very little theorizing is available for interrogating, indeed even critically talking about, heterosexuality/identity within the context of teacher identity formation, teaching practices, and curriculum. The following broad questions, thus, are raised, implicitly and explicitly, throughout the volume: (1) What would constitute the work of queering straight teachers within the context of teacher education? (2) In what ways would the project of queering straight teachers contribute to, even radically reconstitute, the discourses of multicultural education, pedagogy, and curriculum? (3) In what significant ways might the work of queering straight teachers link the institution of schooling and education (including teacher education) to broader societal initiatives for gender, sexual, and social justice?

Works Cited

Fiske, J. (1994). *Media matters: Everyday culture and political change*. Minneapolis: University of Minnesota Press.

Foucault, M. (1978). *The history of sexuality: An introduction (Vol. 1)*. New York: Random House.

Ingraham, C. (2005). Introduction: Thinking straight. In C. Ingraham (Ed.), *Thinking straight: The power, the promise, and the paradox of heterosexuality* (pp. 2–11). New York: Routledge.

Schlichter, A. (2004). Queer at last?: Straight intellectuals and the desire for transgression. *GLQ,* 10(4), 543–564.

INTRODUCTION

A Queer Conversation, Toward Sustainability

William F. Pinar

As Nelson Rodriguez—who conceived and labored this collection[1]—observes in his preface, Critical Heterosexual Studies represents an emphasis within queer theory. A key concept is, Nelson explains, the "heterosexual imaginary," a concept specifying "'that way of thinking that conceals the operation of heterosexuality in structuring gender and closes off any *critical* analysis of heterosexuality as an organizing institution.'" An ideology with nothing "natural" about it, heterosexuality is a historical and political phenomenon, appearing some one hundred years ago in the West. What caused heterosexuality? Evidently homosexuality caused heterosexuality (see Jagose, 1996, p. 16). If "we"[2] precipitated "it," we can queer it.

To queer how gender, sexuality, and sexual identity are addressed by prospective and practicing teachers, we pose the following questions[3]:

1. What would constitute the work of queering straight teachers within the context of teacher education?
2. In what ways would the project of queering straight teachers contribute to, even radically reconstitute, the discourses of multicultural education, pedagogy, and curriculum?
3. In what significant ways might the work of queering straight teachers link the institution of schooling and education (as well as teacher education) to broader societal initiatives for gender, sexual, and social justice?

These are momentous questions. In engaging them the contributors have created a queer conversation, indeed.

Most scholars and educators "steer clear of queer theory," Liz Meyer acknowledges in the opening chapter. How well I know. My first queer theory piece[4] was greeted with snickers when it appeared in 1983. The first queer theory in education collection (Pinar, 1998) received no attention from the major—straight—journals. The status of queer theory within the academic field of education is an ongoing scandal. In a profession presumably dedicated to diversity and equal opportunity, queers remain the last legitimate target of "straights."

Meyer reminds us how persistent homophobia is, how even the most basic right to school safety—bullying is one issue on which Meyer focuses—cannot be guaranteed until broader issues of sexism are also addressed. (As Guy Hocquenghem [1978, p. 126] suggested: "It is as if society could not bear to see in man what it demands to see in women, as if to dominate women and to repress homosexuality were one and the same thing.") Even when basic survival is not at stake, Meyer observes, gender codes limit the opportunities available to students and teachers. Meyer addresses language and discourse as modalities of power; they prove primary, she suggests, in the reconstruction of school culture.

Key to reconstructing school culture, then, is revising the language comprising the school curriculum, especially those discourses considered central: the sciences. "We again live," Jane Lehr observes, "in a period in which biological explanations are dominant." In the second chapter, Lehr reviews those science-based assertions that homosexuality is natural and unchangeable, that it should be understood as "just another human variation" much like hair color or height.[5] This political employment of scientific knowledge challenges religious fundamentalism, but in so doing installs an uncritical and ahistorical view of "science." In using science to combat religious fundamentalism, Lehr asserts, we substitute for it "scientific fundamentalism."

Science then, not the Bible, presumes to guide personal and public decision-making. Moreover, by employing a discourse of genetic difference, Lehr cautions, gay, lesbian, bisexual, transgender, and queer (GLBTQ) activists and allies may inadvertently legitimate the public's pathologizing of homosexuality. Might "the gay gene" be used for fetal testing? Might insurance companies refuse coverage for individuals with the "gay gene" because they may have a greater risk of becoming HIV-positive? Lehr is also concerned that reliance upon genetic explanations of difference undermines other social justice initiatives. Lehr recommends historicizing scientific knowledge and sexuality[6] in order to critique the distinction between homosexuality and heterosexuality, thereby providing opportunities to queer straight teachers, straight students, and ourselves.

"Straightness is performed and nourished so that it may perpetuate itself," Reta Ugena Whitlock observes in the chapter that follows, "but queer happens." Reta should know, having taught for fourteen years in conservative Alabama schools. "Somehow," she continues in a style for which I predict she will become well-known, "I did not win an Academy Award for 'Best Female Queer in the Role of a Heterosexual' during the six months following my divorce, despite the 'cast of thousands' in the production." As the humor implies, this was a serious affair, simultaneously queer and fundamental, adjectives she claims as integral to her identity. Reta admonishes her fellow Christians to engage in dialogue in order to honor Jesus' command to love one another.

There was not much dialogue concerning the use of *The Heterosexual Questionnaire* in a high school in the Australian state of Victoria in 2003, as Mary Louise Rasmussen, Jane Mitchell, and Valerie Harwood explain in chapter four. The *Questionnaire* included the following questions: (1) What do you think caused your heterosexuality? (2) If you have never slept with a person of the same sex, is it possible that all you need is a good lesbian/gay lover? (3) How can you become a whole person if you limit yourself to compulsive and exclusive heterosexual behavior? In response, the Premier of Victoria called not for collective self-examination but for an official inquiry. The hapless teacher involved was never interviewed by the press; even the authors of the training program came to concede that the *Questionnaire* was inappropriate for use with high school students. "Is the use of the *Questionnaire* in this context," Rasmussen, Mitchell and Harwood ask wryly, "a classic case of curriculum intervention gone awry?" You will find their answers provocative and insightful.

Schooling is a form of masculine agency, Yin-Kun Chang reminds, "where ideologies, discourses, representations and material practices systematically privilege straight boys and men." During the fall of 1999, Chang interviewed queer teachers in Taiwan. Chang met teachers resisting heterosexual hegemony, including teachers who were not queer identified, but who nonetheless affiliated themselves with queer political struggles. This was "my first time inquiring among those who have devoted themselves to resist heterosexual hegemony while having unambiguously straight identities." To make sense of what he learned, Chang introduces the intriguing notion of a "euphemistic" strategy of resisting heterosexism. Such a euphemistic set of practices implies, Chang suggests, modes of meaningful action ignored in the West.

In my chapter I play with the notion of "punk'd"—desexualized in the popular media to mean merely "tricked"—to describe the political situation of U.S. teachers under Bush. True enough, all teachers are tricked, but they are also turned into "tricks" by politicians pimping them to parents in pathos. Straight male teachers are also punk'd in the prison sense, no longer "men," something, of course, no man is (see DiPiero, 2002). Snapshots of the one-hundred-year-old (and ongoing) crisis of masculinity provide glimpses into how men's distrust of mothers morphed into the scapegoating of those women (and men) who care for children in schools.

In her chapter, Cris Mayo suggests that even the most straight are some-times queer (and vice versa) and, on occasion, these intragender sexual differ-ences draw young women into queer associations they find surprising. Through narrations of female same-gender attraction on campus, in pre-service teacher classrooms, and in teacher education practicum settings, Mayo shows how queerness "sparks alliance and interest across other differences—or highlights differences through attraction." From straight girls making out while waiting to use the restroom to girls dating guys as a ritualized performance for other girls (a phenomenon not uncommon among boys; see, for instance, Pi-nar, 2001, p. 917), Mayo finds that "queered heterosexuality was not particu-larly queer at all," as it revolved around boys and challenged no one's sexual identity.

If, as Mayo asserts, "queerness is about flirtation with the possible" and "angry critique of the obstacles," then her discussion of the emotions of queer politics intensifies both sets. She theorizes "shame" as a "strategy that can be used to stop interactions, to buy time, and to redirect the force of criticism from…introspection, change, and reconciliation." Her "favorite affective strategy," however, is anger, invoking an emotion long associated with lesbian politics (see De Veaux, 2004, p. 293). "Anger is less interested in emotional response than in political change," she asserts. All emotions are complicated in Mayo's piece. As she points out, distinctions between queer and straight in the tales she has narrated are not easy to make. Recalling Erica Meiners' (1998) critique of "queer," Mayo notes "when sexual identity becomes another fash-ion, anyone can try it on and take it off if it becomes inconvenient."

John Petrovic and Jerry Rosiek situate their chapter in "teacher knowledge research," wherein teacher knowledge, rather than teacher behavior, is emphasized. (It has long seemed to me [see, for instance, Pinar, 2004, pp. 196–197] that teacher knowledge—communicated in speech acts—constitutes teacher "behavior.") According to this research, teachers themselves are the ones best positioned to make judgments about the character of teaching. How can we acknowledge the value of teachers' practical insights, Petrovic and Rosiek ask, while questioning the cultural foundations of those insights? To answer that important question, Petrovic and Rosiek call upon the work of Judith Butler and John Dewey, characterizing the great philosopher as a "supplement." Readers will judge whether this "queer marriage" (the authors' phrase) makes for a more perfect union or a cocktail of contraries.

Karen Anijar and Angelika Foerst begin their chapter at a public school, where Karen visits a teacher named Leigh, a straight teacher sensitive to LGBTQ issues. Karen speaks as well with close friends and family members, connecting these conversations to "the larger public political pedagogy." Such research requires, she suggests, a "kitchen table methodology." What emerges from this *mélange* of sources is a searing indictment of the Bush Administration's suppression of science (except in educational research, where it is now legislated). The hypocrisy (Karen recalls both Mark Foley and Roy Cohn) of such "straightforward" indoctrination in the normalizing name of "bioethics" fails to register politically as the public is distracted by the demonization of queers. Given the advent of such "theocratic hyper-capitalist fascism," Anijar and Foerst wonder: will there even be queers in the future?

Reading David Ruffolo's chapter, we're left wondering if there will be, in the future, straight teachers. Ruffolo theorizes "a radical politic of the self" informed by queer theory. "Queer theory's theoretical shift from *identities* to *identifications* highlights," he points out, "the negotiations of differences, rather than similarities, amongst subjects." This shift situates the "straight" self as "an implicated subjectivity of circulating norms," including disavowed queer (anti)norms. For Ruffolo, then, queering straight teachers does not mean substituting a "straight" identity with a "queer" identity; it requires understanding how and why "straight" "identities" become intelligible. As Ruffolo puts it, "straight teachers can become queerly intelligible by giving an account of queer." He concludes that "there are no *straight* teachers."

In the concluding chapter comprising this queer conversation, Nelson Rodriguez distinguishes between two classes of straight people: one who would do us harm, and those who would not. Even this second class is vulnerable to arguments of "separate but equal," Nelson notes. "What links these two classes of straights," he suggests, "is a lack of *critical* engagement with (hegemonic) heterosexuality." He invokes the notion of "straight panic"—I wonder how evenly distributed this "panic" is: I suspect it is primarily straight men's—to account for "the mixed, and oftentimes illogical and irrational, not to mention contradictory, reactions to gay marriage by straight America."

Drawing on the work of Foucault, Butler, Annamarie Jagose, Calvin Thomas, and Annette Schlichter, Nelson emphasizes the historical and constructed character of sexual identities. "If heterosexuality is unstable and incoherent," he points out, "then it is this very aspect of it—its instability—that becomes the condition for its possible rearticulation." Rodriguez finds evidence for that rearticulation in the emergence of the paradoxical figure of the queer straight, which, he suggests, creates "a major opening for straight participation in queer critical practice." Such a queering of straightness blurs the overdetermined distinction between straight and queer. Emphasizing heterosexuality's dependence on the queer while proliferating the figure of the queer straight contributes to the queering of straight teachers.

How might we queer straight teachers is, you recall, the first of Nelson's questions structuring this collection. As Kate Evans (2002) has noted, teachers are supposed to be straight. (One hundred years ago, female teachers weren't even supposed to be sexual.) In this collection (in Reta Ugena Whitlock's and David Ruffolo's chapters specifically), we see how slippery straightness can be. Even straight teachers can be queer-identified, if in a political sense, as the Chang and Anijar/Foerst chapters testify. In my chapter I show how, in the United States at least, male teachers have been politically positioned as punks. Given the historic conflation of breast with penis and the attendant suspicion of wet nurses (Pinar, 2006a, pp. 34–40), female schoolteachers aren't exactly ladies themselves.

Does the inclusion of queer subjects in teacher education—and multiculturalism and curriculum studies, as in Nelson's second question—function politically like those girls kissing each other Cris Mayo describes? In whose gaze and for whose desire do we perform queer (and do straights perform straightness)? Obviously, what you see is not necessarily what you get. What could make things perfectly queer (Doty, 1993)? Should we supplement Butler with Dewey, as Petrovic and Rosiek recommend? Will that cocktail render teachers' knowledge less Edenic, more worldly? Does the curriculum controversy that Mary Louise Rasmussen, Jane Mitchell, and Valerie Harwood describe constitute teacher knowledge after the Fall? Certainly the questionnaire they narrate constitutes knowledge of the flesh, at least to our fundamentalist friends, perhaps even to our fundamentalist science friends, who think they can keep our sin confined to a gene. As gay boys know, it's not so hard to slip out of jeans.

Boxers or briefs, Congressman Foley wanted to know. What binds the pages of the straight school curriculum, who bequeaths us our professional personae, what psychic undergarments organize our and invite others' desire? For queers, where is the "culture" in a queered multiculturalism, and what is its status? Is it both a cover-up and an undergarment? Or, to change metaphors, is multiculturalism the Ladies Room in the line for which some of us perform queer for others while waiting our turn at inclusion? By insisting on culture's political primacy, on its constitutive relation to identity, are we (only? also?) titillating those trapped in traditional drag, waiting in the wrong line while legislating straightness from the House floor? If we stop reading straight, as Deborah Britzman famously advised, if we appreciate desire as relational rather than object-focused, does it matter what we wear, or with whom we undress? Is pedagogy, after Britzman, always already queered?

Even queer pedagogy is subsumed within the curriculum (Pinar, 2006a, pp. 109–120). What characterizes a queer curriculum? Dennis Sumara and Brent Davis (1998, pp. 215–217) provide six provocative answers to that question, among them examination of the "heterosexual closet" (1998, p. 216), a call to Critical Heterosexual Studies *avant la lettre*. Surely a queer curriculum incorporates our pedagogic performances of the knowledge we teach. We can queer a straight script, yes, but it surely helps if the subject we wish to queer is already queer itself, a textbook (for instance) that cannot be consumed straight-on (Pinar, 2001, p. 24), a juxtaposition of scholarship structured as differentiation and dissonance. In teaching such textbooks, we concoct a perverse brew, containing both, let us say, degenerate discipline and strict spontaneity. Questions are posed, subjects debriefed, replies performed. And by providing such "queer critical care for the straight self" (Nelson's phrase), we are queering not only straight teachers: we are queering straight students as well, fulfilling the paranoid fantasies of those parents and politicians with pedophilia already and always on their minds.

In setting up Judith and John, are we fantasizing straightness, if of the queer kind? What is the primal scene (Pinar, 2004, p. 57) of a queer progressive dream (Pinar, 2001, pp. 19–33)? Surely it includes that exhibitionistic *ménage a trois* (homophobia, heterosexism, misogyny, as Liz Meyer points out) while that fourth perverted participant—racism—hides between the sheets. Excoriating their corrugated corruption is a peculiar project to which I have tried to contribute (2001, 2006b).

In exorcising these demons from the body politic, what forms of coalitional practices can we invoke? Are identity-differentiated struggles against misogyny, homophobia, heterosexism, and racism collectivized by subsuming them, as neo-Marxists have demanded, in anticapitalism? Or is "social justice" the catalytic collectivizing concept, as Nelson's third question implies? What binds identity-politics dissidents together when the unjust public sphere is itself forever fragmented by capitalism, an incoherence articulated, but hardly healed, by identity politics? Can a queered subjectivity (Miller, 1998) contribute to a queered sociality, or, as Leo Bersani (1995, p. 7) has argued, is "queer" by definition a form of antirelationality? Such questions reverberate through Dennis Carlson's post-Marxist questioning of identity politics. Carlson (1998, p. 218) argued that:

> If the promise of multicultural education is to be realized, it must be committed to helping young people learn the technologies of self that will allow them to work together strategically across as well as within various identity boundaries to advance common democratic projects.

The method of *currere* is, of course, one such "technology" of subjectivity, but what is, today, the status of the notions of "common" and "democratic"? In Dewey's formulation, the labor of subjective and social reconstruction was to be conducted through education. Can queer's emphasis on differentiation and difference be reassembled as a "common democratic project"?

"Queer" emerged from the self-affirmative politics associated with the lesbian and gay liberation movements of the 1960s and 1970s.[7] Queer theory questioned what "self" was being affirmed while it wondered what "liberation" looked like. Carlson's conception of "common democratic projects" recalls the progressivism of an earlier era, but today, in the United States, community has long been eclipsed by consumerism. Indeed, the future itself is foreclosed, as society seems not only beyond social reconstruction but, according to some ecological forecasts, beyond survival.

Still a wager made for the sake of a shared future, a queer progressivism today is (despite deconstruction) structured by—even as it disclaims— binaries. Yes, our enemy is "straightness." But, as queers know, that "them" cannot bind "us" together forever, as "they"—in this collection, and elsewhere—have already been queered, at least in our minds. (And, if "straight panic" is any indication, they have been queered in theirs as well.) In the polarized political landscape in which we labor today, any promise of coalitional progressive politics requires an "other" in order to call into social formation a "we," that pronoun prerequisite to a "common democratic project." On the horizon I see only one enemy worthy of all of us: namely the loss of the horizon, the collapse of the biosphere of which we, whatever our identity politics or economic allegiances, are part. It is the apocalyptic loss of Life itself that might enable those of us nursing identity wounds to mobilize with others—including "them"—for the sake of sustainability, cutting capitalism down to size in the bargain.

Central to any conception of sustainability—it is, today, our one and only "common democratic project"—is the realization that homophobia, heterosexism, misogyny, and racism have been in that nasty bed with each for at least one hundred years, the century of overpopulation and plunder of the planet. As ecofeminists have pointed out, misogyny and the ongoing rape of the earth are hardly unrelated (Salleh, 1997). Straightness—in the 1960s we used the term not in a sexually specific sense but to refer to anyone who was not "hip" —that is, anyone who accepted uncritically the official cultural and political "curriculum"—is killing us, all of us, everything, everywhere. Antiracist Paul Hoch (1979, p. 137) understood: "The rape of nature—and the ecological disaster it presages—is part and parcel of a dominating masculinity gone out of control." Contrary to heterosexist propaganda, straightness—not degeneracy—is the inversion of sustainability.

It is, then, not only the ongoing crisis of capital that imperils the planet. Through relentless, aggressive, often violent tactics of "recruitment," heterosexists command their sons and daughters—everyone's daughters and sons— to copulate and produce offspring, generations of progeny now promising to overwhelm the earth's collapsing ecosystem. While overpopulation is often acknowledged in the public press as a major cause of the escalating ecological crisis, its relation to heterosexism is not. Sustainability constitutes our queer common democratic project. Queering straight teachers helps.

Notes

1. The concept of the book is Nelson's. It is Nelson who issued invitations to the contributors, edited their chapters, wrote a preface and chapter, and formatted the book. In my secondary and passive role, I contributed a chapter, composed this introduction, and provided an index. Despite the heterosexual verbs employed in the text above, I am hardly the husband here.

2. The use of "we" as a totalizing concept is spurious, as lesbian theorists have made clear. If "queer" means anything, it means difference and differentiation. Only vis-à-vis "them," does a "we" make sense (see Bersani, 1995, p. 42).

3. The questions are Nelson's.

4. That first piece—two parts gay liberationist, one part queer theory—celebrates matrifocality through anal eroticism. In their chapters, both Yin-Kun Chang and Jane Lehr underscore the prominence of anal intercourse in homophobia.

5. This is the argument my good friend and former LSU colleague Ron Good makes (see Good, 2005). Lehr quotes Smith and Drake: Smith is a Ph.D. student of Good's.

6. A valuable resource for studying the history of sexuality is the journal by that name, published first by the University of Chicago Press and now by the University of Texas Press. See: http://www.utexas.edu/utpress/journals/jhs.html. Retrieved from the Internet on November 2, 2006.

7. And they from the movements before them: see Sears, 2006.

Works Cited

Bersani, L. (1995). *Homos*. Cambridge, MA: Harvard University Press.

Britzman, D. P. (1998). Is there a queer pedagogy? Or, stop reading straight. In W. F. Pinar (Ed.), *Curriculum: Toward new identities* (pp. 211–231). New York: Garland. [Originally published in 1995 in *Educational Theory*, 45(2), 151–165.]

Carlson, D. (1998). Who am I? Gay identity and a democratic politics of self. In W. F. Pinar (Ed.), *Queer theory in education* (pp. 107–119). Mahwah, NJ: Lawrence Erlbaum.

De Veaux, A. (2004). *Warrior poet: A biography of Audre Lorde*. New York: Norton.

DiPiero, T. (2002). *White men aren't*. Durham, NC: Duke University Press.

Doty, A. (1993). *Making things perfectly queer*. Minneapolis, MN: University of Minnesota Press.

Edelman, L. (2004). *No future: Queer theory and the death drive*. Durham, NC: Duke University Press.

Evans, K. (2002). *Negotiating the self: Identity, sexuality, and emotion in learning to teach*. New York: Routledge.

Good, R. (2005). *Scientific and religious habits of mind: Irreconcilable tensions in the curriculum*. New York: Peter Lang.

Hoch, P. (1979). *White hero, black beast: Racism, sexism and the mask of masculinity*. London: Pluto Press.

Hocquenghem, G. (1978). *Homosexual desire*. London: Allison & Busby.

Jagose, A. (1996). *Queer theory: An introduction*. New York: New York University Press.

Meiners, E. (1998). Remember when all the cars were Fords and all the lesbians were women? Some notes on identity, mobility, and capital. In W. F. Pinar (Ed.), *Queer theory in education* (pp. 121–140). Mahwah, NJ: Lawrence Erlbaum.

Miller, J. L. (1998). Autobiography as a queer curriculum practice. In W. F. Pinar (Ed.), *Queer theory in education* (pp. 349–364). Mahwah, NJ: Lawrence Erlbaum.

Pinar, W. F. (Ed.). (1998). *Queer theory in education*. Mahwah, NJ: Lawrence Erlbaum.

Pinar, W. F. (2001). *The gender of racial politics and violence in America*. New York: Peter Lang.

Pinar, W. F. (2004). *What is curriculum theory?* Mahwah, NJ: Lawrence Erlbaum.

Pinar, W. F. (2006a). *The synoptic text today and other essays: Curriculum development after the reconceptualization*. New York: Peter Lang.

Pinar, W. F. (2006b). *Race, religion, and a culture of reparation*. New York: Palgrave Macmillan.

Salleh, A. (1997). *Ecofeminism as politics: Nature, Marx and the postmodern*. London: Zed.

Sears, J. T. (2006). *Behind the mask of the Mattachine: The Hal Call chronicles and the early movement for homosexual emancipation*. New York: Harrington Park Press.

Sumara, D. & Davis, B. (1998). Telling tales of surprise. In W. F. Pinar (Ed.), *Queer theory in education* (pp. 197–219). Mahwah, NJ: Lawrence Erlbaum.

PART ONE

Queering Straight Teachers:
Theoretical Interventions in Curriculum,
Pedagogy, and Teacher Education

CHAPTER ONE

"But I'm Not Gay": What Straight Teachers Need to Know about Queer Theory

Elizabeth J. Meyer

Introduction

Most scholars and educators steer clear of queer theory because the word "queer" has a long history of being a pejorative term for gays and lesbians or anyone perceived to be different. What many people do not understand is that in the past twenty years, this term has been actively under reconstruction and has been infused with new meanings and applications. Although "queer" is still often used with the intent to harm, in scholarly contexts it has come to represent new concepts that, when applied in the school setting, can have a liberatory and positive influence on the way schools work today.

Another common misunderstanding about queer theory is that it is a synonym for gay and lesbian studies. Although queer theory emerged from the work of scholars in this field, it has evolved to become much more broad and encompassing than gay and lesbian studies. Queer theory goes beyond exploring aspects of gay and lesbian identity and experience. It questions taken-for-granted assumptions about relationships, identity, gender, and sexual orientation. It seeks to explode rigid normalizing categories into possibilities that exist beyond the binaries of man/woman, masculine/feminine, student/teacher, and gay/straight. Queer theory offers educators a lens through which educators can transform their praxis so as to explore and celebrate the tensions and new understandings created by teaching new ways of seeing the world. This chapter will introduce some key tenets of queer theory and describe how the application of these ideas by all educators can create classrooms that are more liberatory, inclusive of diversity and socially just.

The first section describes how the persistence of homophobia and the related tool of sexism in schools harm everyone in the community and how the most basic expectation of school safety for all cannot be attained until these issues are addressed. The second section describes how gender codes work to limit the opportunities available to students and teachers in schools and society. The third section addresses the concepts of language and discourse and how understanding this form of power is essential to understanding how to transform school cultures. The fourth section explains several of the key ideas in Queer Theory that are most relevant to educators working in schools today. Finally, this chapter concludes with a brief summary of key points and a description of how queer theory and an application of queer pedagogies can move schools toward being more liberatory, inclusive, and socially just.

The Harmful Effects of Homophobia and Heterosexism

In recent years there has been growing attention paid to the important issue of violence in schools. The issue of bullying and harassment is one aspect of school violence that has received a significant amount of attention from the media as well as from school officials and community members. It is encouraging that this important issue is getting widespread attention, but much of the information about bullying and harassment is flawed because it fails to address some of the underlying social forces at work. As Martino and Pallotta-Chiarolli (2003) point out in their study of masculinities, *So What's a Boy?: Addressing Issues of Masculinity and Schooling*, the problem of bullying has been depoliticized and examined as isolated acts of teasing or violence rather than as a form of policing and enforcing the norms of our culture. They explain that, "bullying needs to be understood in terms which acknowledge the regime of normalizing practices in which sex/gender boundaries are policed for adolescent boys" (p. 54). These same processes shape adolescent girls' behaviors and relationships as well (Brown, 2003; Duncan, 2004). Since much of the bullying that occurs in schools is discriminatory in nature (Coalition, 2004; Harris, 2001; Kosciw & Diaz, 2006; Reis, 1999; Reis & Saewyc, 1999), it is clear that these behaviors act to create and support a social hierarchy that privileges mainstream identities and behaviors over marginalized ones.

This form of school violence is closely linked to the problems of homophobia and sexism in schools and has resulted in several court battles over how families, students, and teachers who do not conform to traditional notions of heterosexual masculinity and femininity are allowed to participate in schools. A sample of recent North American cases includes the questions of censoring literature that represents same-sex families in a positive light ("Chamberlain v. Surrey School District No. 36," 2002); to educators being fired for being gay, lesbian or bisexual ("Vriend v. Alberta," 1998; "Weber v. Nebo School District," 1998); to the right of student groups to meet and discuss issues relating to relationships, sexuality, and sexual orientation ("East High Gay/Straight Alliance v. Board of Education of Salt Lake City School District," 1999); to students being violently and repeatedly harassed with homophobic taunts and slurs ("Nabozny v. Podlesny et al," 1996; "School District No. 44 v. Jubran," 2005). These cultural battles are being waged everyday in schools. Educators need to have accurate information and support to educate their students and communities around issues of gender, sex, sexual orientation, and how discrimination based on any of these grounds harms everyone in schools. By developing a more critical understanding of gender, sex, sexual orientation and how these identities and experiences are shaped and taught in schools, educators can have a profound impact on the way students learn, relate to others, and behave in schools.

How Gender Works to Limit Students' Opportunities

The first aspect of queer theory that is important for teachers to understand is the function of traditional heterosexual gender roles in reinforcing and maintaining harmful power dynamics in schools and society. Many people have never questioned or examined how gender shapes our daily behaviors. The invisible nature of how masculinity and femininity are taught to children contributes to its strength. The purchasing of gender-"appropriate" toys and clothes for babies and young children is one way adults perpetuate these lessons. This is a good example of how hegemony works. Antonio Gramsci's concept of *hegemony* explains how groups in power are able to maintain structures that benefit them through gaining the consent of subordinate groups (1995). It is not done through overt or forceful means, but rather through subtle, yet powerful, messages that repeatedly permeate daily life.

Madeline Arnot (2002) explains that, "one of the ways in which male hegemony is maintained is obviously through schooling, where it is most easy to transmit a specific set of gender definitions, relations and differences while appearing to be objective" (p. 119). She describes how gender categories are taught in schools and provide evidence for how these "arbitrary social constructs" (Arnot, 2002, p. 118) are reproduced through various social structures such as schools, families, religious institutions, and the media. One example of this is the role of adults in schools actively reinforcing these gender norms. It is not uncommon for students to be told to act more feminine if they are a girl, or more masculine if they are a boy in order to blend in and avoid harassment and discrimination at school. One student said that when she reported harassment, "they told me to get over it. That maybe if I acted more like a girl that I wouldn't get harassed so often" (Kosciw & Diaz, 2006, p. 39). This is why it is important for all educators to understand how gender codes function and how we can work against these narrow definitions that hurt us all.

Judith Butler's (1990) groundbreaking work *Gender Trouble* provides a framework for understanding how the social category of gender works. She takes a poststructural understanding of gender and explores it in-depth. Her concepts of gender performativity and the heterosexual matrix are of significant interest to understanding how homophobia and sexism work in schools. Butler shows how gender has been theorized as a "performance" of identity and how the narrow structures—or matrix—of heterosexuality contribute to our existing notions of gender. What this means is that our daily behaviors that signify our gender (separate from, but often related to, biological sex), such as clothes, hairstyle, manners of speech and body language, are external representations that are chosen and fall within a wide spectrum of masculinities and femininities. When these representations adhere to traditional expectations of a masculine male who partners with a feminine female, they are never questioned. However, if just one aspect of this equation is changed (for example, two masculine males walking together holding hands, or simply an androgynous or gender nonconforming person alone), the individuals become curiosities and are often subject to harassment or other unwanted attention.

Children learn very early in their lives about what cues represent boys and girls in our culture. They begin their school careers with this knowledge and work alongside their teachers to practice and perform these gender norms. Gender theorist Sandra Bem recounts an illustrative tale about when her son first attended nursery school. She prefaces the story by explaining the fact that she has taught her children that "being a boy means having a penis and testicles; being a girl means having a vagina, a clitoris, and a uterus; and whether you're a boy or a girl, a man or a woman, does not need to matter unless and until you want to make a baby" (Bem, 1993, p. 149). She goes on to tell about the following experience:

> Both the liberation that can come from having a narrow biological definition of sex and the imprisonment that can come from not having such a definition are strikingly illustrated by an encounter my son, Jeremy, had when he naively decided to wear barrettes to nursery school. Several times that day, another little boy insisted that Jeremy must be a girl because 'only little girls wear barrettes.' After repeatedly insisting that 'wearing barrettes doesn't matter; being a boy means having a penis and testicles,' Jeremy finally pulled down his pants to make his point more convincingly. The other boy was not impressed. He simply said, 'Everybody has a penis; only girls wear barrettes.' (p. 149)

This anecdote demonstrates that children learn at a very early age that it is not biological sex that communicates one's gender to the rest of society; rather it is the signifiers we choose to wear that will identify us as male or female. These choices are informed by codes that are explicitly and implicitly taught to children. Some examples of explicitly taught rules include comments like, "boys don't wear dresses" or "Mommies wear makeup to look nice." Implicitly taught, dress codes are more invisible and pervasive and include the layout of clothing stores, models in the media, and parental and peer influences.

The fact that most people wear clothes and accessories that are consistent with the gender role expectations for their biological sex demonstrates the strength of hegemony in the gender codes that we have been taught. Lyn Mikel Brown (2003) describes the harmful impacts of these codes in shaping young women's experiences in school,

> By high school, many girls have become practiced in voicing these misogynistic cultural stereotypes of girls and women and ascribing them to other girls. It's as though girls become voluntary spokespersons for the status quo, missionaries for the heterosexual script when they claim that 'other' girls are 'hos' and 'bitches.' 'Other' girls are those held up to and judged through a male gaze, against male standards of behavior and beauty, cast in those now familiar derogatory roles: good girls or bad, Madonnas or whores. Cultural messages and childhood patterns of girlfighting have become crystallized for adolescent girls; they have become social reality. (p. 138)

All individuals are constrained by these gender codes. The strict expectations that accompany them severely limit girls' opportunities to be assertive, physically strong, and competitive; boys' opportunities to be creative, sensitive, and cooperative; and gender nonconforming youths' opportunities to express their gender freely. A nationwide study conducted in the United States by the Human Rights Watch supports this assertion,

> It quickly became obvious from our research that the abuse of lesbian, gay, bisexual, and transgender youth is predicated on the belief that girls and boys must strictly adhere to rigid rules of conduct, dress, and appearances based on their sex. For boys, that means they must be athletic, strong, sexist, and hide their emotions. For girls, that means they must be attentive to and flirtatious with boys and must accept a subordinate status to boys. Regardless of their sexual orientation or gender identity, youth who violate these rules are punished by their peers and too often by adults. (Bochenek & Brown, 2001, p. 49)

Gendered harassment, which includes homophobic harassment, (hetero) sexual harassment and harassment for gender nonconformity, is one very clear way that society polices and reinforces this heterosexual matrix. By targeting students who openly identify as gay or dress and act in gender non-conforming ways, heterosexual male hegemony is supported and marginalized identities continue to be oppressed. Additionally, when schools fail to intervene or punish perpetrators appropriately, the structure of the school system is supporting these psychologically harmful policing behaviors in order to support existing dominant ideologies. The psychological harm caused by these behaviors has tangible and long-term effects. Students who are targeted for harassment in schools have been shown to have increased feelings of depression, lower self-worth, and are at a greater risk to abuse drugs and alcohol as well as to attempt suicide (Bond, Carlin, Thomas, Rubin, & Patton, 2001; GLSEN, 2005; Hand & Sanchez, 2000; Reis & Saewyc, 1999). Schools also actively silence and censor any discourse that could be seen as positive toward homosexuality. These concepts of power and control lead us into a discussion of how the use of language and activities of surveillance in schools contribute to homophobic attitudes and to reinforcing the heterosexual norm.

How Ignoring Homophobia Teaches Intolerance

Language is power. The ability to name and create concepts through discourse is a form of control and domination. These concepts were introduced by such theorists as Derrida (1986a; 1986b), Lacan (1957/1986), and Foucault (1975, 1980, 1986a, 1986b). They explored the power of words as signifiers to constitute a subject and his/her experiences as well as the structures in society that police and reinforce the dominant ideology through discursive practices. McLaren (1998) clarifies how these forces work:

> discourse and discursive practices influence how we live our lives as conscious think-ing subjects. They shape our subjectivities (our ways of understanding in relation to the world) because it is only in language and through discourse that social reality can be given meaning. Not all discourses are given the same weight, as some will ac-count for and justify the appropriateness of the status quo and others will provide a context for resisting social and institutional practices. (pp. 184–185)

Historically, society has constructed homosexuality as an illness, a deviance, and a sin. This discourse was created through psychological research, religious ideologies, and the political and financial privileging of heterosexual and mo-nogamous family structures by the state. This discourse has been disrupted and challenged by the gay rights movements that gained momentum in the 60s and 70s. Many authors have examined the social, historical, and political forces that have worked together to construct the idea of the homosexual and then demonize it (Bem, 1993; Foucault, 1980; Jagose, 1996; Sears, 1998; Weeks, 1985).

Heterosexism, compulsory heterosexuality (Rich, 1978/1993), the het-erosexual matrix (Butler, 1990), and gender polarization (Bem, 1993) are all different terms that seek to explain the discursive practices that present oppo-site-sex attraction and sexual behavior as the dominant and assumed social practice. The concept of homosexuality, and subsequently, heterosexuality by oppositional definition, is just over a century old (Jagose, 1996, p. 17). The resulting prejudice against those who deviate from this social script has been carefully developed by institutional heterosexism through the powerful institu-tional discourses of organized religion, medicine, sexology, psychiatry, and psychology (Bem, 1993, p. 81). Sandra Bem explains how the cultural lens of *gender polarization* works to reinforce heterosexuality by serving two major functions, "first, it defines mutually exclusive scripts for being male and fe-male. Second, it defines any person or behavior that deviates from these scripts as problematic...taken together, the effect of these two processes is to construct and naturalize a gender-polarizing link between the sex of one's body and the character of one's psyche and one's sexuality" (1993, p. 81).

These powerful social discourses are generated through various institu-tions including schools. Educational structures wield extraordinary ideological power due to their role in teaching what the culture has deemed as important and valuable to future generations. Ministries of Education, textbook publishers, and teachers determine what lessons are passed on to students and whose knowledge or "truth" is valued (Apple, 1990, 2000). Subsequently, schools are important sites that contribute to the normalization of heterosexual behavior. In Richard Friend's article, "Choices, Not Closets," he exposes two ways that such lessons are passed on in schools through the processes of systematic inclusion and systematic exclusion. Systematic inclusion is the way in which negative or false information about homosexuality is introduced in schools as a pathology or deviant behavior. Systematic exclusion is "the process whereby positive role models, messages, and images about lesbian, gay and bisexual people are publicly silenced in schools" (Friend, 1993, p. 215). Ironically, schools make efforts to desexualize the experience of students while they simultaneously affirm heterosexual behavior and punish those who appear to deviate from it. Epstein and Johnson explain,

> Schools go to great lengths to forbid expressions of sexuality by both children and teachers. This can be seen in a range of rules, particularly those about self-presentation. On the other hand, and perhaps in consequence, expressions of sexuality provide a major currency and resource in the everyday exchanges of school life. Second, the forms in which sexuality is present in schools and the terms on which sexual identities are produced are heavily determined by power relations between teachers and taught, the dynamics of control and resistance. (1998, p. 108)

These acts of surveillance are rooted in Foucault's (1975) concept of the Panopticon—an all-seeing, yet completely invisible source of power and control. This type of surveillance and control is particularly effective because we all unknowingly contribute to it unless we actively work to make it visible by questioning and challenging it. Another example of this panopticonic power is seen in what Mills (1996) calls "containment discourses." He explains how these methods of control are employed to limit work by teachers that push the boundaries of what is "comfortable,"

> The discourse of teacher 'professionalism' is one of the most powerful educational discourses in its containment of teacher-student challenges to the existing heteronormative order. It regulates and monitors the boundaries between students and teachers so that much remains deliberately unspoken or unconsciously unseen. Teachers who resist the heteronormativity of the school, of one's teaching peers, are liable to be accused of unprofessional activity or have their careers ended. (cited in Martino & Pallotta-Chiarolli, 2003, p. 227)

This is one of the most powerful ways that schools reinforce heterosexism. Through the surveillance and policing of bodies and language, school structures mandate hyperheterosexuality using the curriculum and extracurricular activities. The heterosexuality of the curriculum is invisible to many, but some examples include: the exclusive study of heterosexual romantic literature, the presentation of the "nuclear" heterosexual two-parent family as the norm and ideal, and teaching only the reproductive aspects of sexuality and abstinence-only sex education. Other forms of relationships and the concept of desire, or *eros,* are completely omitted from the official curriculum (Britzman, 2000; Pinar, 1998). Extracurricular functions that teach this hyperheterosexuality include Valentine's Day gift exchanges, kissing booths at school fairs, and deeply entrenched prom rituals that include highly gendered formal attire (tuxedos and gowns) and the election of a "king" and a "queen." This prom ritual has begun to be subverted by alternative proms often organized by gay-straight alliances and community youth groups. At these events there are sometimes two kings (a male king and female "drag king") and two queens (a female queen and a male "drag queen").

Art Lipkin's (1999) groundbreaking work, *Understanding Homosexuality, Changing Schools*, provides in-depth accounts of the discrimination experienced by gay, lesbian, and bisexual educators as well as the painful and enduring stories of students who were emotionally and physically harassed for their perceived or actual nonheterosexual, nongender conforming performance of identity. In other words, schools are not safe for "guys who aren't as masculine as other guys" or "girls who aren't as feminine as other girls" (Coalition, 2004). Although the people in control of the school are not directly inflicting the harassment and harm on the nonconforming students (in most cases), it is their lack of effective intervention in cases of homophobic and sexual harassment (Coalition, 2004; Harris, 2001; Kosciw & Diaz, 2006; NMHA, 2002) along with the invisible scripts of the school that are reinforced through surveillance and discipline that sends the message that these borderland identities are not valued or welcomed.

Heterosexism and its more overt partner, homophobia, are very clearly linked to cultural gender boundaries and are informed by the imbedded practice of misogyny. The most effective challenge to any boy's masculinity is to call him "gay," "homo," "fag," or "queer" (Epstein & Johnson, 1998; Mac an Ghaill, 1995; Martino & Pallotta-Chiarolli, 2003). What is being challenged is his masculinity—his gender code—but it is being done by accusing him of being gay, which is equated with being "feminine." Girls are also subject to similar kinds of policing (Brown, 2003; Duncan, 2004), but research shows that it is much more prevalent among male students (Coalition, 2004; Harris Interactive, 2001). It is for this reason that some activists and educators are pushing for a deconstruction of gender codes and delabeling of sexual orientations. By continuing to live within prescribed linguistic and behavioral matrices, the hierarchical binaries of male-female and gay-straight remain unchallenged. This work of dismantling socially invented categories is necessary to create educational spaces that liberate and create opportunities as opposed to limiting and closing down the diversity of human experiences. We must move toward understanding identities and experiences as falling on a continuum of gender expressions and sexual orientations. In order to move in this direction, understanding the work of liberatory educational theorists is essential to initiating educational practices that seek to transform oppressive educational spaces.

How Queer Pedagogy Can Transform Schools

South American educator and activist Paulo Freire (1970/1993) is widely recognized for advancing the concepts of liberatory pedagogy and consciousness-raising, or conscientização. He worked with oppressed groups to resist and counteract social structures in order to critically interrogate and transform them. This concept of education as praxis was influential for many educators and activists who shared Freire's ideals of creating a nonoppressive and equitable society. Although Freire has been widely criticized by feminists for his sexist language and assumptions, many thinkers have taken his ideas and built upon them to include antisexist and antiracist work as a form of liberatory pedagogy. In education, feminist pedagogy has built on Freire's concepts to work toward more liberatory educational experiences for all students. In her article, "Rereading Paulo Freire," Kathleen Weiler (2001) points out many of the similarities in the feminist and Freirean pedagogies. She writes, "Like Freirean pedagogy, feminist pedagogy emphasizes the importance of consciousness raising, the existence of an oppressive social structure and the need to change it, and the possibility of social transformation" (p. 68). She goes on to make the distinction that feminist pedagogy is different in that it includes an analysis of patriarchy and attempts to develop an education that is supportive to women. Many scholars of color, lesbian scholars, and Marxist theorists have critiqued much feminist work as being narrowly centered in the realm of white, middle class, heterosexual privilege. Gay and lesbian researchers have also had a history of working from a white, middle class, patriarchal perspective. Although many poststructural feminists and critical theorists have worked to address these issues, queer theory has learned from this history. Queer theorists have consciously worked to understand the many intersecting layers of dominance and oppression as possible. Liberatory pedagogy and queer pedagogy are mutually reinforcing philosophies that share a radical vision of education as the path to achieving a truly equitable and just society.

In April 2004, the Lesbian and Gay Studies Special Interest Group (SIG), at the annual meeting of the American Educational Research Association, voted to change its name to Queer Studies. This marked an important shift in focus and demonstrates where the work in the area of sexual orientation, gender, and education is headed. In her review of the literature, *Come Out, Come Out, Wherever You Are: A Synthesis of Queer Research in Education*, Janna Jackson (2001) demonstrates the evolution in research and language examining homosexuality and schooling. In studies predating 1990, she noted that they presented homosexual youth as victims, focusing primarily on the experiences of gay men, and none of the studies presented teachers as political agents. As research in this field evolved, later studies (1994–1996) began questioning the construction of gender roles and viewed youth as active agents in creating their own identities. Finally, Jackson noted that every study post-1997 addressed the hidden curriculum of schools, "transmitting dominant heterosexist ideology to the younger generation" (Jennings cited in Jackson, 2001, p. 26). Thus her review of research recorded how the field of gay and lesbian studies has made a radical shift from studying an imagined, unified experience of being gay in schools to a more broad and open understanding of how categories of gender and sexuality are learned and experienced in schools, and has clearly documented the epistemological and pedagogical effects of the emergence of Queer Theory.

Queer pedagogues have continued to build on the ideals of critical theory and feminism, but move them further into the realm of the postmodern. The concept of "queer" as a more inclusive and empowering word for the gay and lesbian experience emerged in the early 1990s as a controversial and deeply political term (Jagose, 1996, p. 76). "Queer" is understood as a challenge to traditional understandings of sexual identity by deconstructing the categories, the binaries, and language that supports them. Butler's *Gender Trouble* and Sedgwick's "Epistemology of the Closet" (1990/1993) were influential works for this emerging school of thought. Jagose explains that queer theory's most influential achievement is to specify "how gender operates as a regulatory construct that privileges heterosexuality and, furthermore, how the deconstruction of normative models of gender legitimates lesbian and gay subject-positions" (Jagose, 1996, p. 83). What the concept of queer truly seeks to do is disrupt and challenge traditional modes of thought and, by standing outside them, examine and dismantle them. Deborah Britzman (1995), a leading theorist in this field, explains how she understands Queer Theory and its role in learning,

> Queer Theory offers methods of critiques to mark the repetitions of normalcy as a structure and as a pedagogy. Whether defining normalcy as an approximation of limits and mastery, or as renunciations, as the refusal of difference itself, Queer Theory insists on posing the production of normalization as a problem of culture and of thought. (p. 154)

In Kevin Kumashiro's (2002) work *Troubling Education: Queer Activism and Antioppressive Pedagogy*, he writes, "learning is about disruption and opening up to further learning, not closure and satisfaction" (p. 43) and that "education involves learning something that disrupts our commonsense view of the world" (p. 63). While marginalized groups employ new strategies to challenge dominant ideologies, these entrenched discourses push back. Resistance is offered up by the dominant structures of society to forces that try to change them. Britzman (2000) presents the queer theoretical approach to understanding this opposition in outlining three forms of resistance to sexuality: structural, pedagogical, and psychical. She asserts the need to challenge all forms of resistance. She specifically addresses how sexuality is currently inserted into the school curriculum. She notes, "this has to do with how the curriculum structures modes of behaviour and orientations to knowledge that are repetitions of the underlying structure and dynamics of education: compliance, conformity, and the myth that knowledge cures" (p. 35). *Structural resistance* is especially resilient to change as it refers to the "very design or organization of education" (p. 34). In discussing how to challenge *pedagogical* forms of resistance, she encourages educators to recognize the power that *eros* can play in teaching. By understanding sexuality as a force that "allows the human its capacity for passion, interests, explorations, disappointment, and drama" and "because sexuality is both private and public—something from inside of bodies and something made between bodies—we must focus on sexuality in terms of its contradictory, discontinuous, and ambiguous workings" (p. 37). Finally, in addressing *psychical* forms of resistance, Britzman advocates working through internal conflicts and ambivalence toward sexuality in order to "raise rather serious questions on the nature of education and on the uses of educational anxiety" (p. 35).

This disruption and open discussion of previously taboo issues can be a very difficult one for teachers to navigate. A liberatory and queer pedagogy empowers educators to explore traditionally silenced discourses and create spaces for students to examine and challenge the hierarchy of binary identities that is created and supported by schools, such as jock-nerd, sciences-arts, male-female, white-black, rich-poor, and gay-straight. In order to move past this, teachers must learn to see schooling as a place to question, explore, and seek alternative explanations rather than a place where knowledge means "certainty, authority, and stability" (Britzman, 2000, p. 51).

Kumashiro, an emerging leader in Queer Theory and antioppressive pedagogy, offers four different approaches that can be used to challenge multiple forms of oppression in schools: "education for the Other, education about the Other, education that is critical of privileging and Othering, and education that changes students and society" (Kumashiro, 2002, p. 23). He advocates most strongly for the application of the latter of these four approaches. In true postmodern fashion, Kumashiro explicitly states that his is not a prescriptive program. He explains,

> I do not aim to offer strategies that work. Rather, I hope to offer conceptual and cultural resources for educators and researchers to use as we rethink our practices, constantly look for new insights, and engage differently in antioppressive education…I encourage readers to think of reading this book as an event that constitutes the kind of antioppressive educational practices that I articulate throughout its discussion. It is queer in its unconventionality and it is activist in the changes it aims to bring about. In this way, my book is not a mere exercise, and not a final product, but a resource that I hope can be in some way helpful to the reader, as it was for the researcher, and as I hope it was for the participants. (Kumashiro, 2002, pp. 25–26)

In this explanation, he is challenging us to find our own ways of creating useful knowledges and understanding the world. He refuses to be placed in the position of authority where his work will be read unquestioningly and used as a one-dimensional text. Instead he is pushing educators to find new methods to destabilize traditional ways of learning and offers different tools with which we

can build that understanding. This is what a queer and truly liberatory pedagogy is about.

Conclusion

Historically, schools have been institutions that have filled an important cultural role of teaching children to learn what has been deemed important by the
people in power. As a result, children emerge from schools having learned
only the language, the history, and the perspectives of the dominant culture.
The recent shifts toward critical pedagogy since the civil rights movement and
the feminist movements of the 1960s have begun to question this type of
schooling in search of a way to create students and citizens who will be critical, engaged, independent thinkers in order to move our society in a more
egalitarian direction. In better understanding how the forces of hegemony and
discursive power work to shape gender and sexual identities, educators will be
more equipped to create classrooms that embody the ideals of a queer liberatory pedagogy.

Queer theory is just another step further down the road initially paved by
critical pedagogy, poststructural feminism, and theories of emancipatory education. In calling on educators to question and reformulate through a queer
pedagogical lens: (1) how they teach and reinforce gendered practices in
schools, (2) how they support traditional notions of heterosexuality, and (3)
how they present culturally specific information in the classroom, we will be
able to reduce and eventually remove all forms of gendered harassment and
other related forms of discrimination from schools and, consequently, from
most realms of society. Schools need to begin to challenge and disrupt traditional ways of knowing and encourage students to question and "trouble" all
that is passively assumed and taken for granted in society. Institutions of learning must redefine themselves in order to move toward a truly liberatory and
emancipatory learning experience. This project is building on and extending
the work of critical pedagogy. Barry Kanpol (1994) affirms,

> the critical pedagogue always seeks just and fair ways to alter a system which, by and
> large, and despite seemingly good intentions, has effectively oppressed many of its
> members. Critical postmodernism, then, is not only about passive judgment but also
> about active engagement in change and reform issues that seek to sever inequalities
> and other forms of social and cultural injustices. (p. 33)

By doing away with the docile, submissive, "banking" style of learning in schools, we can open up more educational possibilities and socially just experiences for future citizens rather than confine them with ideologies of traditional hegemonic, heterosexist, gender roles. In order to move in this direction, it is important to apply the lenses offered by Queer Theory to creatively work through the current obstacles that prevent teachers from teaching passionately and connecting with their students and communities in meaningful ways.

Works Cited

Apple, M. (1990). *Ideology and the curriculum.* New York: Routledge.

Apple, M. (2000). *Official knowledge: Democratic education in a conservative age* (2nd ed.). New York: Routledge.

Arnot, M. (2002). *Reproducing gender: Selected critical essays on educational theory and feminist politics.* London: Routledge-Falmer.

Bem, S. (1993). *The lenses of gender: Transforming the debate on sexual inequality.* New Haven: Yale University Press.

Bochenek, M., & Brown, A. W. (2001). *Hatred in the hallways: Violence and discrimination against lesbian, gay, bisexual, and transgender students in U.S. schools.* Human Rights Watch.

Bond, L., Carlin, J. B., Thomas, L., Rubin, K., & Patton, G. (2001). Does bullying cause emotional problems?: A prospective study of young teenagers. *BMJ: British Medical Journal*, 323(7311), 480–484.

Britzman, D. (1995). Is there a queer pedagogy?: Or, stop reading straight. *Educational Theory*, 45(2), 151–165.

Britzman, D. (2000). Precocious education. In S. Talburt & S. Steinberg (Eds.), *Thinking queer: Sexuality, culture, and education* (pp. 33–60). New York: Peter Lang.

Brown, L. M. (2003). *Girlfighting: Betrayal and rejection among girls.* New York: New York University Press.

Butler, J. (1990). *Gender trouble.* New York: Routledge-Falmer.

Chamberlain v. Surrey School District No. 36 (Supreme Court of Canada 2002).

Coalition, C. S. S. (2004). *Consequences of harassment based on actual or perceived sexual orientation and gender non-conformity and steps for making schools safer.* Davis: University of California.

Derrida, J. (1986a). Différance. In H. Adams & L. Searle (Eds.), *Critical theory since 1965* (pp. 120–136). Tallahassee: University Press of Florida.

Derrida, J. (1986b). Of grammatology. In H. Adams & L. Searle (Eds.), *Critical theory since 1965* (pp. 94–119). Tallahassee: University Press of Florida.

Duncan, N. (2004). It's important to be nice, but it's nicer to be important: Girls, popularity and sexual competition. *Sex Education*, 4(2), 137–152.

East High Gay/Straight Alliance v. Board of Education of Salt Lake City School District (81 F. Supp. 2d 1166, 1197 [D. Utah 1999] 1999).

Epstein, D., & Johnson, R. (1998). *Schooling sexualities.* Buckingham: Open University Press.

Foucault, M. (1975). *Surveiller et punir: Naissance de la prison.* Paris: Gallimard.

Foucault, M. (1980). *The history of sexuality, volume I: An introduction*. New York: Random House.

Foucault, M. (1986a). The discourse on language. In H. Adams & L. Searle (Eds.), *Critical theory since 1965* (pp. 148–162). Tallahassee: University Press of Florida.

Foucault, M. (1986b). What is an author? In H. Adams & L. Searle (Eds.), *Critical theory since 1965* (pp. 138–148). Tallahassee: University Press of Florida.

Freire, P. (1970/1993). *Pedagogy of the oppressed*. New York: Continuum.

Friend, R. (1993). Choices, not closets. In L. Weis & M. Fine (Eds.), *Beyond silenced voices: Class, race, and gender in United States schools* (pp. 209–235). Albany: State University of New York Press.

GLSEN, H. I. a. (2005). *From teasing to torment: School climate in America, a survey of students and teachers*. New York: GLSEN.

Gramsci, A. (1995). *Further selections from the prison notebooks* (D. Boothman, Trans.). Minneapolis: University of Minnesota Press.

Hand, J. Z., & Sanchez, L. (2000). Badgering or bantering?: Gender difference in experience of, and reactions to, sexual harassment among U.S. high school students. *Gender and Society*, 14(6), 718–746.

Harris, I. (2001). *Hostile hallways: Bullying, teasing, and sexual harassment in school*. Washington, D.C.: American Association of University Women Educational Foundation.

Jackson, J. (2001, April 10–14). Come out, come out, wherever you are: A synthesis of queer research in education. Paper presented at the American Educational Research Association Annual Meeting, Seattle, WA.

Jagose, A. (1996). *Queer theory: An introduction*. New York: New York University Press.

Kanpol, B. (1994). *Critical pedagogy: An introduction*. Westport, CT: Bergin & Garvey.

Kosciw, J. G., & Diaz, E. M. (2006). *The 2005 national school climate survey: The experiences of lesbian, gay, bisexual and transgender youth in our nation's schools*. New York: Gay, Lesbian, and Straight Education Network.

Kumashiro, K. (2002). *Troubling education: Queer activism and antioppressive pedagogy*. New York: Routledge-Falmer.

Lacan, J. (1957/1986). The agency of the letter in the unconscious or reason since Freud. In H. Adams & L. Searle (Eds.), *Critical theory since 1965* (pp. 738–756). Tallahassee: University Press of Florida.

Lipkin, A. (1999). *Understanding homosexuality, changing schools*. Boulder, CO: Westview Press.

Mac an Ghaill, M. (1995). *The making of men: Masculinities, sexualities, and schooling*. Philadelphia: Open University Press.

Martino, W., & Pallotta-Chiarolli, M. (2003). *So what's a boy?: Addressing issues of masculinity and schooling*. Buckingham: Open University Press.

McLaren, P. (1998). *Life in schools: An introduction to critical pedagogy in the foundations of education*. New York: Longman.

Mills, M. (1996). 'Homophobia kills': A disruptive moment in the educational politics of legitimation. *British Journal of Sociology of Education*, 17(3): 315–26.

Nabozny v. Podlesny, et al (7th Cir. [Wis.] 1996).

NMHA. (2002). *What does gay mean?* Teen Survey Executive Summary: National Mental Health Association.

Pinar, W. F. (1998). Understanding curriculum as gender text: Notes on reproduction, resistance, and male-male relations. In W. F. Pinar (Ed.), *Queer theory in education* (pp. 221–244). Mahwah, NJ: Lawrence Erlbaum Associates.

Reis, B. (1999). *They don't even know me: Understanding Anti-gay harassment and violence in schools*. Seattle: Safe Schools Coalition of Washington.

Reis, B., & Saewyc, E. (1999). *83,000 youth: Selected findings of eight Population-based studies*. Seattle: Safe Schools Coaltion of Washington.

Rich, A. (1978/1993). Compulsory heterosexuality and lesbian existence. In H. Abelove, D. M. Halperin, & M. A. Barale (Eds.), *The lesbian and gay studies reader* (pp. 227–254). New York: Routledge.

School District No. 44 (North Vancouver) v. Jubran, 2005 BCCA 201 (BCSC 6 2005).

Sears, J. T. (1998). A generational and theoretical analysis of culture and male (homo)sexuality. In W. F. Pinar (Ed.), *Queer theory in education* (pp. 73–105). Mahwah, NJ: Lawrence Erlbaum.

Sedgwick, E. K. (1990/1993). Epistemology of the closet. In H. Abelove, D. M. Halperin, & M.A. Barale (Eds.), *The lesbian and gay studies reader* (pp. 45–61). New York: Routledge.

Vriend v. Alberta (1 S.C.R. 493 1998).

Weber v. Nebo School District (29 F. Supp. 2d 1279, 1290 n. 10 [D. Utah 1998] 1998).

Weeks, J. (1985). *Sexuality and its discontents*. New York: Routledge.

Weiler, K. (2001). Rereading Paulo Freire. In K. Weiler (Ed.), *Feminist engagements: Reading, resisting, and revisioning male theorists in education and cultural studies* (pp. 67–87). New York: Routledge.

CHAPTER TWO

Beyond Nature: Critically Engaging Science to Queer Straight Teachers

Jane L. Lehr[1]

Introduction

Within today's conservative sociopolitical context, the idea that scientific knowledge can be used as a tool for social justice is compelling due to the link made between science and truth. Thus, employing scientific knowledge as a tool for social justice works to "speak truth to power," establishing credibility for social justice efforts by bypassing the need to establish the authority of certain moral or political claims over others. Instead, these moral or political claims become "objectified" and thus less "objectionable" within public and private spheres. "Science as a tool for social justice" is the dominant approach to arguing for civil rights for gay, lesbian, bisexual, transgendered, and queer (GLBTQ) individuals in our country—employed by social justice–oriented educators both inside and outside science education to combat homophobia.[2]

Within an often hostile and increasingly violent environment, the possibility of enrolling one of the most dominant forms of knowledge within our culture—science—to justify demands for equality for GLBTQ members of our communities and to make space to even talk about GLBTQ discrimination within educational settings is tempting, and at least initially appears to be a "win-win situation." This science-based discourse for equality is grounded, almost solely, on the argument that homosexuality is natural and unchangeable, and should be understood as "just another human variation" much like hair color or height. This use of scientific knowledge works as a strategic way to challenge religious fundamentalism, both within our classrooms and the larger world, and to resist legislative efforts aimed at further criminalizing homosexuality—particularly at a time in which our discourses of "diversity," "tolerance," and "multiculturalism" seem to have failed or been appropriated.

However, certain dangers exist when we employ scientific knowledge to authorize our social justice work, particularly around issues of sexuality. This essay seeks to push social justice educators to ask ourselves what we risk when we employ the "homosexuality and science" discourse—that is, "science as a tool for social justice"—to challenge the moral condemnation of homosexuality. Estelle Freedman and John D'Emilio (1997) identify three arenas of knowledge in which homosexuality is policed: religion, medicine/science, and the law. Is it most strategic to argue for human rights and equality by using one of these discourses against another, or can we find a way to move beyond these constraints? Does advocating this approach within our classrooms engage the moral condemnation of homosexuality—or move it aside without critique? Finally, when we employ "scientific fundamentalism" to combat "religious fundamentalism," what relationship between scientific knowledge and non-scientist citizenship does "science as a tool for social justice" naturalize for our students?

Is it possible to move "beyond nature" to teach for equality and justice? In the concluding section of the chapter, I argue that we have the opportunity and responsibility to challenge the normative relationship between science and public(s) by critically engaging science to teach for social justice. As social justice educators, *it is never enough to ask what we gain through science, but we must also ask what we risk and what we lose.* Using science as a tool for social justice creates a situation in which the authority of science goes unchallenged, thereby limiting what counts as appropriate behavior for our students in relation to science and to the state. They are positioned to acquiesce to the authority of science in all personal and public decision-making practices. Is this a risk with which we can live? In this context, my answer is "no." Instead, I show how work within the field of Science & Technology Studies (STS) can serve as a resource to support the development of oppositional relationships between science and public(s) in our classrooms.

What is Science & Technology Studies? STS research over the past two decades provides alternative models of science and scientific knowledge production. What I am calling STS research includes work by scholars in cultural studies, ethnic studies, and women's studies, among other disciplines, that critically engages science, technology, and medicine, as well as work on these topics in anthropology, history, sociology, philosophy, and policy studies. By STS research, I mean more the critical interrogation of science, technology, and medicine rather than any specific institutional or disciplinary affiliation of the researcher. STS case studies produced from these different vantage points show that all sciences and technologies do have a politics, and thus provide a way of introducing a critical analysis of science into social justice pedagogies. In his introduction to the field, David Hess writes that STS provides:

> …a conceptual tool kit for thinking about technical expertise in more sophisticated ways. Science Studies tracks the history of disciplines, the dynamics of science as a social institution, and the philosophical basis of scientific knowledge. It teaches, for example, that there are ways of developing sound criteria for evaluating opposing theories and interpretations, but also that there are ways of finding the agendas sometimes hidden behind a rhetoric of objectivity. In the process, Science Studies makes it easier for laypeople to question the authority of experts and their claims. It teaches how to look for biases, and it holds out a vision of greater public participation in technical policy issues. (Hess, 1997, p. 1)

Through the lens of STS research, we can see that how we are trained to think about science—or not think about science—embodies different understandings of the status of its knowledge, knowledge production practices, authority, and expertise. These understandings then shape our ability (or lack of ability) to challenge science and form the context for the models of nonscientist citizenship in which we participate.

STS research on sexuality and genetics provides an alternative strategy to teach and work for GLBTQ equality by allowing us to question the very naturalness of categories like homosexuality and heterosexuality—situating us, and our students, to question the naturalness of privileging one category of sexuality (heterosexuality) over all others. By questioning nature, we create the opportunity for the practice of oppositional models of scientifically literate citizenship and the creation of new relationships between science and public(s). This approach may be used in conjunction with or as a replacement to the genetic reductionist strategy so prevalent in current work for GLBTQ equality, thus allowing "queered" straight teachers to act more fully to transform our world.

Teaching About Homosexuality in Virginia: A Place of Danger

As an antioppressive educator within a public university in Virginia, I have watched my K–12 and university colleagues, as well as preservice students, struggle with the question about whether homophobia and antigay violence should even be discussed within the public school system because of the conservative and even dangerous environment in which we live. The fear of educators in Virginia—for themselves and their students—is justifiably palpable, as it is across the country. At Virginia Tech, for instance, the Board of Visitors (BOV) (the university's governing board) rescinded a faculty offer (approved at all previous levels of university governance) made to the lesbian partner of the highly courted new graduate dean—making the homophobic climate of Virginia Tech into a legally questionable policy overnight. The new BOV policy translated unofficially into "no partner hires for unmarried, queer couples" though the publicly declared reasons included vague references to "budget cuts"—even though partner hires for married, heterosexual couples continues. In addition, the BOV also unilaterally removed sexual orientation from the university's equal opportunity/antidiscrimination clause in March 2003. (This decision was reversed in April 2003 after public outcry, but the position of the BOV on sexual orientation—and the Commonwealth Attorney General who had supported this move—is clear.)

At the state level, lawmakers refused to remove the antisodomy law from the law books even after a U.S. Supreme Court decision in 2003 found a similar law in Texas unconstitutional. Persons charged with performing lewd acts in public in Virginia face radically different punishments based on the sex of the persons involved. Virginia preemptively banned gay marriage in 1997 and, as Jonathan Rauch (2004) of the Brookings Institution points out, Virginia is "the only state to forbid even private companies, unless self-insured, from extending health insurance benefits to unmarried couples" (np). And in 2004, Virginian lawmakers passed the Marriage Affirmation Act, which states that "A civil union, partnership contract or other arrangement between persons of the same sex purporting to bestow the privileges and obligations of marriage is prohibited" and that any such union, contract or arrangement entered into in any other state, "and any contractual rights thereby," are "void and unenforceable in Virginia" (Rauch, 2004, np). As Rauch continues,

> In the Marriage Affirmation Act, Virginia appears to abridge gay individuals' right to enter into private contracts with each other. On its face, the law could interfere with wills, medical directives, powers of attorney, child custody and property arrangements, even perhaps joint bank accounts.... It is by entering into contracts that we bind ourselves to each other. Without the right of contract, participation in economic and social life is impossible; thus is that right enshrined in Article I, Section 10 of the Constitution. Slaves could not enter into contracts because they were the property of others rather than themselves; nor could children, who were wards of their parents. To be barred from contract, the founders understood, is to lose own-

ership of oneself. To abridge the right of contract for same-sex partners, then, is to deny not just gay coupledom, in the law's eyes, but gay personhood. It disenfranchises gay people as individuals. It makes us nonpersons, subcitizens. By stripping us of our bonds to each other, it strips us even of ownership of ourselves. (Rauch, 2004, np)

The situation for the GLBTQ communities and their allies in Virginia is dire. In addition to the challenges posed by these laws, Virginia is also home to some of the most public faces of the Religious Right—Pat Robertson and Jerry Falwell.

Within my own classes—including work with preservice teachers in the Social Foundations of Education, as well as other courses in the fields of Women's Studies, Science and Technology in Society, and History—almost all of my students condemn homosexuality. For many of the students at Virginia Tech, the approach of "hating the sin, loving the sinner" is a "progressive" stance on GLBTQ individuals. Heterosexism and homophobia are accepted as natural parts of the community. For instance, students consistently address me as "Mrs. Lehr," even though, each semester, I consciously introduce myself as "Jane" or "Ms. Lehr." I respond, each time, by asking my students to think about exactly how many assumptions about me are required to decide that I should be called "Mrs. Lehr." Each time, we count at least four significant assumptions: (1) heterosexuality; (2) a willingness to marry; (3) a married state; and (4) the choice to take my husband's name in a professional setting. Every semester, I encourage or require my students to read Kate Evans' (1999) essay entitled, "Are You Married? Examining Heteronormativity in Schools," in which Evans asks:

> How does an assumption of heterosexuality (or other hegemonic structures) play out within a school? And in what ways are heterosexism and homophobia—indeed, "compulsory heterosexuality" (Rich, 1980, p. 637)—inscribed and reinscribed? How might our interactions with others actively "reproduce compulsory heterosexuality and homosexual repression" (Pinar, 1994, p. 194)? And in what ways is compulsory heterosexuality being resisted and reinterpreted in schools? (Evans, 1999, p. 8)

However, my students—some of whom amaze me with their passion and insightfulness in our conversations about race, class, and gender—are consistently unwilling to critically examine their own assumptions regarding sexual orientation. One student in a Gender and Science course in Spring 2004 actually told me that his calling me "Mrs. Lehr" was an attempt to show respect that I shouldn't reject—despite the fact that he rejected my identity by continually calling me "Mrs. Lehr."

Far more painful than being called "Mrs. Lehr," however, are the overt expressions of disgust and hatred that many students are willing to voice both publicly and privately. As an illustration of the challenges facing educators in Virginia, let me revisit the class I taught on October 22, 2002. The class topic for the day in the Social Foundations of Education was heterosexual privilege and homophobia in U.S. educational contexts. In our previous classes that semester, we had focused on the role of class, race, and gender in shaping historical and contemporary educational practices. In each case, we asked: "How do historical and contemporary discourses about difference shape educational institutions and practices in the United States?"

At the beginning of class, we watched selected excerpts from *It's Elementary: Talking About Gay Issues in School* (Chasnoff & Cohen, 1996), a film aimed at K–12 educators that features discussions with students in 1st through 8th grades and their teachers and administrators, as well as some parents—gay and straight. The film argues that talking about "gay issues" in public schools is necessary because of the ways in which even the youngest of students are already dealing with discourses about what it means to be gay—and know (from playground talk, media sources, and perhaps their parents or older siblings) that they need to do everything possible to not be gay, to not be labeled this way. The film connects these emergent homophobic and heterosexist attitudes to antigay violence, and thus pushes all educators interested in issues of student safety to take responsibility to prevent antigay prejudice at all school ages.

Prior to each meeting of this class, the students were required to complete readings and prepare to discuss questions I provided beforehand. Our discussion questions for the day were:

- How are masculinity and femininity shaped by heterosexuality, heterosexism, and homophobia?
- How have we learned to speak/not speak, teach/not teach about issues of sexuality and heterosexuality, and lesbian and gay culture and families?
- How are students affected by maintaining "silence" about these issues in our classrooms?[3]

However, this is not what we spoke about.

Instead, my students steered—or rather, pushed—the discussion in two overlapping directions: the first, religious; the second, biological. In both cases, the argument enunciated focused on the perceived naturalness of homosexuality—or rather, the unnaturalness of it. My students enrolled scientific facts that are common to condemnations of homosexuality in the United States: for instance, that same-sex sexual behavior does not occur in any other animals; that same-sex sexual behavior is unhealthy; that same-sex sexual behavior is a treatable disease. At the same time, the same students drew upon biblical and religious sources to identify homosexual behavior as a sin.

As I continued the conversation with my students, I discovered that what they found most "unnatural" is anal intercourse, intercourse that could not be traced to a script of reproduction. I can still picture one student (an ex-Marine) squirming near the front of the classroom, as he tried to enunciate how "disgusting" the thought of two men having sex was to him. In my frustration, after asking a few questions about birth control and heterosexual sex for nonreproductive purposes, I exclaimed, "Well, maybe not here at Virginia Tech, but in other places I *know* that even heterosexual couples sometimes have anal intercourse!" (Shock all around—was the shock because of the sexual practice or because I said anal intercourse as part of our discussion?) By the end of the class, the vocal critics of homosexuality did not appear to be moved. They still did not see the place for even a *discussion* of sexual orientation in any class, including this one.[4]

Science as a Tool for Social Justice in Gay-Inclusive/ Antihomophobia Curricula

How can this type of virulent homophobia be addressed? How can educators protect themselves at the same time as engaging in the struggle for justice and equality for GLBTQ individuals? Within antihomophobia and gay-inclusive curricula, three answers exist. First, some educators frame the discussion of "alternative" sexual orientations in terms of the physical, mental, and emotional right to safety and human dignity of all students, teachers, administrators, and community members. Second, educators engage the religious condemnation of homosexuality by arguing for alternative interpretations of the religious texts commonly used to portray homosexuality as a sin. (In the Bible, these are Leviticus 18:22 and 20:13; Genesis 19:4-11 and Judges 19:22;

Romans 1:26-32; I Corinthians 6:9-10 and I Timothy 1:5-10; and the Gospels.) For instance, Universalist minister F. Jay Deacon (2000) rejects what he calls a "literal" and "legalist" understanding of the Bible. Others have pointed out that it doesn't make sense to only apply a "strict" reading of the Bible to passages dealing with homosexuality—in a literal sense, parts of the Bible also sanction slavery, racism, and sexism.

However, by far the most common approach to combating homophobia and heterosexism from what appears to be a safe place is to enroll scientific authority to argue that, in fact, homosexuality is natural—that is, homosexuality is genetic. In fact, when I gave a talk that included a discussion of my experiences trying to disrupt homophobia as a teacher educator in the conservative state of Virginia at the first International Conference on Teacher Education and Social Justice in June 2003, numerous audience members shouted out during my session that homosexuality is *natural, not unnatural!* This science-based discourse for equality is grounded, almost solely, on the argument that homosexuality is natural and unchangeable, and should be understood as "just another human variation" much like hair color or height. The use of "science as a tool for social justice" in this context is understood to make moral or political claims more objective, and thus less "objectionable" within public and private spheres. In this section, I provide examples of the ways in which social justice educators employ a genetic reductionist approach to sexuality to argue for GLBTQ equality in nonscience and science classrooms.

Sexual Orientation and Scientific Knowledge in the Nonscience Classroom

Warren Blumenfeld has played a key role in establishing the dominance of the genetic and immutable understanding of sexual orientation within education literature. I have used Blumenfeld's work in my own teacher-educator seminars and he is cited in many of the gay-inclusive/antihomophobia resources that I have examined. For that reason, I include his definitions of sexual orientation, sexual behavior, and sexual identity in full here. In his essay, "Adolescence, Sexual Orientation & Identity: An Overview," originally written in 1994 for the Gay, Lesbian, and Straight Education Network's educational materials and Web site, Blumenfeld writes that:

> **Sexual (or erotic) orientation.** This is determined by whom we are sexually (or erotically) attracted—our sexual/erotic drives, desires, fantasies. Categories of sexual orientation include homosexuals—gay, lesbian—attracted to some members of

the same sex; bisexuals, attracted to some members of both sexes to varying degrees; heterosexuals, attracted to some members of the other sex; and asexuals, attracted to neither sex. *Sexual orientation is believed to be influenced by a variety of factors including genetics and hormones, as well as unknown environmental factors.* Though the origins of sexual orientation are not completely understood, it is generally believed to be established during early childhood, usually before the age of five.

Sexual behavior. This is what we do sexually and with whom. Though the culture has little or no influence over a person's primary sexual attractions (sexual orientation), our culture can heavily influence peoples' actions and sexual behaviors. For example, one may have a "homosexual" orientation, but due to overriding condemnations against same-sex sexual expression, may "pass" by having sex only with people of the other sex.

Sexual identity. This is what we call ourselves. Such labels include "lesbian," "gay," "bisexual," "bi," "queer," "questioning," "undecided" or "undetermined," "heterosexual," "straight," "asexual," and others. Sexual identity evolves through a multistage developmental process, which varies in intensity and duration depending on the individual. *Our sexual behavior and how we define ourselves (our identity) is usually a choice. Though some people claim their sexual orientation is also a choice, for the vast majority, this doesn't seem to be the case.* (Blumenfeld, 1994, np) [italics added]

In these definitions, Blumenfeld sets up a sharp distinction between nature and culture. Sexual orientation is natural and unchangeable. Sexual behavior and sexual identity, on the other hand, may shift in response to cultural pressures and personal choices. This distinction allows Blumenfeld to hold simultaneously to a biological explanation for sexual orientation and recognition that people identify as GLBTQ at all stages of life. Thus, persons who "come out" at later stages of their lives are read as culturally oppressed, and now finally able to realize their "biological destiny."

Blumenfeld's typology is visible throughout gay-inclusive/antihomophobia curricula and projects. For example, an online Web site called "SEX, ETC.," staffed by sexuality and health experts who "answer [teens'] questions with honest, accurate information" and are "teachers, doctors, and social workers who know a lot about sexuality and health issues," includes this in its Frequently Asked Questions: "I feel I'm homosexual and don't want to be. Can I change my sexual orientation?" The answer is "No." It reads:

Basically your sexual orientation is something that is a part of you—just like the color of your eyes and the shape of your nose. So, in general, no, you can't change your sexual orientation.

Some conservative and religious groups claim people change their sexual orientation through prayer or therapy. But this just isn't true. People might change their sexual behavior. Maybe they start having sex with a member of a different gender. Or they might stop having sex altogether. But, that doesn't change their inner feelings of who they find attractive.

In other cases, people's understanding of their sexual orientation changes. Our society generally accepts being heterosexual as "normal." That puts a lot of pressure on lesbian, gay and bisexual people to suppress their true feelings and try to fit in. It seems easier, even if it means being someone you're not. A lot of times, though, people realize they can't pretend for their whole life. So, they come out. They haven't "become" lesbian, gay or bisexual. They've just accepted who they are. (SEX, ETC!, 2004, np)

Likewise, a recent Gay, Lesbian & Straight Education Network (GLSEN) publication entitled "GLSEN Safe Space: A How-To Guide for Starting an Allies Program" states that "Though the origins of sexuality are not completely understood, it is generally believed to be established before the age of five" (GLSEN, 2003, pp. 29–30). And, Youth Pride, Inc., a nonprofit organization in Providence, Rhode Island, serving "youth and young adults affected by issues of sexual orientation" via a drop-in center, support groups, counseling, social activities, and victim assistance advocacy, among other activities, states in its resource guide for school staff, that sexual orientation is "probably one of the many characteristics that people are born with" (Youth Pride, 1997/2003, np).

The Youth Pride resource guide includes an exercise developed by Denise Johnson at Barrington High School that helps students develop an orientation timeline (Figure 1). Again and again, the main tool in these examples to argue for equal human rights for GLBTQ persons is the idea that sexual orientation is a natural, unchangeable aspect of each individual.

ORIENTATION TIMELINE

Concepts:

- orientation is **established** by age 4 or 5
- orientation is **realized** during puberty
- people **self-identify** as lesbian, gay, straight or bisexual at many different ages

This timeline activity is to help students understand concepts of the development of sexual orientation. Student responses should be kept confidential. The purpose of this activity is to think about how and when sexual orientation develops. Sexual orientation is something that is NOT CHOSEN. Homosexuality, however, is often viewed as chosen and something that can be changed. Review the concepts for this activity and explain that lesbian and gay people struggle with "coming out" to friends and family. Cultural and societal factors may cause lesbian and gay people to self-identify at a much older age. This activity encourages discussion about when sexuality is formed. Explain to students that heterosexuality is assumed until expressed otherwise. Have students draw a timeline.

- Have them write their **date of birth** at the beginning of the timeline.
- Next, have them write their **present age** at the end of the timeline.
- Have them draw a circle around the age when they think their sexual orientation is **established**.
- Have them draw a star around the age when people have a first crush or first love (attraction).
- Next, have them underline the age when people know or **realize** they are gay, lesbian, straight or bisexual.
- Finally, have students draw a cloud around the age when people tell others about their orientation (self-identify).

Figure 1: Orientation timeline exercise.

Sexual Orientation and Scientific Knowledge in the Science Classroom

Some gay-inclusive/antihomophobic curricula and projects provide suggestions for specific subject areas—most commonly, life science or biology classes. In the same way that the use of scientific knowledge "objectifies" arguments for equal rights, the science classroom is seen as a neutral, apolitical, objective site of education. Thus, scientific subject areas are understood as an ideal site to speak "truth to power." For instance, the P.E.R.S.O.N. Project Organizing Handbook (Public Education Regarding Sexual Orientation Nationally) states that, "Regardless of the content of their discipline all science teachers have a contribution to make in anti-homophobia education. Of course teachers of the hard sciences will have less occasion to relate sexuality to their subjects; however they can do some things" (Marshall, Kaplan, & Greenman, 1996, np). In biology and life sciences, the P.E.R.S.O.N. Project recommends that:

1. Teachers may present some of the latest research and theory on the biological etiology of homosexuality.
2. Teachers may present examples of same-gender sexual behavior among other species.
3. Teachers may present the scientific facts about Human Immunodeficiency Virus (HIV) and its transmission in the context of explaining how AIDS is not a gay disease.
4. Teachers may explain the biology of hermaphroditism and transsexuality, emphasizing the differences between these and the homosexual orientation. (Marshall, Kaplan, & Greenman, 1996, np)

These recommendations are reiterated within a 2001 article from the journal *American Biology Teacher* entitled "Suicide & Homosexual Teens: What Can Biology Teachers Do to Help?" Authors Mike Smith and Mary Ann Drake write that,

> The first step toward being able to help these students is to understand more about them. One of the most common questions about homosexuality heard today is whether sexual orientation is determined by genetics or by early upbringing and societal influences (nature vs. nurture). For example, male homosexuality is widely believed to be the result of having a "strong" mother and a "weak" father. Recent scientific studies, however, have convincingly demonstrated that homosexual orientation is not caused by adverse conditions in upbringing, such as abnormal parenting, sexual abuse, etc. (Bell, Weinberg, & Hammersmith, 1981; Remafedi, 1990) (Smith & Drake, 2001, p. 3)

Smith and Drake emphasize that in the United States a majority of people "lean toward the 'nurture' rather than the 'nature' explanation for sexual orientation by a 47 to 31% margin (Newport, 1998)…. In contrast, fully 75% of the gay respondents in the recent *Newsweek* poll endorsed the 'nature' position"

(p. 3). This poll seems to confirm the assertion that linking homosexuality and scientific knowledge is a safe and effective strategy.

Smith and Drake see three primary ways in which biology teachers can help homosexual teens:

- Start with a Personal Inventory—including "What do you know about recent work in behavioral genetics, about the biology of sexual orientation, about same-sex behaviors across species, etc.?" (p. 6)
- Reexamine the Atmosphere in Your Classroom (p. 6)
- Address Sexual Orientation in the Biology Curriculum (p. 7)

They recommend that biology teachers "discuss the current biological under-standings of sexual orientation as an example of behavioral genetics" (Smith & Drake, 2001, p. 7). Smith and Drake point out that "most human heredity (including sexual orientation) is not determined by simple Mendelian alleles but is polygenic and multifactorial"; however, they simultaneously argue that while "science takes no position on whether homosexual behavior is right or wrong…the scientific evidence about the causes of homosexuality and its occurrence can influence a person's opinion about such non-scientific questions" (p. 7).

Smith and Drake endorse a "biopsychosocial model of sexual orientation determination" in which sexual orientation is "determined by a combination of both genetic and environmental factors (Huwiler & Remafedi, 1998, p. 4). However, they also hold that homosexuals cannot change their sexual orientation (p. 5) and that homosexuality is natural.

> …one of the most common arguments against homosexuality is the mistaken notion that same-sex behavior does not occur among animals, i.e. that homosexuality is "unnatural" and therefore unacceptable/immoral. A recent review of published field studies of mammals and birds, however, reveals that same-sex behavior occurs in almost every species studied. In fact, "exclusive homosexuality of various types occurs in more than 60 species of nondomesticated animals and birds, including at least 10 kinds of primates and more than 20 other species of mammals" (including lions, giraffes, gorillas, orangutans, and chimpanzees) (Bagemihl, 1999). (Smith & Drake, 2001, p. 5)

Primarily, Smith and Drake draw upon three studies that support the genetic determination of homosexual orientation, moving from what they see as the weakest to the strongest case. First, Smith and Drake point to Simon LeVay's

1991 "discovery of physical differences in the autopsied brains of homosexual males compared to heterosexual males" (p. 3).[5] Second, the authors cite twin studies by Bailey & Pillard (1991), Eckert, Bouchard, Bohlen, & Heston (1986), and Whitam, Diamond, & Martin (1993) that offer the conclusion that there is a "preponderance of identical twins who are both homosexual, compared to [a] lower frequency of concordant fraternal twins which is more similar to siblings," which, for Smith and Drake, "strongly supports the conclusion that homosexuality has a large heritable component" (p. 4).

Finally, Smith and Drake summarize the molecular genetic work of Hamer (Hamer & Copeland, 1994; Hamer, Hu, Magnuson, Hu, & Pattatucci, 1993), who, in examination of the chromosomes of 40 gay brothers, found that "Among these siblings, a statistically significant number—33 pairs—had received the same region of their X chromosome (q28) from their mother (only 20 would have been expected by chance)" (p. 6). Based on this report, Smith and Drake write that, "not only had Hamer found evidence supporting the genetic heritability of homosexual orientation among these men, but he had mapped the determining locus (sometimes called the 'gay gene') on the X chromosome, explaining earlier observations that homosexuality tends to occur in an X-linked pattern in some families" (p. 6). While noting that Hamer's work has been criticized for various reasons, Smith and Drake write that, "Regardless of these criticisms, Hamer's work is now widely recognized as supporting the conclusion that, at least in some families, homosexual orientation has a strongly inherited component" (p. 6).

The Risks of a Science-Based Approach to GLBTQ Rights

I recognize that as a strategy for gay-inclusive/antihomophobia curricula, arguing that homosexuality is natural, innate, and unchangeable—and that differences in sexual orientation are akin to differences in eye color and height—can accomplish a number of goals. First, it positions the educator as speaking from a place of objectivity and neutrality. Second, it addresses the question: "Does talking about homosexuality encourage it?" Wiggsy Sivertsen and Terri Thames (1995) write that, "A major objection that lies behind many educators' reluctance to discuss gay and lesbian issues with their students is the belief that young people may be 'recruited' into a lesbian and gay lifestyle. This reluctance rests on the belief that people make a choice to be gay or lesbian and that children are vulnerable to being swayed into being homosexual" (np). More broadly, as Sivertsen and Thames continue:

> Continuing to believe in the idea of "choice" leads to continuing to debate about the issues of free will, sin, and morality with groups which see it as a "choice," and wastes time which could be spent in more productive discussions. Continuing to believe in the idea of "choice" leads to the perpetuation of pain, guilt, and anger that parents of gay and lesbian young people often feel.... Continuing to believe in the idea of "choice" implies that children or adolescents who are gay or lesbian decide to be "that way," perhaps having heard a presentation about homosexuality or perhaps wanting to "get" their parents somehow. (1995, np)

This genetic reductionist approach to sexual orientation is perhaps particularly compelling from the perspective of current and future teachers because it also can be used to protect one's self and colleagues from charges that GLBTQ teachers are compelled to seduce their students by disrupting the link between homosexuality and a deviant "lifestyle" by positioning homosexuality as natural.

As a strategy, this approach also provides a way to move beyond a discussion of religious beliefs about homosexuality, and sin more broadly, within the classroom and create bridges between those who oppose homosexuality on religious grounds and those who are homosexual. For instance, the free resource book entitled "What We Wish We Had Known: Breaking the Silence, Moving Toward Understanding—A Resource Guide for Individuals and Families" (no date), which was developed by members of the congregation (First Tuesday Group) of the Presbyterian church in Mt. Kisco, New York, uses "new scientific information" to initiate dialogue between gay and lesbian individuals and their estranged families. Framing one's antihomophobic work via genetics also allows educators to address the debate about where students should learn about sexual orientation (home vs. school, parents vs. teachers), and argue against reparative therapy as championed by organizations such as the National Association for Reparative Therapy (NARTH) and the "exgay" movement.

Very understandably, then, many social justice educators draw upon scientific knowledge and its genetic reductionist approach to sexual orientation to address homophobia in our classrooms. This move to enroll scientific knowledge is also found within arguments and practices aimed at the project of queering, which is perhaps different than the types of projects described above. For instance, James Sears, co-editor of the book *Queering Elementary Education: Advancing the Dialogue about Sexualities and Schooling*, writes,

> Although sexual identity is constructed within a cultural context, the predisposition for sexual behavior is biologically based....The precise biology for the "cause" of homosexuality has not been found.... However, the argument that—absent ironclad evidence—homosexuals choose their "lifestyle" is the "equivalent of saying that since we haven't found the gene that governs left-handedness—and we haven't—then left-handed people choose to be left-handed (or, at a minimum, we can't determine if they do so)" (Burr, 1996, p. 9). Genetic evidence coupled with hormonal research, neurobiological science as well as evidence drawn from anthropology to zoology, overwhelm the etiological debates. Thus the old nature/nurture debate is really two sides of the same coin. Sexual identity is constructed from cultural materials; sexual orientation is conditioned on biological factors. The degree to which this predisposition for (homo)sexual behavior is realized is, in fact, a measure of social coercion and personal resolve. The question, thus, for educators who teach queerly is not what causes homosexuality but what factors contribute to the homophobia and heterosexism that make coping with one's sexual orientation so difficult. (1999, p. 7)

This argument by Sears is strikingly similar to the distinctions made by Warren Blumenfeld (discussed above). Sears writes that, "teaching queerly demands we explore taken-for-granted assumptions about diversity, identities, childhood and prejudice" (p. 5). For Sears, this critical lens is not turned on scientific knowledge—scientific knowledge remains positioned as objective and authoritative.

As cultural historian and STS scholar Jennifer Terry (1995, 1999) carefully documents in her work on science, medicine, and homosexuality in modern U.S. society, the historical relationship between those who identify or are identified as homosexuals and scientific knowledge is long and complex. At different points and in different contexts, GLBTQ persons have exhibited both skepticism and faith in scientific and medical knowledge—and they have been both empowered and disempowered, in some cases simultaneously. In the 1960s and 1970s, lesbian and gay rights activists challenged the authority of science to define homosexuality as a disease. Today, for reasons including those discussed above, lesbian and gay rights activists often draw upon a discourse of scientific knowledge to make homosexuality "natural."

Many have responded to this strategy by offering critiques of the "science" of today's "gay science" and its proponents for being incomplete or lacking objectivity. This critique has emerged across the political spectrum—from the

Traditional Values Coalition to Jennifer Terry, a progressive educator and researcher. For example, Terry writes that

> The argument for homosexual immutability betrays a misreading of the scientific research itself. Nothing in any of these studies can fully support the idea that homosexuality is biologically immutable; each study leaves open the possibility that homosexuality is the result of a combination of biological and environmental factors, and several suggest that homosexuality may be tied to a predisposition in temperament that could manifest itself in a number of ways. All agree that biological, social, and psychological factors interact to produce and change the signs of homosexuality. Furthermore, these studies cannot comment effectively on the frequency of homosexuality in the general population. (1999, p. 394)

However, my primary purpose here is not to raise questions about the validity of these particular research findings. I am more concerned with what it means for GLBTQ activists, educators, and allies to believe (1) that this science does, or can, or will provide us with the objective truth about sexual orientation; and (2) that this should serve as the bedrock from which we build our case for equal human rights. Broadly, I want to question whether this strategy is, in fact, a "safe" strategy.

In the following sections, I identify risks in our enrollment of "science as a tool for social justice" to argue for GLBTQ equality by asking:

- What models of citizenship and democracy does this biologically based argument reflect?
- Is there a distinction between the perceived and actual safety of this argument?
- What will happen to our efforts and arguments for equality when scientific explanations shift?
- How does our support for and reliance upon scientific knowledge in this case directly contradict simultaneous social justice work?
- What is lost in this "normalization" of homosexuality?

What Kind of Nonscientist Citizenship? What Kind of Democracy?

One of the keenest dangers of adopting a science-based approach to GLBTQ rights to combat religious fundamentalism is that we participate in maintaining the "scientific fundamentalism" that currently competes for the domination of our culture. By "scientific fundamentalism," I mean the dominant model of scientifically literate citizenship found in the U.S. national science education standards and K–12 science education, as well as the broader culture, in which science is assumed to be "an important force for human improvement,… offering a uniquely privileged view of the everyday world" (Irwin & Wynne, 1996, p. 6). Scientific fundamentalism argues that all personal and public decision-making processes should be guided by scientific knowledge. As Karen Barad writes, this particular type of scientific literacy and non-scientist citizenship has been hailed as:

> the basis for democratic decision-making about public issues; necessary for global economic competitiveness and national security; crucial for the promotion of rational thinking; a condition for cultural literacy; necessary for gainful employment in an increasingly technologized world; the basis for personal decision-making about health related issues; and necessary for the maintenance of the public image of science. (2000, p. 225)

The dominant model of scientifically literate citizenship found in the U.S. national science education standards aims to train (future) nonscientists to acquiesce to the authority of science and the state by actively demarcating science from nonscience, experts from nonexperts, and the rational from the irrational so that scientific knowledge is privileged in all personal and public decision-making practices. This produces a system of acquiescent democracy that creates boundaries and serves to reproduce divisions between scientists and nonscientists, reducing the role of the nonscientist citizen to one of docile acquiescence to technical experts (Lehr, 2006).

While, in this case, "we" become the "experts," this model offers a particularly constrained understanding of nonscientist citizenship—a model grounded in concepts of "neutral authority" and "value-free knowledge" that seems antithetical to basic tenets of social justice education. This approach limits our ability to use other forms of knowledge and alternative arguments for equality by participating in a discourse that legitimates science as the one true lens for understanding our world.

Scientific Knowledge—Perceived or Actual Safety?

The use of scientific knowledge to justify the right to safe space raises further questions about what counts as safety. Terry cautions that, regardless of scientists' "attempts to control the implications of their research, there is a growing popular trend regarding biological evidence for things like homosexuality as a possible means for targeting 'carriers' and removing them from the gene pool"

(1999, p. 396). Biologist and science critic Ruth Hubbard (1997) poignantly argues that while,

> Most of us would be horrified if a scientist offered to develop a test to diagnose skin color prenatally so as to enable racially mixed people (which means essentially everyone who is considered black and many of those considered white in the Americas) to have light-skinned children. And if the scientist explained that because it is difficult to grow up in black America, he or she wanted to spare people suffering because of the color of their skin, we would counter that it is irresponsible to use scientific means to reinforce racial prejudices. Yet we see nothing wrong, and indeed hail as progress, tests that enable us to try to avoid having children who have disabilities or are said to have a tendency to acquire a specific disease or disability later in life. (1997, p. 187)

By participating in and, in fact, emphasizing a discourse of genetic difference, GLBTQ activists and allies may be strengthening public opinions that condemn homosexuality and the wish to root out the "disease" from our population—pathologizing or "abnormalizing" rather than "normalizing" sexual orientation variation through our reliance on scientific knowledge. What guarantees exist that Hamer's work on the "gay gene" will not be used within the context of fetal testing? What guarantees exist that will keep insurance companies from refusing to provide coverage for individuals with this "gay gene" because it is perceived that they have a greater risk of becoming HIV-positive or contracting other sexually related diseases? In a state like Virginia—a state that has outlawed contracts between persons of the same sex—what guarantees exist that hate and fear and genetic truths will not combine to create an opportunity to institutionalize even more oppressive regulations?

What Will Happen When Scientific Explanations Shift?

Cultural historians of sexuality and sexed and gendered bodies provide ample evidence that medical and scientific explanations shift. More importantly, these histories trouble a narrative of linear scientific progress. That is, the dominant framings and findings of research on sexuality often contradict—rather than build off of—the dominant framings and findings of the previous research paradigm and those of the dominant paradigm that followed. Terry's work, for instance, maps a series of shifts between 1869 and 1948 (the publication date of Alfred Kinsey's *Sexual Behavior in the Human Male*), in which homosexuality "moved from being understood in terms of an innate biological condition afflicting certain individuals to being considered one of the many possible forms of sexual behavior practiced by all kinds of people" (1995, p. 130).

Today, we again live in a period in which biological explanations are dominant. However, between 1952 and 1973, for instance, homosexuality was classified as a psychiatric illness by the American Psychiatric Association (APA)'s *Diagnostic and Statistical Manual of Mental Health Disorders (DSM)*. According to the *DSM*, homosexuality was treatable with psychopharmaceuticals, lobotomy, psychoanalysis, and aversion therapy (Terry, 1999, p. 368). What does all of this tell us? Standard historical accounts of medicine and science—found today, for instance, in textbooks, popular media, and medical practice—often assume that the knowledge of today is superior to that which existed before. However, the lesson we can learn from these more recent cultural histories is that there is no guarantee that today's explanatory model of choice will continue to be dominant or even play a role in tomorrow's explanations. Thus, we must prepare ourselves for the realistic expectation that the dominant explanations of homosexuality will shift. We must also then prepare ourselves for the effect this shift will have on our ability to argue for equality.

Even today, however, while genetic explanations may be dominant, they are by no means the only framework available. While genetics continues to play a role in these other paradigms, it is at once more complex and less central. For instance, as described by Anne Fausto-Sterling (2000), today's neuroscientists provide examples in which social interactions produce physical changes in the nervous system—pointing to the conclusion that brains and nervous systems are plastic. As Fausto-Sterling argues, a more "likely" explanation of homosexuality will necessarily focus on dynamic interactions between a range of factors including genetics, social experience, cognitive development, and so forth. Notably, these interactions will be ongoing and nonhierarchical. In fact, a more exhaustive review of current research frameworks across disciplines may show that the genetic reductionist approach to homosexuality currently advocated by GLBTQ teachers and activists only exists as dominant in textbooks, the popular media, and other arenas of popular culture.

How Does Our Support for and Reliance Upon Scientific Knowledge in This Case Directly Contradict Simultaneous Social Justice Work?

The discussion of the APA's/*DSM* highlights my fourth concern about the use of scientific knowledge as the primary argument for GLBTQ equality. In 1973, the APA removed homosexuality from the second edition of the *DSM* as a result of the gay and lesbian rights movement's efforts to challenge the pathologization of homosexuality, specifically within psychiatric discourses. This important change in the conceptualization of homosexuality occurred at the same time as second-wave feminists argued that, "biology is not destiny, and that male and female roles are learned—indeed that they are male political constructs that ensure power and superior status for men" (Koedt, 1973; cited in Terry, 1999, p. 378). Jennifer Terry, as well as other cultural critics, has raised the question about how and why a second shift occurred from this moment in the early 1970s to the early 1990s and today, in which gay journalists like Chandler Burr choose to publish statements such as:

> Homosexuality's invitation to biology has been standing for years. Homosexuals have long maintained that sexual orientation, far from being a personal choice or lifestyle (as it is often called), is something neither chosen nor changeable; heterosexuals who have made their peace with homosexuals have often done so by accepting that premise. The very term "sexual orientation," which in the 1980s replaced "sexual preference," asserts the deeply rooted nature of sexual desire and love. It implies biology. (Burr, 1993; cited in Terry, 1999, p. 378)

By returning to the "biology is destiny" argument, GLBTQ rights advocates seem to undercut earlier work in the gay and lesbian rights movement to de-pathologize homosexuality and troubles efforts to demand equality for individuals who do not identify with one of the binary poles of homosexuality and heterosexuality. Perhaps just as importantly, however, this move undercuts simultaneous social justice work occurring today.

For instance, within an era of increased high-stakes testing and a constant discourse of failing schools, failing teachers, and failing students, many of us—as teacher educators—seek to challenge the biologically deterministic link often made between race and poor test performance. Instead, we point to social rather than biological inequities to provide explanations for this persistent "achievement gap" at the same time that we question what high-stakes tests actually can and do measure. While questioning scientific knowledge may not be our primary goal in this project, this challenge is implicit as we move beyond genetics to seek other explanations for differences in performance. At a time in which the draw of genetic explanations continues to increase, however, what happens when we base our arguments for social justice in some instances on scientific knowledge and in others reject the notion that this same type of knowledge has any basis at all?

Finally, our reliance upon genetic explanations of difference intersects with the project of liberal multiculturalism—again undercutting other social justice efforts. Liberal multiculturalism primarily focuses on addressing issues related to social diversity by celebrating differences, for instance, including non–Anglo American foods, holidays, or cultural traditions within the educational space. However, liberal multiculturalism ignores the social inequalities attached to these cultural differences, marginalizing the difference that matters—who has power and who does not? Instead of paying attention to these social patterns of haves and have-nots, liberal multiculturalism focuses on individuals, taking for granted that "if individuals are taught to give up their individual prejudices and treat everyone the same, we will 'all get along,' and any remaining limits to equal opportunity will simply disappear" (Berlak & Moyenda, 2001, p. 94). The genetic science of sexuality also supports an individualist rather than social understanding of difference. By teaching our students that variations in sexual orientation are akin to differences in hair color or height, we teach them to ignore the history of oppression of GLBTQ persons. Further, liberal multiculturalism allows students to "opt out" from challenging homophobia and heterosexism embedded within institutional structures, as long as they are "nice" to their "gay friends." In the meritocracy of liberal multiculturalism, the "failure" of any GLBTQ individual is the result of individual choices—not genetics, not sexual orientation, and definitely not any social structures.

What Is Lost in the "Normalization" of Homosexuality?

I want to briefly turn to the discussion of the "normalization" of homosexuality, although space does not permit a full exploration. I am aware that many gay and lesbian activists will find my position "queer"—and indeed, that is intentional. The debate over the genetics of sexuality within the broader GLBTQ and allies' communities highlights a tension between liberal and radical politics—much as the related debate over gay marriage does. However, even those of us who choose monogamous relationships must ask ourselves:

What does it mean to talk about GLBTQ sexuality as "just like" heterosexuality? What do we lose in this process? Again, I turn to Jennifer Terry who asks:

> What would it mean if "homosexuality as we know it today" became reduced in the popular imagination to a strip of DNA, or to a region of the brain, or to a hormonal condition? What would we lose in the defensive move to believe science to be our rational savior and to base our politics in biology? What does science do *for* us? What does it do *to* us? And where can we turn for new questions of the self and new ways of *performing*—as opposed to biologically manifesting—deviance? (1999, pp. 396–397)

As we struggle to contain sexuality in the two poles of monogamous heterosexuality and monogamous homosexuality, how many individuals are we silencing in the same way that we have been silenced and made invisible? When we accept monogamous heterosexuality as the model for our relationships—which we seem to do when we rely upon genetic explanations for sexuality—what political stakes are tied to this decision?

Beyond Nature: Critically Engaging Science to Teach for Social Justice

I was working on revisions to this chapter two days after the 2004 election cycle ended—sitting in the very same coffee shop that I sit now one-and-a-half years later, as I revise, yet again, the conclusion to this chapter. On November 2, 2004, the U.S. public reelected George Bush as president of the United States and 11 states passed ballot initiatives that not only constitutionally outlawed gay marriage, but also, in many cases, made civil unions between same-sex partners illegal. On November 4, 2004, the cover of the *Daily Mirror* (United Kingdom) asked: "How can 59,054,087 people be so DUMB?" Similar questions were being asked within democratic and progressive circles in this country—however, it may be inaccurate to point to ignorance as a determining factor in the election. Instead, it appears as if U.S. voters deliberately chose homophobia (and imperialism). In response to the election results, the mainstream press had provided a narrative about "Moral Moms" and "Values Voters." When did hate become a moral value?

Of the countless press releases and election analyses I received in my in-box in the 48 hours after the election occurred in response to these very visible and deliberate efforts to deny GLBTQ persons equal human rights in this country, one commentary in particular stood out. A medical student named

Ian Hoffman (UMDNJ) posted a commentary to the Direct Action Interest Group listserv of the American Medical Students Association entitled, "What happened 11/2/2004?" In this public post, Hoffman asked: "Why did it happen?" and answered: "Our morals are the new battleground of political thought. There is a movement that is officially entrenched in American politics to make morals *the* issue of our times, and it is framing every issue in politics, from foreign to domestic." Instead of acquiescing to the moral framing of homosexuality and gay marriage, however, Hoffman calls on his readers to see that, "Same-sex marriage is not an attack on family, not a denigration of the moral fiber of America, it is an issue of all people being equal, regardless of their *biology, biology such as the color of their skin, their ethnic origins, their abilities, and especially now, the biological programming of their brain in terms of their sexual preference*" [italics added].

In the next section of his posting, Hoffman asked: "How did it happen?" Here, speaking to the mostly medical student members of this listserv, Hoffman wrote: "We failed. Simple. The medical community who understands the issue of the *biological basis for sexual preference*, failed in its ability to even attempt to address this issue in a wide-spread way.... I have to say that we, as the medical community, are complicit in allowing this to happen.... We failed to recognize that we had ballot measures that attacked entire segments of our population based on their *biologically-based sexual* preference.... As physicians, future physicians, and health-care providers who care about how policy effects our patients, we had a duty to let the American public know about the *biological issues at hand*. Yet not once in the last 6 months leading up to the election did I hear us talking about this issue in any capacity that would make a difference. It was allowed to slip under the radar of us all, and now we are waking up to a world that we can hardly believe" [italics added].

Finally, in a section entitled "What can we do about it?" Hoffman wrote: "This is where the pep-rally speech comes in. It is hard to muster the strength right now, but let's see what happens. Start by asking yourself a question: '*Do you feel that sexual preference is governed by biological factors such as the hardwiring of the brain?*' Keep on moving down a line of thought: 'Do you feel that two adults who have a loving, committed, beautiful relationship, should be sanctioned by the state?' Okay, keep going: 'Do you think that laws that prevent the state from sanctioning certain adult members in loving relationships should be allowed?' Finally, ask yourself the most important question of all: 'If you would have been capable of taking part in the civil rights movement of the

1950's and 1960's, would you have gotten on the buses to go to Alabama, Georgia, Louisiana, knowing what you know today about civil rights?' …So ask yourself the famous question, 'are you on the bus?' And more importantly, are you willing to get on that bus, and put your fight for rights above all else, at the cost of putting all else aside, all the other issues we hold dear. Today is not a day of mourning. It is the birth of a new civil rights era. November 3, 2004 is a call to action. Let's get ready to get on the bus" [italics added].

Since November 2004, attacks against the rights of GLBTQ individuals have continued in this country. In this increasingly dangerous climate, it may seem as if "science as a tool for social justice"—that is, the genetic reductionist approach to GLBTQ rights—is our only option to fight religious fundamentalism, bigotry, and intolerance. However, as social justice educators, *it is never enough to ask what we gain through science, but we must also ask what we risk and what we lose.* In this chapter, I have identified some of the real risks of adopting a genetic reductionist approach to sexual orientation. Using science as a tool for social justice creates a situation in which the authority of science goes unchallenged, thereby limiting what counts as appropriate behavior for our students in relation to science and to the state. They are positioned to acquiesce to the authority of science in all personal and public decision-making practices. Is this a risk with which we can live? Or do we need to locate other options and more oppositional or radical models of scientifically literate citizenship?

This is not the first work to propose the construction of oppositional models of scientifically literate citizenship. For instance, Mark Elam and Margarita Bertilsson (2003) argue for a model of public confrontation with science based on radical democracy. Drawing from Chantal Mouffe (2000), Elam and Bertilsson argue that, "By connecting scientific citizenship to the alternative model of a radical and pluralist democracy, room is created for legitimate forms of public confrontation with science and technology outside of deliberative contexts and a new vision of the virtuous scientific citizen" (Elam & Bertilsson, 2003, p. 245). Their call for radical scientific citizenship parallels Richard Sclove's (1995) argument for strong democracy in technical decision-making, in which the authority of scientific and technical experts and knowledge is countered by a "due sensitivity to experts' deep and abiding shortcomings on the specific subject of democracy and technology, and in a manner that ensures that, with respect to experts, lay citizens reclaim their rightful political sovereignty, formally and in practice" (Sclove, 1995, pp. 50–51) and are recognized as experts on the "social."

However, what theorists of new, more equitable and democratic relationships between science and the public(s) often seem to miss is the connection between formal education and practices of citizenship, and the ways in which formal education can serve as a site of intervention and transformation in the production of (future) citizens. As educators we have the opportunity and responsibility to challenge the normative relationship between science and public(s) by critically engaging science to teach for social justice. While enrolling scientific knowledge as a tool to teach for social justice in our classrooms *is* powerful in the context of religious fundamentalism and virulent homophobia, another way is possible. What if, instead of relying upon scientific knowledge to naturalize homosexuality, we historicize the science of homosexuality to denaturalize all categories of sexual orientation as an educational strategy for GLBTQ rights?

In the preceding sections, I drew heavily upon the work of Jennifer Terry and other cultural historians and STS scholars on the history of homosexuality to argue that the scientific knowledge upon which we rely today will shift— and it may shift in ways that harm our ability to use it to make the case for GLBTQ rights. In fact, as I indicated, contemporary or future scientific knowledge may be used for exactly opposite purposes, in which case we will have participated in our own (re)pathologization. An alternative to relying upon scientific knowledge to authorize our arguments for GLBTQ rights involves the introduction of Terry's narrative—or a similar account—of historical change in the science of sexuality into science and nonscience classrooms.

Terry's history allows us to ask questions about the very naturalness of categories like homosexuality and heterosexuality—situating us, and our students, to question the naturalness of privileging one category of sexuality (heterosexuality) over all others and participate in the creation of an oppositional model of scientifically literate citizenship. While some research in STS on the history of sexuality can be dense and therefore somewhat inaccessible, it is possible to ask critical questions about the science of sexuality in other ways and with other, more accessible texts and activities. For instance, Alice Dreger's work on hermaphrodites is very accessible and yet nuanced, and forces readers "to realize how variable 'normal' sexual traits are...and [to] start to wonder how and why we label some traits and some people male, female, or hermaphrodite. We see that the boundaries are drawn for many reasons; and could be—and have been—drawn in many different ways, and that those boundaries have as many complex affects as they do causes" (1998, p. 5).

Teachers can use Dreger's work to then make parallels to the history of the classification of sexual orientation—describing how, for instance, the category of homosexuality was "invented" in the 18th and 19th centuries. In the same way, Suzanne Kessler's (1990) work on "intersexuality" shows the arbitrariness of the sexual categories that most of us believe are based in biological fact. If sex as male and female is not natural, how can categories of sexuality be? As a final example, Kate Bornstein's gender workbook (1998) provides a fun way to explore serious and challenging questions about gender and sexual orientation. While many readers may already be familiar with Bornstein's gender aptitude test (found in chapter one), the rest of the book elaborates upon a nuanced account of the relationships between bodies, genders, and sexual practices with close attention to power and the ways in which we are taught to do gender and sexual identity—and how we can disrupt this training.

What can be gained by denaturalizing rather than naturalizing categories of sexual orientation? In general, logics of classification rely upon (constructed) oppositions between terms or groups in order to assign meanings. Thus, we understand social categories of race—say, white—by paying attention to what it means to be black. While some classifications appear arbitrary, most are embedded within a deep social and political history—as terms like "normal" and "abnormal" become attached to distinctions like that between white and black, half of the binary opposition becomes privileged, the other marginalized. As Terry argues, following Foucault, heterosexuality—the normative, privileged practice in our country—can only be understood by what it is not: homosexuality. Reinforcing that distinction via genetic reductionism may, in fact, reify the gap between privileged and marginalized practice. A way into a new type of discussion about homosexuality and heterosexism may be to focus on this project of classification to trouble the meanings of the distinction between homosexuality and heterosexuality. We can thus make the social and historical nature of scientific knowledge explicit—instead of insisting on that very difference by enrolling scientific knowledge as an objective authority. This allows us to argue for GLBTQ equality beyond nature to teach for social justice and work to create oppositional practices of citizenship with our students. It creates an opportunity for us to queer straight teachers, straight students, and ourselves.

Notes

1. Since June 1, 2006, the author has been supported by a grant from the National Science Foundation (ESI-0119787) to the Center for Informal Learning and Schools, a collaboration between King's College London, the Exploratorium, and UC-Santa Cruz as part of the Center for Teaching and Learning grants program. Any opinions, findings, conclusions or recommendations expressed in this chapter are those of the author and do not necessarily reflect the views of the National Science Foundation or the Center for Informal Learning and Schools.

2. Many readers of this chapter will be familiar with—and perhaps hold—queer or other social justice–oriented critiques of genetic explanations of sexual orientation. However, the dominant "liberal" or "politically correct" position in this country remains the idea that sexual orientation is solely the result of genetics. (For instance, this position is articulated as the only nonoppressive way to understand sexual orientation within the 2005 film *The Family Stone* [Bezucha].) Likewise, as will be shown in this chapter, the genetic reductionist approach to sexual orientation remains the dominant approach for challenging homophobia within K–12 education.

3. My syllabus and teaching practices in the Social Foundations of Education have been significantly influenced by the work and course syllabi of Megan Boler.

4. One of the class assignments was to turn in 5 video responses to films we watched as a class. Students were asked to answer the following questions: What are the film's strengths and weaknesses? Why was the film useful or not useful for this class and in conjunction with the day's assigned readings? In what other contexts would the film be appropriate? Would you consider showing this film in your classroom? Why or why not? As I recently reviewed these responses—turned in at the end of the Fall 2002 semester—I found that over half of the students wrote that they do not think that GLBTQ issues should be discussed in school—whether because these issues were not a part of the required curriculum and/or moral reasons.

5. Smith and Drake do note that, "all of the gay males in [LeVay's] study died of AIDS, which could have caused the dimorphism" (2001, p. 3).

Works Cited

American Psychiatric Association (APA). (1952). *Diagnostic and statistical manual of mental health disorders* (1st ed.). American Psychiatric Publishing, Inc.

Bagemihl, B. (1999). *Biological exuberance: Animal homosexuality and natural diversity*. New York: St. Martin's Press.

Bailey, J. M., & Pillard. R. (1991). A genetic study of male sexual orientation. *Archives of General Psychiatry*, 48, 1089–1096.

Barad, K. (2000). Reconceiving scientific literacy as agential literacy, or learning how to intra-act responsibly within the world. In R. Reid & S. Traweek (Eds.), *Doing culture + science*. New York: Routledge Press.

Bell, A. P., Weinburg, M. S., & Hammersmith, S. K. (1981). *Sexual preference: Its development in men and women*. Bloomington: Indiana University Press.

Berlak, A., & Moyenda, S. (2001). *Taking it personally: Racism in the classroom from kindergarten to college*. Philadelphia: Temple University Press.

Bezucha, T. (Director). (2005). *The family stone* [Motion picture]. United States: Twentieth Century Fox Film Corporation.

Blumenfeld, W. J. (1994). Adolescence, sexual orientation & identity: An overview. Retrieved Sept 7, 2004, from http://www.outproud.org/article_sexual_identity.html

Bornstein, K. (1998). *My gender workbook: How to become a real man, a real woman, the real you, or something else entirely*. New York and London: Routledge.

Burr, C. (1993, March). Homosexuality and biology. *The Atlantic Monthly*, 271(3), 47–65.

Burr, C. (1996). *How biology makes us gay*. New York: Bantam Press.

Chasnoff, D., & Cohen, H. (Director). (1996). *It's elementary: Talking about gay issues in school* [Documentary]. San Francisco, CA: Women's Educational Media.

Deacon, F. J. (2000). What does the Bible say about homosexuality? In M. Adams, W. J. Blumenfeld, R. Castañeda, H. W. Hackman, M. L. Peters, & X. Zúñiga (Eds.), *Readings for diversity and social justice: An anthology on racism, antisemitism, sexism, heterosexism, ableism, and classism* (pp. 290–293). New York and London: Routledge.

Dreger, A. D. (1998). *Hermaphrodites and the medical invention of sex*. Cambridge, MA, and London: Harvard University Press.

Eckert, E. D., Bouchard, T. J., Bohlen, J., & Heston, L. (1986). Homosexuality in monozygotic twins reared apart. *British Journal of Psychiatry*, 148, 421–425.

Elam, M., & Bertilsson, M. (2003). Consuming, engaging, and confronting science: The emerging dimensions of scientific citizenship. *European Journal of Social Theory*, 6(2), 233–251.

Evans, K. (1999). "Are you married?": Examining heteronormativity in schools. *Multicultural Perspectives*, 1(3), 7–13.

Fausto-Sterling, A. (2000). *Sexing the body: Gender politics and the construction of sexuality*. New York: Basic Books.

First Tuesday Group, Mt. Kisco, New York, Presbyterian Church (no date). What we wish we had known: Breaking the silence, moving toward understanding—A resource guide for individuals and families, Version 5. Retrieved Sept 12, 2004, from http://www.mkpc.org/ Blue_Book_V5.pdf

Freedman, E., & D'Emilio, J. (1997). *Intimate matters: A history of sexuality in America*, 2nd expanded edition. Chicago: University of Chicago Press.

Gay, Lesbian & Straight Education Network (GLSEN). (2003). *GLSEN safe space: A how-to guide for starting an allies program*. Retrieved Sept 10, 2004, from http://www.glsen.org/binary-data/GLSEN_ATTACHMENTS/file/294-2.PDF

Hamer, D., & Copeland, P. (1994). *The science of desire: The search for the gay gene and the biology of behavior*. New York: Simon and Schuster.

Hamer, D., Hu, S., Magnuson, V. L., Hu, N., & Pattatucci, A. M. (1993). A linkage between DNA markers on the X chromosome and male sexual orientation. *Science*, 261, 321–327.

Hess, D. J. (1997). *Science studies: An advanced introduction*. New York and London: New York University Press.

Hoffman, I. (2004, Nov 4). What happened 11/2/2004? Message posted to: Direct Action Interest Group listserv of the American Medical Students Association, available at: http://www.amsa.org/direct/

Hubbard, R. (1997). Abortion and disability: Who should and who should not inhabit the world? In L. Davis (Ed.), *The disability studies reader* (pp. 187–200). New York and London: Routledge.

Huwiler, S. M. S., & Remafedi, G. (1998). Adolescent homosexuality. *Advances in Pediatrics*, 45, 107–144.

Irwin, A., & Wynne, B. (1996). *Misunderstanding science?: The public reconstruction of science and technology*. New York: Cambridge University Press.

Kessler, S. J. (1990). *Lessons from the intersexed*. New Brunswick, NJ: Rutgers University Press.

Kinsey, A. (1948). *Sexual behavior in the human male*. Philadelphia: W.B. Saunders.

Koedt, A. (1973). Lesbianism and feminism. In A. Koedt, E. Levine, & A. Rapone (Eds.), *Radical feminism* (pp. 246–258). New York: Quadrangle Books.

Lehr, J. L. (2006). *Social justice pedagogies and scientific knowledge: Remaking citizenship in the non-science classroom*. Unpublished doctoral dissertation, Virginia Polytechnic Institute and State University.

LeVay, S. (1991). A difference in hypothalamic structure between heterosexual and homosexual men. *Science*, 253(5023), 1034–1037.

Marshall, D., Kaplan, R., & Greenman, J. (1996). *P.E.R.S.O.N. project organizing handbook (Public Education Regarding Sexual Orientation Nationally)*, version 1.4. Retrieved Sept 7, 2004, from http://www.youth.org/loco/PERSONProject/Handbook/contents.html

Mouffe, C. (2000). *The democratic paradox*. London: Verso.

Newport, F. (1998). *Americans remain more likely to believe sexual orientation due to environment, not genetics*. Retrieved Aug 26, 1999, from http://www.gallup.com/poll/release/pr908725.asp

Pinar, W. (1994). *Autobiography, politics and sexuality: Essays in curriculum theory 1972-1992*. New York: Peter Lang.

Rauch, J. (2004, Jun 13). Virginia's new Jim Crow, *The Washington Post*, page B07. Retrieved Sept 19, 2004, from http://www.brookings.edu/views/op-ed/20040613rauch.htm

Remafedi, G. (1990). Fundamental issues in the care of homosexual youth. *Medical Clinics of North America*, 74(5), 1169–1179.

Rich, A. (1980). Compulsory heterosexuality and lesbian existence. *Signs: Journal of Women in Culture and Society*, 5(4), 631–660.

Sclove, R. (1995). *Democracy and technology*. New York: Guildford Press.

Sears, J. T. (1999). Teaching queerly: Some elementary propositions. In W. J. Letts, & J. T. Sears (Eds.), *Queering elementary education: Advancing the dialogue about sexualities and schooling* (pp. 3–14). Lanham, Boulder, New York, and Oxford: Rowman & Littlefield Publishers, Inc.

SEX, ETC. (2003, Mar 24). *I feel I'm homosexual and don't want to be. Can I change my orientation?* Retrieved Sept 6, 2004, from http://www.sxetc.org/index.php?topic=FAQ&sub_topic=GLBTQ&content_id=590

Sivertsen, W. D., & Thames, T. B. (1995). Each child that dies: Gays and lesbians in your schools. In J. M. Novak & L. G. Denti (Eds.), *Multicultures, unity through diversity—A monograph of diversity in the field of education*, Vol. 1. Retrieved Sept 8, 2004, from http://www.outproud.org/article_each_child.html

Smith, M., & Drake, M. A. (2001, March). Suicide & homosexual teens: What can biology teachers do to help? *American Biology Teacher*, 63(3), 154–163. Retrieved Sept 19, 2004, from http://www.bioone.org/pdfserv/i0002-7685-063-03-0154.pdf

Terry, J. (1995). Anxious slippages between "us" and "them": A brief history of the scientific search for homosexual bodies. In J. Terry & J. Urla (Eds.), *Deviant bodies: Critical perspectives on difference in science and popular culture*. Bloomington and Indianapolis: Indiana University Press.

Terry, J. (1999). *An American obsession: Science, medicine, and homosexuality in modern society*. Chicago and London: The University of Chicago Press.

Whitam, F., Diamond, M., & Martin, J. (1993). Homosexual orientation in twins: A report of 61 pairs and three triplet sets. *Archives of Sexual Behavior, 22*, 187–206.

Youth Pride (1997/2003). *Creating safe schools for lesbian and gay students: A resource guide for school staff*. Retrieved Sept 7, 2004, from http://members.tripod.com/~twood/guide.html

CHAPTER THREE

Queerly Fundamental: Surviving Straightness in a Rural Southern High School

Reta Ugena Whitlock

"You can't be queer and a fundamentalist." That was what seemed to me a dismissive rejection of my submission by the editor of a prominent curriculum journal. The editor seemed to object to my reluctance to scathingly and utterly renounce the ideals and practices of fundamentalist Protestantism, the first and only Christian faith I have ever known. I suspect the editor's concern was compounded by my writing as a "queer theorist" focused a bit too fondly on "Old Time Religion." Regardless, the editor (you have, of course, noticed my annoying repetition of the antecedent to retain anonymity that would be lost with pronoun usage) doubted the relevance of my little story to a curriculum studies readership in a post-911 world. I consider fundamentalism more relevant to curriculum studies today than at any other time in its 200-year history, and it is central to my discussion of queering straight teachers.

Now, my work has since been published, and the reader can judge its quality and appeal for him- or herself; lousy articles must be rejected for the integrity of our field. I only know that whenever I present my research on queer fundamentalism, invariably someone approaches me afterward. "I grew up Baptist," or "My fundamentalist parents have just recently accepted my partner," or "I still remember the words to the songs...." This is because everywhere I present my narrative, my colleagues in curriculum studies, who are both queer and fundamentalist, who are struggling with one or both, make a point to connect with me in a moment of washed-in-the-blood solidarity. And while each may not be technically *practicing* one or both—queer or fundamentalist Christianity—each clearly felt that his or her *being* was to an extent both queer and fundamentalist. Being both queer and fundamentalist, *queerly fundamental* as I call it, is not uncommon; nor is it uncomplicated. For fourteen years I was an English teacher living a straight—and narrow—life. Five of those years were spent at a conservative Christian school that required daily chapel and Bible classes. So the intriguing prospect of queering straight teachers appeals to me in that it allows me to continue to acknowledge and deconstruct complexities that may not be apparent at first glance. Despite the contradictions, then, one can indeed be queer and fundamentalist.

As for being relevant in a postmodern world, understanding the convergence of fundamentalist Christian sociopolitical thought with corporate models of education is crucial for any meaningful reconstruction of curriculum and schooling. Susan Talburt (2000a) sites the "rise of fundamentalisms" as a phenomena whose relation to "class, race, national, ethnic, gender and sexual oppressions have been dramatized (and theorized) in multiple spheres, including education" (p. 3). She emphasizes "...the need for researchers and educators to closely consider," among other concerns and issues in the 21st century, "the Christian-corporate nexus in schools..." (p. 4), an unholy alliance within the public school curriculum "that emphatically seeks to produce docile teachers, students, workers and citizens" (p. 5). It is my contention that herein also lies the root of maintaining straightness in schools and schooling.

I take up the paradox of identity construction and lived experiences as I reflect upon my upbringing as a member of the Church of Christ from my peculiar, queer perspective. As the title suggests, *Queer* and *fundamentalist Christian* converge in complexities and contradictions of identifications and desires. Further, the title implies the play of language on the concept of "queerly fundamental" subjectivities. *Queer* and *fundamental* converge autobiographically as I consider myself as queer, fundamentalist, queerly fundamental and fundamentally queer. I consider not only the queerness of fundamentalism, but also its queer peculiarity. "Queerly Fundamental" is set in a small rural community where the two most distinctive structures are the church and school, located side by side with blurred boundaries of influence. A member of the church and an English teacher at the school, I consider how the school, ensconced within a staunchly fundamentalist community, cultivates a discourse of straightness that reinforces and affirms straightness in its students and faculty.

So how *does* a fundamentalist Protestant counter deeply engrained gender and sexual expectations? I can negotiate the tensions apparent in, for example, my Southernness or my white-working-class-woman status and make some meaning of self in relation to other. But in matters of sexuality, I find myself grappling with fundamentalism much as Jacob wrestled with the angel. It has shaped my identity and informed my pedagogy, so my examination of straightness, in this case within the educational setting, of necessity includes forays into fundamentalism. Admittedly, I have done my share of ranting against the patriarchal structures within organized religion, sometimes wallowing in self-pity as a victim of doctrine. Part of my growth process. But I have come to the realization that the faith to which I cling is as much a part of my identity as my queerness; they are both my ways of being in the world. I am, as Anzaldúa phrases it, on "both shores at once" (1987, p. 78). I love the simple elegance of the Church of Christ's worship and fundamental doctrine. I am comfortable with this no-frills religion that has as its heart "walking in the light" (I John 1:7). It is the earliest source of my spirituality, and as such, continues to be a presence in my life. However, I continue to explicitly critique narrow fundamentalist practices, which seem to me to be primarily manifest not in the daily life of individual Christians, but in organized political activity of ultraconservative groups such as the Christian Coalition. Such predatory organizations I am happy to renounce.

With the passage of time my work has taken a turn toward desire for reconciliation and deeper understanding and appreciation for my churchgoing past. And while I continue to interrogate intolerance and condemnation as they may be employed for control—a kind of *piety for power* strategy—the spirit of my work is changing. For me to make any meaning, any meaningful application, from my Protestant upbringing, I evoke the very best it has to offer, that which is at its heart: the fruits of the spirit. Love, joy, peace, patience, kindness, goodness, faithfulness, gentleness, self-control—against such there is no law (Galatians 5:22–23). I am becoming a mellower queer. It is with a spirit of love and hope that I negotiate the brick wall of dogma because love is, as Edgerton (1996) contends, "a very real and necessary condition" (p. 67).

My purpose here is to explore the meanings and practices of the identity category, "straight teacher," within the secondary school setting and with the effect of "queering" straight teachers. This study employs a recursive, spiral— a queer, if you will—approach to straightness as normalized identity: queer me looks back at straight me in a queerly straight world or a straightly queer world as I myself become increasingly queered and the recipient of my own straight gaze. If queer and nonqueer identities are mutually constructed and associated, I survived straightness by looking for clues to my identity in places where they intersect. If straight teachers—and the straight curriculum, school-ing, and administrative structures of the No Child Left Behind (NCLB) vari-ety—are to be queered, it will be through the intersectionality of queer and nonqueer ways of being.

Surviving Straightness

If, as Luhman (1998, p. 151) contends, "Normalized identities such as straight and stable gender identities work through, invoke, produce, constitute, as well as refuse its other," what is the impact when the field upon which epic warfare takes place is within one little Southern gal? What overt and covert discourses from conservative ideology and political activism by the Religious Right are the vanguards of straightness in teachers and within curriculum? How might we designate such ideologically based activism *oppressive* without succumbing to the delicious bitterness of vengeful confrontation? What possi-ble range of discourses can be produced to construct a transformative straight teacher? Perhaps the conversation can begin within the driving force of Chris-tianity, love. Surviving straightness, whether one is straight or gay, requires an active, emancipatory love of common union with the self and other. The way to get to communion is to be able to know one another, and that cannot be accomplished from either side of the closet door. I am convinced that one is either gay, has a gay relative, or has a close friend or neighbor or co-worker who is gay. This includes fundamentalist Protestants. Surviving straightness is queerly fundamental; we must overcome fear and begin to know one another.

In his call for scholarship, Hawley (1994) muses, "many important ques-tions remain to be asked…most obviously, one ought to ask what differences are apt to ensue when women, not men, speak the language of fundamental-ism" (p. 34). It was then that I realized that, far from being monolingual, fundamentalism is my native tongue. Working within the definition of funda-mentalism by Altemeyer and Hunsberger (1992) and Hill (1998), I examine the conflict between the ultra-Right with all things queer and the further inad-vertent marginal positioning of the very fundamentalist Christians for whom they claim to speak. Hawley (1994) and Balmer (2000) consider the nature of American fundamentalism and the "ideology of gender that reconstructs an idealized past and attempts to reshape the present along the same lines" (Haw-ley, p. 30). This "missionary zeal" concealing political lust influences public perception and provokes antagonism in order to entice its followers, 20 to

30% of the population, to the polls. Hunsberger (1995), Opfer (2000), and Lugg (2000, 2000) provide some insight into the appeal and gendered nature of the Religious Right.

Fundamentalists hold unwavering beliefs about gender roles and sexual behavior. I know this because I grew up hearing quite a bit about sin, and of course, hell. For me, it has always been perfectly normal to believe, for example, that women are forbidden to hold positions of authority over men in the Church, that the only grounds for divorce is adultery, and that homosexuality is a sin. I was taught to be in gracious submission to my husband long before the Southern Baptist Convention exhorted Baptist women to do so; after all, man is the head of woman as Christ is the head of the Church (Ephesians 5:23–24). According to Balmer (2000),

> American fundamentalists remain on the defensive, trying to shore up what the broader culture now considers a quaint, anachronistic view of women. Whatever the merits of their arguments, the fundamentalist political agenda…may represent, at some (albeit subconscious) level, a battle for their own survival, as well as a struggle for the preservation of a 19th century ideal. (p. 59)

I know the arguments and scriptural references about the place of women and about the depravation of homosexuality. I have also heard gay-friendly interpretations, which sound suspiciously like rationalizations to fundamentalist me. Complications abound. If I cling to fundamental, literal interpretations of the New Testament, am I not my own enemy? Does not my same-sex love openly conflict with Paul's teachings, which I believe are divinely inspired? Is there middle ground?

I concur with Hill's (1998) observation that "interpretation is no issue" for fundamentalists; nevertheless, literal interpretation is still interpretation. Without openness to more contextual interpretations, there is no avenue for dialogue, whether it pertains to the spiritual or the secular—in our case, education. Dialogue, intertwined with desire and questioning and the space of possibilities (Martusewicz, 1997), is itself interpreted by the fundamentalist as betrayal to the literal, divinely inspired Word. If pushed on matters of, say, Sears' "isms": evolutionism, ecumenicalism, secular humanism, and multiculturalism (1998, p. 41), conservative Christians will side with whomever has the Bible open to an applicable verse, and this will usually be the "high profile," (Sewall, 1998, p. 78) "secondary-level male elites" (Lawrence in Hawley, 1994, p. 38).

I engage autobiographical narrative, and thereby lived experiences, as text, as ways-of-knowing, ways-of-being-in-the-world. Emergent themes thread together, but not neatly in a pattern. For example, I scrutinize my own complicity—*as* a Southern fundamentalist Christian *with* Southern fundamentalist Christian patriarchal structures. Yet as a low-to-middle–class educated white lesbian feminist woman from the country (whew!), I find disruptions that form a tangle like the balled-up thread that has been at the bottom of Mama's sewing box for as long as I can remember. While it would be much easier to put the lid back on the box, it is time to put on my glasses, turn on the lamp, and attack the thread-demon, for, as Pinar (1998) writes, "To attack patriarchy and fascism in their graduated and symbolic forms requires attacking one's own internalizations of them, however subtle their expression" (p. 231). Perhaps an unknotting of the tangled implications (Britzman, 1997) rooted in place and culture, particularly the religious subculture, will point the way to transformative theory that welcomes articulated voices of the marginalized.

I recall my last two years at a rural Southern high school, to which I have lovingly assigned the fictional name Lick Skillet High School (LSHS). (There is actually a Lick Skillet community in Alabama, and the name was too good not to use.) Although compulsory heterosexuality was the understood state of affairs at LSHS, a queer reading of place as text discloses cracks in the wall of straight pedagogy. I propose that the nonqueer stakeholders were blind to the queer fissures, as I myself had been for most of my tenure there. I return for a reflective visit to Lick Skillet's hallowed halls, but this time with a "queered gaze" (Doll, 1998, p. 287) of memory.

In addition to narrative reflection, I examine a variety of sources that address the different tensions within my little story. Curriculum theorists whose expeditions to the margins found queer happily flourishing there decenter the compulsory heteronormative beast that is education. William Pinar, Janet Miller, Mary Aswell Doll, and Marla Morris (in Pinar, 1998) examine curriculum as gendered text and thus definitively link queer to education. Susan Talburt's (2000b) collection extends queer thinking that would affect educational change so that it reaches toward culture and politics. While Randall Balmer's (2000) work on the evangelical subculture in America and Hawley's (1994) gendered look at the nature of fundamentalism ground my account of being a queerly fundamentalist Christian, Sears (1991) helps me reflect on what it means to be a *fundamentally queer* Christian. Huebner (1999) and Edgerton (1996) provide for weaving together the untangled threads with love.

Fundamental Perspectives

Lick Skillet is a rural and growing community on the expanding border of a technologically significant city in the Deep South. It is a community that very much enjoys reaping the benefits of its proximity to technology, yet its members wish for the conservatively close-knit cultural makeup to remain intact. There is no greater representation of this than the two buildings, the largest in greater Lick Skillet, that stand side by side in the middle of a flat expanse of what was until recently farmland. The first, LSHS, is a state-of-the-art education complex and the prototypical flagship high school of the county. The other is the Clearview Church of Christ, also an architecturally elegant compound made up of several buildings, including the Bible education building, the fellowship hall, daycare center, benevolence thrift shop, and, of course, the auditorium that seats up to 2,000. A queer duality in its own way for sure, considering the penetration by church into state, yet a good vantage point for looking at the same duality that is found inside those very same buildings. I know about what is contained inside because, for several years, much of my week was spent in one or the other; I taught at LSHS and worshiped at Clearview.

I return, mostly in memory, to a place where I never thought I would. My teaching home changed for me in time from being a place that felt like family and home folks to a place where I felt the gaze, including my own, so strongly that I felt the pressure physically. In rethinking it, I realize that my colleagues, students, their parents, and community members did not change. Institutional life is notorious for *not* changing. Rather, the change was mine. In my rural Southern fundamentalist Christian world, the straightness had been embedded within the school culture clearly and plainly all along; but I could not see it until my gaze was queered.

According to Hawley (1994), fundamentalists "see themselves as a holy remnant of an idealized past and as the vanguard of a future yet to be revealed" (1994, p. 21). Restoring this idealized, mythical, straight way of life is what allowed Robertson and Falwell, for example, to speak for God after September 11, 2001, when they declared that America "got what it deserved." The terrorist attacks, according to them, were natural consequences—the wages of sin (in Harris, 2001). Conservative Christian organizations such as the Christian Coalition, Focus on the Family, and Concerned Women of America often seek to advance a political agenda by professing great love for the sinner, positioning their family organizations as the "good cop" to Falwell's bad. As Mel White and Soulforce prepared to enter the America's Center in St. Louis at the 2002 Southern Baptist Convention (SBC), SBC President James Merrit admonished delegates to respond with grace and love. "We love homosexuals. God loves homosexuals. But he loves them too much to leave them homosexuals" (Miller, 2002).

The "truth" that Focus on the Family's *Truth in Love* ad campaign lovingly offers is that homosexuality is a sinful choice that one may conquer in order to return to the natural state of the hetero. While the Right may profess love as the impetus for political actions, something other than love prompted Falwell's response to the terrorist acts of September 11. "I really believe that the pagans, and the abortionists, and the feminists, and the gays and the lesbians who are actively trying to make that an alternative lifestyle, the ACLU, People for the American Way—all of them who have tried to secularize America—I point the finger in their face and say, 'You helped this happen'" (Harris, 2001). Christ got really good and mad one time: when the moneychangers, the finance folks, came into the synagogue, a place for the spiritual, and started conducting business. He was mad enough to do more than point a finger. But he never expressed anger, or any other negative thought, toward the nature of human love.

I cannot resist including here one of Pat Robertson's most publicized quotations and one that underscores his political strategy with his skewed logic: "Feminism encourages women to leave their husbands, kill their children, practice witchcraft, destroy capitalism, and become lesbians"... (1992 fundraising letter, http://www.intercom.net/~dayna/index.html). There is grim irony to note that Bev Russell, a devoted Coalition member, would come home from hanging Robertson campaign posters (during Robertson's run for president in 1988) and then molest his stepdaughter. Her name is Susan Smith; and when she grew up—after many years of being molested—she killed her children (see above quote) by drowning them in order to attract a man (Klein, 1996).

But why are gay people the principle targets of these campaigns? Of all kinds of evils in the world—poverty, racism, violence—why malign people solely based on gender issues? One answer lies in Arthur Miller's (1953) notes in Act I of *The Crucible,* as he seeks explanations to why the Puritans of Salem could persecute (mostly) women of the community for being witches.

> ...the necessity of the Devil may become evident as a weapon, a weapon designed and used time and time again in every age to whip men into a surrender to a particular church of church-state....Our difficulty in believing the—for want of a better word—political inspiration of the Devil is due in great part to the fact that he is called up and damned not only by our social antagonists but by our own side, whatever it may be....A political policy is equated with moral right, and opposition to it with diabolical malevolence. Once such an equation is effectively made, society becomes a congerie of plots and counterplots and the main role of government changes from that of the arbiter to that of the scourge of God....Sex, sin, and the Devil were early linked, and so they continued to be in Salem, and are today. (p. 3335)

I would impose a curricular meaning from Miller's parallels between Puritan theocratic structures and the radical conservatism of the McCarthy era, for the *Devil* remains a potent weapon, one still linked in fundamentalist ideology, the scriptural standard for morality, with sex and sin. But why the gendered embodiment of evil? Consider again Miller's observation: "Sex, sin, and the Devil were...linked" (p. 3335). The Devil as weapon becomes gendered because sex and sin for the fundamentalist are so deliberately conflated and thus, gendered.

Pinar (2001) contends that gender as a social construct completes a "triumvirate" (p. 1157) with racism and misogyny. He further argues that anti-queer prejudice is, in fact, mutated racism and sexism. Fundamentalists play the "queer card" because, unlike outright racial or sexist sentiments, they *can* do so without penalty of public outcry. He writes,

> Do they (the Religious Right) feel cornered, desperate for an issue which they fantasize will bring down God's wrath and make America the heavenly state they imagine it was always meant to be? Homosexuality appears to be that issue. Does this issue come to the surface now in these reactionary groups because the other two elements of the 'triumvirate,' 'race' and 'women's bodies,' are beyond their grasp? ...the right wing clings to what's left of their hatred, that is, what's left that they can express publicly: that which is the 'queer.' (p. 1157)

While Miller rightly links the sexual, religious, and political, Pinar *queers* the structure, suggesting that power and passion are intertwined with all three elements. Sex sells. It sells shoes, clothes, and soft drinks—and it sells a message to disenfranchised evangelicals that sexually liberated (and therefore male-threatening) feminists and sexually perverted queers have infiltrated the schools and are influencing—even recruiting!—their children. Christians react to the taboo—the titillating—the thing that good girls and boys do not do or even talk about or even "lust in their hearts" over. The trigger here is the deliciously forbidden universal obsession: sex.

Straight and Narrow

LSHS is an interesting place to deconstruct straightness. Of the approximately fifty teachers and administrators, at least four of us were queer. I am designating queer here myself; none of the people referenced, unless otherwise noted, has publicly stated that he or she is gay. I use queer in a broad sense, based on Morris' (1998) idea of the queer aesthetic, or queer sensibility: "Queer suggests a self-naming that stands outside the dominant cultural codes; queer opposes sex-policing, gender-policing, heteronormativity, and assimilationist politics." Careful not to codify, she offers three feature "ingredients":

a) Queerness as a subject position digresses from normalized, rigid identities that adhere to the sex-equals-gender paradigm;

b) Queerness as a politic challenges the status quo, does not simply tolerate it, and does not stand for assimilation into the mainstream;

c) Queerness as an aesthetic or sensibility reads and interprets texts as potentially politically radical. (pp. 276–277)

Lick Skillet pedagogues who exemplify queerness are those who do not overtly perform straightness. It is not my intention to solidify a queer/straight identity binary; rather, establishing queer is the proactive act by which to examine straightness within the school culture. This time, queer is the standard, and offcenter is where I am aiming. Of course, when we completely extract sexuality from queer and broaden it to encompass those who do not practice patriarchical conformity, then our little school, as do many others, becomes a much queerer place. I have written in other places (Whitlock, in press) about our queer (my designation) principal, his very visible companion, and the very queer assembly held for our students my last year there, so I will discuss surviving straightness by reclaiming another queered memory involving another enigmatic colleague, Miss Reed.

Miss Reed was the first woman inducted into the state Sports Hall of Fame for her 32 years of success as a girls' volleyball coach. In addition to the esteem in which she was held professionally, Coach Reed was loved by her girls, the Lady Spartans. She is a spinster who, despite a very public and celebrated professional life, keeps her private life closely guarded. In a world where heterosexuality is worn like a badge, the absence of heterosexual proclamation may distinguish one as queer. Although Pollak (in Garber, 1994) suggests that "a role model who is in the closet is not a role model at all," (p. 132) when the role model is not merely a part of the institution but an institution herself, something much more important than a message of sexual identity is modeled. Talburt (2000b) explains that, "to codify queer…is to doom ourselves to repeating the terms of our identities, to keeping the 'space of the possible' small and contained" (p. 10). There was nothing small or contained about Coach Reed. Thirty-two years and a case full of state championship trophies was how she navigated her own possible spaces.

Miss Reed's presence within the school culture is as a kind of "grand dame" icon, a fitting presence in a search for straightness. Her longevity has put her in the position of having taught many of the members of the community, those same members who attend the fundamentalist churches on Sunday. Icons may not be ridden out of town on a rail. Winning icons are local treasures. Coach Reed, like Miss Dove, is formidable; when they are in her presence, school board members, central office administrators, and church deacons are once again fourteen years old and have that tardy-to-class feeling. I only remember having two conversations with her that could remotely be considered queer. It was the same conversation, twice. Late in my year of queer transition, she asked me twice if I had made any men friends online whom I planned to meet. Looking back through my handy-dandy decoder glasses, I can feel the stress on the word *men*, see the slight nod of her head and raised eyebrow. A stretch, I know, but a queer one.

The Right and Prejudice

Britzman (2000) asks, "What would a curriculum be like if the curriculum began with the problem of living a life?" (p. 49). My own curriculum began during my last year at Lick Skillet. That marked the first time that I recall feeling the weight of prejudice upon me, and it felt mighty queer. It happened so suddenly; one day, I was part of the fold—by gosh, people liked me. Next day, I was still me, but I felt something that I came to recognize as distance. I was both bewildered and brokenhearted by the walls that had gone up. I realize that internal and external homophobia were working together to amplify my emotions, but I was incredulous about two things: that the turnaround was such a marked about-face by some of my closest colleagues and that they would abandon *me*. The question arises: How can people, who as New Testament Christians believe in a "law of liberty" (James 1:25) and a loving God, buy into rhetoric that targets somebody like me as a threat to the moral fabric of America? The Religious Right is able to capture the public's attention and play upon its collective emotions because queers (and feminists, and others) are tangible representations of the forces of darkness; again, Miller's *Devil* (1953, p. 35). The problem of living a life for me, then, was that not only was I no longer walking in the light, but I was part of the darkness.

Fundamentalist Christians who ascribe to antiqueer rhetoric do so because queer sex is sin, but what of the "sinner"? How are we so easily vilified? One answer lies in the relationship between religion and prejudice. Hunsberger (1995) speculates that the extent to which fundamentalist people are authoritarian generally determines the extent to which they are also prejudiced, primarily because both "religious fundamentalism and authoritarianism encourage obedience to authority, conventionalism, self-righteousness, and feelings of superiority" (p. 121). People who demonstrate the characteristics of right-wing authoritarianism are often likely to become fundamentalists; at the same time, religious fundamentalism tends to foster the right-wing authoritarian personality (p. 121).

Hunsberger is careful to leave open the possibility of free agency for the individual Christian; he appears to realize the sensitive nature of the empirical research and its margin of error before he would use it to generalize that all fundamentalists are doomed to lives of prejudice. Rather, he holds that prejudice is most likely to occur when the two factors, fundamentalism and authoritarianism, are entwined. He explains, "Religious people who hold that their religious beliefs represent the absolute truth, that they must constantly be alert to Satanic influence in the world around them, that the world can be divided into 'Good' and 'Evil'...and who also tend to be high right-wing authoritarians, tend to hold prejudiced attitudes" (p. 124). Although all fundamentalist Christians are not prejudiced—the radicals do not represent all practitioners—Hunsberger clearly shows that they/we have the *propensity* to be. With the soil so very fertile, all that remains is the mobilization under authoritarian leadership of today's political Religious Right.

In 1998, the Southern Baptists declared that a wife should "submit herself graciously to the servant leadership of her husband" (Baptist Faith and Message, 2000). Later that year, the SBC in its official statement of *Faith and Message* prohibited women from becoming pastors. The same statement urged Christians to oppose racism and homosexuality (Baptist Faith and Message, 2000). (What a difference the official policy might have made if it had denounced *sexism* instead of *homosexuality*.) The president of the convention, Dr. Paige Patterson, offered a bold justification: "Somebody said the other day that we were trying to set things back 200 years and we felt like that was a big mistake. We're trying to set them back 2,000 years. We want to go all the way back to Jesus and the Bible" (2000). However, as Hawley (1994) observes, although fundamentalist ideals are rooted in nostalgia, it is not a nostalgia for that of Jesus' time, "but of home and community life in the small towns of rural, nineteenth-century America" (p. 16).

More recently, in October 2002, President Bush proposed Dr. W. David Hager as his choice to head the Food and Drug Administration (FDA) panel on women's health policy. Hager is the author of *As Jesus Cared for Women: Restoring Women Then and Now* and co-author of *Stress and the Woman's Body*, which prescribes scripture reading and prayer for headaches and premenstrual syndrome. In his practice he refuses to prescribe contraceptives to unmarried women and, in August 2002, he joined the Christian Medical Association in protesting FDA approval of RU-486, the "abortion pill." The panel that he is slated to head is the same panel that recommended approval of RU-486 in 1996. Presently the Reproductive Health Drugs Advisory Committee, which he would chair, is studying the highly controversial hormone replacement therapy (HRT) for menopausal women. HRT contains similar compounds as birth-control pills, and according to *Time*, "some conservatives are trying to use doubts about such therapy to discredit the use of birth-control pills" (Tumulty, 2002, p. 26). With Hager's appointment, the boundaries separating public health/medical policy, religious activism, and gender have been blurred.

Opfer (2000) correlates the increase of antigay activity by the Religious Right with increased public acceptance of homosexuals, noting that over the same period in which this acceptance has occurred, the fundamentalist population has actually declined (p. 95). In June 1998, Pat Robertson broadcast a condemnation of not only Disney World, but also the entire city of Orlando for purchasing and displaying flags celebrating "Gay Days." He said: "And I would warn Orlando that you're right in the way of some serious hurricanes and I don't think I'd be waving those flags in God's face if I were you" (Robertson quoted in Talburt, 2000, p. 85). Within two weeks, fires blazed across central and north Florida. Robertson, on the June 24, 1998, *700 Club*, explained their presence:

> ...we had quite a flap the other day when we were talking about that gay pride day in Orlando and everybody laughed...And what happens to these fires in Florida could be a prelude to some things that are going on all around the world. It just has to do with terrible drought, but it also is caused by lightning. Lightning keeps striking...And I saw on CBS last night the reporter said these fires cannot be stopped by man and says nature is not cooperating. (Robertson in Talburt, 2000, p. 86)

Following the *Lawrence v. Texas* sodomy case in June 2003, in addition to controlling the elements, Robertson suggests a petition for divine yet morbid intervention in the constitutional system of checks and balances:

> Now, the Supreme Court has declared a constitutional right to consensual Sodomy and...has opened the door to homosexual marriages, bigamy, legalized Prostitution, and even incest....But no culture has ever endured which has turned openly to homosexuality. One justice is 83 years old, another has cancer, and another has a heart condition. Would it not be possible for God to put it in the minds of these three judges that the time has come to retire?...(Robertson in NGLTF *Know Thy Enemy*)

Using a different, less abrasive, strategy, on July 13, 1998, a coalition of fifteen different religious groups formed at a Focus on the Family meeting in Colorado, purchased advertising space in *The New York Times*, *The Washington Post*, and *USA Today*. Thus began the now famous "Truth in Love" ad campaign, in which concerned and compassionate fundamentalists claim that through repentance and conversion, a homosexual can become heterosexual. The focus of "Truth in Love" is that homosexual sex is sexual sin, thereby a choice that the "sinner" makes; that through "God's healing love" (Gersen, 1998), gay people can change. Opfer contends that the Christian Right does not practice paranoid, reactionary politics; rather, using the Devil as a weapon is a rational and calculated strategy. Prophesying God's wrath on the reprobate and compassionately offering queers the opportunity to choose *not* to sin as easily as we chose *to* sin represent proactive antiqueer campaigns.

Straighten Up and Gaze Right

I somehow did not win an Academy Award for "Best Female Queer in the Role of a Heterosexual" during the 6 months following my divorce, despite the "cast of thousands" in the production. The whole school community was supportive, offering encouragement, as well as dating hints and "fix-ups." One important tenet of compulsory heterosexuality is the assumed participation in the gendered mating rituals, including the expressed and implied gender expectations. Brownmiller (1984) writes,

> …in this patriarchal culture, women socially have to validate their femaleness in addition to their gender. In other words, to emphasize gender identity, you have to dress, to behave, to think, to react, to emote, to fear, to love, to nurture, and to look 'like a woman' in order to be a woman. (p. 212)

After a respectable time had passed, I began to date again; the women faculty made ready the offering. I remember well the day of the makeover consultation. It happened, of all places, in the principal's office. I have reproduced their tips on "How to Attract a Man" here so that others may benefit from them:

- "Let your hair grow; get a softer cut."
- "Walk (stand, etc.) more like this." (Demonstration following.)
- "Get him to talk about himself."
- "If you have to wear slacks, then get some nice outfits with really feminine pants."

And this one from the principal himself:

- "Wear sandals and paint your toenails. There is nothing sexier than a woman with painted toenails."

The piece de resistance:

- "Be yourself."

I bought those sexy sandals; I spent a hundred dollars on Merle Norman makeup. ("It's thick so it covers difficult blemishes.") I bought a little black dress for the faculty Christmas party because the band director was single, but

I consider my lowest point dying my hair in the sink in the faculty bathroom before the Homecoming game. Performing het can be hell.

That year, I taught juniors. They once completely manufactured a secret admiration between the junior varsity soccer coach and me, two young divorced colleagues who would be just perfect for each other. My vexation multiplied when he good-naturedly joined in. Valentine's Day was particularly fun that year, with a public "outing" of my secret admirer in the cafeteria, complete with his presenting me, on bended knee no less, with a carnation. Very near this time I had a queer epiphany: if I completely remake every fiber of myself, voice, hair, clothes, gait and mannerisms, attitude, and personality, then I just *might* be presentable enough for a man to find me attractive. I change; he chooses.

While I have made every effort to prevent this from being a coming out story, two telling indicators of straightness discourse occurred to me as straight teacher transitioning to queer. It is the way in which two different colleagues responded to my taking them into my confidence. The first is a happy surprise; the second is a sore disappointment. The very first friend and co-worker to whom I sounded out the idea of maybe being not so very heterosexual was Joy. She appeared to be an open-minded person, and she was. Although married to a traditional head-of-the-household man 20 years her senior, Joy fought hard to carve for herself a niche as a slightly bohemian teacher. Perhaps because she practices pedagogy with a queer aesthetic (Morris, 1998, p. 276) or because of her fascination and belief in people, I felt safe in declaring to my friend that I was not entirely revolted by the thought of loving a woman. She responded with all of the warmth and support that every het-on-the-brink could hope for in her time of emotional flux. It is important to note here that my queerly eccentric and accepting friend is not a fundamentalist Christian, no Sister in Christ.

My first queer conversation with a Clearview Christian came a few weeks later, after a failed fix-up date with a fellow who had found me to be, in his words, "peaches," while I considered him more of the pits. At the time, my work had been suffering because my personal life was severely testing my professional one. Sensing this, Dora, who had arranged the date, gained my confidence by relating her own divorce and aftermath stories, including confronting the expectations and demands of parents, church, and community. I ventured softly into the same territory as I had with Joy: that my intrigue and titillation had led me to approach women online to talk to. As I write it today, I feel foolish. Dora's expression never changed from one of sweet concern as I na-ively sought some sort of validation for my actions. I remember thinking what a swell person she was—*and how easy this was going to be after all.*

One of the recurring themes in fundamentalist Christian doctrine is that God "hates the sin but loves the sinner." That principle is the guiding force behind the Christian Right–supported exgay movement, in which gay people are welcomed into the flock where they undergo an onslaught of reparative, or conversion, therapy. Straightness is the state of loving the sinner and hating the sin, whether the sin is being queer, poor, below average intelligence/ ability, nonwhite, different. So out of concern and for my own good, Dora went to her old friend, our assistant principal of curriculum and instruction, and informed her of my confusion about my sexual orientation. Now, I am sure that the reader saw that coming, as well as the spreading of the glad queer tidings like seed thrown into the wind, but I did not.

Attending to Straightness

The Christian Right molds straightness in curriculum and stakeholders through educational policy that is decidedly antiqueer. Nelson Rodriguez writes, "In-deed, combining heterosexism with schooling is an insidious way of educating youth to promote 'sexual fascism'; no doubt it is part of the moral right's 'hid-den curriculum'" (1998, p. 177). Conservative Christians would openly hearken back to a nostalgic ideal with traditional back-to-basics, family values– laden public school curriculum—nothing hidden there. I contend that it is much more effective for the Right to infuse, rather than impose, straightness into education structures. It is not so much that the curriculum is hidden; more likely it is subdued. Straightness, compulsory heterosexuality, and by extension heterosexism, are quietly nurtured in the school culture in much the same way that team pride is built by the football players wearing suits and ties on gameday.

The Right finally recognizes what Freire knew: education is political (1993, p. 127), and it is the medium through which capitalism, and thus patri-archal democracy, will be perpetuated. And so we see more overt measures, apparent in the quantification of school accountability and in the zealous fixa-tion on standardized test scores. Publish district test scores and promise merit raises or school choice based on performance; pedagogy and curriculum be-come centered around content standards, leaving the children on the margins in their own classroom. Where is the participatory and transcendent education (Darder, 2002) of fellowship and dialogue? Conservatism and corporatism, the "power of commodified identities within capitalism" (McLaren, 2000, p. 187), have bound the wonder and inquiry of teachers and students in the classroom, holding them hostage to the "bankrupt logic of standardization" (Darder, 2002, p. 58). The suppression of zest keeps things straight.

When overt measures are undertaken, according to Lugg (2000b), they take one of two forms: re-Christianizing the schools and deinstitutionalization. Re-Christianizing public schools would replace the secular with the Judeo-Christian version of the spiritual by promoting religious activities and curricula—a "redemptive mission" (p. 622)—within the schools. Lobbying for creationism and for an abstinence-only sex education curriculum falls into this category. Multiculturalism would be eliminated, yet religious-sponsored school activities would be endorsed. The school prayer movement and the 1999 Hang Ten promotion, sponsored by the Family Research Council (Dr. James Dobson's Washington lobbying group), that set out to post a copy of the Ten Commandments in every public school in America, are attempts at re-Christianization (FRC quoted in Lugg, 2000b). The introduction of Bible electives, particularly those developed and marketed by the National Council on Bible Curriculum in Public Schools, into public school curriculum, is a current example.

Lugg's second category of Christian Right activism is *deinstitutionalization.* A more far-reaching goal than re-Christianization, it implies a breakdown, rather than a restructuring, of the system of public schooling as it exists. I like to think of it as the "take my ball and go home" variety of school reform: if schools are not being run to suit us, then we will withdraw our children and educate them ourselves. For example, home schooling, unrestricted vouchers, and charter schools present alternatives to school. A conservative Christian agenda will increasingly affect not only the scope of public education, but it will also continue to shape straight teacher identity. Ironically, among the most immediate victims of (ultra-Conservative) Christianization of schools would be the minority population of fundamentalist children who, marginalized from the mainstream, stand to benefit from a multicultural, pluralistic, democratic education (McConnell, 1998, p. 33) from a queer education.

To achieve its education policy goals, the ultra-Right must therefore find ways to induce the public out of its voting apathy so that Right-supported elected officials can then advance this far-reaching philosophical and curricular/pedagogical agenda. The formula that seems to yield the greatest results contains (1) variables to which the public will react passionately: children, sex, and queers; and (2) the threat of disenfranchisement of the fundamentalist population by school policymakers. Such polarization pushes Christian voters to an ultimatum, and they answer by turning to the safe, known entity: the fellow holding the Bible. We make a choice because we perceive no other choice, when, in fact, issues such as those above do not represent the "normative desires of traditional Christians in school reform" (Sewall, 1998, p. 78). The alternative is risky: Christians must resist the militant, reactionary, exclusive course, acknowledge that there are issues in question that conflict with a literalist interpretation of the Bible, and turn to dialogue.

What may on the surface appear to be a return to old-fashioned Christian values—a focus on the family, rededication of husbands and fathers, the promotion of abstinence—is actually a very modern political strategy. A closer examination of what these value-laced ideals stand for will illumine what they stand against. Fundamentalist activism goes beyond a nostalgic back-to-basics, back-to-God campaign, for in order to entice the people to embrace this agenda, the movement must vilify those responsible for the falling away. Queers are easy targets because gender-related issues make up what Bowman (2000) calls "the last acceptable prejudice" (p. 1). Acceptable prejudice is what gives Alabama Supreme Court Chief Justice Roy "Ten Commandments" Moore license to suggest violent implications in reference to a custody case involving a lesbian mother:

> The State carries the power of the sword, that is, the power to prohibit conduct with physical penalties, such as confinements and even execution. It must use that power to prevent the subversion of children towards this lifestyle, to not encourage a criminal lifestyle. (Rostow, 2002, p. 13)

Moore's seat is an elected one; had he believed that his career as Alabama Supreme Court justice would be in any way jeopardized by asserting the power of the state to execute queers as subversive criminals harmful to children, then he would not have done so. The conflict is gendered, with implications that cross the threshold of the classroom. And for the sake of advancing a conservative political agenda, the last acceptable prejudice has led to the last acceptable form of oppression.

The Greatest of These

How is straightness infused into the school culture, compulsory heterosexuality propagated among pedagogues? The key, I think, lies within the curriculum. "When values become institutions," writes Doll, "they become dangerous. Whoever controls the accepted notion of God, presides over what is socially acceptable" (2000, p. 43). When that notion is of a heterosexual God with 19th century ideals, and when the institution is the school culture, then it is straightness that is socially acceptable. What actual curriculum undercurrents propel accountability, "scientifically" based research, Grade Level Expectations, and Highly Qualified Teachers (NCLB, 2001)? How is it that we can expect to close the achievement gap between white, middle class children and minority subgroups (NCLB, 2001) with Norm- and Criterion-Referenced Test mandates? Education in this country is rooted in patriarchal structures; pedagogy, curriculum, and epistemology must not be. No Child Left Behind is the culmination of 20 years of conservative Right political activism that began during the Reagan Administration. NCLB is legislated straightness. The queerly fundamental course of action that I propose for education is based on love, and love seems like a deceptively uncomplicated creature.

An educator for 16 years, I see a decided absence of love in pedagogy and curriculum at all levels. A conservative wave of corporatism and performance propels education; we are in the *business* of educating youngsters—we always have been preparing workers, but the jobs have become more sophisticated. Now, three- and four-year-old prekindergarten students will have mandated performance standards, and reading will be taught from scripted, directed "curricula" (Open Court, Language, Voyager). There is no room for the dialogue-sparking spiritual element just beneath the surface of human nature, no room for what Noddings calls "moral education as a form of life" (in Sears & Carper, 1998, p. 44). Dialogue might lead to critical consciousness, which might in turn engender unity in diversity in our students, which might finally result in our acceptance and appreciation of each other. Freire maintained that if we would live free—whatever our oppression, whether pedagogical, societal, political—we must "risk an act of love" (1970, p. 35). Love is not to be found in a quest for higher scores; it is present when teaching becomes a "personal calling to actualize the transformation of identity" (Wexler, 1996, p. 149).

Huebner (1999) holds that education is the "lure of the transcendent," (p. 462) conceding that the risk involved is threatening. He continues,

> How can we face the threat of the unknown and the threat of the stranger outside of us and inside of us? It is not easy. We need the assurance that we will not be destroyed, that life will indeed be enhanced rather than destroyed. Love is that assurance. We can face the threat of the unknown and of the stranger if we are not alone; if we are in the presence of love which affirms life. (p. 363)

Huebner's call for the infusion of the spiritual into the secular world of education has as its foundation a powerful, active love that is to be utilized, a love that assures and affirms rather than denies and negates. Acts of love require courage. Before stakeholders, at every level and from all "sides," can use love as a liberatory tool, they must have the courage to open their hearts and minds to love as an impetus for progressive change. Love must gain admittance to the discourse.

Love-in-action, revolutionary love, inspires dialogue. Love without dialogue is a theoretical ideal, fruitless, and dialogue without love is talk, analogous to the Biblical syllogism in James: faith without works is dead; works without faith are barren (2:14–18). Strike (1998) suggests, "The key to dialogue is the virtue of reasonableness" (p. 68), the belief that both parties approach the dialogue with openness that is based on faith and trust. Dialogue grounded in reason is supported by precepts that are undeniably embraced by Christians: faith, hope, love; and the greatest of these is love (I Corinthians 13:13). Along with openness, reason, and love that we bring to the dialogue table, we must also, however, come with the expectation that we might leave the table in (dis)comfort.

The concept of dialogue in which I am investing such hope is based upon that of "analytic dialogue" (1997, p. 115), which Ellsworth (1989/1994, 1997) incorporates into her discussion of the "repressive myths of critical pedagogy" (1989) and pedagogical "modes of address" (1997). She positions dialogue as a form of pedagogy that is a practice "historically and culturally embedded" (1997, p. 48) in raced, classed, and gendered "networks of power, desire, and knowledge" (p. 49). She dismisses simplistic, unquestioned tenets of dialogue, as well as the neutral understanding that is assumed as its logical outcome, as not only ineffective, but repressive, doing more harm than good to efforts at critical pedagogy. Neither phlegmatic nor unitary, Ellsworth's analytic dialogue embraces ruptures and unsettles its participants (Could this dialogue be queer?) as it moves participants toward the *play* of understanding. The task may be, she suggests, "building a coalition among the multiple, shifting, intersecting, and sometimes contradictory groups carrying unequal weights of legitimacy within the culture" (1989/1994, p. 317). It is from *processes* of analytic dialogue that we grapple toward the self-understanding from which "self-mobilization in the service of social reconstruction" (Pinar, 2004, p. 201) might spring.

I call on fundamentalist Christians to dedicate ourselves to the principles to which we have dedicated ourselves: "As I have loved you, so you must love one another. By this all men will know that you are my disciples, if you love one another" (John 13:34–35). I propose the following roadwork: fundamentalist Christians must acknowledge that homophobia and the other "isms"—racism, sexism, classism, ageism, etc.—impede spirituality, and recognize that celebrating the agency of all people strengthens the spirit—both our individual and collective spirits. When the discourses that construct straight teachers become instilled with openness, trust, and propensity for dialogue, then unity in diversity might also emerge. Perhaps then the sacred might permeate pedagogy then culture then society, which might then lead to Wexler's (1996) exploration of the "implications of religious theory and practice for creating new models of educational theory and practice" (p. 151).

A pedagogy of love requires a leap of faith—faith that the risks, that the difficult knowledges can make ready the course for transformative, coalition-building discourses. Ellsworth (1994) writes, "Educational researchers attempting to construct meaningful discourses about the politics of classroom practices must begin to theorize the consequences for education on the ways in which knowledge, power, and desire are mutually implicated in each other's formations and deployments" (p. 316). Education reform that begins with curriculum design—standards, assessments, best practices—picks up in the middle. Knowledge, power, and desire are risky entanglements of love; but this time the queer tangle stays at the bottom of the box with a gaggle of policymakers sitting on the lid.

As for me, I still feel the strong pull to "come back to Jesus" by coming back to straightness. If queer pedagogy unsettles curriculum, I am the embodiment of how it can shake up a faculty—or an identity perception. For at least the year of my own queer gazing, LSHS had to steady itself as it was forced to consider its own queerness. For a community of compulsory heterosexuality that cultivates dispositions of straightness in its resident stakeholders, it is queerer than it knows. Queer is scary because it does indeed "unrest" and "trouble" curriculum (Morris, 1998, p. 285), while straight strives to reach the peaceful center of the known with the comfort of standardization. Shooting for this center is the ultimate straightness discourse within the local school culture, positioning the evolution of straight teachers as part of the natural order of things. Straightness is performed and nourished so that it may perpetuate itself, but queer happens. Christian values, along with other sets of humanizing values important to stakeholders, might find space in education structures through the embracing of queer ruptures. It will be the queering of straight teachers and of curriculum that will offer the hope of infusing them with the sacred. It will be the decentering of straightness that will present the greatest possibility of its continued being.

Works Cited

Allen, J. (Ed.). (1990). *Lesbian philosophies and cultures*. Albany: SUNY Press.

Altemeyer, B. & Hunsberger, B. (1992). Authoritarianism, religious fundamentalism, quest, and prejudice. *International Journal for the Psychology of Religion*, 2(2), 113–133.

Anzaldúa, G. (1987). *Borderlands La Frontera: The new mestiza*. San Francisco: Aunt Lute Books.

Asher, N. (2002). (En)gendering a hybrid consciousness. *Journal of Curriculum Theorizing*, 18(4), 81–92.

Balmer, R. (2000). *Mine eyes have seen the glory: A journey into the evangelical subculture in America* (3rd ed.). New York: Oxford University Press.

Bowman, D. (2000). *The last acceptable prejudice*. Retrieved October 29, 2001, from http://www.salon.com/sex/feature

Britzman, D. (1997). The tangles of implication. *Qualitative Studies in Education*, 10(1), 31–37.

Britzman, D. (1998). *Lost subjects/contested objects: Toward a psychoanalytic inquiry of learning*. Albany: SUNY Press.

Britzman, D. (2000). Precocious education. In S. Talburt & S. R. Steinberg (Eds.), *Thinking queer: Sexuality, culture, and education* (pp. 33–59). New York: Peter Lang.

Brownmiller, S. (1984). *Femininity*. New York: Linden Press, Simon and Schuster.

Charpentier, S. (1996). *Gender, body and the sacred: Heterosexual hegemony as a sacred order*. Retrieved October 22, 2001, from http://www.Ars-Rhetorica.net

Darder, A. (2002). *Reinventing Paulo Freire: A pedagogy of love*. Cambridge, MA: Westview Press.

Detwiler, F. (1999). *Standing on the premises of God: The Christian Right's fight to redefine America's public schools*. New York: New York University Press.

de Lauretis, T. (1990). Eccentric subjects: Feminist theory and historical consciousness. *Feminist Studies*, 16(1), 115–149.

Doll, M. A. (2000). *Like letters in running water: A mythopoetics of curriculum*. Mahwah, NJ: Lawrence Erlbaum Associates.

Doll, M. A. (1998). Queering the gaze. In W. F. Pinar (Ed.), *Queer theory in education* (pp. 287–298). Mahwah, NJ: Lawrence Erlbaum Associates.

Edgerton, S. H. (1996). *Translating the curriculum: Multiculturalism into cultural studies*. New York: Routledge.

Ellsworth, E. (1989/1994). Why doesn't this feel empowering? Working through the repressive myths of critical pedagogy. In L. Stone (Ed.), *The Education Feminist Reader* (pp. 300–327). New York: Routledge.

Ellsworth, E. (1997). *Teaching positions: Difference, pedagogy, and the power of address.* New York: Teachers College Press.

Fitzgerald, S. (Ed.). (1979). *Letters of Flannery O'Connor.* New York: Farrar, Straus, and Giroux.

Freire, P. (1970). *Pedagogy of the oppressed.* New York: Continuum.

Freire, P. (1993). *Pedagogy of the city.* New York: Continuum.

Garber, L. (Ed.). (1994). *Tilting the tower: Lesbians teaching queer subjects.* New York: Routledge.

Gersen, M. (1998, July 28). *Out of the political closet.* Retrieved November 2, 2001, from *U.S. News and World Report* Web site: http://ask.elibrary.com

Gilmore, L. (1994). *Autobiographics: A feminist theory of women's self-representation.* New York: Cornell University Press.

Gourdine, A. (2003). *The difference place makes: Gender, sexuality, and diaspora identity.* Columbus: Ohio State University Press.

Gross, R. M. (1996). *Feminism & religion: An introduction.* Boston: Beacon Press.

Harbeck, K. (Ed.). (1992). *Coming out of the classroom closet: Gay and lesbian students, teachers and curricula.* New York: Harrington Park Press.

Harding, S. (1991). *Whose science? whose knowledge?* New York: Cornell University Press.

Harris, J. (2001). *God gave U.S. 'what we deserve,' Falwell says.* Retrieved September 14, 2001, from *The Washington Post* Online Web site: http://www.washingtonpost.com

Hawley, J. (Ed.). (1994). *Fundamentalism & gender.* New York: Oxford University Press.

Hill, S. (1998). Fundamentalism in recent Southern culture: Has it done what the Civil Rights Movement couldn't do? *The Journal of Southern Religion.* Retrieved October 29, 2001, from http://jrs.as.Wvu.edu/essay.htm

Hillis, V. & Pinar, W. (Eds.). (1999). *The lure of the transcendent: Collected essays by Dwayne E. Huebner.* Mahwah, NJ: Lawrence Erlbaum.

hooks, b. (1990). *Yearning: Race, gender, and cultural politics.* Boston, MA: South End Press.

Huebner, D., Hillis, V., & Pinar, W. (Eds.). (1999). *The lure of the transcendent: Collected essays by Dwayne E. Huebner.* Mahwah, NJ: Lawrence Erlbaum.

Hunsberger, B. (1995). Religion and prejudice: The role of religious fundamentalism, quest, and right-wing authoritarianism. *Journal of Social Issues*, 51, 113–129.

Jennings, K. (Ed.). (1994). *One teacher in ten: Gay and lesbian educators tell their stories.* Los Angeles: Alyson Publications.

Khayatt, M. (1992). *Lesbian teachers: An invisible presence.* Albany, NY: SUNY.

Kimmel, M. S. (1996). *Manhood in America: A cultural history*. New York: Free Press.

Kincheloe, J., & Pinar, W. (Eds.). (1991). *Curriculum as social psychoanalysis: The significance of place*. Albany, NY: SUNY Press.

King, F. (1995). *The Florence King reader*. New York: St. Martin's Press.

Klein, M. (1996, January). *The sex lies of the religious right: How conservatives distort the facts of life*. Retrieved October 29, 2001, from The Playboy Forum Web site: http://www.radical-sex.com

Lugg, C. (2000a). *For God and country: Conservatism and American school policy*. New York: Peter Lang.

Lugg, C. (2000b). Reading, writing, and reconstructionism: The Christian Right and the politics of public education. *Educational Policy*, 14, 622. Retrieved November 8, 2001, from http://ftviewer.epnet.com

Luhman, S. (1998). Queering/quering pedagogy? Or, pedagogy is a pretty queer thing. In W. F. Pinar (Ed.), *Queer theory in education* (pp. 141–156). Mahwah, NJ: Lawrence Erlbaum.

Martin, W. (1997). *With God on our side: The rise of the Religious Right in America*. New York: Broadway.

Martusewicz, R. A. (1997). Say me to me. In S. Todd (Ed.), *Learning desire: Perspectives on pedagogy, culture, and the unsaid* (pp. 97–113). New York: Routledge.

McConnell, M. W. (1998). Commentary, in Encounters in law, philosophy, religion, and education. In J. T. Sears & J. C. Carper (Eds.), *Curriculum, religion, and public education: Conversations for an enlarging public square*. New York: Teachers College Press.

McLaren, P. (2000). *Che Guevara, Paulo Freire, and the pedagogy of revolution*. Lanham, MD: Rowman & Littlefield.

Miller, A. (1953). *The Crucible*. New York: Penguin Books.

Miller, D. W. (2000, June). Striving to understand the religious right. *Chronicle of Higher Education*, 56(43), A17–A18.

Miller, N. (2002, June 11). *'We love homosexuals,' James Merritt tells SBC*. Retrieved June 12, 2002, from *BP News* Web site: http://www.bpnews.net

Mintz, B., & Rothblum, E. (Eds.). (1997). *Lesbians in academia: Degrees of freedom*. New York: Routledge.

Molick, C. (2001). *Quotes: Homophobia and sexism*. Retrieved October 29, 2001, from http://www.bible.org/quotes/phobia

Morris, M. (1998). Unresting the curriculum: Queer projects, queer imaginings. In W. F. Pinar (Ed.). *Queer theory in education* (pp. 275–286). Mahwah, NJ: Lawrence Erlbaum.

Munro, P. (1998). Engendering curriculum history. In W. Pinar (Ed.), *Curriculum: Toward new identities* (pp. 263–294). New York: Garland Publishing.

Munro, P. (1998). *Subject to fiction: Women teachers' life history narratives and the cultural politics of resistance*. Philadelphia: Open University Press.

National Education Association. (2001). *The Religious Right*. Retrieved October 29, 2001, from National Education Association Web site: http://www.nea.org/publiced/paycheck

National Gay and Lesbian Task Force. (2003). *Know thy enemy: A compendium of recent quotes about the Supreme Court sodomy ruling and the same-sex marriage backlash* (July 30, 2003 ed.) [Brochure]. : Author.

New International Version Study Bible. (1985). Grand Rapids: Zondervan.

Nicholson, L. (Ed.). (1990). *Feminism/postmodernism*. New York: Routledge.

No Child Left Behind (2001). Retrieved on March 15, 2007, from http://www.ed.gov/nclb/

Opfer, D. (2000). Paranoid politics, extremism, and the Religious Right: A case of mistaken identity? In S. Talburt & S. Steinberg (Eds.), *Thinking queer: Sexuality, culture, and education* (pp. 85–103). New York: Peter Lang.

Pinar, W. (1994). *Autobiography, politics and sexuality*. New York: Peter Lang.

Pinar, W. (2001). *The gender of racial politics and violence in America*. New York: Peter Lang.

Pinar, W. (2004). *What is curriculum theory?* Mahway, NJ: Lawrence Erlbaum.

Pinar, W. (Ed.). (1998). *Queer theory in education*. Mahwah, NJ: Lawrence Erlbaum Associates.

Pinar, W., Reynolds, W., Slattery, P., & Taubman, P. (1996). *Understanding curriculum*. New York: Peter Lang.

Pitt, A. (2003). *The play of the personal: Psychoanalytic narratives of feminist education*. New York: Peter Lang.

Political Research Associates, the Policy Institute of the National Gay and Lesbian Task Force, and Equal Partners in Faith. (October 1998). *Calculated compassion: How the ex-gay movement serves the Right's attack on democracy* [Brochure]. : Author.

Reaves, J. (2000, June 13). *Are Southern Baptists flirting with a schism?* Retrieved October 29, 2001, from http://www.time.com

Rodriguez, N. (1998). (Queer) youth as political and pedagogical. In W. Pinar (Ed.), *Queer theory in education* (pp. 173–185). Mahwah, NJ: Lawrence Erlbaum.

Rofes, E. (1997). Gay issues, schools, and the right-wing backlash. *Rethinking Schools*. Retrieved Spring 1997, from http://www.rethinkingschools.org

Rostow, A. (2002, May). Judging Roy. *Girlfriends*, 12–14.

Schoolfacts. (n.d.). Retrieved October 29, 2001, from Schoolfacts Web site: http:// www.pflag.org/schools/schoolsfacts.htm

Sears, J. T. (1991). *Growing up gay in the South: Race, gender, and the journeys of the spirit*. New York: Harrington Park Press.

Sears, J. T. (1998). Crossing boundaries and becoming the other. In J. T. Sears & J. C. Carper (Eds.), *Curriculum, religion, and public education: Conversations for an enlarging public square* (pp. 38–58). New York: Teachers College Press.

Sewall, G. T. (1998). Religion and the textbooks. In J. T. Sears & J. C. Carper (Eds.), *Curriculum, religion, and public education: Conversations for an enlarging public square* (pp. 73–84). New York: Teachers College Press.

Smith, S. (Ed.). (1998). *Women, autobiography, theory: A reader*. Madison: University of Wisconsin Press.

Smith, S., & Watson, J. (2001). *Reading autobiography: A guide for interpreting life narratives*. Minneapolis: University of Minnesota Press.

Southern Baptists to vote against women. (2000, June 13). Retrieved October 29, 2001, from http://www.cnn.com

St. Pierre, E. (1995). *Arts of existence: The construction of subjectivity in older, white, Southern women*. Unpublished dissertation. Columbus: The Ohio State University.

Stone, L. (Ed.). (1994). *The education feminism reader*. New York: Routledge.

Strike, K. A. (1998). Dialogue, religion, and tolerance: How to talk to people who are wrong about (almost) anything. In J. T. Sears & J. C. Carper (Eds.), *Curriculum, religion, and public education: Conversations for an enlarging public square* (pp. 59–69). New York: Teachers College Press.

Swomley, J. (1996, January 11). Promises we don't want kept. *The Humanist*. Retrieved November 2, 2001, from http://ask.elibrary.com

Talburt, S. (2000a). *Subject to identity: Knowledge, sexuality, and academic practices in higher education*. Albany: SUNY Press.

Talburt, S., & Steinberg, S. (Eds.). (2000b). *Thinking queer: Sexuality, culture, and education*. New York: Peter Lang.

The Baptist Faith and Message. (2000). Retrieved on March 15, 2007, from http://www.sbc.net/bfm/bfm2000.asp

Trebilcot, J. (1990). Dyke methods. In J. Allen (Ed.), *Lesbian philosophies and cultures* (pp. 15–29). New York: SUNY Press.

Tumulty, K. (2002, October 14). Jesus and the FDA. *Time*, 26.

Walker, A. (1989). Everyday use. In *Adventures in American literature* (Pegasus Edition). Dallas: Harcourt Brace Jovanovich.

Weedon, C. (1999). *Feminism, theory, and the politics of difference*. Malden, MA: Blackwell Publishers.

Weiler, K. (1991). Freire and a feminist pedagogy of difference. *Harvard Educational Review*, 61, 449–474.

Wexler, P. (1996). *Holy sparks: Social theory, education, and religion*. New York: St. Martin's Press.

Whitlock, R. U. (In press). *This corner of Canaan: Curriculum studies of place and the reconstruction of the South*. New York: Peter Lang.

Williams, T. (1974, 1947). *A streetcar named desire*. New York: Signet.

Woog, D. (1995). *School's out: The impact of gay and lesbian issues on America's schools*. Boston: Alyson Publications.

CHAPTER FOUR

The Queer Story of "The Heterosexual Questionnaire"

Mary Louise Rasmussen
Jane Mitchell
Valerie Harwood

"Protest over school sex survey"
(28 October 2003) *The World Today*

"Sex class quiz inquiry"
(10 October 2003) *The Adelaide Advertiser*

"Sex survey probe; Questionnaire was meant for teachers"
(29 October 2003) *Herald Sun* (Melbourne)

"SURVEY UPROAR"
(28 October 2003) *Courier Mail* (Brisbane)

"Sex survey shocks; School asks teens questions on *homosexuality*"
(28 October 2003) *Herald Sun* (Melbourne)

"Gay sex questions 'in the curriculum'"
(29 October 2003) *The Australian*

The headlines featured above all accompanied a news story related to the use of *The Heterosexual Questionnaire*[1] in a high school in the Australian state of Victoria in 2003. In this chapter we discuss the debate generated by this news story and analyze the authorized and unauthorized readings of this questionnaire, and associated implications for teacher education curriculum. The *Questionnaire* was part of an education program called "Talking Sexual Health: National Framework for Education About STI's, HIV/AIDS and Blood Borne

Viruses in Secondary Schools" (1999) that was designed by the Australian Research Centre in Sexual Health and Society at Victoria's La Trobe University to develop teachers' sex education skills (Hoare, 2003). The *Questionnaire* was not, according to the authors, a classroom tool. The program did not become controversial until last year when a relieving teacher,[2] who was taking a Year 9[3] Health Education class at Wodonga High, administered the *Questionnaire* and parents and community members objected.

The *Questionnaire* includes questions such as the following:

What do you think caused your heterosexuality?

If you have never slept with a person of the same sex, is it possible that all you need is a good lesbian/gay lover?

How can you become a whole person if you limit yourself to compulsive and exclusive heterosexual behavior?

Following on from the *Questionnaire* readers are asked to consider "What assumptions are made about heterosexuality?" The *Questionnaire*, it appears, is very focused on the production of heterosexual identity. Insofar as this *Questionnaire* is designed to provoke readers to interrogate their assumptions related to sexual identity, one might say that the exercise was very queer. Hence, on first glance, it may be perceived as an instance of queerly critical teacher education within a secondary educational setting. As the *Questionnaire*, at least in this instance, was designed specifically for teachers, it might also be read as a considered attempt to queer straight teachers' understandings of heterosexuality. However, as the newspaper headlines above suggest, the implementation of the *Questionnaire* within a school setting caused some controversy. The Premier of Victoria, Steve Bracks, called for an inquiry; the authors of the training program insisted that the *Questionnaire* was considered inappropriate for use with high school students; and the teacher involved was never heard from in the press.

For the purpose of this chapter we have chosen to organize our analysis of the *Questionnaire* into two parts. We commence with what we term authorized readings of the *Questionnaire*, and here we document the use of the *Questionnaire* as a government-sanctioned antihomophobic curriculum device in educational settings in Australia and in the United States. In so doing we consider ways in which knowledge about same-sex attraction is rendered in the curriculum for particular audiences. More specifically we ask: What are the intentions that might underlie the inclusion of the *Questionnaire* in school or teacher education curricula? How is the *Questionnaire* understood in practice in the Victorian context? And is the use of the *Questionnaire* in this context a classic case of curriculum intervention gone awry?

In part two of this article we draw attention to the tensions that adhere to the production of "straightness" in educational settings, even when that "straightness" takes the form of a tongue-in-cheek questionnaire. We also consider how readings of the *Questionnaire* may vary according to the place and space in which the *Questionnaire* is conducted. Our aim here is not to suggest a correct reading of the *Questionnaire*, but rather to demonstrate how diverse the readings of this curriculum document might be. This process points to some possibilities and limitations regarding the use of the *Questionnaire* and, potentially, similar curriculum devices that might be used to queer "straight" and "gay" teachers. At the outset, it is also worth highlighting the difficulties associated with any attempt to queer straight or gay teachers when we can't assume any agreement about what constitutes the work of queering. For instance, can one assume that the *Questionnaire*, by its very existence in this teacher-training program, is an example of queering the straight teacher?

Part One: *The Heterosexual Questionnaire* as an Official Curriculum Device

The Heterosexual Questionnaire was one, admittedly small, part of a set of resources produced as part of the "Talking Sexual Health: National Framework for Education About STIs, HIV/AIDS and Blood Borne Viruses in Secondary Schools" (Commonwealth of Australia, 1999). Used in Australia from 1999 to 2004, *Talking Sexual Health* was designed to provide a national framework for education about sexually transmitted infections (STIs), HIV/AIDS, and blood borne viruses (BBV) in secondary schools. Far from producing some fact sheets on STIs, HIV/AIDS, and BBV for distribution to schools, *Talking Sexual Health* located these issues within a broad and far-reaching set of principles and practices pertaining to education about sexuality and sexual health in schools. The principles and practices included:

- Taking a whole school approach
- Acknowledging young people as sexual beings
- Acknowledging and catering to the diversity of all students
- Providing an appropriate and comprehensive curriculum context
- Acknowledging the professional development needs of the school community (Commonwealth of Australia, 1999, p. 5)

Each of the above points is elaborated on in the *Talking Sexual Health* document and through the activities and strategies presented in three associated sets of resource materials: a Professional Development Resource for Teachers; a Parent's Resource; and Teaching and Learning Resources for use with students in classrooms. As a curriculum tool, *Talking Sexual Health* had considerable purchase, both because of its conceptual breadth and depth, and because it was a national project that was supported by state education jurisdictions and other educational and research groups concerned with young people, their health and sexuality.

For the purposes of this chapter, the elaboration of the principles mentioned above and their manifestation in the resource materials touches on two salient points. First, as part of the concern to acknowledge and cater to the diversity of students, the authors of *Talking Sexual Health* seek to explicitly recognize same-sex attraction and challenge heteronormative assumptions. The document argues that most current school-based programs concerned with sexuality education do not include young people who are attracted to members of their own sex. *Talking Sexual Health* recommends that schools remedy this and examine health education programs and resources to ensure they are inclusive of all students.

Second, the authors of *Talking Sexual Health* argue that appropriate professional development is lacking for those teachers working in the sexuality education field. They suggest that successful delivery of programs requires teachers who are "qualified, sensitive, and trusted by students" (Commonwealth of Australia, 1999, p. 58) and that this requires a comprehensive professional development strategy. Thus *Talking Sexual Health* seeks to build a strong professional development focus into both policy and practice. One part of this professional development strategy was the production of materials and activities designed to support teachers' professional learning, some of which aimed to assist educators to understand and cater for the diversity noted above. The specific professional development approach for teachers associated with the *Talking Sexual Health* materials was a two-day workshop facilitated by Family Planning, an Australian body that provides a wide range of services related to sexual and reproductive health.

As mentioned above, *The Heterosexual Questionnaire* was one of a number of strategies in the *Talking Sexual Health* resource materials. But what was its purpose and for whom was it intended? In the controversy surrounding the use of the *Questionnaire* in the Wodonga High School, there is some dispute over the answers to the questions. The media reported comments from those central to the debate: Steve Bracks, the Premier of Victoria; Paul Barber and Jan Watson, spokespersons for the Victoria Department of Education and Training (DET); Ann Radowski, Education and Training Manager for Family Planning Victoria, the group responsible for delivering the professional development; and Peter McLean, the Principal of Wodonga High School. Their views are noted below:

In a radio interview, Premier Steve Bracks argued:

> I understand it was not meant to be distributed to students and was distributed by the emergency teacher, and obviously some action will be taken by the region on this matter. The Regional Office will examine that pretty closely. (Australian Broadcasting Commission, 28 October 2003)

A newspaper reported spokespersons from the Victoria DET as follows:

> Department of Education spokesperson Paul Barber said the 17 question survey was created as a training resource for teachers conducting the health education course and was never meant for students' eyes. "The teacher who was running this course went to hospital and a trainee teacher took over her class and it appears grabbed this (survey) from their manual thinking it was part of the course" Mr. Barber said. (*Australian National News Wire*, Australian Associated Press, 28 October 2003)

> Jan Watson, from Victoria's Department of Education and Training, said the survey had been 'taken out of context' by the school and claimed it was designed to be used 'in the context of a two day training program for teachers.' ("Gay Sex questions 'in the curriculum,'" *The Australian*, 29 October 2003)

Ann Radowski, Education and Training Manager for Family Planning Victoria, the deliverers of the *Talking Sexual Health* professional development program for teachers:

> said the questionnaire was designed…to develop teachers' sex education skills and was 'not a classroom tool.' ("Gay Sex questions 'in the curriculum,'" *The Australian*, 29 October 2003)

The view of the school principal, as reported in *The Australian* newspaper, differed sharply regarding the audience and purpose of the survey:

> They [school teachers who attended the workshop] were given clear instruction, he [the Principal] said, that the survey was appropriate for students from Year 9 upwards. "It was a worksheet which clearly states that as an activity, students should read the following and answer and discuss the questions at the end of the attached questionnaire" he said. ("Gay Sex questions 'in the curriculum,'" *The Australian, 29 October 2003)

The portrayal of different points of view regarding the purpose and use of the *Questionnaire* provides a useful illustration of both the politics and unpredictability of systemic intention and local interpretation of the curriculum (Bernstein, 1990) in teacher education and school contexts. The comments by the Premier, the departmental spokespersons, and the professional development deliverers were public attempts to (re)inscribe an "official" view of the curriculum, post the controversy—that is, that the *Questionnaire* was not intended to be used in classrooms and that it was inappropriate for Year 9 students. The comments made by the principal in the media represented one contestation of this "official" view at the local school level. According to the principal, the use of the *Questionnaire* was about "values clarification" and "educating young people to be tolerant" (Australian Broadcasting Corporation, *The World Today*, 28 October 2003). The actual use of the *Questionnaire* by the teacher likewise represented a probably unwitting yet publicly volatile, local interpretation of a curriculum document. Our concern here is not to arbitrate and say that one party was right and the other wrong regarding the intended audience and use of the *Questionnaire*, but rather to illustrate the very public tension that emerged in this case regarding local interpretation and systemic control of the *Questionnaire* as a curriculum resource. Moreover, given one newspaper report that the principal had withdrawn the *Questionnaire* from the curriculum ("Gay Sex questions 'in the curriculum,'" *The Australian,* 29 October 2003), we can only assume that some greater degree of "after-the-fact" systemic control may have been exercised in this case.

It is interesting, yet perhaps not surprising, that the focus for attention in this case was principally on the use of the *Questionnaire* with school-age students. The use of the *Questionnaire* as part of professional development materials was not scrutinized in the public debate. Nor were any of the principles and practices pertaining to the recognition of diverse sexualities embedded in the *Talking Sexual Health* documents. By implication, however, and as we discuss further in the next section of this paper, the *Questionnaire* and associated debate symbolized and carried a set of regulatory and heteronormative messages regarding the discussion of sexuality in the school curriculum. Such messages served to undercut related professional development materials and the *Talking Sexual Health* principles.

In contrast to the intended and "official" use of *The Heterosexual Questionnaire* in *Talking Sexual Health,* other educational providers within and outside Australia do include the *Questionnaire* as a potential classroom strategy that can assist students to examine their assumptions about sexualities. For example, Planned Parenthood of Connecticut lists the *Questionnaire* as a resource. In so doing it provides some recommendations and advice regarding its use: to be used for high school+ age groups; it is given a 201 rating (101 beginners; 201 and 203 more advanced); it may need to be adapted to "developmentally-based age appropriate levels"; and teachers should make the goals and objectives of the workshop explicit. While the example above authorizes the use of the *Questionnaire* with students, the context in which it is presented was very different from the supposed authorization of the *Questionnaire* in the Wodonga High School/*Talking Sexual Health* debate. In the Planned Parenthood context, the *Questionnaire* was a resource for teachers to use if they chose; it is not part of a formal state or district curriculum mandate. The concern in the Wodonga case, at least in its media representation, was that the *Questionnaire* might be part of the compulsory curriculum; in other words, that it was to be used with all students and be outside teachers' decision making. The irony in this case, and reflecting the unpredictability and in some ways (despite systemic intentions) uncontrollable nature of the curriculum, is that a teacher who had not been to the workshop chose to use it with students.

Part Two: Unauthorized Versions of a Queer Story

In this second part of the chapter we turn to a consideration of the *Questionnaire* from the perspective of unauthorized discourses. These discourses incorporate community objections to the administration of the *Questionnaire* in a school setting as well as associated media reporting surrounding the *Questionnaire*. Under the heading of unauthorized discourses, we also venture a queer reading that asks three questions. First, can *The Heterosexual Questionnaire* fulfill the goal of disturbing normative heterosex? Second, what are the queer pedagogical possibilities that might arise from conducting the *Questionnaire*? And, third, do curriculum frameworks such as *Talking Sexual Health* effectively queer straight and gay teachers? Here we are exploring tensions between what the *Questionnaire* is intended to do and what it sometimes does.

Somewhat ironically, and perhaps unsurprisingly, the newspaper headlines and reporting generated by the administration of *The Heterosexual Questionnaire* tended to portray the document as a homosexual survey. The *Questionnaire* thus moved from a device to make sexuality education more inclusive of diverse groups to a tool for promoting a "gay lifestyle." This slippage is witnessed, in part, by some reporters' focus on the content of *The Heterosexual Questionnaire*, specifically questions such as "If you have never slept with a person of the same sex, is it possible that all you need is a good lesbian/gay lover?" However, this is only one explanation of how a document called *The Heterosexual Questionnaire* becomes branded as homosexual. In the media reports analyzed below it is possible to see how questions about heterosexuality come to be associated with the "promotion" of homosexuality—potentially the most unauthorized discourse in secondary schooling.

Prior to making its way to Australia, *The Heterosexual Questionnaire* has been used as a device in teacher education and high school sexuality education in the United States (see part one of this chapter). Nor is controversy surrounding the use of *The Heterosexual Questionnaire* in educational settings confined to Australia. In 1999 the *Questionnaire* was explicitly linked to the "gay agenda" in schools by Beverly La Haye's conservative Christian group, Concerned

Women for America (Parker, 1999). When the *Questionnaire* was used in Orleans County, Vermont, critics also characterized it as an example of the "gay agenda" infiltrating schools (*Education Reporter*, 2001). FortheChildrenInc (2006), on a Web page headed "Promoting Homosexuality in Vermont Schools—How to Make a Questioning Youth," make the following observations relating to the *Questionnaire*:

> In these questions, you can see the so called alternative lifestyle being proposed to school children. Aren't these questions an obvious attempt at creating questioning youth by undermining the influence of their parents? By the use of false assumptions, half truths, and outright distortions, the questioners are trying to "soften up" the children and bring them under the influence of homosexuals.

The sentiments expressed above provide one explanation of how *The Heterosexual Questionnaire* comes to be transformed into the homosexual survey. The unnamed author proposes that asking probing questions about sexuality potentially provokes students to question their own sexuality. Such questioning, it is further argued, is a necessary precursor to falling "under the influence of homosexuals." Thus it comes to pass that calling on students to question heterosexuality is tantamount to promoting homosexuality. In a similar vein, a representative of the Sacramento-based group Campaign for California Families, Randy Thomasson, objected to the passage of Sex Education Bill SB71 explicitly on the grounds that it would allow for the use of the "Heterosexuality Questionnaire" in the classroom. In justifying his objection Thomasson associates the *Questionnaire* with the Gay, Lesbian and Straight Teachers Network (*WorldNetDaily*, 2003). There is an implication that associating the *Questionnaire* with a gay rights group is, in and of itself, sufficient justification of the *Questionnaire*'s pedagogical unworthiness.

In the Australian context, religious objections to the *Questionnaire* echoed those seen in the United States. The Senior Pastor of Wodonga Faith City, Warren McMartin, describes the *Questionnaire* as follows:

> ...a push for children to consider that having a homosexual affair was the most reasonable and normal thing for a young person to be thinking about, and felt like that it was a real push poll by a homosexual lobby or whatever else to mainstream the homosexual lifestyle. (*The World Today*, 28 October 2003)

For McMartin, what was problematic about the *Questionnaire* was not only that it might provoke students to consider the viability of having a homosexual affair, but that the *Questionnaire* also endeavored to normalize homosexuality.[4] What the objections above suggest is that *The Heterosexual Questionnaire*, whether it is used with students or with teachers, is often inextricably linked to debates about how lesbian and gay issues in education should be represented in the school curriculum. It also appears, at least in the Australian instance reported above, that the pedagogical possibilities that may potentially be opened up by the use of the *Questionnaire* couldn't be countenanced, at least in the State of Victoria.

What isn't made explicit, at least in official discussions relating to the use of the *Questionnaire* in Wodonga High School, is exactly what the government found most objectionable about the document. In the following reported radio exchange between an announcer and the Victorian Premier, it is apparent that the Premier thinks the *Questionnaire* is inappropriate, but he doesn't advise listeners as to why it is inappropriate[5]:

ELIZABETH JACKSON: Is it fair to ask a high school student whether their heterosexual behaviour is just a phase? Is it right to ask them if their heterosexuality stems from a neurotic fear of others of the same sex? They're the questions being asked at Wodonga High School on the Murray in Victoria.

The Premier Steve Bracks says the questions are offensive and he's asked his bureaucrats to investigate. But the school principal says the questions come from a Government-approved program, and they're supposed to be offensive, to make students think about how a minority might feel when pressured by others.

Rafael Epstein reports.

RAFAEL EPSTEIN: The sex survey at Wodonga High School has hit the airwaves across Victoria. First, the questions were put to the Premier on Southern Cross radio.

RADIO ANNOUNCER: Is it possible that your heterosexuality is just a phase you may grow out of? Yes or no, Premier.

STEVE BRACKS: I don't think...

RADIO ANNOUNCER: Is it possible your heterosexuality stems from a neurotic fear of others of the same sex, Premier?

One interpretation of the above exchange is that the Premier felt that the questions were so obviously *inappropriate* that he did not need to explain to listeners why they should not have been distributed to students and why it was necessary to take action in the region. Furthermore, he also states that it is inappropriate for the interviewer to pose them. Here not only is there the issue of the authorization of the *Questionnaire* within a school context, there is also, according to the Premier, the question of a radio announcer being able to pose them. This concern, then, not only deauthorizes the use of the *Questionnaire* in a classroom text—but also seems to raise doubts about its positing to adults, and by extension, teachers who are undergoing professional development.

If such discourses relating to sexuality are unauthorized in the educational context, why is this so? This prompts the question of which discussions of sexuality should be authorized? Those who would endeavor to queer straight (and lesbian, gay, bisexual, and transgendered) identified teachers, ourselves included, might argue the importance of curriculum devices such as *The Heterosexual Questionnaire*. Such devices are, to our minds, apposite because they do encourage an interrogation of the strategic deployment of particular tropes of sexual and gender identity. And, if we are lucky, they may even result in young people considering "that having a homosexual affair is the most reasonable and normal thing for a young person to be thinking about." Maybe this is the inappropriate outcome to which the Premier gestures above. As the Premier is not explicit about why the *Questionnaire* is inappropriate for students, we can only speculate on what sort of sexuality education might be considered appropriate.

From a queer theoretical perspective, curriculum devices such as *The Heterosexual Questionnaire* may, as we indicate above, be useful pedagogical tools. Such devices have the potential to provoke debate, requiring students and teachers to consider how particular tropes of identity become fundamental to people's conceptions of individuals and groups within their culture. Moreover, it may be argued such devices will enable people to see that they are not neutral; instead, everybody is implicated in the process of reinscribing particular essentializing or constructivist positions relating to sexual and gender identity.

Following our consideration of the potential that may be attached to *The Heterosexual Questionnaire*, we now consider some possible limitations that may arise from the use of such a document in educating teachers about sexuality. We also explicitly explore tensions we identify between what the *Questionnaire* may be intended to do and what it sometimes does. Our raison d'être in undertaking such an analysis is that even though the *Questionnaire* may not be taken up in Victorian schools following the public debate, it is used within Australia and the United States as a curriculum device within sexuality education programs.

To our minds the queer pedagogical potential inherent within the *Questionnaire* is, in part, linked to the capacity of students and teachers to engage in the process of deconstructing the document. As such, we preface this study of how the *Questionnaire* might be taken up in classroom settings with a brief outline of our interpretation of the process of deconstruction. In seeking a movement beyond essentialism and constructivism, Judith Butler places an emphasis on the value of deconstruction (1998). Deconstruction is a term most closely associated with the work of Jacques Derrida. Chris Barker defines Derridean deconstruction as the:

> ...'undoing' of binaries of western philosophy....In particular, deconstruction involves the dismantling of hierarchical conceptual oppositions...which serve to guarantee truth by excluding and devaluing the 'inferior' part of the binary. (Barker, 2000, p. 33)

In *Epistemology of the Closet*, Sedgwick makes use of this notion of deconstruction to:

> ...demonstrate that categories presented in a culture as symmetrical binary oppositions—heterosexual/homosexual, in this case—actually subsist in a more unsettled and dynamic tacit relation according to which, first, term B is not symmetrical with but subordinated to term A; but, second, the ontologically valorized term A actually depends for its meaning on the simultaneous subsumption and exclusion of term B; hence, third, the question of priority between the supposed marginal category of each dyad is irresolvably unstable, an instability caused by the fact that term B is constituted as at once internal and external to term A. (Sedgwick, 1990, p. 10)

Sedgwick's deconstructive study of the heterosexual/homosexual binary is not an endeavor to disable this dyad; rather, she suggests deconstruction enables a study of how language is used to determine and negotiate ways of understanding. Potentially, following Sedgwick's formulation, a deconstruction of *The Heterosexual Questionnaire* could enable teachers and students to see who is privileged and who is harmed by the valorization of particular types of "straight" subjects. However, the pedagogical effects of deconstruction are by no means straightforward, so inspired by Jordana Rosenberg (2003), one might consider what happens when the joke implicit within *The Heterosexual Questionnaire* "fails," or is taken all too literally.

More generally, Rosenberg draws our attention to the disconnect she perceives:

> …between queer theory's conceptualization in terms of its (unmanageable) audience and queer theory's conceptualization in terms of the field of theory more widely…[she] imagines a conflict between queer theory's life in the hands of its queer readers and its life among its theoretical peers. (2003, p. 395, brackets in original)

In short, Rosenberg notes that readers of texts, even "hungry" readers, might not "get the queer joke." Presumably those readers who do "get" the queer joke, will, in accordance with Sedgwick's conceptualization of deconstruction above, read the *Questionnaire* as an attempt to underscore heterosexual privilege. Going further, a queer theoretical reading might also conclude that the *Questionnaire* simultaneously reinscribes the heterosexual/homosexual binary. This second queer reading, that perceives the *Questionnaire* as giving sustenance to the heterosexual/homosexual binary, suggests one of the potential limits of this curriculum device. Will teachers in both school and teacher education contexts come to trouble the heterosexual/homosexual binary through the use of curriculum devices such as *The Heterosexual Questionnaire*? From a queer theoretical perspective, part of "getting the joke" implicit in the *Questionnaire* is a recognition that the heterosexual/homosexual binary is passé. However, teachers learning about sexuality education using the *Talking Sexual Health* framework might not engage such a deconstructive maneuvre, a maneuvre that we would argue is fundamental to the project of queering straight and gay teachers.

Our suspicion that *Talking Sexual Health* represents potential conflicts "between queer theory's life in the hands of its queer [and straight] readers and its life among its theoretical peers" (Rosenberg, 2003, p. 395) is also raised by a follow-up activity[6] that appears in the same module of this framework. This activity, entitled "Opposite ends of the pole," poses several scenarios, including the following:

Sally

Sally is a college student who had a two-year sexual relationship with her female room-mate. When the relationship broke up, she began dating a male student. She has married him and enjoys their sex life.

Bruce

Bruce says by the time he was seven or eight years old, he knew he was different from other boys. Now middle-aged, he has never had sex with a woman, although many of his friends are women. Since adolescence he has been involved in a series of sexual relationships with men.

Kym

Kym is married and has three children. His only experiences with sexual intercourse have been with his wife. When he masturbates, he fantasizes only about men. Although he does not intend to act out his fantasies, he is sexually attracted to several of his male friends.

Ginny

After 20 years of marriage and two children, Ginny divorced her husband under bitter and hostile circumstances. She moved in with another divorced woman. After several months, the two of them began a loving, sexual relationship that has continued for several years. Before this experience Ginny had never fantasized about sex with another woman or considered the possibility.

After reading each scenario, participants are invited to work in groups of five or six using the "sexual trichotomy model of sexuality (to) decide the sexual identity, sexual orientation and sexual behaviour" of the people featured in the scenarios. Teachers are then asked to contrast the sexual trichotomy to how they might have identified these people using "traditional binary thought" (see Table 1). In this formulation the sexual trichotomy may be posited as the "preferred" way of conceptualizing diverse sexualities.

	Sexual Orientation	Sexual Identity	Sexual Behaviour	How would traditional binary thought identify this person?
Sally				
Bruce				
Kym				
Ginny				

Table 1. Possible tool for examining two different models of sexuality.

Upon reading these scenarios, it is salient to inquire into the perceived pedagogical benefit of requiring teachers to determine the orientation, behaviour, and identity of each of the subjects listed above. If participants were to take such an exercise at face value, they may take away the knowledge that the sexual trichotomy offers a more nuanced understanding of sexuality than "traditional binary thought." At the very least participants may come away recognizing that terms such as orientation, identity, and behaviour are interconnected in complex ways. Such a trichotomy also has the potential to focus participants on discerning the "truth" of one's sexuality (presumably one's sexual orientation in this formulation). From a queer theoretical perspective, these outcomes, while a useful beginning, might not be the most desired. Like *The Heterosexual Questionnaire* it appears that this exercise has the capacity to reinscribe sexual difference, rather than destabilizing essential notions of the sexual subject.

Returning to the three questions posed at the beginning of this section, we would argue that *The Heterosexual Questionnaire* has the potential to fulfill the goal of disturbing normative heterosexuality but that the queer pedagogical possibilities that might arise from conducting the activities we describe above are somewhat limited. Therefore the *Talking Sexual Health* strategies discussed in this chapter might not be particularly effective devices for queering straight and gay teachers. Our reticence in recommending the two strategies outlined above is borne from our concern that participants in this workshop might not get the joke (i.e., that liberal notions of the subject, implicit in the two activities discussed above, reinforce the heterosexual/homosexual binary).

Drawing on Rosenberg, we read such a failure as part of a broader problem within the project of queer deconstruction, a problem that for her "is distinguished not in terms of what it can see but of what it would enable a rigorous reader *not* to see" (2003, p. 401, our emphasis). What Rosenberg's analysis implies is that queer theorists might be too smug for their own good. To be more specific, if the process of queering teachers and students is predicated on the performance of complex acts of deconstruction, then such a process might expect to fail, or at least fall short. The process of queering teachers is a complex task and is subject to the existence of certain "conditions of possibility for deconstructive reading" (Rosenberg, 2003, p. 404). A "bad" reading of documents such as *The Heterosexual Questionnaire*, according to Rosenberg's theory, should not be perceived as "the subject's loss of agency but rather as deconstruction's 'loss' of insight about itself" (p. 408). Such a formulation puts the lie to the supposition that queer deconstruction is somehow more self-reflexive than those who "fail" to get the joke implied by texts such as *The Heterosexual Questionnaire*.

The lesson we take from Rosenberg is that those interested in the project of queering straight and gay teachers might take pause before relying on the tool of queer deconstruction in achieving such a task. It cannot be presupposed that a two-day training workshop provides participants with the conditions of possibility for deconstructive reading that Rosenberg points to above. In the absence of such conditions it is wise not to be smug about "bad" readings, but rather to design pedagogical devices that more explicitly involve readers in disturbing normative notions of gender and sexuality, which is not to say that the *Questionnaire* could not, at least potentially, be such a device.

Conclusion

What this queer story of *The Heterosexual Questionnaire* tells us is that the project of queering teachers needs to be cognizant of its "unmanageable audience." The "unmanageable audience," in this case, the Premier, the Pastor, the Principal, the Departmental Spokespersons, the Professional Development Provider, the Teacher, and the Press, interpreted the sexuality curriculum in ways that rendered the *Questionnaire* an "unmanageable" pedagogical and curricular device. The device was "unmanageable" not only because of the overt controversy it caused, but also because of the unstated and unutterable difficulties that appear to be associated with the project of queering sexuality education curriculum.

Intricately linked to the process of queering teachers is the necessity of being mindful of recurring misconceptions about what language and related acts of deconstruction can do. With this awareness, we suggest there is a need to consider how these pedagogical devices can be differently designed, taken up or interpreted and the therefore "unmanageable" ways that they may be put into play. Perhaps, then, there is a justification for including in such curriculum resources information about this "unmanageable audience" and the varying interpretations such an audience can have. Conceivably, there is also need for some explication of the possibilities for responding if things do go awry. We also suggest there is credence in making queer pedagogical devices more explicit. If we are attempting to queer teachers, then why not be clear that that is our purpose? This is to propose that the audience can be let in on the act—for isn't one of the hopes that not only will such pedagogical devices assist the teacher in questioning the heteronormative, but also that they may better understand how these pedagogical devices work?

Notes

1. The first version of the *Questionnaire*, attributed to Martin Rochlin, was devised in 1972.

2. A relieving teacher is a qualified teacher from outside the school who takes classes temporarily in the absence of permanent teaching staff.

3. Year 9 students in Victoria are aged 14 to 15 years old.

4. Contrary to McMartin, we are not so concerned about curriculum documents that provoke students to consider the viability of having "a homosexual affair."

5. This radio transcript is from an Australian Broadcasting Corporation program, *The World Today*. Elizabeth Jackson is the program presenter. The report presents an excerpt from a radio interview with the Premier broadcast on another radio station, Southern Cross Radio. The name of the announcer posing the questions is not supplied in the ABC transcript of this radio report.

6. This exercise is listed as Activity 3, Module 5.

Works Cited

Australian Associated Press. (2003*). Australian National News Wire*, 28 October.

Australian Broadcasting Corporation. (2003). "Protest over school sex survey," *The World Today,* 28 October.

Barker, C. (2000). *Cultural studies: Theory and practice.* London: Sage.

Bernstein, B. (1990). *The structuring of pedagogic discourse.* London: Routledge and Kegan Paul.

Butler, J. (1993). *Bodies that matter: On the discursive limits of "sex."* New York: Routledge.

Butler, J. (1998). Left conservatism, II. *Theory and Event*. Retrieved 7 July 2000, from http://calliope.jhu.edu/journals/theory_&_event/v002/2.2butler.html.

Commonwealth of Australia. (1999). *Talking sexual health: National framework for education about STI's, HIV/AIDS and blood borne viruses in secondary schools.* Commonwealth of Australia.

Epstein, D. (1993). Practising heterosexuality. *Curriculum Studies*, 1(2), 275–286.

Epstein, D. (Ed.). (1994). *Challenging lesbian and gay inequalities in education.* Buckingham [England]: Open University Press.

Epstein, R. (2003). *The World Today, Australian Broadcasting Corporation.* Retrieved 10 April 2004, from http://www.abc.net.au/worldtoday/content/2003/s976956.htm.

ForTheChildrenInc. (2000). Promoting homosexuality in Vermont schools—How to make a questioning youth. Retrieved 25 July 2006, from http://www.forthechildreninc.com/issues/homsexuality/TheAgenda/introduction.html

Foucault, M. (1996). Friendship as a way of life. In S. Lotringer (Ed.), *Foucault live: Collected interviews, 1961-1984* (pp. 308–312). New York: Semiotext(E).

Gard, M., & Meyenn, R. (2000). Boys, bodies, pleasure and pain: Interrogating contact sports in schools. *Sport, Education and Society*, 5(1), 19–34.

Gay sex questions "in the curriculum." *The Australian*, 29 October 2003.

Gov. Davis signs controversial sex-ed bill: Opponents say it promotes promiscuity, circumvents parents. *WorldNetDaily*, 4 October 2003.

Hoare, D. (2003). *The Australian*, 29 October.

Jackson, E. (2003). *The World Today, Australian Broadcasting Commission.* Retrieved 10 April 2004, from http://www.abc.net.au/worldtoday/content/2003/s976956.htm.

Macgillivray, I. K., & Kozik-Rosabal, G. (2000). Introduction. *Education and Urban Society*, 32(3), 287–302.

Parker, K. (1999). Education should be a sole agenda. *Kansas City Star*. Retrieved 25 July 2006 from http://www.youth.org/loco/PERSONProject/Alerts/States/Missouri/editorial.html

Rosenberg, J. (2003). Butler's "lesbian phallus"; Or, what can deconstruction feel? *GLQ*, 9(3), 393–414.

Sedgwick, E. K. (1990). *Epistemology of the closet*. Berkeley: University of California Press.

Sex class quiz inquiry, *The Adelaide Advertiser*, 10 October 2003.

Sex survey probe; Questionnaire was meant for teachers, *Herald Sun* (Melbourne), 29 October 2003.

Sex survey shocks; School asks teens questions on *homosexuality*, *Herald Sun* (Melbourne), 28 October 2003.

Sexual orientation survey sparks outcry. *Education Reporter*, 182, March 2001.

Sullivan, N. (2003). *A critical introduction to queer theory*. Melbourne: Circa Books.

Survey uproar, *Courier Mail* (Brisbane), 28 October 2003.

Wright, S. (1999). Sexuality education: What Australian parents and teachers are saying. *Sexualities: The Australian Kaleidoscope Conference on Sexology*. University of Adelaide, Adelaide: Unpublished Conference Paper.

CHAPTER FIVE

Beyond Soldiers in the Closet:
Creating Queer Carnival and Aesthetic
Dimensions in the Classroom

Yin-Kun Chang

> Without a shared vision (however contingent and provisional) of democratic community, we risk endorsing struggles in which the politics of difference collapses into new forms of separatism...We need to retain some kind of moral, ethical, and political ground—albeit a provisional one—from which to negotiate multiple interests. (McLaren, 1994a, p. 207)

Opening Story: The Classroom as a Site of Resistance and Refutation

Schooling is a form of masculine agency; indeed, certain dominant definitions of masculinity are affirmed within schools, where ideologies, discourses, representations and material practices systematically privilege straight boys and men. Until recently, in Taiwan's elementary and high schools, it was an established fact that one could not find gender equity in the formal curriculum,[1] and one can still sense the bias and hostility toward queer issues. The mainstream discourse in education combines the complex of heterosexual hegemony with homophobia. Thus, many papers adopt the notion of the "closet" as a metaphor to describe the queer-oppressive situation in the school. However, although the notion of the closet can be highly developed in a Western cultural context, in Taiwan queer teachers have a great deal at stake in developing a "euphemistic"[2] strategy to resist heterosexism, as I discovered in my participant observation; this euphemistic set of practices offers meaningful action which Western culture tends to ignore in my view. Euphemism signifies a politically correct, tactful or less explicit term used to avoid the direct naming of an unpleasant, painful, or frightening reality. Scott (1990, pp. 152–153) describes euphemism as "an accurate way to describe what happens to a hidden transcript when it is expressed in a power-laden situation by an actor who wishes to avoid the sanctions that a direct statement will bring....What is left in the public transcript is an allusion to profanity without a full accomplishment of it." In my fieldwork, I found that when teachers teach queer issues using a euphemistic strategy, they resist the logic of heteronormative schooling while simultaneously obeying certain rules. Regardless, if homophobia is indeed pervasive, perhaps we need to be happy with the fact that schooling has failed to restrict homosexuality despite its best efforts.

During the fall of 1999, I interviewed several queer teachers in Taiwan. These interviews offer "hidden transcripts" exhibiting methods of resisting heterosexual hegemony. But while conducting my dissertation fieldwork from Winter 2003 to Summer 2004, I continued to gain access not only to queer teachers, but also to "queering straight teachers"—teachers who, while not queer themselves, affiliate themselves with queer struggles. This is my first time inquiring among those who have devoted themselves to resist heterosexual hegemony while having unambiguously straight identities. This is also especially interesting because there is little relevant literature or research into how collective resistance or cooperation between queers and straights can counter heterosexual hegemony in schooling. One interesting case in my observation comes from a social science workshop taught cooperatively by three female teachers (two straight teachers and one lesbian teacher) who are all members of the Association of Gender Equal Education. Their goal was to build emancipatory gender and queer curricula and to facilitate mutual respect, gender equity, and resistance to hegemonic power. This workshop,[3] held in the one high school north of Taiwan, consisted of 18 males and 29 females for one semester (one hour per week). Their workshop included eight topics: gender stereotypes; going beyond gender stereotypes; gender inequity, in particular, the story of one boy's death in Taiwan[4]; gender and space; understanding homosexuality; the gender culture in heterosexual love; understanding sexual harassment; and date rape.

Before this workshop, when one teacher was preparing the handout and some teaching materials for students, she could sense the mood of excitement, expectation, and disquietude pervading the air. In order to understand the bias against and stereotypes of queerness, as well as the degree of acceptance, one of these teachers asked students to fill out a questionnaire before class. The questionnaire asks: (1) Have you ever encountered queers? How about your relationship with queers? What are your feelings about queerness? (2) Have you ever searched queer Web sites? What content struck you? (3) If a queer should out himself to you, what would be your reaction? The responses to this survey indicated that over 50% of the students neither accept nor reject queers. One teacher asked students this question: When you see the term homosexuality, what is the first thought that comes into your mind?[5] Students' responses tended toward neutral terms like "gay" or "lesbian." However, this teacher also required students to write down their first reaction in advance of two group discussions about homosexuality. The first group expressed their preconceptions about queers with the following words and phrases: "gay," "abnormal," "dirty," "disgusting," "strange," "sex activist," "AIDS," "transsexuality," and so on; the second group's thoughts included "small chrysanthemum" (euphemism for the anus in the Chinese context), "AIDS carrier," "glass" (euphemism for the anus in the Cantonese context), "transvestite," "disgusting," "inequality," "scurrilous," "sissy," "dirty," "wild fights of fancy," "sorrowful," "fool," "social problem," "minority group," "social discrimination," "fear," "terrorist," "no confidence," and so on. This process helps to create a space for rethinking what is "queer" in everyday life among students and teachers.

This workshop presents a clear picture that most students look upon queerness with biases and stereotypes. Although few students have very positive feelings about this issue, they are forced to spend their time trying to reverse false ideology while discussing queerness in small groups. Teachers told me one interesting phenomenon: that they cannot find any neutral or positive term for naming queerness in the Chinese context. In my mind, this also represents the reason why queer issues are almost absent in the school, and only a few homophobic terms are used (like abnormal, dirty, etc.). In other words, this also represents that there are few queer-friendly terms or discourses in Taiwan's society.

Activities and assignments for this workshop included reporting on the historical development of the queer movement, staging a drama charged with social injustice, and challenging the queer-blindness of popular texts such as fiction and comic books. The way in which each actor dialogues and interacts with each other throughout this process has attributes of the carnivalesque. Unlike the traditional classroom, this gender and queerness workshop did not lock students into passive spectator roles. Like participants in carnival, students experienced a blurring of performance and spectator roles in the classroom, moving in and out of the roles of narrator and audience. Generally speaking, in this workshop, these three teachers are challenged with the fact that gay men are always imagined as feminine guys in the mainstream vision. This forces upon gay men a crisis of masculinity. These three teachers instructed students to rethink the binary logic of gay-equals-sissy, lesbian-equals-tomboy, and transvestite-equals-transsexual. After observing dialogues and interactions, I can tell that the key problem is that some students always feel that homosexuality is a disgusting issue due to its association with anal intercourse. This queer stereotype comes from pop culture, including public media like film, TV, and fiction, and it is more powerful than teachers' instruction and institutional settings in schools. Fortunately, not all students have a false or rigid ideology about queerness, and both affirmation and opposition exist in this process. Thus, this situation is a good opportunity for teachers to develop a resistance moment and for students to cultivate a queer-friendly atmosphere and language.

In my mind, a critical educator's task is to name the world, to build collectively an education that is counterhegemonic and is part of the larger terrain of struggle over what counts as literacy, who should control it, and how critical literacy connects to the real struggles of real people in real relations in real communities. From this point of view, these teachers' workshop represents the concept of "counter-text" and "counter-memory" presented by Henry Giroux (1997). Some students gained a deep impression from this workshop, expressing that they have gradually shifted their attitudes toward queers and accept queers as friends, or deeply understand what homosexuality is and how to respect queers. Some students examined novels or comic books to discuss how queers are presented and represented in popular texts and analyzed how stereotypes functions in these texts. Then, some students shared their identity confusion in their private interactions. In my view, this gender and queerness workshop represents the plastic sexuality proposed by Giddens (1992). Students must have the right to speak freely: this is the only way to create possibilities for unofficial and even antiofficial space. In other words, this is a good way to transgress the boundaries embedded in the hegemonic cultural world-view.

In this paper, I theorize the conditions necessary for queer teachers to create an atmosphere of carnival and heteroglossia in school through theoretical debates; that is, I will build up my own concept of the aesthetic dimension of critical pedagogy. Thus, I need to remind readers that my purpose in this paper is not to exhibit any details of my case study in Taiwan; instead, I want to focus on the phenomenon of queer teachers' resistance in their classroom. I've adopted the phrase "beyond soldiers in the closet" to name those who are not passive anymore and adopt a positive stance that allows them to go beyond the common queer closet situation.

Preface

In common sense, schooling itself still represents "a mode of social control" (McLaren, 1994b, p. 173), a name by which to produce particular forms of subjectivity, and not only to elicit particular forms of participation in social life, like queerness, but also to suppress it. According to the opening story, there is no denying that teachers rarely have a place to talk about eros or the erotic in the school. bell hooks (1994, p. 113) describes that "entering the classroom determined to erase the body and give ourselves over more fully to the mind, we show by our beings how deeply we have accepted the assumption that passion has no place in the classroom. Repression and denial make it possible for us to forget and then desperately seek to recover ourselves, our feelings, our passions in some private place—after class." Thus, hooks considers that we should transform stereotyped consciousness, and provide students with ways of knowing that enable them to better themselves and live in the world more fully. She also believes that to some extent we must rely on the presence of the erotic in the classroom to aid the learning process. In other words, eros and desire in all kinds of sexualities are crucial issues in schooling, not just abstracted knowledge.

However, queer issues seem like "shadow structures"[6] in the curriculum, and we feel it difficult to find their proper location in schooling. Kate Evans (1999, p. 242) sought an answer, focusing on the possibility that the key problem lies in a teacher's role in creating queer stereotypes. Evans found that the tensions, conflicts, and ambiguities of negotiating queer and teacher identities gained in intensity when the participants talked about queer teachers in relationship to their students. In *Negotiating the Self*, Evans (2002) further examines the experiences of gay and lesbian teachers in the school setting. She uses several different preservice teachers and their experiences of teaching to convey the message of the difficulties homosexual educators have in the school system. Evans extends further this realm of experiencing difficulties while teaching to include any teacher, regardless of race, sexual orientation, religion, or creed. Every educator negotiates themselves during teaching because of their own personal identities that they do not wish to reveal to their students in order to keep a job and maintain respect in their school. This is the most important question Evans asks in her book: "Why couldn't I just keep my 'private life' out of teaching?" (2002, p. 3). As in Evans' study, one of the teachers I spoke to explained to me that parents always worry that if the teacher is gay, he will teach the kid to become gay in the future. This is not just a kidding remark. Clearly, stereotypes about the teacher describe both a heterosexual-centered and respectable pattern held all over the world.

Unfortunately, the reductive transmission or "banking" approach to pedagogy underscored in Taiwan's current educational system cancels out most possibilities of making queer knowledge relevant to certain students' lives, providing a supportive environment in which queer students can survive, and developing a range of teaching approaches and forms of sexuality not based on abstract and moralized knowledge. Even though this is quite bleak, classrooms as sites of knowledge production, signification, and representation are necessarily implicated in the practices of multiple voices and standpoints. bell hooks (1994, p. 12) stirs up this possibility with her real experiences: "The classroom remains the most radical space of possibility in the academy...I add my voice to the collective call for renewal and rejuvenation in our teaching practices...I celebrate teaching that enables transgressions—a movement against and beyond boundaries. It is that movement which makes education the practice of freedom." Relating this to my opening story, I find that these three teachers are devoted to creating classrooms implicated in the dynamic negotiation for gender and queer equality. This may be a good example of what Ira Shor and Paulo Freire (1987) call "teaching for liberation," which is more challenging and more likely to be challenged than is teaching that supports the status quo. In my view, the ambition of these three teachers fights to go beyond the current closet situation like soldiers; hence, I name this ambition "beyond soldiers in the closet."

In addition, the definition of queer teachers will be a little bit changed here. In general, using the term queer effectively combines references to gay men and lesbian women, along with bisexual, transsexual, and transgendered people. In this paper, however, I take a relational stance, meaning that the term "queer teacher" not only refers to teachers' sexualities, including lesbian, gay, bisexual, and transgender (LGBT), but also refers to some heterosexual teachers who already have been engaging in complex processes of knowledge production about LGBTQ others within the context and concerns of schooling, education and social justice. In other words, the former are individual queer teachers and the latter are the relational queer teachers, which I will call "queering straight teachers." These two groups are affiliated with each other in the educational field. In the following discussions, I will examine the queer-oppressive situation in everyday lives; and I will also introduce the idea of the aesthetic dimension of critical pedagogy, which is an important mechanism for creating queer carnival and heteroglossia in the classroom.

The Situation of the Queer Closet

There is no denying that queer theory offers an influential impact on the issue of queer oppression, insofar as it interrogates normative sexual categories and the heterosexual matrix. Eve Sedgwick's (1990) metaphor of the closet is the defining structure of homosexual oppression, and the normalization of sexuality has created and continues to reinforce the closet. Generally speaking, the nature of queer oppression is characterized by a daunting ubiquity: as stigmatized others, queers have been constructed within a multiplicity of discourses and genres; thus, the enterprise of deconstruction entails intervention within cultural politics. Even before this occurs, the mere recognition of queer existence and articulation of queer voices tends to disrupt the unquestioningly heterocentric practices of the academy. Within queer theory the idea of revolutionary activism that might challenge the material power differences between the sexes, of which gender is simply the expression, had been replaced by the idea, derived from Judith Butler's work, that "transgression" on the level of dress and performance is revolutionary and will bring down the gender system. Similarly, Jeffery Weeks (2000, p. 70) is enthusiastic about the importance of transgression: "The moment of transgression, in which the whole social order is symbolically challenged, is actually necessary, it seems, to achieve citizenship. This is the attraction of queer theory and queer politics: they provide a theoretical justification for transgression, and practices of sexual dissidence and subversion which challenge the symbolic order."

Running counter to this is the criticism that queer theory sometimes neglects narratives in favor of theoretical orientations that emphasize abstract explanation. For instance, leading scholars in the queer theory camp, such as Judith Butler and Eve Sedgwick, draw nourishment from the perspective of poststructuralism, particularly Foucault's thought. Foucault asserts that people are not self-directed, autonomous agents, but are rather produced by the matrix of power/knowledge relations within which they find themselves inextricably bound. Subjects are entities that are constituted by the discursive and disciplinary configurations that have accompanied the emergence of the carceral society. That is, modern forms of power tie the subjectivity (conscience, identity, self-knowledge) of the individual to that individual's subjection (control by another). The subject is thus one who is both under the authority of another and the author of her or his own actions. I quite recognize the significance of this powerful (and sometimes elegant) rhetoric or discourse within queer theory; however, if we follow queer theory to analyze the phenomenon I mentioned in the opening story, it seems quite difficult to conceive of how social actors (like queer teachers in this context) could possibly engage in alternative forms of action or formulate "counter-disciplines" in reality. That is, critiques of textualism in queer theory usually rest on the presumption of a gulf between cultural or textual analysis on the one hand, and social or political effect on the other. However, critique is not a purely intellectual exercise; rather, it must be in synchronicity with the actual sociohistorical process and baseline of everyday life. Only then, as Lefebvre (1991, p. 76) suggests, "can we transform abstract thought into a dialectical consciousness of life, *in life*: the unity of the mediate and immediate, of the abstract and concrete, of culture and natural spontaneity. Whereas dominant ideologies define and sanction certain patterns of life as natural or inevitable—which helps to give the everyday the unreflexive and taken-for-granted quality that such phenome-nologists as Berger and Luckmann allude to—such transgressive moments problematize, 'make strange,' and thereby subvert the ideological and bureau-cratic structuring of everyday life."

We need to remember that most times the situation of a queer teacher in the school is of course different than that of a straight teacher, and that queer teachers' oppression is always characterized by "invisibility," denial of reality, and denial of the significance or even the very existence of queers and queer relationships. Queer issues are particularly unspeakable (at least, directly or positively) in certain cultural backgrounds, such as that in Taiwan, almost all the time. Thus, I name this culturally unspeakable manner of treating a taboo-like phenomenon, in which one ignores by avoiding talking about or acting on it in everyday life, and in which most people will choose silence, as "cultural aphasia." The oppression of sexual minorities in education has therefore been orchestrated through a series of techniques of selection and exclusion (Pop-kewitz, 1998), as well as through the construction of particular discourses, which are placed at the center of homosexual normality. Not surprisingly, the notion of queerness is designated a silent issue by all kinds of techniques, such as inclusion and exclusion, in order to meet with heterosexual rules. In sum, cultural aphasia is not only the avoidance of speaking but also the forbidding of naming; it is also the identification of rules that delimit the sayable (which are never rules of closure) and the identification of rules that create the spaces in which new statements can be made. Voices from sexual minorities are always mute or distorted in schooling, and this also means they are prohibited from being. Thus, finding ways to dig out the queer voices or narratives in schooling becomes the core mission for critical educators.

According to the relevant literature, certain books already overview queer issues in the educational field. These books offer some practical evidence from schoolteachers, but they lack attempts to develop theoretical discussions; e.g., *Tilting the Tower*, edited by Linda Garber (1994), which documents the voices, personal experiences, teaching strategies, and activist efforts to diversify the curriculum, the classroom, and the campus; Donovan R. Walling's (1996) *Open Lives, Safe Schools: Addressing Gay and Lesbian Issues in Education*, which fo-cuses on antigay discrimination in schools from kindergarten to graduate school, and also examines circumstances in which students, parents, educators, and others in the school community are allowed to live openly in terms of sexual orientation. In addition, although Gerald Unks (1995) published *The Gay Teen: Educational Practice and Theory for Lesbian, Gay, and Bisexual Adolescents*, which deals with theoretical and practical perspectives, this book seems just to offer certain ideal principles, such as identity politics, resistance and sexuality, and moral panic, and is not built on real fieldwork from real participant observation and real interaction in everyday life. Also, certain books about life stories also showcase influential stories that examine the closet situation, such as Kevin Jennings' (1994) *One Teacher in 10: Gay and Lesbian Educators Tell Their Stories* and Rita Kissen's (1996) *The Last Closet: The Real Lives of Lesbian and Gay Teachers*. Both of these books tell the stories of lesbian and gay educators as they struggle for dignity in the face of homophobia. In my opinion, these works still fall into the same problem; that is, they do not theorize their findings, only vividly describing schoolteachers' oppressive experiences.

In addition, with regard to classroom interaction and school roles, Britzman (1995) has begun to explore the ways in which tenets of queer theory can be applied within classrooms. The common characteristic is that placing homosexuality within a wider and more universalizing discourse of difference is one way to begin to address the needs of both straights and queers. Britzman applies cultural reproduction theories to queer studies and suggests that the notion of sexual capital may help us to understand how sexual identities become normalized and also outlawed. In other words, the "political economy of sexualities" can account for differences between the use and exchange values of heterosexuality and homosexuality in schools (Britzman, 1995, p. 69). In addition, Davis (1993) identifies primary schooling as a site where young boys learn how to be heterosexual men. The textual narratives contained within fairy tales and adventure stories that operate as the basis of knowledge for boys on how they should constitute themselves as men reinforce ideas of heroism and toughness. Indeed, boys in schools learn to be "tough," learn not to cry, and learn to suppress their emotions. Quinlivan (2002, pp. 20–21) is also concerned with the role that "at-risk" schooling discourses play in marginalizing and abnormalizing representations of queer sexualities. Thus, she focuses on the framing of queer youth in schools as "at-risk" individuals whose sexuality is framed as their individual problem. This process reinforces notions of disease and deviance and simultaneously operates to normalize heterosexuality. Thus, queerness seems to be a "plague" in the educational field.

On the whole, local popular culture in schooling is saturated with homophobia and scapegoating mechanisms. This results from heteronormative ideology and stereotypes. However, a stereotype's power to harm does not inherently reside in the stereotype itself, as if the words that express the stereotype are somehow imbued with meaning and harm. Rather, an iteration of a stereotype has both a meaning which people generally understand, and a power to produce a particular material effect—such as the power to harm people because it cites past iterations of that stereotype. After listening to many queer teachers' narratives in Taiwan and reading the relevant literature, I conclude that we must go beyond merely describing the pragmatic activities of social agents within particular social settings such as the queer closet. On the contrary, I am curious about how queer teachers develop an insider's knowledge of particular social processes and utilize this understanding to develop a critical knowledge of their everyday lives. Queer teachers' resistances in the classroom have been almost neglected, particularly in queer theory. Queer teachers' arguments have usually been excluded because they do not fit the proper formal mold of schooling. Thus, their voices have been more fragmentary, multidimensional, and temporally disjunctive. But here we can mobilize Melvin Pollner's (1991) important term "radical reflexivity," whereby people can develop a heightened understanding of their circumstances and use this comprehension as the basis of conscious action designed to altar repressive social conditions. I always ask myself this question: how can we begin to formulate new strategies that authentically promote transgression for all constituencies? In my opinion, this mechanism will be the aesthetic dimension of critical pedagogy. For this reason, I am strongly interested in the possibility of creating the atmosphere and activity of carnival and heteroglossia in schooling. This also means "queering" education, defined by James Sears (1999, p. 5) as "bracketing our simplest classroom activities in which we routinely equate sexual identities with sexual acts, privilege the heterosexual condition, and presume sexual destinies. Queer teachers are those who develop curricula and pedagogy that afford every child dignity rooted in self-worth and esteem for others. Queer teachers imagine the world through a child's eyes while seeking to transform it through adult authorship."

The Aesthetic Dimension of Critical Pedagogy

The three queer or queering straight teachers in the opening story perform the aesthetic praxis. This praxis could be named the aesthetic dimension of critical pedagogy. In the work of the Frankfurt School critical theorists (e.g., Adorno, Benjamin, Marcuse) or postmodernists (e.g., Jameson, Baudrillard), the focus of the aesthetic has been relocated and radically expanded to include those aesthetic signifiers commonly lost or left unattended in the flotsam and jetsam of everyday life. Aesthetic, in my opinion, is not only a dynamic performance signifying a movement toward the realization of social phenomena, but also a rehearsal of a revolutionary act, i.e., a rehearsal to acknowledge the multiple rather than monolithic forms of power exercised through various institutions and diverse forms of representation, both resisting and transcending false consciousness and organizing for revolutionary action.[7] As John Dewey (1934) announced, for any educative act to be truly educative, it must have an aesthetic component. Similarly, Shor and Freire (1987, p. 118) state: "Education is naturally an aesthetic exercise. Even if we are not conscious of this as educators, we are still involved in a naturally aesthetic project." For instance, when teachers and students deliberate and act to face queer issues in the classroom, as in the opening story, they perform a type of critical aesthetics.

What is the aesthetic dimension of critical pedagogy? In my argument, it's based on basic elements of what scholars call a "language of critique and possibility" in critical pedagogical terms. I regard the aesthetic dimension of critical pedagogy as operating on two linguistic levels. The first level is determined by the language of critique, and I see its function in terms of *ways of seeing*. The second level is designated by the language of possibility, and I consider this *a performance of radical democracy*. The purpose of the aesthetic dimension of critical pedagogy is intricately linked to the fulfillment of what Paulo Freire defined as radical "vocation"—the mark of truly humanized social agents in the world. For instance, the critical aesthetic urges teachers to create opportunities for students to discover and perform educational essence. In the queer context, educational essence needs to teach students how to be proud of themselves regardless of their sexual orientation.

Critical Pedagogy

Here, I want to briefly summarize the key point of critical pedagogy. Generally speaking, critical pedagogy is a collective and diverse term including different viewpoints on the political implications of education as a series of cultural formations. According to McLaren (1995, p. 231), "critical pedagogy brings [us] into the arena of schooling practices that are insurgent, resistant, and insurrectional modes of interpretation. These practices set out to imperil the familiar, to contest the legitimating norms of mainstream social life, to render problematic the comportment on which social interactions are premised, and attempt to construct a new vision of the educational issues." In other words, critical educational theorists view schooling as a form of cultural politics; this permits educational theorists to highlight the political consequences of interactions between teachers and students, who come from dominant and subordinate cultures within the educational sphere. In its first instance, critical pedagogy begins with the assumption that educational institutions are essential sites for organizing knowledge, power, and desire in the service of extending individual capacities and social possibilities. It provides a critical account of how individuals are constituted within schools as human agents according to different moral and ethical discourses and experiences. Fundamentally concerned with the centrality of politics and power in our understanding of how school works, a number of classic works on critical pedagogy center their attention on the political economy of schooling, the state and education, the representation of texts, and the construction of student subjectivity. To sum up, critical pedagogy attempts to analyze and unsettle extant power configurations, to defamiliarize and make remarkable what is often passed off as the ordinary, the mundane, the routine, and the banal. Therefore, the major objective of critical pedagogy is to empower teachers and students "to intervene in their own self-formation and to transform the oppressive features of the wider society that make such an intervention necessary" (McLaren, 1988, p. xi).

However, critical pedagogy also suffers from challenges because certain critiques and actions reside in the male perspective. These arguments at times lack sexuality and gender considerations, such as Freire's failure to include the experience of women or to analyze or to even acknowledge the patriarchal grounding of Western thought.[8] For instance, Weiler (1994, pp. 16–17) points out that, "from a feminist perspective, *Pedagogy of the Oppressed* is now striking in its use of the male referent. That is, not only the use of 'men' for 'human being,' but also that the model of oppression implied in the Freirean context is based on an immediate male oppressor." Weiler also noticed that the teacher is presented as a generic man, whose interests will be with the oppressed as they mutually discover the mechanisms of oppression in a theorized Freieran context. In reality, of course, teachers are not abstract, but are raced, classed, gendered individuals of particular ages, abilities, locations, and sexual orientations. This failure exists even in Freire's final books published in the late 1990s. Weiler (2001, p. 76) states "that Freire continued his presentation of a liberatory teacher as transparent, and his failure to locate the teacher or to consider the various ways in which the teacher is imagined, and positioned because of race or gender, remains troubling. What he fails to envision are the complexities of the intersection of the private and public, the density of everyday life." Thus, a feminist perspective challenges the assumptions and political effects posited by gender-blind critical pedagogy. From a feminist position, the discourse of critical pedagogy constructs a masculine subject, which renders its emancipatory agenda for gender theoretically and practically problematic. Similarly, we also need to rethink queer issues in the same way, and it seems that studies of queer issues in the critical pedagogy camp are still very marginal.

Aesthetic Theory

My interpretation of this concept includes theoretical references like the Marxist tradition, pragmatism, and cultural studies. In the Marxist tradition, many theorists in the Frankfurt School emphasize aesthetics and ideology, including Horkheimer, Adorno, and Marcuse. Particularly, Herbert Marcuse held that reified social relations, invested with a repressive ideology of control and false needs, permeate everyday life and thus insert themselves in the unconscious and in personality dispositions. In Marcuse's one-dimensional society, art and aesthetic experience remain one of the few junctures at which individuals gain access to critical insight. Marcuse's argument about the aesthetic dimension provides a meaningful theorization of a source of aesthetic sensibility or cognition that leads to critical insight and a movement against a one-dimensional society. In Marcuse's context, it is necessary to develop an aesthetic taste for differences in order to escape one-dimensionality through the ability to see another universe. In other words, the universe of the aesthetic dimension provides the space for a second interpretation of reality or for people to want something different from their lives as they now live them. Without the insights into how life could be regained through aesthetic experiences, we would be trapped inside the problems of a one-dimensional universe. Thus, an aesthetic sensibility brings with it radical action. As Marcuse points to the connection between thought and action in dialectical thought, he asserts, "dialectical thought starts with the experience that the world is unfree; that is to say, man and nature exist in conditions of alienation, exist as other than they are...its [dialectical thought's] function is to break down the self-assurance and self-contentment of common sense, to undermine the sinister confidence in the power and language of facts, to demonstrate how their internal contradictions leads necessarily to qualitative change" (Marcuse, 1960, p. ix). Marcuse presupposes a second dimension as the normal human state that remains a latent but mostly obscured potential for experience. By articulating the basis for a two-dimensional society, Marcuse means that there was an officially sanctioned reality associated with work and the state, and a separate personal reality in which individuals could develop according to their own rules and values. Marcuse calls this second dimension an "inner dimension of the mind in which opposition to the status quo can take root" (Marcuse, 1964, p. 11).

In addition, Marcuse presents the aesthetic experience as an opportunity for the contradiction of a one-dimensional reality. He considers that "every authentic work of art would be revolutionary, i.e., subversive of perception and understanding, an indictment of the established reality, the appearance of the image of liberation" (1978, p. xi). Marcuse argues that through the aesthetic experience, art creates an opportunity to recognize a vision of life and reality that diverges from one-dimensionality. Aesthetic experience creates an image of reality that is independent of normative reality and such experience asserts the validity of the image as a contradiction to normative reality. Through aesthetic experience, the individual regains the second dimension of thought which fosters an individual critical awareness.

In the pragmatist tradition, John Dewey reminds his readers of how necessary it is for their imaginative and perceptual energies to reach toward a painting or a poem if it were to be transmuted into an aesthetic object for their perceptions. Dewey (1934, p. 54) continues to insist that the aesthetic is not an intruder from without, not an affair "for odd moments." Dewey writes about how important it always is to attend actively, to order the details and particulars that gradually become the more visible as we look into integral patterns or experienced wholes. He argues, "There is work done on the part of the percipient as there is on the part of the artist. The one who is too lazy, idle, or indurated in convention to perform this work will not see or hear. His appreciation will be a mixture of scraps of learning with conformity to norms of conventional admiration and with a confused, even if genuine, emotional excitation" (Dewey, 1934, p. 54). That is, art objects are made to seem remote to ordinary people, as are many fine fictions that reach beyond our daily horizons and much music that reaches beyond our accustomed gamut of sound. Art forms are removed from the scope of common or community life.

Moreover, Greene (1978, p. 171) also points out how Dewey considers aesthetic experience "a challenge to that systematic thought called philosophy." She considers aesthetic experience in Dewey's context as a challenge to linear, positivist thinking, as well as to the taken-for-grantedness of much of what is taught. Dewey calls the aesthetic an experience in its integrity, an experience freed from the forces that impede and confuse its development as experience. Greene (1978, p. 175) thinks aesthetics involve an exploration of the questions arising when people become self-reflective about their engagements with art forms. For instance, Greene (1987, pp. 15–18) has helped to create the Lincoln Center Institute, which seeks to initiate students and teachers into "aesthetic" practices of freedom. The Institute helps participants move beyond a simplistic consumerist approach to art and artistic creation, encouraging them to "make a deliberate effort to combat blankness and passivity and stock responses and conformity." In other words, the critical aesthetic can create domains where there are new possibilities of vision and awareness.

Finally, Willis proposes a grounded aesthetic functioning in everyday life from the perspective of cultural studies. Cultural studies turns away from a literary-textual approach toward a nonreductionist social analysis of culture. For instance, Willis (1989, p. 14) expresses that "a grounded aesthetic is a view of an aesthetic not necessarily enclosed in a single artifact, but one articulated as the creative quality in a process wherever meanings are carried." This also suggests suspension of traditional canons of evaluation along with suspension of the notion that artistic activity is *sui generis*, unconnected with other social practices. He defines a grounded aesthetic as follows:

> The grounded aesthetics are the specifically creative and dynamic moments of a whole process of cultural life, of cultural birth and rebirth. To know the cultural world, our relationship to it, and ultimately to know us, it is necessary not merely to be in it but to change the cultural world. This is a making specific of the ways in which the received natural and social world is made human to them and made controlled by them. The grounded aesthetic produces an edge of meaning which not only reflects or repeats what exists, but transforms what exists—received expressions and appropriated symbols as well as what they represent or realizing different futures, and for being in touch with the self as a dynamic and creative force to bring them about. (Willis, 1990, pp. 22–23)

To sum up the above, I consider these different approaches to aesthetics in order to construct a concept of the aesthetic dimension of critical pedagogy with strong and synthetic theoretical backgrounds. In the following section, I will focus on the language of critique and possibility in aesthetic meaning.

Language of Critique: A Way of Seeing

Critical pedagogy is the act of reading the word and world, as Freire and Macedo (1987, p. 29) conceived it, by taking the measure of the world's indwelling in us as we are constructed as ethical and political subjects. Thus, the language of critique, in my opinion, needs to create the way of seeing (or reading) toward social events like queer issues. Moreover, complex intersections of text/context and word/world remind us that a curriculum is not simply seen as the sum of its pasts—curriculum design, instructional techniques, and assessment methods; it is fundamentally about how knowledge is constructed in relations of power. In other words, it is necessary to teach students to read the word, image, and the world critically, with an awareness of the cultural coding and ideological production involved in each of these various social dimensions. For example, McLaren and Giroux (1997, p. 37) considered that "this means teaching students to read, to interpret, and to criticize. In reading we produce a text within a text; in interpreting we create a text upon a text; and in criticizing we construct a text against a text. To read the world and the word means understanding the cultural and generic codes that enable us to construct words into a story—stories we can tell in our own words, and from different points of view." In other words, the category of the aesthetic may sound very much like what is commonly called deconstructive reading. In this vein, as Marcuse (1978, p. 9) expresses it, aesthetic transformation becomes a vehicle of recognition and indictment.

Although critical pedagogy may engage aesthetic cognition in its ideal agenda, it is quite difficult for schoolteachers and students to master this blurred concept; that is, I am curious about how to read the word and the world in the classroom. In order to face this problem, it is necessary to remember that a text does not indicate a static situation; instead, a textual approach underscores the dynamics of social construction. To put it differently, we have to notice the form of the text and the possible formation of the text without ever being given a definition directly. For example, in my analysis of the textbook industry in my dissertation, I designated the final content of the textbook as a "text" and I revealed why queer issues are always missing in the production process as the "context." In this light, social phenomena like queer issues can be read as text by teachers and students. Such reading constitutes a negotiation between the subject's experience and the demands, suggestion, or implications of the text.[9] Negotiation of meaning refers to evidence that audiences are not passive recipients of the communications of others; rather, they actively, and unpredictably, construct diverse and sometimes contradictory meanings for the same text, just as in the opening story, different students had divergent opinions about queerness. For this reason, the meanings given by any particular text will be constructed differently depending on the discourses, knowledge, prejudices, or resistances brought to bear on it by an audience (Ellsworth, 1989, p. 61). The process of negotiation is not merely an unproblematic picking and choosing between the multiplicity of meanings that a text seems to suggest. Rather, each process of text interpretation takes place within a context of socially constructed, unequal, and competing versions of reality embedded within the text. In other words, texts aid in having multiple and contradictory meanings. They may articulate dominant ideologies that naturalize and normalize inequalities, but the contradictory meanings of texts allow for readers to resist dominant ideologies or to refashion textual meanings in empowering ways—such as subversive, ironic readings.

To summarize the above, we might ask: what does a text mean? Texts, in my opinion, create particular meanings and modes of understanding that need to be investigated, and one can read or observe a text for the social phenomena it conveys. We can also reflect, deliberate, and redefine the possible meanings of these social phenomena. Texts would be analyzed as part of a social vocabulary of culture that points to how power names, shapes, defines, and constrains relationships between individuals and their culture, and constructs and disseminates what counts as knowledge. For instance, Weedon points out the paucity of texts involving women's historical resistance to patriarchy, which has deprived history students of alternative and resistant subject positions that would illustrate the nonnatural status of current gender norms. She furthermore emphasizes that "while we need texts that affirm marginalized subject positions...it is important to be constantly wary of the dangers of fixing subject positions and meanings beyond the moment when they are politically productive" (Weedon, 1987, p. 172). To be sure, texts need to be understood in their historical, political, and cultural specificity; and further, texts do not mean in the same way for readers who occupy different contexts, or different historical junctures. Most importantly, Chandra Mohanty (1990, p. 185) points out that a more comprehensive view of reality would include "uncovering and reclaiming subjugated knowledge."

In addition, Giroux (2000, p. 63) argues that texts are now seen not only as objects of struggle in challenging dominant modes of racial and colonial (or heterosexual) authority, but also as pedagogical resources for rewriting the possibilities for new narratives, identities, and cultural spaces. Focusing on the politics of representation, critical pedagogy calls attention to the ways in which texts mobilize meanings in order to suppress, silence, and contain marginalized histories, voices, and experiences. It has reasserted the power of symbolic reading and understanding as a pedagogic force in securing authority, and a pedagogical strategy for producing particular forms of contestation and resistance. A public text such as film presents particularly powerful teaching material for wide groups of young students. For instance, Giroux (2002, p. 10) points out that film is a good teaching form, which often puts into play issues that enter the realm of public discourse, debate, and policymaking in diverse and sometimes dramatic ways—"whether we are talking about films that deal with racism, challenge homophobia, or provide provocative representations that address the themes of war, violence, masculinity, sexism, and poverty." Giroux (2003, p. 135) points out that films can be interrogated initially by analyzing both the commonsense assumptions that inform them, the affective investments they evoke, and the absences and exclusions that limit the range of meanings and information available to audiences. Analyzing such films as public discourses also affords pedagogical opportunities to engage those complex institutional frameworks that are brought to bear in producing, circulating, and legitimating the range of meanings associated with such cultural texts. Similarly, two famous and important fake weeding films in East Asia, *Okoge* from Japan and *The Wedding Banquet* from Taiwan, which engage gay identity in relation to the Confucian family tradition, are excellent texts for students to discuss.

Then, after we read the established text, the most important thing is to restore this text back to its context, while following the idea of critical pedagogy. The German sociologist Habermas (1972) calls this established text a "mutilated text," because it is full of omissions and distortions resulting from power-based or hegemonic relations. Habermas also considers that textual omissions and the distortions that they rectify have a systematic role and function. The meaning of a corrupt text of this sort can be adequately comprehended only after it has become possible to illuminate the meaning of its corruption. The ongoing text of our everyday language, or speech and actions, is disturbed by apparently contingent mistakes: by omissions and distortions that can be discounted as accidental and ignored, as long as they fall within the conventional limits of tolerance. Habermas points out that the mistakes in the text are more obstructive and are situated in the pathological realm as symptoms. Although Habermas does not focus on the educational field or queer studies, I think that this metaphor is still quite striking here. Thus, the first step is to find the paradox, contradiction, and irony in the text. As Apple mentions, we have to pose the conflict in the curriculum, for only then can we recognize what mechanism dominates and controls schooling knowledge. He calls this "performative contradiction"; that is, to pose contradiction is more crucial than to introduce knowledge directly.[10] When we restore the established text back to context, we can easily recognize that ideology of heteronormative knowledge is inscribed as dominant knowledge into the learner's mind and body; that is, heterosexual knowledge in the dominant curriculum model is treated primarily as a realm of objective facts. However, results are not always preordained. Apple's (1990) *Ideology and Curriculum* offers a good example that the curriculum is the result of constant struggle and compromise. His argument leaves much space for the aesthetic dimension, because it is possible to develop the critical recognition, and bodily practice.[11] In other words, we need to cultivate aesthetic sensibility and cognition in the educational field. Aesthetic criticism helps us to see the curriculum as a cultural political text, assuming that the social, cultural, political, and economic dimensions are the primary categories for understanding an educational context. Particularly in this paper, aesthetic criticism reveals the social construction of sexuality and its hegemonic function. However, critical recognition alone is not enough to transform the cultural configuration of individuals' relations within a repressive institutional context. The aesthetic dimension of critical pedagogy includes critical recognition in addition to radical action. In the following section on the language of possibility, I will focus on the level of action.

Language of Possibility: The Performance of Radical Democracy

Critical pedagogy also refers to a deliberate attempt to construct specific conditions through which educators and students can think critically about how knowledge is produced and transformed in relation to the construction of social experiences informed by a particular relationship between the self, others, and the larger world. That is, critical pedagogy not only remains powerful at the moment of critique; it also aims its critical force at transformation. Especially in Freirean discourse, liberation and dialogue are the basis for a transformative educational praxis. Thus, the language of possibility is based on real action as well as politics of empowerment,[12] and it gives life to practices of cultural struggle. In my opinion, the aesthetic dimension of such a language of possibility is therefore a democratic performance. But in different approaches, the concept of democracy is defined in different ways, such as liberal, social and radical democracy. In the language of possibility, I think the concept of democracy in critical pedagogy is strongly linked to radical democracy. In contrast to these other models, radical democracy stresses the primacy of cultural difference, and it considers that class is not the only form of domination. It is to their credit that some New Left theorists have made visible the diverse and often interconnected forms of oppression organized against women, racial minorities, gay men and lesbians, the aged, the disabled, and others.

Generally speaking, radical democratic theorists[13] have tried to theorize the conditions that would increase opportunities for public-minded, participatory democracy in diverse communities. They imagine an ideal political community whose members sustain a great deal of individual autonomy and who debate many of their own assumptions. The radical definition of democratic politics goes beyond conventional political thinking into the far more dynamic domain of cultural representations and social practices. Democracy is defined at the level of social formations, political communities, and social practices, which are regulated by principles of social justice, equality, and diversity. Thus, radical democracy begins with a radical critique of current forms of representation that limit the populace's decision-making regarding choices over who will govern. Members of such a community increasingly realize their individual potentials as they replace unquestioned traditions or habits with open discussion between free and equal individuals about their community's priorities. To put it differently, radical democracy facilitates the critical educational practice directly as well as indirectly. As Freire (1998, p. 45) states, "one of the most important tasks of critical educational practice is to make possible the conditions in which the learners, in their interaction with one another and with their teachers, engage in the experience of assuming themselves as social, historical, thinking, communicating, transformative, creative persons; dreams of possible utopias, capable of being angry because of a capacity to love." Indeed, democracy is a process that depends on participation—the willingness and belief that the actions and voices of individuals can have an effect on the collective totality. In part this constitutes an exercise in political imagination; in part it is a consequence of positive agency that convinces an active citizenry that its constituents are their own rulers.

If we consider Habermas and Freire to be crucial scholars in this area, we need to look back upon Dewey's argument. There is no denying that the greatest influence on Habermas' thought is the work of John Dewey, and Freire is also influenced by a tentative dialogue with Dewey as introduced in Brazil by Anisio Teixeria, who studied with Dewey at Columbia University (Morrow & Torres, 2002, p. 3). It is relevant to our discussion of radical democracy that Dewey (1980, p. 354) also states, "knowledge as an act is bringing some of our dispositions to consciousness with a view to straightening out a perplexity, by conceiving the connection between ourselves and the world in which we live." Dewey considered it necessary for people to understand the process of change in order to constitute a democratic public. In my opinion, it is necessary for us to value highly the concept of deliberation in Dewey's debates. He defined it as follows:

> Deliberation is a dramatic rehearsal of various competing possible lines of action…Deliberation is an experiment in finding out what the various lines of possible action are really like. It is an experiment in making various combinations of selected elements of habits and impulses; to see what the resultant action would be like if it were entered upon…Deliberation means precisely that activity is disintegrated, and that its various elements hold one another up. While none has force enough to become the center of a redirected activity, or to dominate a course of action, each has enough power to check others from exercising mastery. (Dewey, 1988, pp. 132–133)

In other words, all deliberation is a search for a way to act, not for a terminus. But Dewey reminds us that deliberation has both rational and irrational characteristics.[14] He states, "deliberation is irrational in the degree in which an end is so fixed, a passion or interest so absorbing, that the foresight of consequences in warped to include only what furthers execution of its predetermined bias." And yet, "deliberation is rational in the degree in which forethought flexibly remarks old aims and habits, institutes perception and love of new ends and acts" (Dewey, 1988, p. 138).

How can we apply the idea of radical democracy to the educational field? In my opinion, a teacher can reflect upon and transform his/her own social practice which means that s/he is attentive to the concrete social, economic, cultural and gender/sexuality issues in schools, and examines the relationships between teachers and students.[15] This also echoes Freire's (1998, p. 95) idea about the beauty of the teaching practice: "I am a teacher proud of the beauty of my own teaching practice, a fragile beauty that may disappear if I do not care for struggle and knowledge that I ought to teach. If I do not struggle for the material conditions without which my body will suffer from neglect, thus running the risk of becoming frustrated and ineffective, then I will no longer be the witness that I ought to be, no longer the tenacious fighter who may tire but who never gives up. This is a beauty that needs to be marveled at but that can easily slip away from me through arrogance or disdain toward my students." In spite of the fact that the influence of the public sphere within the educational field is increasingly present in all kinds of formations, such as teacher unions and studying groups at both formal and informal levels, school-teachers are still largely silenced. Thus, the perpetual goal of radical democracy is to redistribute power from elites to various local publics, and radical democracy creates the conditions necessary for marginalized groups to invest in the debates over the meaning of education as both discourse and critical practice. This process seems to be what C. Wright Mills had in mind when he spoke of the need to link private troubles to public issues (Sehr, 1997, p. 71). In the same way, sex-orientation is not merely a personal issue but instead a form of cultural politics. Thus, the idea of connecting private life and public life recalls the powerful feminist slogan that *the personal is political.* In my thinking, the struggle over meaning and values is the performance of aesthetics. The aesthetic dimension of a language of possibility is based on action and grass-roots democracy, enacted through reflection and deliberation in the public sphere or counterpublics. Freire referred to this as achieving a "radical form of being" which he associated with "beings that not only know, but know that they know" (Freire, 1978, p. 24). Freire's radical education insists that learners become subjects in their own education by critically engaging through dialogue and debate the historical, social, and economic conditions that both limit and enable their own understandings of power. Critical pedagogy in this meaning is not only linked to challenging forms of oppression; it is also turned into a theory to be enacted from the perspective of historical realities and material circumstances.

Walking on Water: Building Queer Carnival and Heteroglossia in the Classroom

I also consider that the performance of the aesthetic dimension of critical pedagogy is a form of carnival. Carnival offers opportunities for queer teachers and students to symbolically invert the usual hierarchies and imagine different roles and relationships. In Bakhtin's definition, the carnival refers to "the right to emerge from the routine of life, the right to be free from all this is official and consecrated" (1984, p. 257). First, carnival is both unofficial and antiofficial. For instance, unofficial comes from the notion that carnival loosened the grip of established norms and relations and allowed alternatives to emerge in their place; antiofficial because carnival engendered and supported the criticism and mockery of the official social order and ideology. Carnival refers to a mobile set of symbolic practices, images, and discourses which were employed throughout social revolts and conflicts. Second, carnival also opens up a narrative space that affirms the contextual and the specific while simultaneously recognizing the ways in which such spaces are shot through with issues of power. In other words, performance is a cultural practice, and a practice of representation. Thus, the implication is that carnival may often act as a catalyst for and site of actual and symbolic struggle.

In the opening story, I found that queer teachers or queering straight teachers in Taiwan evoke complex polyglot worlds of negotiation by developing their own teaching materials and holding workshops. These worlds of negotiation through both critical recognition and radical action are best captured in the concept of the "carnivalesque," whose significant contributions include the rise of the public discussion of queerness, its celebration of anti-hierarchical worldviews, and its associated participation in the rise of a heterological voice. In this meaning, carnival is life turned inside-out and upside-down. This disruption of life's routine, and especially the temporary abolition of powerful social hierarchies, allows participants to experience relations with each other and the world that are unavailable to them in their everyday lives. In this way, carnival serves as a cultural and political form. Carnival, according to Bakhtin, functions to make individuals aware of a different mode of being, one in which the individual represents "a material bodily whole." This bodily whole then moves beyond "the limits of its isolation," and the private and the universal are thus blended "in a contradictory unity" (Bakhtin, 1984, p. 23). Also, Bakhtin conceives of the carnival and its capacity for disguise and misrule as possible motivating forces for real action. According to Bakhtin, in late medieval and Renaissance society, the boundaries between high and low culture, and between official and unofficial spheres of activity, were much more fluid and permeable, and daily life was not as rigidly compartmentalized as it is today. Bakhtin found succor in the carnival, which for him revealed the arbitrariness of established linguistic or literary conventions, as well as a whole range of institutional arrangements and social roles right down to our conceptions of history, of individuality and sexuality, and even of time, space, and nature. To put it differently, carnival "discloses the potentiality of an entirely different world, of another order, another way of life [which] is lived by the whole man, in thought and body" (Bakhtin, 1984, p. 48). In the queer context, all such forms of defamiliarization may encourage the conceptualization of existing modes of experience and perception from a different point of view, allowing us to grasp the reification of social relations under heterosexual hegemony, and demonstrate that other, less hierarchical and exploitative social relations are possible.

Carnival functions to reverse the estrangement of humanity from itself and transgress the usual norms and rules that govern the more routinized and habitual aspects of everyday life. Thus, carnival is typified by "incompleteness, becoming, ambiguity, indefinability, non-canonicalism—indeed, all that jolts us out of our normal expectations and epistemological complacency" (Clark & Holquist, 1984, p. 321). In the carnival, the "order of the ordinary" is suspended. New social orders and modes of association proliferate, and free and familiar contact among people reigns. Thus, the concept of carnival will be a good framework for analyzing the phenomenon I described in the opening story, as Bakhtin emphasizes the ceaseless battle between official (monologizing, centralizing) and unofficial (dialogizing, multiform) sociocultural forces. Using the concept of carnival to analyze the opening story, we can realize that every aspect of consciousness and every practice a person engages in is constituted dialogically, through the flowing multitude of deliberation. Unlike the monologic world, which always gravitates toward itself and its referential object, the dialogic word is locked into an intense relationship with the word of another. It is always addressed to someone, real or imaged—a witness, a judge or simply a listener—and it is accompanied by the keen anticipation of another's response. In my participant observation in this social science workshop as I mentioned in the opening story, I found that many students responded to stereotypes and shared their own opinions and experiences, which constructs mutual dialogue about queerness through hearing opinions and sharing experiences. Hence, dialogism renounces the imposition of abstract theoretical schemas onto the concrete sociohistorical world. Dialogue, in Bakhtin's view, is not simply a form of linguistic exchange that occurs between two existing entities or consciousnesses. Rather, dialogism constitutes a generalized perspective, a "model of the world" that stresses continual interaction and interconnectedness, relationality, and the permeability of both symbolic and physical boundaries. By the time Bakhtin (1990) wrote "Author and Hero in Aesthetic Activity," he came to realize that this process of value-creation could not take place outside the "contraposition" of self and other, in which incarnate subjects live their lives in distinct times and places, but co-participate in a shared lifeworld and act to consummate each other's life narrative by providing an exotopic viewpoint, a "surplus of vision." The effort to break the heterosexual-centered myth is not only to focus on queer (self) agents, but the relationship to the straight other. In sum, carnival is not chaos; it is an act of communal signifying, which, like any dramatic ritual, must be composed, coordinated, and performed.

In a practical sense, how does a classroom create carnival moments? Grace and Tobin (1997) argue that video production opens up a space where students can play with the boundaries of language and ideology and enjoy transgressive collective pleasures. This boundary-crossing and pleasure-getting activity by the students in the midst of the curriculum pushes teachers to think about their authority in new ways. In other words, video production elicits an outpouring of transgressive, excessive moments that push us to question heterosexism. I am also of the opinion that sincere dialogue between teachers and students is the best example of this phenomenon. Paulo Freire (1970/1993, p. 71) expresses that "dialogue...requires an intense faith in humankind, faith in their power to make and remake, to re-create...Faith in people is an *a priori* requirement for dialogue." In this process, knowledge emerges in a dialectical relationship wherein meaning is made as a product of dialogue between or among individuals. Meaning is constructed through reciprocal dialogue and not within a single person or subject. This reciprocal dialogue helps us to recognize, understand, and critique current social inequalities such as race, class, gender, and sexual orientation. Bakhtin's idea of heteroglossia[16] theorizes *a priori* the characteristic of dialogue. That is, the various discourses are analogous to "the social diversity of speech types" that Bakhtin labels heteroglossia (1981, p. 263): one's own voice is defined in relation to these surrounding discourses. For Bakhtin, "language" is not understood in a general, singular or unitary sense; it is always defined in terms of diversity and changeability. "Language is never unity," says Bakhtin; "actual social life and historical becoming create a multitude of concrete worlds, a multitude of bounded verbal-ideological and social belief systems" (1981, p. 228). That is, carnival represents the plurality of social situations and standpoints through dialogues among a multiplicity of languages.

In the opening story workshop, these three queer teachers incorporate some issues of eros and desire into the curriculum. Queer carnival and heteroglossia in this classroom are representing both an expression and an enforcement of particular relations of antiheteronormativity; in other words, the classroom is an important location for looking at eros and desire. Eros and desire do not have to be denied for learning to take place. bell hooks (1994, pp. 115, 199) encourages us to "find again the place of eros within ourselves and allow the mind and body to feel and know desire," and "to understand the place of eros and eroticism in the classroom we must move beyond thinking of these forces solely in terms of the sexual." However, I need to confess that carnival is a moment with ideal and romantic characteristics, and queer teachers in the current situation are still in danger of losing the soul of teaching, particularly as it is governed by preservice and in-service processes. Maybe this is a specific case that cannot be representative of the real whole in Taiwan, but the possibilities of creating queer carnival in the classroom seem like walking on water. Thankfully, outreach efforts from the queer movement have already gradually reduced prejudice in teacher education programs. Despite the continual existence of heterosexual hegemony in preservice and in-service projects, it is not difficult to find many colleges that acquiesce to queer student organizations, allow queer activities on university premises, offer relevant courses on homosexuality, and grant tenure to openly gay professors. This challenge will indirectly and gradually contribute to changing teacher education programs in the future.

Conclusion

I consider that we need more space for imagination, instead of standardized content about how to teach queer issues. Queer teachers or queering straight teachers who were into drag consider that heterosexuality is the regime of the truth in need of challenge, and that by posing sexual problems in schooling they were helping to destroy this myth. They were doing what might now be called "queer as performance" (as per Judith Butler) in a very direct and politically motivated way. If gender roles are purely a cultural construction and the options offered by cultural norms are limited to binary oppositions, it must surely follow that men and women would obligingly fit into these categories—but this rule is not always followed in reality. Queer carnival and heteroglossia bring the democratic experience necessary to disrupt this binary. Ideally, the democratic person is a being who speaks, which is also to say a poetic being, a being capable of embracing a distance between words and things which is not deception, but humanity; a being capable of embracing the unreality of representation.

How can queer carnival and heteroglossia become possible? In this paper, I have argued that an aesthetic dimension of critical pedagogy should be regarded as a rethinking and reenvisioning of subjectivity, identity politics, and identity formation. In a language of critique, new visions regarding the location of interpretative power that resides in texts and contexts create new understandings of the social world, and these new visions help to mobilize people in the struggle for social change. On the one hand, the aesthetic dimension of critical pedagogy needs to create this new way of seeing. On the other hand, a language of possibility serves to develop the ability of citizens to become active agents, working toward a more radical democracy. In other words, concrete action will be translated directly out of critical reflection. For me, a radical educator enjoys his or her teaching, and through observation and imagination, masters relevant and dominant issues in schooling. Of course, when we must deal with the language of critique and the language of possibility at the same time, we can master text and context, and we may then act upon reflection and deliberation toward such social phenomena as educational issues.

This suggests, as Paul Freire (1985, p. 48) points out, the need for a theory of pedagogy willing to develop a "critical comprehension of the value of sentiments, emotions, and desires as part of the learning process." The relationships among the aesthetic dimension, queer praxis, and critical pedagogy in this context are always seen as part of an ongoing struggle over what constitutes the social, and how carnival moments are shaped within classrooms that allow for a proliferation of discourse, language, and questioning.

Notes

1. In June 23, 2004, Taiwan started to implement the *Law of Gender Equity in Education*. This law requires schools to implement gender-relevant curricula. For instance, at the elementary and secondary educational level, it requires at least 4 hours of relevant inclusive curricula or activities per semester. At the high school level, schools must have inclusive curricula concerning gender equity. At the college level, this law encourages colleges to offer more gender-relevant courses. Queer pedagogy will be one significant element of this law. Ideally, teaching queer issues will not be taboo once this law is fully implemented. Relevant gender equity curricula in this law include: emotional education, sex education, queer education, psychical education, technology education, media education, and career planning (from udn.com, 2004, pp. 12–14). However, this ideal comes from the juridical perspective, and it remains to be seen whether it will be realized.

2. *Euphemism* means a less distasteful word or phrase used as a substitute for something harsher or more offensive; that is, safe expression of aggression against a dominant figure serves as a substitute for real and direct aggression. For instance, subversive humor expresses the discontents of the present. Scott (1990) argues that subversive humor expresses discontent with anger, frustration, fear, and anxiety. These emotions are responses to "the social experience of indignities, control, submission, humiliation, forced deference and punishment associated with any form of domination" (p. 111). Similarly, in the Chinese world, collectivism and deference to authority have been so central to life that value is placed upon "harmony-in-hierarchy" (Bond & Hwang, 1986, pp. 213–214); for example, I find certain specific practices in queer teacher's everyday life, such as strategies of "judgment for things proper in speech or behavior" and "obeying publicly but disobeying privately" (we call it "nanhie-fenchuen" and "yangfeng-yinwei" in Chinese pronunciation) toward authority.

3. In Taiwan, there are two important strategies for teaching queer issues in school: one is using professional research as a reason to ask permission from the school administration, as in this workshop. However, queer issues are only one topic in this workshop, and this would endanger its success. The other way is to teach queer issues secretly and never report the real plan to the school administration. Both of these strategies embody euphemistic meanings.

4. The story is that one male student in a junior high school south of Taiwan suffered discrimination from his classmates due to his "sissy" temperament. Many of his classmates mocked him as being womanish scum and felt quite disgusted with his behaviors. Many students had beaten him up and jointly took off his pants, supposedly to make sure whether he had a penis and testicles or not. Thus, he was afraid to go to the restroom during break time and he instead used to go alone during class time. On April 20, 2000, he went to the restroom after getting permission from a teacher during class time, but he

never returned back to the classroom. Later, many students found him in a pool of blood (from *China Times*, 01 June 2000); that is, someone unknown killed him.

5.　Similarly, sociologist Michael Kimmel (1993) asks his students to list all the things that count as evidence that a man is a gay. They mention, among other things, effeminate gaits or gestures, flamboyant or colorful dress, expressing affection toward other men, expressing psychological sensitivity about anything, expressive vulnerable emotions like sadness or grief, expressing strong aesthetic reactions, and engaging in traditional feminine activities like cooking or sewing.

6.　"Shadow structure" refers to a vulnerable and neglected academic margin when compared with high visible "surface structure" of the traditional issues in academe (Charles Lemert, 1990, qtd from Klein, 1996).

7.　In "Aesthetics and Politics in Education," Apple (1992) extended Dwayne Huebner's arguments in new directions and considered that we must go beyond static thinking and turn our attention to the dynamic political, economic, and ideological conditions. He points out that the aesthetic helps us go beyond current limits: to situate the reduction of the entire range of human values to the technical. Through more widespread social dynamic analysis, the aesthetic has a major impact on so many people inside and outside of education. That is, aesthetics as unveiled meaning that is built by the speaking and acting of participants, like the teacher as artist and aesthetic critic. Thus, the aesthetic—when linked to the real experiences of people—can make a profound difference in education in aesthetic and political ways.

8.　In fact, Freire also responds to feminist criticisms in the foreword to Peter McLaren and Peter Leonard's *Paulo Freire: A Critical Encounter*. Freire addresses them as follows: "I also appreciate the attempts by feminist critics and educators to rethink my work through their own specific struggles. Since the 1970s I have learned much from feminism and have come to define my works as feminist, seeing feminism closely connected to the process of self-reflexivity and political action for human freedom." But Weiler (2001, p. 80) asserts that here or elsewhere Freire fails to provide us with any examples of what he means by feminism.

9.　For instance, Giroux (1992) uses Leon Golub's painting as an example and considers that aesthetics may be seen as rupturing the complacency of bourgeois hegemony and revealing the most unstated or silenced social conditions. Golub's art attempts to engage rather than command the viewers. It provides images that in their raw immediacy attempt to both open up and peel away those layers of ideological repressions that tie all of us to the prevailing system of control and oppression.

10.　Apple says, "the curriculum should stress hegemonic assumptions, ones which ignore the actual working of power in cultural and social life and which point to the naturalness of acceptance, institutional beneficence, and a positivistic vision in which knowledge is divorced from the real human actors who created it. The key to uncovering this, I believe, is the treatment of *conflict* [italics added] in the curriculum" (Apple, 1990, p. 82).

11. Here I mean that the body of the subject is to be understood as neither a biological nor a sociological category but rather as a point of overlap between the physical, the symbolic, and the social.

12. At present, the word "empowerment" is used by both liberal and radical educators; however, there is a clear distinction between usages of the term. While for liberal educators the term empowerment means personal empowerment, radical and critical educators use the term in a social and political context. Giroux and McLaren (1986) define the term as referring to the process whereby students acquire the means to critically appropriate knowledge existing outside of their immediate experience in order to broaden their understanding of themselves, the world, and the possibilities for transforming the taken-for-granted assumptions about the way we live (p. 229).

13. I do not want to overstate affinities here between Mouffe and Habermas as radical democracy theorists. It is fair to place these theorists in the same general camp because they all advocate an extension of democratic freedoms into realms of life otherwise bound by uncritically accepted communal standards, unequal relations, or assumptions about a consensus that may not exist. However, Spivak (1996, p. 142) asserts that Laclau and Mouffe's model of radical democracy is "appropriate only to liberal democracies and/or postindustrial societies of the North Atlantic model."

14. Similarly, this concept can compare with Freire's idea of problem-solving and problem-posing in *Pedagogy of the Oppressed*, and Habermas' concept of nonreflexive and reflexive learning in *Legitimation Crisis*.

15. Gale and Densmore (2003, p. 6) propose some criteria about engaging teachers who are empowered with a radical democratic agenda for schooling: (1) believe it is possible for ordinary people to have real decision-making authority over those things that most affect them; (2) assume the obligation of transforming everyday practices so that the norms and symbols that ordinarily go unquestioned and analyzed can change in ways that no longer oppress others; (3) simultaneously enhance the individual and advance the community; (4) exercise and develop their creative and problem-solving capacities by participating in the lives of communities; and (5) help others and let themselves become transformed through their participation in common work.

16. The notion of heteroglossia refers to the fact that any language is always stratified into the forms and meanings constructed by the various regional, social, professional or generational groups that use it (Bakhtin, 1981). Thus, society, in fact, is always linguistically diverse, stratified or heteroflossic. As Bakhtin (1981, p. 288) says: "actual social life and historical becoming create a multitude of concrete worlds, a multitude of bounded verbal-ideological and social belief systems." Thus, language is never unity, namely, het-

eroglossia. The social stratification of language is parallel to the diversity of social groups. Each social group is associated with particular activities, social relations, and ideologies, and each develops its own speech genres which gradually fashion differentiated accents, styles, dialects, and languages. In this sense, these languages have both a formal side and a semantic one. The languages, dialects, styles, and accents are thus a product of the dialogical process.

Works Cited

Apple, M. W. (1990). *Ideology and curriculum* (2nd edition). New York: Routledge.

Apple, M. W. (1992). Aesthetics and politics in education. In N. C. Yakel (Ed.), *The future: challenge of chance* (pp. 33–47). Reston, VA: National Art Education Association.

Bakhtin, M. M. (1981). *The dialogical imagination: Four essays*. Austin: University of Texas Press.

Bakhtin, M. M. (1984). *Rabelais and his world*. Bloomington: Indiana University Press.

Bakhtin, M. M. (1990). Author and hero in aesthetic activity. In *Art and answerability: Early philosophical essays* (pp. 4-256). Austin: Texas University Press.

Bond, M. H., & Hwang, K. K. (1986). The social psychology of the Chinese people. In M. H. Bond (Ed.), *The psychology of the Chinese people* (pp. 213–226). Oxford: Oxford University Press.

Britzman, D. (1995). Is there a queer pedagogy?: Or, stop reading straight. *Educational Theory*, 45(2), 151–165.

Clark, K., & Holquist, M. (1984). *Mikhail Bakhtin*. Cambridge, MA: Harvard University Press.

Davis, B. (1993). *Shards of glass: Children reading and writing beyond gendered identities*. Cresskill, NJ: Hampton Press.

Dewey, J. (1934). *Arts as experience*. New York: Minton Balch.

Dewey, J. (1980). *Democracy and education*. (The middle works of John Dewey, vol. 9: 1916.) Carbondale: Southern Illinois University Press.

Dewey, J. (1988). *Human nature and conduct*. (The middle works of John Dewey, Vol. 14: 1922.) Carbondale: Southern Illinois University Press.

Ellsworth, E. (1989). Educational media, ideology, and the presentation of knowledge through popular cultural forms. In H. A. Giroux & R. I. Simon (Eds.), *Popular culture, schooling, and everyday life* (pp. 47–66). South Hadley, MA: Bergin & Garvey.

Evans, K. (1999). When queer and teacher meet. In W. J. Letts IV & J. T. Sears (Eds.), *Queering elementary education: Advancing the dialogue about sexualities and schooling* (pp. 237–246). Lanham, MD: Rowman & Littlefield.

Evans, K. (2002). *Negotiating the self: Identity, sexuality, and emotion in learning to teach*. New York: RoutledgeFalmer.

Freire, P. (1970/1993). *Pedagogy of the oppressed*. New York: Continuum.

Freire, P. (1978). *Pedagogy as process: The letters to Guinea-Bissau*. New York: Seabury.

Freire, P. (1985). *The politics of education: Culture, power and liberation*. South Hadley, MA: Bergin & Garvey.

Freire, P. (1998). *Pedagogy of the freedom: Ethics, democracy, and civic courage*. Lanham, MD: Rowman & Littlefield.

Freire, P., & Macedo, D. (1987). *Literacy: Reading the word and the world*. South Hadley, MA: Bergin & Garvey.

Gale, T., & Densmore, K. (2003). *Engaging teachers: Towards a radical democratic agenda for schooling*. Philadelphia: Open University Press.

Garber, L. (Ed.). (1994). *Tilting the tower: Lesbians, teaching, queer subjects*. New York: Routledge.

Giddens, A. (1992). *The transformation of intimacy: Sexuality, love and eroticism in modern societies*. London: Polity.

Giroux, H. A. (1992). *Border crossing: Cultural worker and the politics of education*. New York: Routledge.

Giroux, H. A. (1997). *Pedagogy and the politics of hope: Theory, culture, and schooling*. Boulder, CO: Westview.

Giroux, H. A. (2000). *Impure acts: The practical politics of cultural studies*. New York: Routledge.

Giroux, H. A. (2002). *Breaking into the movies: Film and the culture of politics*. Oxford: Blackwell.

Giroux, H. A. (2003). *The abandoned generation: Democracy beyond the culture of fear*. New York: Palgrave Macmillan.

Giroux, H. A., & McLaren, P. (1986). Teacher education and the politics of engagement: The case for democratic schooling. *Harvard Educational Review*, 56(3), 213–238.

Grace, D. J., & Tobin, J. (1997). Carnival in the classroom: Elementary students making videos. In J. Tobin (Ed.), *Making a place for pleasure in early childhood education* (pp. 159–187). New Haven, CT: Yale University Press.

Greene, M. (1978). *Landscapes of learning*. New York: Teachers College Press.

Greene, M. (1987). Creating, experiencing, sense-making: Art worlds in schools. *Journal of Aesthetic Education*, 21(4), 11–23.

Habermas, J. (1972). *Knowledge and human interests*. Boston: Beacon.

hooks, b. (1994). *Teaching to transgress: Education as the practice of freedom*. New York: Routledge.

Jennings, K. (Ed.). (1994). *One teacher in 10: Gay and lesbian educators tell their stories*. Boston: Alyson.

Kimmel, K. (1993). Masculinity as homophobia: Fear, shame, and silence in the construction of gender identity. In H. Brod & M. Haufman (Eds.), *Theorizing masculinities* (pp. 119–141). Thousand Oaks, CA: Sage.

Kissen, R. M. (1996). *The last closet: The real lives of lesbian and gay teachers*. Portmouth, NH: Heinemann.

Klein, J. P. (1996). Crossing boundaries: Knowledge, disciplinarities, and interdisciplinarities. Charlottesville, VA: University Press of Virginia.

Lefebvre, H. (1991). *Critique of everyday life: Volume I*, introduction. London: Verso.

Marcuse, H. (1960). *Reason and revolution*. Boston: Beacon.

Marcuse, H. (1964). *One dimensional man: Studies in the ideology of advanced industrial society*. Boston: Beacon.

Marcuse, H. (1978). *The aesthetic dimension: Toward a critique of marxist aesthetic*. Boston: Beacon.

McLaren, P. (1988). Foreword: Critical theory and the meaning of hope. In H. A. Giroux, *Teachers as intellectuals: Toward a critical pedagogy of learning* (pp. ix–xxi). Granby, MA: Bergin & Garvey.

McLaren, P. (1994a). Multiculturalism and the postmodern critique: Toward a pedagogy of resistance and transformation. In H. A. Giroux & P. McLaren (Eds.), *Between borders: Pedagogy and the politics of cultural studies* (pp. 192–222). New York: Routledge.

McLaren, P. (1994b). *Life in school: An introduction to critical pedagogy in the foundations of education* (2nd edition). New York: Longman.

McLaren, P. (1995). *Critical pedagogy and predatory culture: Oppositional politics in a postmodern era*. New York: Routledge.

McLaren, P., & Giroux, H. A. (1997). Writing from the margins: Geographies of identity, pedagogy, and power. In P. McLaren, *Revolutionary multiculturalism: Pedagogies of dissent for the new millennium* (pp. 16–41). Boulder, CO: Westview.

Mohanty, C. (1990). On race and voice: Challenges for liberal education in the 1990s. *Cultural Critique, 14*, 179–208.

Morrow, R. A., & Torres, C. A. (2002). *Reading Freire and Habermas: Critical pedagogy and transformative social change*. New York: Teacher College Press.

Pollner, M. (1991). Life of ethnomethodology: The rise and fall of radical reflexivity. *American Sociological Review, 56*, 370–380.

Popkewitz, T. (1998). *Struggling for the soul: The politics of schooling and the construction of the teacher*. New York: Teacher College Press.

Quinlivan, K. (2002). Whose problem is this? Queering the framing of lesbian and gay secondary school students within 'at risk' discourses. In K. H. Robionson, J. Irwin, & T. Ferfolja (Eds.), *From here to diversity: The social impact of lesbian and gay issues in education in Australia and New Zealand* (pp. 17–31). New York: The Haworth Press.

Scott, J. (1990). *Domination and the arts of resistance: Hidden transcript*. New Haven: Yale University Press.

Sears, J. T. (1999). Teaching queerly: Some elementary propositions. In W. J. Letts IV & J. T. Sears (Eds.), *Queering elementary education: Advancing the dialogue about sexualities and schooling* (pp. 3–14). Lanham, MD: Rowman & Littlefield.

Sedgwick, E. K. (1990). *Epistemology of the closet*. Berkeley: University of California Press.

Sehr, D. T. (1997). *Education for public democracy*. Albany: State University of New York Press.

Shor, I., & Freire, P. (1987). *A pedagogy for liberation—dialogues on transforming education*. Granby, MA: Bergin & Garvey.

Spivak, G. C. (1996). *The Spivak reader: Selected works of Gayatri Chakravotry Spivak*. New York: Routledge.

Unks, G. (Ed.). (1995). *The gay teen: Educational practice and theory for lesbian, gay, and bisexual adolescents*. New York: Routledge.

Walling, D. R. (Ed.). (1996). *Open lives, safe schools: Addressing gay and lesbian issues in education*. Bloomington: Phi Delta Kappa Educational Foundation.

Weedon, C. (1987). *Feminist practice and poststructuralist theory*. New York: Basil Blackwell.

Weeks, J. (2000). *Making sexual history*. Cambridge: Polity.

Weiler, K. (1994). Freire and feminist pedagogy of difference. In P. McLaren & C. Lanksher (Eds.), *Politics of liberation: Paths from Freire* (pp. 1–34). New York: Routledge.

Weiler, K. (2001). Reading Paulo Freire. In K. Weiler (Ed.), *Feminist engagements: Reading, resisting, and revisioning male theorists in education and cultural studies* (pp. 67–87). New York: Routledge.

Willis, P. (1989). Art or culture? An inquiry. In H. A. Giroux & R. I. Simons (Eds.), *Popular culture, schooling, and everyday life* (pp. 131–146). Granby, MA: Bergin & Garvey.

Willis, P. (1990). *Common culture: Symbolic work at play in the everyday cultures of the young*. Boulder, CO: Westview.

PART TWO

Queer(ing) Discourse and Identity in Education

CHAPTER SIX
Punk'd

William F. Pinar

> Gender and race conflate in a crisis.
> Henry Louise Gates, Jr. (1996, p. 96)

The crisis this time is the political subjugation of America's schoolteachers, not only a matter of social justice, but of the very possibility of education itself. As college and university professors have long appreciated, academic—intellectual—freedom is a prequisite to scholarship and teaching. Without liberty—without professional, that is, intellectual discretion over the curriculum we teach and the means by which we assess students' study of it—we cannot teach (Pinar, 2006c). Legislated by the Bush Administration to be bureaucratic functionaries who manage "learning," teachers have been punk'd, now pawns in the right-wing's exploitation of "accountability" as a means of political indoctrination.

Gendered female and racialized as black in the political imaginary (see Pinar, 2004), teachers have been forced to abandon their professional obligation to teach *what* they judge to be knowledge of most worth. The consolation prize is the freedom to teach *how* ones wishes, of course, as long as it resembles "best practice" and those test scores rise. In gendered and racial terms, teachers are "free" to do whatever will please their political husbands and bureaucratic masters. If they fail to please, they can be fired, in the name of "accountability."

In a profession gendered female, straight men are double punk'd. Like boys who play with girls during childhood, men who teach are not "real" men. Forced to submit to the political will of (mostly straight male) legislators, straight men suffer gendered positions of "gracious submission," the term Southern Baptists employed to depict the "biblical" relation of wives to their

husbands (Pinar, 2004, p. 65). One of the nation's great historicans—Richard
Hofstadter (1962, p. 320)—wondered to what extent male teachers can be
"men":

> where teaching has been identified as a feminine profession, it does not offer men
> the stature of a fully legitimate male role....The boys grow up thinking of men
> teachers as somewhat effeminate and treat them with a curious mixture of genteel
> deference (of the sort due to women) and hearty male condescension.

"Genteel deference" and "condescension" have become contempt in the era of
No Child Left Behind.

In the late 19th century, many women chose the profession of teaching to
contradict enforced domesticity (Grumet, 1988). Despite resistance, male
administrators reproduced the confinement of the domestic sphere by legislating women's conduct within the public school classroom (see Crocco, Munro,
& Weiler, 1999). In choosing a feminized profession, straight men contami-
nated their claims to hegemonic masculinity. To contradict their ambiguous
gendered professional identity, many identified with those male legislators
who monitor and control women's conduct by proxy (by legislation and the
administrative apparatus). In so doing, they claim, unconvincingly, to be
"men." Legislators prefer to substitute their own gendered symbols—
businessmen or, better yet, exmilitary men—as school administrators, specifically superintendents, and as teachers.

This convoluted gendered situation has been a century in the making.
During the 19th century, many middle-class men took comfort from women's
nurturance of children. The separate spheres ideology[1]—women at home,
men at work—conferred upon this arbitrary gendered arrangement natural
and divine legitimation. Over the course of the 20th century, many men came
to distrust women's role in the upbringing of "their" sons. Suspicious of those
who care for children is, it turns out, centuries old (Pinar, 2006b, chapter
two), and not limited to the United States.

There is a U.S. story to tell, however. Here I suggest its main moments
through summaries of gender developments in four decades: the 1890s, the
1920s, the 1950s, and the 1960s. These summaries provide snapshots of men's
developing distrust of women (and of the men who work with them) in the
upbringing of children. I begin with the 1890s, a decade of "crisis" for white

middle-class men that both reflected and precipitated the destabilization of those gendered arrangements the separate spheres ideology had formalized. In emphasizing this narrative thread—men's distrust of women as childrearers decoded as a defensive and compensatory contradiction of matrifocality—we can appreciate how straight teachers became punk'd by those who claim to care that no child be left behind.

White Men in "Crisis"[2]

Since the prime of the Victorian era,
men had been in retreat.
Peter G. Filene (1998, p. 228)

In the early 1890s both manliness and white middle-class identity—themselves conflated—were under siege. The legendary U.S. historian Henry Steele Commager (1950, p. 44) likened the 1890s to a great watershed in American history, a decade in which "the new America came in as on flood tide." He focused first on the "passing of the old West" (1950, p. 44), by which he means, I suppose, the genocide of Native Americans. (He focuses on the erosion of the frontier line, the decline of the cattle kingdom, the completion of the transcontinental railroad, and the final territorial organization of the West.) The decade also "revealed a dangerous acceleration of the exploitation of natural resources" (1950, p. 44), including the seizure of the best forest, minerals, range, and farmland by large corporations; these developments helped precipitate the conservation and reclamation movements. The center of economic gravity shifted from the rural to the urban. There was an unprecedented degree of control of manufacturing, transportation, banking, and communication industries in trusts and monopolies. The decade saw the rise of big business, including the emergence of the successful businessman as "hero" (1950, p. 45), and the beginnings of the modern labor movement.

Commager mentions mass immigration and "the advent of the New South" (1950, p. 44), although there is no mention that black citizens were being systematically disfranchised state by southern state, that segregation was being institutionalized throughout the region, and that black men's bodies were swinging from southern poplar trees. Southern white men fought violently to maintain relations of racial subjugation, but even pious northern churchmen found themselves challenged by Christian feminists (Haynes, 1998).

Almost as soon as the First Woman's Rights Convention ended in Seneca Falls, New York, in 1848, white men resisted women's participation in the public sphere, a multivariate issue concentrated then on women's right to vote. As they do today, reactionaries invoked the "Law of God" to defend their prejudice. The Reverend John Todd pointed out that women's suffrage constituted a "rebellion against God's law of the sexes, against marriage…and against the family organization, the holiest thing that is left from Eden." James Long invoked the racial analogue, asking:

> How did woman first become subject to man as she now is all over the world? By her nature, her sex, just as the negro is and always will be, to the end of time, inferior to the white race, and therefore, doomed to subjection; but happier than she would be in any other condition, just because it is the law of her nature. (passages in Kimmel, 1996, pp. 57–58)

It is not fortuitous, of course, that white women and black men are, and not only for James Long, conjoined (Pinar, 2001). The same conflation of race with gender (recall Gates' sentence opening this chapter) is evident in the gracious submission of schoolteachers under the Bush Administration.

Not only women's political progress threatened (especially white) men. The "discovery" of "homosexuality" and "heterosexuality" in the late nineteenth century required restructuring men's relationships with each other. Before the 1890s, American men had formed intimate friendships with other men, evidently unconcerned about the consequences of these emotionally and often physically intimate relationships for sexual identity (Yacovone, 1998). "To be sure," Filene (1998, p. 83) writes,

> there were a minority of men, especially in larger cities, who preferred to have sex with other men, behavior that was deemed "unnatural" and illegal. On the other hand, many men embraced in bed without crossing that line and without shame.

They didn't cross that line, I suggest, because they did not speak, and others were evidently not eager to learn, about what happened when men shared the same bed.

The appearance of "homosexuality" as a public identity meant the rapid disappearance of these intimate male friendships. No longer could men share beds without suspicion. As a public identity, homosexuality forced male–male sexual desire to be segregated within a specific population. As "homosexuals," certain men focused upon "desire" often stripped from friendship, while "heterosexual" men struggled to find ways to be close to other men while suppressing their yearning for physical intimacy.

Although these developments undermined earlier versions of manliness, white middle-class men continued to promote them, for to acknowledge the disappearance of traditional manliness felt like acknowledging male power itself was lost. As historian Gail Bederman (1995b, p. 409) puts it:

> Discourses of manliness were embedded in their very identities. They formed their sons into men by teaching them manliness. Especially in the context of challenges from the Gilded Age woman's movement, abandoning familiar constructs of manliness was an unimaginable option.

In crisis, then, late 19th century white middle-class men began to search for new ways to fortify their illusions of manliness, among them new-found enthusiasms for body-building and college football (Pronger, 1990; Kimmel 1996).

White middle-class men began to speak approvingly about something they called "masculinity," a rhetoric that disclosed the fragility of manliness, now understood as heterosexual, as "straight." Although rarely used until the late 1890s, "masculinity" now became the noun of choice, precisely because it connoted new meanings of maleness different from earlier versions of "manliness." Such reformulations were, Bederman (1995b) points out, fragmented and sometimes contradictory of the facts. For example, increasing numbers of middle-class men frequented urban red-light districts.

One such district in turn-of-the-century New York City, the Bowery, was home to a significant and visible homosexual subculture. "Going slumming in the resorts of the Bowery and the Tenderloin was," George Chauncey (1994, p. 36) reports, "a popular activity among middle-class men (and even some women)." Was such activity the inevitable consequence of naturally explosive masculine passions? Did it represent the sordid and degenerate loss of manly self-control? Could this pervasive moral weakness be counteracted? By the turn of the century, such questions plagued many men and, Bederman (1995b, p. 410) tells us, "middle-class manliness had taken on the character of a beloved but fragile friend, whose weakness must at all costs remain unacknowledged." The straight man was punk'd from the outset.

To compensate for their gendered and racial losses and to mythologize what they imagined had once made them powerful, many middle-class white (especially Southern) men scapegoated African Americans. The 1890s were a period of virulent racism and a racially conceived nativism, an epoch of lynching, black disenfranchisement, xenophobia, and imperialism (Williamson, 1984). These phenomena were interrelated (Stoler, 1995).

Many white middle-class men and women gazed with distaste, even disgust, upon increasing numbers of eastern and southern European immigrants; they perceived these newly arrived Americans as cousins of "blacks"; that is, masses of inassimilable "races." As early as 1849, the President of Middlebury College had wondered whether the new immigrants would be assimilated or prove to be to the Republic what the Goths and Huns had been to the Roman Empire. The answer, he thought, would depend in large measure "upon the wisdom and fidelity of our teachers" (quoted in Cremin, 1961, p. 66). A compensatory and defensive curriculum of cultural standardization would continue to characterize the American school into the 21st century (Pinar, Reynolds, Slattery, & Taubman, 1995; Zimmerman, 2002).

A cult of Anglo-Saxonism—fortified with new "scientific" theories of "race"—provided incontrovertible "proof" of white middle-class men's supremacy (Haynes, 1998; Stoler, 1995). By mythologizing white manhood as racial traits cultivated long ago in the forests of Germany, white men once again "knew" they were manly—straight—men. European Americans could take comfort in the knowledge that the Anglo-Saxon race, as Francis Parkman phrased it, was "peculiarly masculine" (quoted in Bederman, 1995b, p. 410). By virtue of its racial inheritance, Anglo-Saxons were independent, adventurous, strong of will, tenacious of purpose, in a word, manly (Bederman, 1995b).

Anglo-Saxons were, many worried, an imperiled "race." To preserve "race" and nation, "real men" were needed. Instead, many late 19th century white men worried, the United States was being undermined by a widespread feminization of American culture. Many identified this deterioration of the nation with the feminization of (white) boyhood. Such emasculation was, many men suspected, the consequence of omnipresence of women in the lives of their sons. What once had been "natural" and divinely ordained under the separate spheres ideology now appeared to be an arbitrary, even dangerous, fact. Not only did women influence boys as their mothers, increasingly (the "feminization" of the teaching profession occurs during the latter half of the 19th century) they dominated the lives of boys as teachers in both elementary and secondary schools.

Many men under seige became alarmed that women were teaching boys. One observer foresaw only two consequences, the "effeminate babyish boy" and "the bad boy"; he declared that masculine influence "is necessary for the proper development" of young boys. Somehow the presence of a man—preferably the son's father—would provide protection against effeminacy. Writing in the *Educational Review* in 1914, one man complained that women teachers had created "a feminized manhood, emotional, illogical, non-combative against public evils." This psychic threat to "masculine nature," he argued, was beginning to "warp the psyches of our boys and young men into femininity" (quoted in Kimmel, 1996, p. 121). Half a century later, fears of feminization—now linked to conflations of homosexuality with communism during the Cold War—would animate 1960's national curriculum reform (see Pinar, 2004, p. 65ff). Always, it seems, straight men were imperiled.

Not only female teachers threatened boys' becoming men, however. The presence of female classmates was evidently also threatening. Influential educators such as Edward Clarke of the Harvard Medical School and G. Stanley Hall, expert on adolescence and the president of Clark University, warned that co-education was dangerous to both boys and girls. Both Clarke and Hall insisted that co-education distorted and deformed the biological, and therefore "natural," natures of males and females. Clarke and Hall worried that mental, let alone physical, exertion by women would reduce their reproductive and maternal capacities, and that schools with a large number of female students and teachers would, according to Clarke and Hall, "feminize" male students (Tyack & Hansot, 1990). Such "a man with feminine traits of character, or with the frame and carriage of a female," warned Dr. Alfred Stillé, president of the American Medical Association, "is despised by both the sex he ostensibly belongs to, and that of which he is at once a caricature and a libel" (quoted in

Kimmel, 1996, p. 122). The resonance of this slur with Hofstadter's is unmistakable. Straight male teachers merit neither modifier. Like punks in prison, they are other men's "bitches" (Pinar, 2001, pp. 1020–1029).

"A Dangerous Instrument"

> Fears of feminization…
> have haunted men for a century.
> Michael Kimmel (1996, p. 321)

In the 1920s, "manhood" (not democracy, as during the Great War, from which many men returned shell-shocked) was threatened, specifically the manhood of America's (white) sons. In J. B. Watson's influential *Psychological Care of the Infant and Child* (1928), the mother's role was positioned as pivotal. This apparent compliment contained, it soon became obvious, unwanted liabilities. In a chapter entitled "The Dangers of Too Much Mother Love," Watson cautioned readers that a "heart is full of love which she [the mother] must express in some way. She expresses it by showering love and kisses." Contrary to intention, maternal love threatened their sons' independence and mental health, reducing potentially virile young men into whining dependent mama's boys. "Mother love is a dangerous instrument," he announced. Mothers must guard against their own impulses in loving their sons overmuch; they must be careful to treat their sons differently from their daughters. "Never hug [boys] and kiss them, never let them sit on your lap," Watson counseled (quoted passages in Kimmel, 1996, p. 203). Evidently, and contrary to popular culture, mother's love did not lure a young man into marrying a woman just like the woman who married dear ole Dad; instead, mother's love threatened to lure young men into *becoming* like the woman who married dear ole Dad.

During the 1920s, "homosexuality hovered like a specter over anxious parents," reports Michael Kimmel (1996, p. 203). Anxious parents watched for signs of effeminacy in their young sons; these foreshadowed adult male homosexuality. Almost a third of Joseph Collins' *The Doctor Looks at Love and Life* (1926), one of the decade's best-selling advice books to parents, focused on male homosexuality. The homosexual was effeminate and unmanly, he warned, a "man of broad hips and mincing gait, who vocalizes like a lady and articulates like a chatterbox, who likes to sew and knit, to ornament his clothing and decorate his face" (quoted in Kimmel, 1996, p. 203). Clement Wood's advice book *Manhood* (1924) assured readers that homosexuality was a stage of development out of which young men would soon (gratefully) pass. Wood informed his readers that a twelve-year-old boy's preferences were 40 percent autosexual, 50 percent homosexual, and 10 percent heterosexual; by puberty the percentages would shift to 20, 30, and 50 percent, respectively (Kimmel, 1996). Many anxiety-ridden parents were not exactly soothed by these statistics.

The seige of straightness was not helped by the failure of the nation to re- turn to "normalcy" after the "Great War," evident also in the decade's divorce statistics. In 1920 there were 7.7 divorces per one-thousand marriages; by 1927 there was one for every six, sixteen times the rate for the 1870s. One ongoing source of stress was men's continuing concern about their status as (straight) men. This stress was intensified by the public practice of mocking fathers and husbands in the popular press of the 1920s, for instance, in new comic strips like *Blondie*. Dagwood Bumstead, Blondie's bumbling, incompe- tent, hopeless husband, parodied 1920's "patriarchs" as inept fools without the intelligence and common sense of their superior and patient wives (Kimmel, 1996). Even straight men—as husbands and fathers were assumed to be (be- fore the period of the "down-low": see below)—were punks.

Like the 1920s, the 1950s were also a politically reactionary decade, ar- gues Jessica Weiss (1998, p. 350), "a flash point for fatherhood." The post-war moment, for all its euphoria, was also a time of masculine dissolution, a "cri- sis" attributable to World War II, a war which had followed, of course, the Great Depression, another period of gendered and racialized as well as eco- nomic difficulty (Pinar, 2001, pp. 723–725). These historical traumas left many men "castrated." Kaja Silverman (1992) shows how Hollywood tried to come to the rescue, creating films—in particular, *Pride of the Marines* (1945), *It's a Wonderful Life* (1946), and most especially *The Guilt of Janet Ames* (1947) —in which women were called "to disavow the male subject's castration, and—by looking at him with her imagination rather than with her eyes—to confer upon him a phallic sufficiency" (1992, p. 8). American women were accustomed to this ploy, having in all likelihood employed it in the South after the Civil War (Faust, 1996).

In addition to the inevitable trauma of battle, military service subverted straightness in another, quite unintended, way: it afforded gay men and lesbians opportunities to meet more easily and in greater numbers (Bérubé, 1990). World War II also made, if only for short periods, gay men and lesbians out of "straights." When soldiers and sailors and airmen were shipped out to the South Pacific or Europe, they were forced into various kinds of physical intimacies. Some army and navy outfits, for instance, instituted a "buddy system," under which pairs of men were responsible for each other's safety. Purely practical relationships sometimes deepened into emotional and, sometimes, sexual ones:

> In the confines of a navy carrier and the stress of danger, buddy relationships often evolved into romantic ones, sometimes sexual, sometimes affectionate. While watching movies at night on the deck of an LST in the Pacific, men held hands, kissed, hugged—not all of them gay men. In other words, the war reopened the continuum that Victorians had enjoyed before the barrier of "homosexuality" was raised. The war, one might say, proved to be a large-scale coming-out event. (Filene, 1998, p. 174)

Despite this experimentation, most men returned, in 1945, to their "rightful" place in the family; marriage license bureaus did more business in 1946 than in any single year before or since (Filene, 1998).

Americans fled to traditional gender roles not only to compensate for the economic deprivation and gender destabilization associated with the Great Depression and World War II but, Elaine Tyler May (1988) argues, to flee the anxieties associated with the Cold War, anxieties that were profoundly gendered (Pinar, 2004, p. 84ff). During the 1950s, the United States sought "containment" of contagion that was the Soviet threat. Government spokesmen as well as social scientists promoted the nuclear family as the cornerstone of American society and security. The American family was, presumably, nothing less than "a psychological fortress" (May 1988, p. 11) on the home front (see, also, Filene, 1998).

The economic and ideological stage was set for a revitalized American family. It was to be a restructured middle-class family in which, experts hoped, men would play a greater role, intervening, presumably, in the matrifocality of home life, ensuring their sons safe passage to straightness. Those family experts in the 1950s who encouraged fathers to become more involved with their children than their fathers might have been with them were not, as we have seen, the first to focus on the topic. Since the turn-of-the-century— characterized, as we have seen, by a widespread "crisis" in masculinity—many had focused on the role of fathers in ensuring "straightness." Declining family size, suburbanization, and a reduced workweek had functioned to restructure family life for many middle-class Americans, whose increased income and leisure made spending more time with the family a realistic goal for many middle-class men. Even then—some sixty years before the publication of the Moynihan Report, to which we attend momentarily—experts were concerned about men's (in this instance, white men's) daily absence from family life. There were many who advised turn-of-the-century fathers to become more engaged and involved fathers (Bederman, 1995a; Weiss, 1998). The subtext of this advice, as we have seen, was fear of the feminization of (white) boys: straightness subverted.

After World War II, many professionals committed to improving family life listed fatherhood near the top of their reform agendas. They encouraged fathers to be more than the agents of discipline in the home; they asked them to be companions and role models for their children. Psychologists again linked fathers to the development of sexual identity and gender roles in their offspring, adding a certain tension to the increasingly public issue of men's role in rearing children. Despite these calls for increased participation at home, few challenged the central role men continued to play as breadwinners. Added to that continuing demand on men's time and energy, recall that the middle-class family was perhaps at its most "nuclear" at this time. Suburban housing spread rapidly in the 1950s. Young couples may have been pleased to escape the crowded urban housing conditions that typified the war years, but they were not always eager to leave behind an extended family and community that had long been, for many, sources of advice and support. Postwar men and women married younger, had children sooner after marriage, and had more of them in a shorter span of time, all of which led to the baby boom (Weiss, 1998).

Isolated from parents who had traditionally offered advice concerning childrearing, young parents sought alternative, "expert" sources of authority and advice. A veritable army of experts sought to capture their attention, chief among them the "calming voice" (Weiss, 1998, p. 352) of pediatrician Dr.

Benjamin Spock. Spock's 1946 *Common Sense Book of Baby and Child Care* was a bestseller; it was revised the first of five times in 1957. His advice brought letters of thanks from suburban parents, one of whom exclaimed: "I've got a copy in the living room, a copy in the bedroom, a copy in the kitchen, a copy in the bathroom" (quoted in Weiss, 1998, p. 353). Spock's book was only one, albeit the most popular, volume in a barrage of how-to books that rushed to instruct insecure baby-boom parents (Weiss, 1998). Like standardized examinations, Spock's manual represented a prosthetic extension of masculine authority into the matrifocal structure of the home (or the classroom in the analogy), ensuring sons' straightness.

Not only did most of these experts agree that fathers should spend more time with their children, many argued that fathers offered contributions to childrearing that mothers could not. Comforting a crying baby had different consequences when it was a man's arms holding the infant: "Father's arms are strong and the child who experiences the security they give him grows up with a warm regard for some of the best qualities of masculinity—tenderness, protection, and strength" (quoted in Weiss, 1998, p. 354). By using such language, experts characterized tenderness and nurturing as male qualities, redefining the meaning of the phrase "real men" and, they hoped, setting the stage for a rather different masculinity in the next generation. With fathers more involved, a certain balance between mothers and fathers would be struck, one that some experts theorized would make more likely that children would learn appropriate sex roles (Weiss, 1998).

"Appropriate sex roles" were of particular concern during the 1950s. Many men who had been sexually involved with other men during the war returned to their wives and girlfriends. Many women who had enjoyed sexual intimacy with other women during the war returned to homes where such love dare not speak its name. Even many gay and lesbian veterans married and had children, suppressing their sexual identities, sometimes quietly engaging in homosexual affairs, unable to find social support to "come out," living lives of quiet desperation. In fact, during the 1950s, "in Cold War culture, there was room only for straight gender identity—straight and narrow" (Filene, 1998, p. 180).

Feeling threatened by communist gains in Eastern Europe and Asia, Right-wing demagogues undertook a witch-hunt at home. The "witches" were not only communists but homosexuals as well. Homosexuals who worked for the government were condemned as "security risks" because, presumably, they were susceptible to blackmail by (evidently seductive) Soviet spies. One Republican party national chairman in 1948 warned that "sexual perverts...have infiltrated our Government in recent years," and they were "perhaps as dangerous as the actual Communists." Two years later, a Senate committee concluded that even "one homosexual can pollute a Government office" (quoted in Filene, 1998, p. 179). These gendered images of containment and contagion (or pollution) would surface again during the HIV/AIDS hysteria of the 1980s.

Gay federal employees were fired in increasing numbers: five per month between 1947 and 1950, sixty a month between 1950 and 1953. Across the nation, F.B.I. agents were instructed to gather information about gay bars, the post office conducted surveillance on subscribers to gay erotic materials, and local police arrested lesbians and gay men in bars, public restrooms, parks, and beaches. In Philadelphia, for instance, there were a hundred arrests per month during the 1950s. On a single night in 1956 in San Francisco, thirty-six lesbians were arrested at the Alamo Club, and that suspension of civil rights was repeated over and over again across the country (Sears, 2006). After a sensational murder case, the county attorney in Sioux City invoked Iowa's sexual psychopath law and committed twenty-nine local gay men to mental institutions (Filene, 1998). Clearly, there was only one place for American men during the 1950s: in the heterosexual family.

Not only was the American man supposed to be a "family man," he was also supposed to be a parenting man. If husbands resisted increased participation in parenting, many suggested, women should make sure they encouraged them to try. Experts worried that many women mistakenly assumed that childrearing was solely their responsibility and subtly (or not) excluded fathers in shared responsibility for parenthood. Experts advised wives to encourage and guide their husbands' interest in the children, as husbands were presumed not to know how to proceed. Weiss (1998) argues that despite this rhetorical emphasis upon fathers and fatherhood during the 1950s, it was still women who were finally responsible for childrearing, even when that included the additional duty of regulating their husbands' sometimes blundering efforts. In this respect, the emphasis upon fatherhood was a setup for mothers: if Dad turned out to be less than a great father and/or if their children were in some way disappointing, she could look only to herself to explain the failure of the family (Weiss, 1998; see also, Doll, Wear, & Whitaker, 2006, p. 155).

While the experts left undisturbed the division of labor in the middle-class nuclear family, their advice did help blur the boundaries. In practice, Weiss tells us, many middle-class men and women did make efforts to find space between the demands of work and family to perform the prescriptive ideals of mothering and fathering. Many more did not, as frustrated and exhausted men, despite their wives' encouragement to spend more time with the kids, remained focused on the financial rewards their hard work brought the family. Indeed, for most fathers of baby boomers, providing remained the cornerstone of fatherhood. They devoted themselves to work and hoped that the financial rewards their labor brought would compensate for their absence from the home (Weiss, 1998).

White middle-class fathers of the 1950s were unable to escape the demands of work. Despite the advice of experts, the encouragement of wives, and their own professed interest in spending more time with their children, middle-class men were by-and-large absentee dads. As a consequence, by the early 1970s, their children grown, most men found themselves psychologically isolated, retiring from the work which had preoccupied them, strangers to those wives and children for whom the work had presumably been about. Weiss (1998, p. 360) concludes: "Two decades of career commitment and limited involvement with now teenaged or grown children left hopes for fatherly intimacy stillborn."

Rather than facing the fact of their absence from their own families (and the fears of sons' effeminacy that absence threatened), many white men focused on the black family. White men blamed the absence of black fathers for the educational underachievement of black sons. In pathologizing the black family for the effects of white racism, were white men, in part, displacing their own sense of failure as fathers onto black men? Both black and white men were absent from childrearing, but the Moynihan Report focused on only absent black fathers, as we see next.

Sons Without Fathers

Forty percent of…children will live a major portion
of their childhood without their fathers.
E. J. Dionne, Jr. (1996, p. 306)

The release of the Moynihan Report in 1965 provoked considerable controversy, as it seemed—especially to black activists and intellectuals—to "blame the victim," (i.e., the black family) for the problems African Americans faced trying to live in a racist society. Entitled *The Negro Family: A Case Study for National Action*, the Report decried "family pathology—divorce, separation, desertion, female family head[s], children in broken homes, and illegitimacy" (Moynihan, 1965, p. 19). The lower-class black family was judged to be a "tangle of pathology," a phrase borrowed from Kenneth Clark (Young-Bruehl, 1996, p. 92). When men were present at all, the Report alleged, they tended to be derelict, even emasculated, characters, forcing women to act as heads of household. Black sons suffered a lack of male role models and were, therefore, at risk for delinquency (i.e., "bad boys"—see above—not at risk for effeminancy and homosexuality, as white men worried about their own sons). The document conflated the "American" family with the white middle-class nuclear patriarchal fantasy of "normalcy" and "stability." The effect was to stigmatize the lower-class African American "matriarchy" (Young-Bruehl, 1996).

Stigmatization was not Moynihan's intention. In the Report, he acknowledged that three hundred years of slavery coupled with one hundred years of postslavery racism had negatively impacted black family life. However, as Elisabeth Young-Bruehl (1996, p. 92) points out, Moynihan "showed no appreciation whatsoever for the strength and resilience in Negro families by speaking only of distortions." Nor did he acknowledge positive facts about black families, such as, for instance, the fact that child molestation is less frequent in African American than it is in white households. While blaming slavery and postslavery institutions for black family "pathology," Moynihan went on to claim that the problem had become self-perpetuating. Throughout his report Moynihan spoke of racism as a virus, also a common image for homosexuality among gender reactionaries. The virus and pathology metaphors located "the disease" in black, not white, people (Young-Bruehl, 1996).

The distortions lacing the Moynihan Report circulated widely, as Young-Bruehl points out. For instance, the Coleman Report employed the same fantasy of white middle-class family "normalcy" to claim that black children failed in schools due to their home and family environments. There was no acknowledgment of racism in schools or in the society in which those homes and schools were located. Despite their authors' antiracist intentions, both the Moynihan and Coleman reports were easily co-opted by conservatives who argued that the federal government was wasting money on programs for compensatory education, like Project Head Start, programs that assumed that intelligence is not based on heredity or race. In 1969, psychologist Arthur Jensen argued just the opposite, that differences in I.Q. scores between black and white children were based on heredity. Such racist nonsense about I.Q. inheritability has surfaced in every white backlash against compensatory education and affirmative action, most recently just over a decade ago in Richard Hernnstein and Charles Murray's *The Bell Curve* (1994; see Kincheloe, Steinberg, & Gresson, 1996).

In her discussion of the Moynihan Report, Hortense Spillers (1987, p. 65) points out that in certain societies, a child's identity is determined through the line of the Mother, but, referring to the report, the United States is evidently "not one of them." She quotes the Moynihan Report: "In essence, the Negro community has been forced into a matriarchal structure which, because it is so far out of line with the rest of American society, seriously retards the progress of the group as a whole, and imposes a crushing burden on the Negro male and, inconsequence, on a great many Negro women as well" (Moynihan, 1965, p. 75; in Spillers, 1987, p. 65). From the point of view of object relations theory, too, every child's identity is determined through the mother (Chodorow, 1978).

Moynihan's fantasy of a "tangle of pathology" sets up the fourth chapter of the report in which the "underachievement" in lower-class black males is attributed to black females, partly because they overachieve and thus, presumably, undermine their brothers' egos. Spillers (1987) quotes Moynihan: "Ours is a society which presumes male leadership in private and public affairs.... A subculture, such as that of the Negro American, in which this is not the pattern, is placed at a distinct disadvantage" (1965, p. 75; in Spillers, 1987, p. 66). Dressed in liberal drag, Moynihan was repeating the white man's historical (and defensive, compensatory) aside to the black that "you're not a real man, I am." Trapped in a "matriarchal" prison, Moynihan was asserting, African Americans are caught in a state of social pathology (Spillers, 1987).

Moynihan's "Negro Family," Spillers (1987) points out, restates a series of historical associations concerning the enslaved. She asks us to recall that, under conditions of captivity, children did not "belong" to their mothers. Despite this fact, African peoples enslaved in the New World still maintained powerful bonds between parents and children. The fact that the "black family" survived against all (white) odds represents, as Spillers (1987, p. 74) notes, "one" of the "supreme social achievements" of enslaved African Americans. This achievement of affiliation and affection was in no minor way the black woman's doing, but, as Spillers notes, this achievement, is recoded as "dominance" and "strength" by later generations—by both black and white—as a "pathology" (1987, p. 74), as threats of castration. Once again, young men's gendered identity—his straightness—is imagined as threatened by the presence of women.

Embracing matrifocality as a psychological achievement against the historical facts of enslavement and racism, Spillers argues, African American men have been "touched...by the mother, handled by her in ways that he cannot escape, and in ways that the white American male is allowed to temporize by a fatherly reprieve" (1987, p. 80). Because the black male slave was stripped of his rights to his children and his spouse, the only parental relation the slave child might experience was through the mother. This brutal fact of American slavery points, Spillers reminds, to that "inexorable difference" among American women, namely that the black woman, due to slavery, "becomes historically the powerful and shadowy evocation of a cultural synthesis long evaporated—the law of the Mother" (1987, p. 80). Understood matrifocally, then, Moynihan's allegations of "illegitimacy" evaporate. This evocation means, Spillers (1987, p. 80) continues, that black men are the "only" community of men in the United States who have "had the specific occasion to learn who the female is within itself.... It is the heritage of the mother that the African American male must regain as an aspect of his own personhood—the power of 'yes' to the 'female' within."

Moynihan was able to focus only upon the absence of the father, an absence white men themselves demanded during enslavement and homoerotically invited afterward (Pinar, 2001). Effacing the past, blind to the affirmative meaning of matrifocality, white men focused instead on absent black fathers. If only the black family could get itself together, then African Americans could get on track and succeed in this country where, after all, anyone can prosper if they only try. Among many whites, this right-wing rhetoric—that blacks (and black family dysfunctionality) are responsible for black poverty and social struggle—has never disappeared, as this excerpt from the August 30, 1993 edition of *Newsweek* indicates:

> Behind the electric clippers, a muscular black man is trimming hedges with the intensity of a barber sculpting a fade; nearby, his wife empties groceries from the car. In most quarters, they might elicit barely a nod. But in this largely black, working-class community, the couple is one of the few intact families on the block. All too common are the five young women who suddenly turn into view, every one of them pushing a baby stroller, not one of them married. Resigned, Caballero says with a sigh, "Where are the men?" (Chideya, 1993, p. 17; quoted in Blount & Cunningham, 1996, p. ix)

As Spillers might have predicated, the misogyny of that question went unchallenged.

Marcellus Blount and George P. Cunningham (1996) not only point out the historical throughline between the 1965 Moynihan Report and the 1993 *Newsweek* article, but they also bring to our attention how this persisting white fantasy, fixated on the absent father, erases much of what has occurred in the meantime, specifically the women's and LGBT movements. While this white fantasy is about "race," it is also, then, about "gender."[3] Blount and Cunningham (1996, p. xi) explain:

> Behind the racial veil, conventional gender and sexual norms are the saviors from the chaos of the "world without fathers." The collapsing of the time that separates the "Moynihan Report" and the *Newsweek* essay neatly elides, or rather squeezes out, all of the discussion of gender that has taken place in the last three decades. A world without fathers projects as its salvation for blacks (and, by implication, for all of American society) a world without feminism, without gays and lesbians. Most importantly, while the "Moynihan Report" was soundly condemned by African Americans in the 1960s, its normative premises and prescriptions have insinuated themselves in contemporary racial discourse, returning to us in the *Newsweek* article in a black voice.

This misogynist matrifocal narrative of masculinity production is not restricted to black families, of course. Today, it is recoded as distrust of schoolteachers, themselves gendered female and racialized as black in the popular imagination, in whose company white male legislators are determined no child shall be left behind. Testing ensures, presumably, no contamination has occurred. White boys will graduate as both "white" and as "men," "straight men."

Conclusion

> [T]he current panic about the absence of fathers
> is really about the presence of homosexuality—
> if the boy has no father to love and introject
> how will he be successfully masculinized?
> What, in other words, is to prevent them
> from being/remaining a queer?
> Mark Simpson (1994, p. 13)

Like the patriarchal libel that the mother is always accountable for sons' failure to become (straight) "men," contemporary conservatives allege that teachers—gendered female and racialized black—are to blame when children do not succeed in school. The phrase "No Child Left Behind" was no doubt intended to exploit black and poor parents' concerns for their children's futures by demanding that schools be held accountable for student learning as measured on standardized examinations. That schools alone—rather than government or the corporate sector or "faith-based" communities—are accountable for the future goes unchallenged in the popular press. Despite compelling evidence that the school "crisis" is "manufactured" (see, for example, Berliner & Biddle, 1996), No Child Left Behind continues to garner bipartisan support. The controversy over the legislation—focused to date on funding and testing issues—fails to acknowledge the absurd assumptions that underpin it; namely, that the school is *the* lever for social and economic improvement and that teachers are responsible for student learning.[4]

Since the first Coleman Report (see Pinar, 2006b, p. 124), public evaluation of the schools has shifted from "inputs" to "outputs." The concept was initially employed by liberals to focus attention on the responsibilities of government (particularly, the federal government) to provide remedial education and other social and economic supports to compensate for the disadvantages poor and minority children faced (supports to be documented by measuring "outputs"). After the conservative restoration in 1968, the emphasis on "outputs" (or "outcomes" in contemporary jargon) was exploited by conservatives to insist that schools alone were responsible for student achievement, thereby obviating the need for governmental intervention. Indeed, by focusing exclusively on school outputs, conservatives distract the public from forty years of conservative assault upon the poor and lower middle class.

Conservatives' outrageous criticism of schools is faced by no other profession (see Pinar, 2006c). Because the school as institution is a gendered and racial symbol for the future of the nation, the history that renders its present political circumstances intelligible is a gendered and racial history. Here I have presented four glimpses of that history, beginning in a late 19th century crisis of white manhood, triggered by a racialized fear of (desire for) black male phallic potency and a related homophobic panic, publicly focused on fears of feminization associated with the primacy of mothers in childrearing and schooling.[5] In the 1920s, this fear focused on mothers' alleged (if inadvertent) undermining of (especially white) boys' masculinity. Fears of emasculation occasioned by the omnipresence of women in boys' lives led to a 1950's preoccupation with (especially white) fathers' participation in childrearing, imagined, in part, as a corrective to the dangers of maternal solicitude. The presence of the father (assumed to be straight) would presumably protect the male child from the allegedly feminizing effects of women.

While perfectly prepared to leave childrearing to women in earlier historical periods, during the 20th century white men came to worry that in doing so they risked producing sissy sons who would become queer. White men expressed few such worries over black boys. Rather than producing effeminate homosexuals, matriarchal black families presumably produce hypermasculine young men who exhibit insufficient patience with schools and those white women who teach them. Instead, white anxiety over "blackened" (integrated) schools derives from the threats white men imagined hypermasculine black boys pose to white female teachers and white children, echoing the nineteenth-century white obsession with black men as sexual predators. No longer politically acceptable to express, this fear is codified in the legislation of white male control of schools.

In this historical and political context, then, the phrase "No Child Left Behind" discloses its gendered and racialized meanings. The phrase expresses the fear that men dare not leave "their" children behind in the company of well-intended but emasculating women and those not-quite-straight "men" who work with them. By legislating how boys—girls' achievement (or gendered development) does not seem to be a likewise lightning-rod issue—turn out (definitely not how they "come out"), mostly male legislators attempt to contradict the matrifocality birth from a woman's body establishes and maternal care extends. No white boy-child will be left behind to become a sissy.

Nor will any white child (or white schoolteacher) be left behind, unprotected, with blacks. Decoded racially, NCLB codifies white male control of black boys in the company of white women and children. Racially, such straight white male concern shifts from the feminization of white boys to the fantasized danger white women and children face in the company of black boys whose hypermasculinity compels underachievement. As the case with white girls, the achievement of black girls is not the lightning-rod issue here.

Distressed over the apparently high incidence of bisexuality (also known as being on the "down-low" or DL[6]) and homosexuality among African American men, black critics Nathan and Julia Hare found racial and gendered reasons for black boys' presumed promiscuity. The Hares charged that black boys were becoming homosexuals due to the preponderance of white female schoolteachers, alleging that "white teachers infiltrate black child centers, nurseries and primary schools, compelling black boys to play with blonde dolls in the name of progress" (1984, p. 66). Not all black critics agree.[7]

NCLB also exploits black parents' conviction that white teachers have failed their children, displacing the racism of the post-1968 conservative assault on African Americans (the antiaffirmative action backlash, for instance) onto the nation's schoolteachers, not all of whom are, of course, innocent of the charge. By forcing teachers to teach to tests measuring "skills," conservatives reduce time available to study "uncomfortable" topics such as lynching, in effect, deracializing the curriculum, and naturalizing the racial status quo.

Straight male schoolteachers have few moves to make. Politically, they must accept their subjugation quietly or risk being gender traitors to (and thereby inviting the rage of) the "real" men who legislate and govern the country. That gendered politics of identification coupled with conservative straight women's acceptance (at least in the public sphere) of men's authority over them means that there has been no mass protest against NCLB (and the political subjugation it signifies) among the nation's schoolteachers. There is, as education professors know, plenty of grumbling in private. Failing to provide leadership, those organizations that (fail to) represent the profession—the NEA and AFT—reflect teachers' passive acceptance of their "accountability"[8] for how boys turn out, just as many mothers in decades past accepted their culpability for boys who failed to coincide with their fathers' fantasies of them.

Because "school deform" cannot be understood apart from the history of racial and gender politics in the United States, feminist and queer theory become key to imagining a different future. Suggestive is Michael Kimmel's (1996, p. 333) sketch of an "American manhood for the future," a manhood not based on obsessive self-control, compensatory control, and defensive exclusion of others. In this context, then, to queer straight male teachers means to accept that the "crisis" of "manhood" is structural not circumstantial, that no man is "straight" (or "white" for that matter; see DiPiero, 2002), and join with our (especially lesbian) sisters in rejecting the ideological indoctrination of everyone's children.

A democratization of the white male "straight self" means, then, reclaiming projected gendered and racialized fragments as well as disavowed identifications, including that preoedipal identification with the mother—matrifocality—as Spillers recommends. Through "affirmative action" for those repudiated "minority" elements of interpellated subjectivity we can transgender our punk'd status from victimization to political mobilization and aggression. Straight male teachers, democratize yourself. Come out of the political closet and, with your female and queer colleagues, TALK BACK. For the children's sake, ACT UP.[9]

Notes

1. For a succinct summary of the cult of domesticity associated with the separate spheres ideology, see http://www.library.csi.cuny.edu/dept/history/lavender/386/truewoman.html. Retrieved October 17, 2006. For more detail, see, for example, Haynes, 1998.

2. Among historians the concept of "crisis" is controversial (see Pinar, 2001, pp. 321–332).

3. Genealogically, "race" is, I argue, in the "white mind," derived from gender (see Pinar, 2006a).

4. The obvious fact is that teachers provide educational opportunities; students and their parents are responsible for taking advantage of them.

5. The appearance of the figure of the "homosexual"—among other historical developments (see above)—also contributed to straight men's sense of being besieged.

6. "Down-low" or "DL" is an African American slang phrase used in the United States for "secret information," as in "Keep it on the down-low" (meaning "Do not make it known"). It can now be used to refer to secret sexual activity. Among some sectors of African American male subculture (called "men on the DL" or "down-low"), same-sex sexual behavior is sometimes viewed as solely for physical pleasure. Men on the "down-low" may engage in regular, secret sex acts with other men while continuing sexual and romantic relationships with women. Some have argued that being openly gay may lead to considerable stigma in the African American community, thus leading men to engage in male-to-male sex in secret while publicly maintaining heterosexual relationships. These men often shun the more commonly known label "gay" as something that refers only to stereotypically flamboyant and effeminate European American men. Many African American men have no feeling of connection or commonality with these European Americans, and find that they have no benefit from the sacrifice required to show loyalty to a minority despised by the larger community that they live in and rely on.

    Another possible explanation for "being on the down-low" concerns lost social status in traditionally masculine-oriented or patriarchal cultures. Homosexual men may not necessarily have a moral problem in such a culture, but often lose social rank if they accept a "passive" sexual role. They are viewed as being "less than a man." Further, men in such cultures who take an "active" sexual role with other men (sometimes openly) often believe that their actions are not homosexual. Finally, a childless man can lose status in any culture that places high value on children, especially if reasonable people consider the man likely to remain childless. The rejection of the label "gay" by men on the "down-low" is thus seen as a combined rejection of the perceived effeminacy of the general gay community, and an effort to preserve a masculine image. Retrieved on October 3, 2006, from http://en.wikipedia.org/wiki/Down-low.

7. Black gay activist Ron Simmons (1991, p. 213) was among those unpersuaded by the Hares' gendered racial analysis: "Nathan and Julian Hare's homophobic raving does not negate the fact that there may be racist genocidal plots against the black community, or that black men are systematically destroyed. Our homosexuality, however, is not part of such plots and our love is not genocidal. It is their divisive homophobic and heterosexist reactions to our natural sexual expression that play into the plot of divide and conquer."

8. Accountability is, I insist, the "face of fascism in America today" (Pinar, 2004, p. 163).

9. Because U.S. schoolteachers are racialized and gendered as female (which for men is to be positioned as not straight, as queer), I employ the phrase "talking back" —associated with black women's courageous resistance to white male slave-owners' threats to them and to their children (see Pinar, 2004, p. 46) —to specify the order of communicative action required to "enter the arena" and contest punk'd teachers' "gracious submission." The second phrase—"ACT UP"—is the acronym for AIDS Coalition to Unleash Power. Schoolteachers face neither enslavement nor death, of course, but the phrases might inspire us to accept our racialized and gendered (and, specifically, queered) status in the American popular imagination, to reverse the discourse (see Pinar, 2006b, p. 162). As in prison (see Pinar, 2001, p. 1059), punks, too, can fight back.

Works Cited

Bederman, G. (1995a). *Manliness and civilization: A cultural history of gender and race in the United States, 1880-1917.* Chicago: University of Chicago Press.

Bederman, G. (1995b). "Civilization," the decline of middle-class manliness, and Ida B. Wells's Antilynching campaign (1892-94). In D. C. Hine, W. King, & L. Reed (Eds.), *We specialize in the wholly impossible: A reader in black women's history* (pp. 407–432). Brooklyn, NY: Carlson.

Berliner, D. C. & Biddle, B. J. (1996). *The manufactured crisis: Myths, fraud, and the assault on America's public schools.* Cambridge, MA: Perseus.

Bérubé, A. (1990). *Coming out under fire: The history of gay men and women in World War Two.* New York: Free Press.

Blount, M., & Cunningham, G. P. (Eds.). (1996). *Representing black man.* New York: Routledge.

Chauncey, G. (1994). *Gay New York: Gender, urban culture, and the making of the gay male world 1890-1940.* New York: Basic Books.

Chideya, F. (1993, August 30). Endangered family. *Newsweek,* 16–27.

Chodorow, N. J. (1978). *The reproduction of mothering.* Berkeley: University of California Press.

Collins, J. (1926). *The doctor looks at love and life.* New York: Doran.

Commager, H. S. (1950). *The American mind.* New Haven: Yale University Press.

Cremin, L. A. (1961). *The transformation of the school: Progressivism in American education, 1876-1957.* New York: Alfred A. Knopf.

Crocco, M. S., Munro, P., & Weiler, K. (Eds.). (1999). *Pedagogies of resistance: Women educator activists, 1880-1960.* New York: Teachers College Press.

DiPiero, T. (2002). *White men aren't.* Durham, NC: Duke University Press.

Dionne Jr., E. J. (1996). *They only look dead: Why progressives will dominate the next political era.* New York: Simon and Schuster.

Doll, M. A., Wear, D., & Whitaker, M. L. (2006). *Triple takes on curricular worlds.* Albany: State University of New York Press.

Faust, D. G. (1996). *Mothers of invention. Women of the slaveholding south in the American civil war.* Chapel Hill: University of North Carolina Press.

Filene, P. G. (1998). *Him/her/self*. [3rd edition; 1st edition published in 1974 by Harcourt, Brace, Jovanovich.] Baltimore, MD: Johns Hopkins University Press.

Gates Jr., H. L. (1996). *Colored people: A memoir*. New York: Alfred A. Knopf.

Gilmore, L. (1994). *Autobiographics: A feminist theory of women's self-representation*. Ithaca, NY: Cornell University Press.

Grumet, M. R. (1988). *Bitter milk: Women and teaching*. Amherst: University of Massachusetts Press.

Hare, N., & Hare, J. (1984). *The endangered black family: Coping with the unisexualization and coming extinction of the black race*. San Francisco: Black Think Tank.

Haynes, C. A. (1998). *Divine destiny: Gender and race in nineteenth-century Protestantism*. Jackson: University Press of Mississippi.

Hernnstein, R. J., & Murray, C. (1994). *The bell curve: Intelligence and class structure in American life*. New York: The Free Press.

Hofstadter, R. (1962). *Anti-intellectualism in American life*. New York: Vinatge.

Kimmel, M. S. (1996). *Manhood in America: A cultural history*. New York: Free Press.

Kincheloe, J. L., Steinberg, S. R., & Gresson III, A. D. (Eds.). (1996). *Measured lies*. New York: St. Martin's Press.

May, E. T. (1988). *Homeward bound: American families in the Cold War era*. New York: Basic Books.

Moynihan, D. P. (1965). *The Negro family: The case study for national action*. Office of Policy, Planning and Research, Department of Labor. Washington, DC: Government Printing Office.

Pfeil, F. (1995). *White guys*. London: Verso.

Pinar, W. F. (2001). *The gender of racial politics and violence in America: Lynching, prison rape, and the crisis of masculinity*. New York: Peter Lang.

Pinar, W. F. (2004). *What is curriculum theory?* Mahwah, NJ: Lawrence Erlbaum.

Pinar, W. F. (2006a). *Race, religion and a curriculum of reparation*. New York: Palgrave Macmillan.

Pinar, W. F. (2006b). *The synoptic text today and other essays: Curriculum development after the reconceptualization*. New York: Peter Lang.

Pinar, W. F. (2006c). Independence. In J. Milam, S. Springgay, K. Sloan, and B. S. Carpenter (Eds.), *Curriculum for a progressive, provocative, poetic and public pedagogy* (pp. xi–xxiii). Troy, NY: Educator's International Press.

Pinar, W. F., Reynolds, W. M., Slattery, P., & Taubman, P. M. (1995). *Understanding curriculum: An introduction to historical and contemporary curriculum discourses.* New York: Peter Lang.

Pronger, B. (1990). *The arena of masculinity: Sports, homosexuality, and the meaning of sex.* New York: St. Martin's Press.

Sears, J. T. (2006). *Behind the mask of the Mattachine: The Hal Call chronicles and the early movement for homosexual emancipation.* San Francisco: Harrington Park Press.

Silverman, K. (1992). *Male subjectivity at the margins.* New York & London: Routledge.

Simmons, R. (1991). Some thoughts on the challenges facing black gay intellectuals. In Essex Hemphill (Ed.), *Brother to brother: Collected writings by black gay men* (pp. 211–228). (Conceived by Joseph Beam. Project managed by Dorothy Beam.) Los Angeles: Alyson Books.

Simpson, M. (1994). *Male impersonators: Men performing masculinity.* (Foreword by Alan Sinfield.) New York: Routledge.

Spillers, H. J. (1987). Mama's baby, papa's maybe: An American grammar book. *Diacritics*, 17 (2), 65–81.

Spock, B. (1946). *Common sense book of baby and child care.* New York: Pocket Books.

Stoler, A. L. (1995). *Race and the education of desire: Foucault's history of sexuality and the colonial order of things.* Durham, NC: Duke University Press.

Tyack, D., & Hansot, E. (1990). *Learning together: A history of coeducation in American schools.* New Haven, CT: Yale University Press.

Watson, J. B. (1928). *Psychological care of the infant and child.* New York: Norton.

Weiss, J. (1998). Making room for fathers: Men, women, and parenting in the United States, 1945-1980. In Laura McCall & Donald Yacovone (Eds.), *A shared experience: Men, women, and the history of gender* (pp. 349–367). New York: New York University Press.

Williamson, J. (1984). *The crucible of race: Black-white relations in the American South since emancipation.* New York: Oxford University Press.

Wood, C. (1924). *Manhood: The facts of life presented to men.* Girard, KS: Haldeman-Julien.

Yacovone, D. (1998). Surpassing the love of women: Victorian manhood and the language of fraternal love. In Laura McCall & Donald Yacovone (Eds.), *A shared experience: Men, women, and the history of gender* (pp. 195–221). New York: New York University Press.

Young-Bruehl, E. (1996). *The anatomy of prejudices.* Cambridge, MA: Harvard University Press.

Zimmerman, J. (2002). *Whose America? Culture wars in the public schools.* Cambridge, MA: Harvard University Press.

CHAPTER SEVEN
Intermittently Queer

Cris Mayo

When I was a waitress I had very, very short hair. I drove a pickup truck. I wore boots to work. I did all that was humanly possible to assert queerness. Sitting down to fold napkins on one of my first days at a new restaurant, Mary, another waitress, asked if I had a boyfriend. I told her that I was a lesbian and had a girlfriend. She seemed momentarily jolted but recovered nicely. The next day—and many days thereafter—we'd be sitting there quietly folding napkins and Mary would ask if I had a boyfriend. While I have never come out to one person as often as I came out to Mary, the intermittency of queerness remains both a constant and a puzzle. How is it that queerness is simultaneously disruptive and forgettable? Why do some moments of queer expression shatter norms at the same time they easily convert back into the norm?

One of the central tenets of queer theory is that all sexualities, indeed all attempts at normativity, are bound to fail because achieving normal is an impossible task. But having pointed out the queerness at the heart and edges of heterosexuality, what then? Indeed having pointed out the queerness of queerness, how do we reckon with the rather intermittent way that queerness operates? Even the queerest of us sometimes inadvertently or intentionally pass. Even the most out person experiences situations which, despite her best spoken or sartorial intentions, are mistaken for normal. Or maybe there are just lurking moments of normalcy in all queers. While theoretically one may assert that there is queerness in normalcy, not all the "normal" people get the same privileges from normalcy. Even normative categories like heterosexuality only pay major dividends to heterosexuals who also belong to racially, ethnically, and class-related dominant groups and certainly gender complicates heterosexual privilege. Cohen's (2005) critique of queer theory and activism argues that both tend to, even as they gesture at the ubiquity of queerness, separate out queers and straights without adequately attending to the complexities that race, ethnicity, class, and gender bring to that separation.

In this paper, I will examine the time and intermittent character of queerness and will show that even the straightest have some queerness, the queerest of us have some normalcy, and sometimes these differences draw young women into queer associations that even they find surprising. Somehow, as I will show through examples of female same-gender attraction on campus, in preservice teacher classrooms, and in teacher education practicum settings, queerness sparks alliance and interest across other differences—or highlights differences through attraction. While I am largely interested in these queer associations, there are still distinctions to be made among the queers in these relationships, and, following the series of examples, it will be clear that differences still do make a difference. I will argue that affect gives us a way to look at the urgencies that bridge intermittent queerness into futurity, however contingent that futurity is. A distinction between shame and anger gives us one way to distinguish among queers. Where anger tries to move identity possibilities and critique into the future, shame largely directs its energy back into consideration of the present with its aim a continuation of self-fascination.

We do know though that because queerness is a hard position to occupy, there are fairly good reasons for people to decide not to be out and as I begin to make some distinctions among queer heterosexuals and queer queers, I do not think this is a simple matter. As Warner (1999) argues, queer people may not share a lot of things, but they do share the understanding that they are supposed to be ashamed of their desires, activities, and identities. This shame emanates from individual experience of social pressures, but also winds up constituting central ethical relations in queer communities. Because queers understand our desires as shameful, he argues, queer politics demands that we move beyond the shame placed on us by dominant culture and to recognize and work through the shaming effects of sexual desire. But queers also understand that that is easier for some than it is for others and that differences may have to do with inclination or weightier issues like race, class, and gender.

In addition, by distinguishing among kinds of intermittent queerness, I do not mean to suggest that I am disrespecting the variety of queernesses, though that disrespect in itself might be a queer act. Eribon (2005) argues that the experience of insult has been central to the constitution of lesbian and gay subjectivity; subjectivity is as much constituted through homophobic discourse as it is in response to it. Part of the experience of insult leads to queer people leaving for more "hospitable" spaces like cities, part of the experience leads to "dissimulation." In other words, queers understand the pressures of homophobia, rely on associations with one another for protection and support, but also learn to be angry at, to hide, and to disparage other queers. What draws queers and queer associations together is the understanding that connections are ambivalent and alliances to one another are structured by intermittency, gaps, and possibilities. Queer ethicality—to take the central concept from Anzaldúa's (1990) mestiza consciousness—is deeply involved in working through and living with ambiguity.

Much of the interaction between queers that I will be discussing has flirtatious play as a central element of their relation. Thorne (1993) notes that "'Play' is a fragile definition; participants have to continually signal the boundary that distinguishes play from no-play, and play and humor easily slide in and out of other, more 'serious' meanings. This ambiguity creates a tension, since one is never sure in what direction it will swing" (p. 79). As I attempt to make some sort of argument out of this ambiguous relationship between queer queers and straight queers, I will also be sorting out shifts in queer affect, largely the vacillation between shame and anger that seem to define the ambiguous and playful relationships between straight queers and queer queers that I will examine. Sometimes, of course, ambiguity is charming and intriguing. At other times, one's inability to read social interactions with any certainty is frustrating. As Harper (2005) puts it, specifically in the context of discussing black queerness, "minority existence itself induces speculative rumination, because it continually renders even the most routine instances of social activity and personal interaction as possible cases of invidious social distinction or discriminatory treatment" (p. 108).

Queers of all sorts generally share an experience of needing to read social interactions carefully and critically, looking for dangers and attractions, remaining open to communications not quite made clear, subjectivities not yet or never fully determined. Whether our attachment to queerness is in the realm of play or seriousness, fantasy and privacy, public identity and politics, or some combination, all queers who learn to read carefully for queerness in others know that they must engage the possibility that things are not what they seem, that situations and identities may turn very quickly from one thing to another, or that identities and relations may remain in the space of uncertainty and ambiguity. Queers engage in readings of subjectivity and reading the subjectivity of others in ways that attend to the plays of meaning, power, and strategy, noting that play of meanings doesn't stop, but moments of negotiation may freeze-play. Play is a very serious and considered activity, but has as its virtue a concept of edging away from intentionality determining the meaning of the activity once and for all. Play's fragility reminds us that there are contextual and varied meanings to activities, as well as openings for readings and misreadings of any intentional strategy. And for play to stay in play, it has to have a future, a point I will return to near the end.

Just the Usual Level of Affection Between Girls

This paper will focus almost entirely on women. On the one hand, women's experience of sexuality is sometimes described as more flexible than men's. Girls and women experience shifts in their gender of object choice and subjectivity all through their sex lives and this points to the shortcoming of concepts like stable sexual identity or orientation. Even while most women maintain that they are heterosexual, many have engaged in fantasies, attractions, and sexual activities involving other women. So to a large extent, sexuality is queerer in practice than in concept. But because women also live in a society where the possibility of their gender and sexual flexibility is denigrated and where their ability to relate closely to other women is considered unimportant to the usual operation of dominant heterosexuality, even the fact of that flexibility may be considered part of the operation of normative heterosexuality. Queering heterosexuality is at once completely commonplace and very difficult, since every variation is easily converted back into something that supports the norm.

Though the following stories are all about preservice teachers, most of my recent research has been in high schools and that experience has helped me to see the intermittency of queerness. At the first Gay Straight Alliance dance I observed, I did not see any girls expressing more than the usual physical affection for one another, which gets me further into a category problem. As anyone who has been to high school dances or undergrad bars in the past decade can attest, there is a fair amount of girl-on-girl public display of affection and attraction in heterosexual public space. A few years ago when discussing Rich's (1993) classic essay, one of the undergraduate women in my class suggested that if I wanted an update on the lesbian continuum I should go stand in the line for the women's bathroom at one of the popular campus bars. She said that part of the reason girls take so long is that they are constantly making out on line. This stood in marked contrast to the other scenes I had observed where girls were clearly flirting and engaging in physical affection for the amusement of young men, or at least that is what it looked like to me, based perhaps on a rather circular line of thought. I imagined that since I was in what I took to be a heterosexual space, whatever queerness I observed was there to bolster heterosexuality. But my student was making a different argument that stressed that young women were finding queer spaces in heterosexual spaces in which to express their attraction for one another and that this was not simple performance for the boys—and it turned out through later conversation that even that simple act of performing for boys was not so simple.

When I raised this distinction between queerness in queer spaces and queerness in straight spaces and mentioned the distinction between kissing another girl in a queer space like a gay bar compared with kissing another girl in highly public heterosexualized space to preservice teachers in a multicultural education course, a cluster of young women approached me after class to dispute my distinction. They countered with the argument that many of the women involved in public displays of affection with other women in heterosexual bars were in fact involved with those women but have found a new place to express that sexuality. They also explained it is possible that they will be dating the young men for whom they are "performing" in addition to dating one another. They suggested that new forms of queer relationships were comfortable in what used to be solely heterosexual spaces.

But there still remained a problem because while these young women felt comfortable being queer in heterosexual spaces, they had yet to see men engaged in same-sex public affection. So even if these were new kinds of queer relationships, they were gendered and the girls all understood that to a large extent they were welcome in those spaces because they were titillating to the young men present. In this and other ways, queer relationships were reconverted back into centralizing male heterosexuality and continuing to keep gay men out of those heterosexual spaces. One of the girls said that the problem with complex relationships in which female same-gender kissing and caressing was acceptable, and even part of heterosexual relationships, was that one girl often felt more for the other girl than she did for the boy, but that the assumption in these trios was that the boy was the first priority. Another young woman said a friend of hers had just gone through that experience and, while the friend did not identify as a lesbian, she had not expected that her attentions were being circuited through the woman to the man. She wanted her relationship with the other woman to be seen as valid on its own. In other words, in this case, queered heterosexuality was not particularly queer at all: it recentered male dominance through a performance of lesbian attraction and, even as it incited that performance, it devalued it. Let me just restate that these were preservice elementary education students and despite my experience with that population as being fairly conservative, these particular girls, though they continued to identify publicly in class as heterosexual, were very tuned into a whole range of queer possibilities, however fraught and intermittent those may have been.

Racialized Queer Attraction

Another queer relationship between self-defined white straight young women in preservice elementary education and Alex, a young Puerto Rican woman at a Latino community center, more closely ties queer attraction to the project of antiracist education. In this case, attraction among the women was structured around mentoring relationships, as Alex mentored the preservice teachers at the community center and they, in turn, mentored her at the university. Though the situation was by no means equal, it was reciprocal, and while there were moments of seriousness, playful attraction also defined much of their interaction. In this example, there are multiple moments where not only are girls playing with identities and attractions, they were also playing each other. That is, they were all overreaching the possibilities that their attractions afforded one another and, in many ways, using queer attraction as the cement to relationships that were on racially troubled ground. Deception and overreaching of the possibilities of the moment are also part of play and intermittency of queerness. Alex's reception by the elementary education students and her experiences at school also underscore Crenshaw's (1995) observation that practices of reading identities as "'woman' or 'person of color' as an either/or proposition...relegate the identity of women of color to a location that resists telling" (p. 357).

Alex's ability to cross gender lines further complicates the difficulty of interpreting the variety of responses she generates, many of which are generated by a collision of race, class, and sexuality and often the "telling" of that complexity misses at least part of what's going on. Doubtless my own recounting is incomplete as well. I use this example also because the white female students who became close to Alex did so through forms of interaction that appear to be only objectifying. But I hope to show that because their attraction was to another woman—even if they initially misrecognized her as a man—the situation complicated their own ideas about sexuality, gender, and race/ethnicity. Further, while Alex knew that the girls' attraction was centered around her racial/ethnic identity, she was also drawn to the possibilities for new interactions and places that they were able to provide, mainly through visits to the university and ways to get out of her house that her parents approved of. So, in many ways, they were all playing one another and playing with their mutual attractions.

I met Alex in the context of working with elementary education students in a practicum for a multicultural education class that met at a Latin American Community Center. This was a space of alliance for Latinas/os in the area, and had been in operation since its start during black community protests during the 1960s that occasioned the longest National Guard occupation of a U.S. city. As the youth coordinator explained, she and other Puerto Rican activists were organizing with black activists who suggested that Puerto Ricans could build their own community space. While there were relatively few Latina/os in the city at the time, the idea had great appeal and the community center became a crucial resource for current and new residents of the city. A space of advocacy, the community center brings together the variety of ethnic, racial, and national groups who work together to improve the educational, economic, health, and political lives of community members. Because the community center is in a neighborhood that was not conducive to safe play for children and young people, the community center runs a substantial after-school program, combining tutoring with arts, dance, sports, and other recreational activities.

The first time I saw Alex, she was being misinterpreted as male by my entire class, whose task at the community center was to work against the segregation under which most of them had lived their lives and begin to understand more fully the lives of Latina/o children, youth, and families, in the hopes that they would bring memories of these experiences with them into public school teaching. Because the children and youth at the center were engaged in activities in a community that supported them, their strengths very clearly shone through and often stood in marked contrast to the evaluations they received at school. In other words, for the elementary education students, as well as for the people at the community center, the after-school program was an association across differences, not only within the community, but also between the almost entirely white elementary education students and the community of color that would be among the communities they would eventually serve. It was clear to my students that Alex was considered to be a youth leader. She had been introduced to them by the youth coordinator who was one of the founding members of the community center and whose confidence in and affection for Alex were very clear.

When Alex, dressed in a baggy 76er's shirt and with a very close buzz cut, was done describing how she worked with university students to introduce them to kids and youth, most of my students were chatting excitedly. As one asked, "who *was* that boy?," Web chats that day centered on how much they all "really enjoyed listening to that boy." Alex's presence and their response was an occasion for them to make gestures of association and perhaps the easiest association they could imagine making with a young Puerto Rican boy was attraction. Part of the excitement the students expressed at meeting Alex was overlaid with their desires to find connections with people of color, to represent their willingness and ability as white people to be attracted to people of color, and to be attracted to the idea of helping kids of color. As one student wrote, "When that sixteen year old boy was talking to us about his experiences with the students from the University…I really feel that we are able to make a difference in the lives of the children at the LACC, as they will make a difference in ours."

As Eugene Matusov and his colleagues (2002) have pointed out, this kind of initial excitement and sense of one's ability to make a difference in these kids' lives is part of a process of objectification. They use their positions as members of the racially dominant group to label, judge, and act with the kids without reference to how the kids fit into the kids' community beliefs and practices. In short, the process of objectification keeps dominant members out of a relationship with kids with whom they are working and keeps them at a remove. In the case of their attractions to Alex, though, the young women in our classes were also edging away from their positions as unproblematically dominant and beginning to extend themselves into a relationship that was clearly structured by mutual attraction. Partially they were all playing with the idea of changing their patterns of racial/ethnic association, but doing so in a personal language rather than racial language, often not fully self-consciously articulated. Web discussions from previous years also show the same level of excitement at meeting Alex, although this time at least the students recognized her gender, likely because she hadn't cut her hair that year.

According to the Web chats, which sound to my jaded ears like dialogue out of lesbian pulp novels, students found her "exciting," "a little dangerous," and as one put it "I think we all know who she is—she always seems to make her presence known. I was a little intimidated by her at first because she does have such a strong personality, but I slowly started talking to her more and more." Another said, "She was…it seemed like she was almost rough" and then their relationship "just kind of…clicked" (M. Smith, anonymous interview, Spring 2002). Another young woman explained that initially, "I thought she was more talk than whatever she did. Like…she appears rough and stuff but…once I started talking to her, she's really not like that at all. She definitely puts on a front" (M. Smith, anonymous interview, Spring 2002). This group of girls brought Alex to campus (during one of her suspensions from school), drove into the city to take her out for meals, and generally began to develop friendships with her. When Alex, who had been dating women her own age for some time, came out to them, they were literally speechless, at least as my colleagues recorded their reactions in interviews. They also were disbelieving of most of the stories she told about why she had been suspended from school as they couldn't imagine a girl her age drinking. They flat out refused to believe her stories about the ease with which one could purchase drugs in her neighborhood. And yet, of course, they were attracted to her, playing with their own attempts at association, and thinking that she was playing them. Deception and attraction, though, structured their increasingly close relationship, the tension between the two reminding them all of their interest in one another but also the difficulty of ethnic, class, and age distance between them. As one of the preservice students put it, she and Alex talked together, understanding the differences in their experiences they would still tell each other stories from their lives. She explained, "Like knowing we would disappoint each other, we would still tell each other. It was weird" (M. Smith, anonymous interview, Spring 2002).

But as much as attraction was part of their transition away from ignorance and segregation that had defined much of their lives, the young white women also used attraction as a form of "playing" relationship, prior to a time when their relationship with Alex and other youth of color would be defined by partial knowledge, as opposed to imaginative fantasy. My colleague and I would watch each semester as preservice students moved from feeling distant from people of color to flirtation with the older youth of color and into feeling, occasionally, sexually harassed. While this was not an ideal stage of relationship, we felt that at least the emptier idealizations and fantasies of racial concord without knowledge were best passed over. Attraction and missionary zeal were often coupled in the ways our white students initially regarded youth of color, and Alex's white women friends were no exception to these dynamics. When the classes discussed sexual harassment, they often came to the conclusion that that was the most easily accessible language of anger that young men of color had in relation to older white women, and they began to understand that their own idealizations of their cross-race relationships had been structured by attraction in order to cover up the discomfort they initially felt in the company of youth of color. When in doubt, flirt.

Even in the midst of all of these complications, the attraction between Alex and the white university women was not one-sided. Alex was also attracted to the white university girls and looked forward to meeting a new group of students. She kept in touch with young women from the previous year and continued going out for meals with them and visiting them on campus. When a colleague asked her what she most liked about working with the students, she said she looked forward to meeting new girls. She also was very keen on seeing what university life was like and had started to think seriously about the possibility of eventually going to the university, which she previously thought was not possible for someone from her neighborhood. Between her relationship with university students and the fact that one of the older girls from the community center had begun going to the university, the distance between the community and university seemed to decrease. But it is also clear that however classic the statements of attraction and interest from the preservice teachers sound, the fact that they maintained heterosexual identities and Alex was younger, Puerto Rican, out, experienced harassment at school, and lost the support of her family, meant that their queer association was a space of differences.

It may be one of the problems of queer association across difference is different levels of urgency about identity. Alex was from a lower income, ethnic minority family in a lower income neighborhood, with all the attendant difficulties of maintaining a safe place to live and move around. She[1] worried about being kicked out of her house and her experiences were quite different from those white, middle-class preservice students who were willing to pass as straight but were still intrigued by queerness in a way that did not necessitate making difficult tradeoffs (at least not right away). There was clearly a different urgency to issues. In addition, while racial/ethnic difference played a part in why the white girls were attracted to Alex (aside from her charisma), that distance also allowed them to be attracted to someone with whom it was unlikely age and social distance would be bridged. The relationship, while it had seriousness and care, was limited.

But there's also this sense of looming tragedy in the women who are drawn to queerness but not willing to risk normalcy, so I don't want to oversimplify. This is also a conversation I often have with students: They say it's hard being normal, holding inside the shame that marks their felt inability to cross the line between thinking about the possibilities of queerness and living queerness. I, being more of an angry queer, argue back that it is very difficult to be queer; hard for kids on the other side of normalcy to negotiate family, schools, communities, and relationships; and then we get into a fairly nonproductive tussle over who's more oppressed. Is it the oppressed themselves or oppressors who'd really rather in their heart of hearts be living with and among the oppressed? I have repeatedly seen this dynamic in gay straight alliances. Straight allies wind up strongly disliking their queer comrades because the queers are too angry, too critical, and set too high a standard for political engagement. Straight queer–identified students also feel that queer anger creates an impossible standard for queerness that doesn't account for the complexity of straight queers, but sometimes their defensiveness is also tinged with shame. It sounds to me that they often begin to dislike the queers not just because queer youth are perpetually too angry, but because the straight queers start to be aggressively ashamed of the excessiveness of queer queerness. They also feel the limitations as well as the pressures of queer queerness and assert their own complexities over the simpler, angrier version of queerness they see in queers. They cement their place in the group by showing that they are more thoughtful and self-critical than those students who are simply queer.

Between Anger and Shame

In these two closing sections, I will argue that in addition to other distinctions one might make between kinds of queers, affect and time are crucial elements of queer differences. In the example of a queer association falling apart in a high school gay straight alliance, shame and anger mark the lines of difference. While queers may all share the common experience of being expected to be ashamed, I do not agree that we all share shame in the same way. The differences in shame are hard to know definitively and I will admit to being cautious at overgeneralizing how people experience shame. But it seems from what I have observed from the shame straight queers experience is that they use their affect to strategically recenter their own complexity over that of queer queers. In the high school group, straight queers were more interested in their own complexity than they were in thinking through the barriers that were angering their queer queer associates. Shame, in other words, makes them more interested in themselves than in queerness and more distant from the queers they view as only excessive in their rage.

In contrast to what I see as a problematic form of shame, Probyn (2005) argues that there are forms of shame that are politically useful. Because shame makes interest urgent at the level of one's own affective disapproval of oneself, as a political affect it may have more problems attending it than other forms of affect that also mark the potential for continuing connections with others. What I want to underscore is how shame allows the one shamed to become more fascinated with themselves than involved in a critique of systems that generate shame. I think this tendency toward self-fascination is one problem with using shame as a political strategy and perhaps this movement away from political critique and toward self-fascination is one distinction among kinds of queers (and this does not fall along lines of queer and straight).

So while I fully agree with Probyn that we do need to be more critical and careful in of the ways we try to shame others in order to stop conversations, I would add to be cautious about how shame is deployed by those feeling it. Quite a lot of recent queer writing raises shame as constitutive of queer identity, and at least some queer writing is quite resistant to that idea. What would account for the difference or how come some queers have no shame? It isn't because the shameless are not connected to social relations or concerned with understanding political identity. They have instead, to use Michael Warner's phrase, "gotten over themselves" without having to deal with shame because shame was not what formed them in the first place. One can, in other words, recognize the normative force of heterosexuality without being particularly compelled into an affective response that entails shame. One can simply get angry.

When I talk to queer youth they seem more to struggle against constraints than take those constraints as seriously defining them as abject. I recently went to a group that had just begun a project in school that would make them more visible. One of their faculty advisors very kindly offered adult support should they encounter anyone attempting to make them feel badly. The students quickly responded that their activity was hardly at the root of that problem: already curricula insulted them on a daily basis, classmates disrespected gay marriage, and teachers opened discussions as if homophobia were an issue with pros and cons that students might debate. The recitation of their grievances was not accompanied by a feeling of shame but rather very clear anger and determination to change the climate of the school. Oddly enough, the faculty advisor, expecting to be called upon to comfort shamed students, could not muster a word of support since the problem was not one that could be dealt with by helping students through their shame; rather, it was a systemic problem that students were already addressing through their critique, anger, and action.

I think that recent queer writing is interested in shame, not so much in order to mount a political critique of the conditions that harm queers, but rather to maintain their own connection to their special status as transgressive. Transgression has become a tiring political strategy, but it did have the promise of centralizing anger and critique to jolt normative structures. Shame, rather than providing that outward jolt, seems to draw the transgressive project thoroughly back into self-regard, even if it is pitched as a moment of community spirit or communal shame. I am, of course, not denying that shame is an important emotion or that it would be wrong to spend a fair amount of time thinking about how political projects either invite disabling, alienating shame or where they might encourage a kind of shame that holds out promise for reconciliation. An understanding of these dynamics are necessary given the wide range of possibilities for shame. While I do want to point out that shame isn't always where one might expect to find it because people are often quite resistant to attempts to shame them, nonetheless I do not deny that shame needs to be understood in more detail.

Shame is also a strategy that can be used to stop interactions, to buy time, and to redirect the force of criticism from a goal that might involve introspection, change, and reconciliation. Stalling and freezing are also, of course, marks of earnest shame, so the manipulations of false shame appear quite similar. But worse than the stalling quality of strategic, false shame, acting as if one is ashamed can be a strategy of reversal that redirects the energy of the shamer—or more to the point, the one who is angry—into trying to comfort the shamed so that both can move on. What they move on to is essentially the same context they started in: the one shamed receives all the attention and the shamer is back to doing supportive emotional work for the one who ought to be changing. In this situation, the affect of shame is a dodge-around responsibility and action—probably most recognizable to all of us who spend any time in a classroom as white guilt.

One of the most intriguing points of Probyn's (2005) discussion is her closing point that "shame can pose the challenge to *learn*, and not to *know*" (p. 106). The larger problem may not be which affect to stimulate but how to stimulate interest that will move beyond present moments where queer associations and other associations structured by difference stall without losing sight of the fact that the obstacle is not just the problem of those who are aggrieved but also enjoying privileges. If I were to choose a favorite affective strategy, it would be anger because it shows the effects of active ignorance and willed privilege. Anger is less interested in emotional response than in political change. I'm not entirely crazy about the passive-aggressive aspects of the Day of Silence that so many queer and ally kids organize at public schools and universities, but it is one example of how anger starts conversations, especially when those who are angry are quiet. In this daylong demonstration, kids hand out cards explaining that they are always silenced on this particular day they are silencing themselves so that other people will notice and learn. Because of the silence, no one gets caught up in false shame or strategic nonreaction; the burden of learning is shifted on to those who didn't know and they are invited to become part of the process of political change. Their shame is completely beside the point.

All of which is to say, the more specific we can get about what is queerness installed in concepts that cannot publicly show themselves and what is queerness that does some more overt form of disruption, the better off our theories will be. Of course we cannot guarantee that a particular act or utterance will work in all situations, nor can we rely on intentionality to sort this out. But these are still conversations we need to go back and forth on. I don't think it's easy to make distinctions and be certain who was queer and who wasn't in any of the situations I've described, but I do at least think that some of the criticisms made of the lesbian continuum are still helpful—by seeing these differences in sexuality as a continuum "the sense of range and gradation...[disappears]" (Thompson, Stansell, & Snitow, as cited in Rich, 1993, p. 247).

Introducing the element of time may help to tease apart a necessary distinction among the players. Part of the problem of associations is not just a problem of trust—will these people really be supportive? are they just playing at being gay?, but also the problem of shared pasts and shared futures, beyond the partial sharing of present situations. I am not arguing that all lesbian, gay, bisexual, transgender (LGBT) people who are already self-identified share the same past and the same future. I do want to suggest that thinking about identity, even thinking about shifts in identity, is a process that takes place over time and that is something that at least some LGBT people share and recognize in one another. I at least have a suspicion that one problem with ideas about play in identity is that it constricts the time of identity to only the present. More than a few queers have expressed their irritation at people who appear to only be playing intermittently at nonnormative identity and who appear to have no commitment to working toward a future where they could actually live nonnormative or minority lives. When sexual identity becomes another fashion, they argue, anyone can try it on and take it off if it becomes inconvenient.

For queers in it for the long run, however shifting their gender and sexual attachments are, queers who seem to be less interested in a commitment to the contingencies of queerness are not part of the practice of queerness. As Bourdieu (1990) puts it, a practice postulates "the continuity of time," however complex the practice itself is. "Urgency, which is rightly seen as one of the essential properties of practice, is the product of playing in the game and the presence in the future that it implies" (Bourdieu, 1990, p. 276). Time and futurity, then, are part of the practice of queerness. Queerness is about flirtation with the possible, angry critique of the obstacles, and however multiple and varied the flirtations, queer urgency demands the action go on.

Note

1.   While she sometimes passed as male, she preferred to use a female pronoun in our conversations and was more comfortable with butch identity than trans.

Works Cited

Anzaldúa, G. (1990). La conciencia de la mestiza: Towards a new consciousness. In G. Anzaldúa (Ed.), *Making face, making soul / haciendo caras: Creative and critical perspectives by feminists of color* (pp. 377–389). San Francisco: Aunt Lute Books.

Bourdieu, P. (1990). *The logic of practice* (R. Nice, Trans.). Stanford: Stanford University Press.

Cohen, C. J. (2005). Punks, bulldaggers, and welfare queens: The radical potential of queer politics? In E. P. Johnson & M. G. Henderson (Eds.), *Black queer studies: A critical anthology* (pp. 21–51). Durham: Duke University Press.

Crenshaw, K. (1995). Mapping the margins: Intersectionality, identity politics, and violence against women of color. In K. Crenshaw, N. Gotanda, G. Peller, & K. Thomas (Eds.), *Critical race theory: The key writings that formed the Movement* (pp. 357–383). New York: New Press.

Eribon, D. (2005). *Insult and the making of the gay self* (M. Lucy, Trans.). Durham, NC: Duke University Press.

Harper, P. B. (2005). The evidence of felt intuition: Minority experience, everyday life, and critical speculative knowledge. In E. P. Johnson & M. G. Henderson (Eds.), *Black queer studies: A critical anthology* (pp. 106–123). Durham, NC: Duke University Press.

Matusov, E., St. Julien, J., & Smith, M. P. (2002). Becoming a culturally sensitive teacher. Paper presented at International Society for Cultural Research and Activity Theory, Amsterdam, Netherlands.

Probyn, E. (2005). *Blush: The faces of shame*. Minneapolis: University of Minnesota Press.

Rich, A. (1993) Compulsory heterosexuality and lesbian existence. In H. Abelove, M. A. Barale, & D. M. Halperin (Eds.), *The lesbian and gay studies reader* (pp. 227–254). New York: Routledge.

Smith, M. (2002). Anonymous interviews.

Thorne, B. (1993). *Gender play: Girls and boys in school*. New Brunswick, NJ: Rutgers University Press.

Warner, M. (1999). *The trouble with normal*. Cambridge, MA: Harvard University Press.

CHAPTER EIGHT

From Teacher Knowledge to Queered Teacher Knowledge Research: Escaping the Epistemic Straight Jacket

John E. Petrovic
Jerry Rosiek

"Teacher knowledge research" is a phrase that refers to a growing movement in the field of teacher education, one that seeks to bridge the gap between educational theory and practice by taking seriously the intellectual dimension of the work of teaching. Contributors to this field reject the idea that teaching can be treated as a set of discreet behaviors whose effectiveness can be measured and which can be prescribed based on those measurements. Instead this emerging field of study focuses on teacher *knowledge*. It frames teachers as thinking professionals who need to be prepared as reflective practitioners, who need to engage in inquiry that informs their teaching practice, and who will occasionally publish original research on their teaching that can inform other teachers' practice.

In a short period of time this movement has produced several very generative programs of research, including research on teachers' practical knowledge (Ball, 1996; Grossman, 1990), craft knowledge (Leinhardt, 1990), personal practical knowledge (Clandinin & Connelly, 1996), and wisdom of practice (Shulman, 1987, 2004). Several subfields such as teacher research (Cochran-Smith & Lytle, 1993, 1999; Noffke, 1992), narrative inquiry (Clandinin & Connelly, 2000), and the scholarship of teaching (Shulman, 2000) have also grown. These programs of research all have one thing in common: they seek to contribute to the development of a naturalistic epistemology of teaching. Instead of building theories about how teachers *should think*, based on the findings of experimental psychology, they examine how teachers *actually do think* and look for valuable insights that arise organically from teaching experience.

Within this common focus there has been considerable debate about how best to accomplish the shared goal of increasing respect for teacher knowledge. These debates have been heated. On one side, claims are made that teachers need to be protected from the imperialism of university researchers who silence their voices and displace teachers' practical concerns with their own more abstract obsessions. Teachers, according to this view, are better positioned than university academics to identify relevant topics for inquiry into the practice of teaching. On another side, accusations are made of naiveté, provincialism, and false consciousness among teachers. Teachers, according to this view, cannot rely on their personal experience and their common sense to guide their inquiries because these have been shaped by taken-for-granted discourses of which teachers are unaware. This concern becomes especially acute when considering the ways teachers address (or fail to address) social justice issues in their practice. Some have claimed that the teacher knowledge research movement is excessively individualistic, and thus lacks the ability to seriously address social justice issues that are structural (Noffke, 1997; Rosiek & Atkinson, 2005).

This essay enters the conversation about teacher knowledge research at its intersection with concerns about the promotion of social justice. Specifically, it asks how teacher knowledge research can address the needs of lesbian, gay, bisexual, transgender, and questioning (LGBTQ) students and how it can examine sexual identity issues in the classroom generally. We take it as a given that a significant portion of schoolchildren will grow up to identify as gay, lesbian, bisexual, or transgender. Others will have parents or other relatives who so identify. Despite a popular culture that encourages students and teachers to "don't ask, don't tell," these identity issues can and do arise in the classroom. Teachers are called upon to respond, and the manner in which they respond affects students. So the question arises: How do we prepare teachers to think constructively about LGBTQ social justice issues?

In what follows, we examine the kind of practical knowledge teachers need in order to respond to the needs of LGBTQ students. Our analysis will show that this knowledge goes beyond knowing something about students. It also requires teachers to have a critical knowledge of themselves—an understanding of their own thoughts, feelings, and values as the product of historical and cultural processes of which they may not be fully aware. This poses a conceptual challenge for teacher knowledge researchers. If the valorization of teachers' experience as a source of foundational insight for teaching practice is too simplistic, then it risks precluding challenges to teachers' homophobic bigotry and heteronormativity. The effort to give teachers some epistemic room of their own in an increasingly bureaucratized profession can become an epistemic "straight jacket" that leaves no room for insisting that the needs of LGBTQ students be discussed.

This essay looks for a framework for thinking about teacher knowledge research that can acknowledge the value of teachers' practical insights, even as the cultural foundations of those insights are problematized. We first review what teachers need to know about LGBTQ youth, how they need to know it, and what this should mean to teacher practice. This review is necessary in order to understand the type and the extent of the work to be done in teacher knowledge research and, ultimately, the goal of such research. After this review, we specify the challenge to teacher knowledge research. Overcoming this challenge requires elaboration of certain conceptual tools, which we find in the work of poststructural social theorists, such as Michel Foucault, Eve Sedgwick, and Judith Butler. A display of these poststructural tools, however, reveals a need for certain others. While it pushes teacher knowledge research toward new vistas, we argue that poststructural theory requires supplementing to provide teacher knowledge researchers with epistemic access to the lived experiences and practices of teachers that are imperative to their work.

Hearing LGBTQ Students: Some Things Teachers Need to Know

Much work has been done to bring attention to the experiences and needs of LGBTQ youth in society and schools. While there have been recent calls to portray the many healthy coping strategies and successes of these students (e.g., successful fights to allow same-sex prom dates, campaigns to include sexual orientation in nondiscrimination clauses, and the formation of on-campus gay-straight alliances), much of the literature in this vein portrays the general, usually negative experiences and school climates that LGBTQ youth endure that create the need for such "fights" and "demands" in the first place.

On a basic level, LGBTQ youth face harm in quite straightforward and overt ways. These students are subjected to verbal, physical, and emotional abuse (Elze, 2003; O'Conor, 1994; Uribe & Harbeck, 1992). In this vein, the 2005 National School Climate Survey completed by the Gay, Lesbian, Straight Educators Network (GLSEN) reports that:

- 89.2% of all youth reported hearing homophobic remarks often or frequently from other students
- Nearly one fifth of all youth reported hearing homophobic remarks from faculty or school staff
- Over one third of lesbian, gay, bisexual (LGB) youth reported at least some experience of physical assault because of their sexual orientation
- Nearly two thirds of LGB youth reported that they felt unsafe because of their sexual orientation

The effects of such abuse are reflected in students' stories of alcoholism, drug use, and poor academic performance. Consider the following not atypical recollections of school days:

> John: "Ninth grade was the worst. I wasn't accepted. I knew I was gay, and I knew everyone else knew because they told me I was a faggot every day. But I was still trying to be straight with the friends that I did have. I stopped doing homework and didn't pay attention to school. I felt like something was exploding inside of me. I started smoking pot too. I was trying to hide from what I really felt." (Bass & Kaufman, 1996, p. 45)

> Michele: " 'More and more I was using alcohol to try to avoid uncomfortable parties and things, where I knew there would be boys.' Michele was aware that she drank a lot, a lot more than her friends and recalls, 'I took the first sips and made sure I had the last.'" (Chandler, 1995)

Other effects of a homophobic school climate are skipping school (GLSEN, 2005) or dropping out entirely (Herr, 1997), and increased suicidal tendencies among LGBTQ youth (Remafedi, 1994; The Center for Population Options, 1992). Fifty-three percent of gay youth served by Los Angeles' Youth Services Department had attempted suicide at least once and forty-seven percent more than once (The Center for Population Options, 1992).

Overt harassment is only one cause of these striking statistics. To this must be added the effect of the malignant neglect of homosexual students' inner needs in a homophobic school culture. Richard Friend (1993) describes this as the difference between systematic exclusion and systematic inclusion. Systematic exclusion is "the process whereby positive role models, messages, and images about gay, lesbian, and bisexual people are publicly silenced in schools" (p. 212). The implicit message here is that heterosexuality is the only acceptable identity. The message becomes particularly insidious when systematic exclusion is paired with the systematic inclusion of homosexuality "only as a pathology, only in regard to sexual behavior and/or framed as dangerous" (p. 215). Additionally, systematic inclusion often holds the message that homosexuality is evil and sinful.

Given these two predominant instructional mindsets, the number of personal narratives depicting school climates that marginalize and do harm to LGBTQ youth is hardly surprising. Further, given the statistics of overt abuse and the silence that tends to surround the entire issue of same-sex orientation (and/or the deadly dialogue a la systematic inclusion), it is not surprising that students report that they create straight identities in order to fit in (Due, 1995; Elze, 1992; Petrovic & Ballard, 2005). As a teen participant in one study commented,

> School was a definite hell hole…Like, you sit in class, right, and all these girls are talking about which boys they like and all that crap. And you make stuff up, like 'oh yeah, he's really cute. Yeah Tom Selleck, wow.' You don't know how many times I wanted to lean over and say, 'hey, what about Julia Roberts? Some fox, huh?' (O'Conor, 1994, p. 9)

Creating façades is a forced "option" for LGBTQ youth. Consider William who tells us that he "wasn't having any harassment problems, but [he] was isolating [him]self from the rest of the students." William continued to explain, "I knew if I came out, there would be consequences, either verbal or physical, and I wasn't willing to do that" (Due, 1995, p. 187). Another student eloquently summarizes the circumstances of LGBTQ youth. When asked what he thought being gay will mean to him, he responded,

> It will mean a lot more secrecy about life. Not being able to show my affection, having to lie to a lot of people, my friends not knowing as much about me as I think they should. Right now I'm worried that it will have a real profound effect, like what kind of friends I'll have and what kind of job I can get. And not to say the least,

> violence. If people would just let me, I would have no problems being gay. I don't know what it does to a person who has to live in that kind of constant fear: Who might know? (Due, 1995, pp. 74–75)

In partial answer to what it means to live in "that kind of constant fear," Al Ferreira, director of a program for LGBTQ youth, observes, "Living with lies destroys the fabric of who we are as people. It imprisons us spiritually—and that's a terrible thing to do to other human beings" (cited in Bass & Kaufman, 1996, p. 68). By being forced to hide a major part of their identity, LGBTQ youth cannot live their lives from the inside out. They cannot engage in the fullness of reciprocal love, caring, and interest because others do not wholly know them (Petrovic, 2000). Those who might assert that sexuality is not a major part of identity need but count in a day the number of times sexuality, especially heterosexuality, is displayed. Count the number of couples passed holding hands, kissing, or flirting. Count the number of family pictures seen on desks in the office place. Count the number of hands with wedding rings. Count the number of second glances at a good pair of legs. Count the number of male comments about how pretty Julia Roberts is and female comments on what a hunk Vigo Mortensen is.

After years of abuse in high school, one student reports on the joy of living from the inside out:

> Now that I'm a junior in college and head of the campus gay group, the best part of my life is a sense of inner peace, a sense of knowing that I'm not lying to myself and that I'm not lying to anyone else anymore. And if someone else has a problem with my being gay, then that's their problem and not mine. (Bass & Kaufman, 1996, p. 24)

Notice here that this student's ability to deal confidently with heterosexism, something he could not do in high school, comes from a community of support. This becomes an important point as we later discuss the importance of discursive communities within which teachers, too, can maintain their commitment to social justice.

In sum, there are two levels at which we can view the experiences of LGBTQ youth. First is the basic level of overt harm, easily recognizable in its forms of physical or verbal violence. Second is the level of discourse, silence being a part of discourse. Of course, these levels are interrelated in much more complicated ways. Certainly, the latter give license to the former and the former is part of the latter. This oversimplification suffices momentarily for our analytical purposes. In the next section, we further divide and fine-tune these levels, looking at calls for action by both educators and LGBTQ youth.

Listening to LGBTQ Students: What Teachers Must (Not) Do

The two levels of LGBTQ experiences outlined above can be more finely tuned upon consideration of what teachers need to know and know how to do. At the basic level of overt abuse, teachers must (1) do no harm and (2) let no harm be done.

The great number of students who report hearing homophobic remarks from teachers necessitates explicit iteration of the first principle. Such occurrences add to the feeling among LGBTQ students that there is nowhere to turn, even, or perhaps especially, to teachers and other school personnel. This feeling is most probably an accurate one. As Sears (1991) found, approximately 80 percent of preservice teachers hold negative views of sexual minority people. Replicating Sears' study more than a decade later, Mudrey-Camino (2002) reports a somewhat lower but equally concerning figure of 70 percent.

The second principle demands that teachers take action to disrupt violence against LGBTQ youth in all its forms. Here we are reminded of a scene from *It's Elementary* (Chasnoff & Cohen, 1996) where a 3rd grader comments, "It's amazing how teachers don't notice all the stuff that's going on." Typically, a distinction can be drawn between not noticing something and turning a blind eye to it. For many teachers that same distinction can be drawn here. However, a poststructural lens, which we develop more fully in a subsequent section, helps to reveal the extent to which not noticing homophobic violence and heterosexism and turning a blind eye to them are part and parcel of the same discursively produced phenomenon.

Given the number of times LGBTQ youth hear homophobic remarks from teachers and/or the number of times these students witness teachers ignoring homophobic remarks coming from students, one place that many teacher educators begin is name-calling. In some circumstances, it will take an act of bravery for a teacher to merely interrupt shouts of "fag," "dyke," or "queer" in the hallways and classrooms. At the very least, stopping name-calling of any type (and other basic, overt forms of violence) seems commonsensical to most teachers.

There are, however, problems with this strategy for teacher educators. First, stopping name-calling typically translates to some generalized notion of "tolerance." Teachers are happy to accept that they must promote tolerance and even respect for all types of difference. But, in taking this tack, they are also quick to combine stopping name-calling with the fear of naming. In other words, while better than nothing, stopping name-calling is quite anemic unless students are educated as to whom they are offending with the name. That person or that group must be named and students must be explicitly educated around the topic.

Here we are reminded of a guest lecture, observed by Petrovic, in which the professor was talking about LGBT issues with a group of preservice teachers. The professor had herself boiled the issue down to stopping name-calling. She was cornered when a perceptive student asked, "But what message does that send to the student who is gay?" Her response was basically that you stopped the name-calling and therefore you have sent a positive message. The student's question, however, went much deeper than this. It went to the fear of naming, the fear of educating around the topic of nonheterosexuality. "But," he continued, "you have made 'gay' a bad word." Unfortunately, the professor simply did not get the depth of his observance and feebly responded, "Yes, that's why no name-calling."

The point here is that, at the level of discourse, "no name-calling" and/or "no beating people up" certainly serve to disrupt, to some degree, the silence around heterosexism. They are, however, small first steps and should never be seen as more than that by qualified educators. Thus, we must consider more meaningful ways to disrupt both silence and heteronormative discourse.

In this vein, recent works consist of calls to and ways to sensitize teachers to the needs of their LGBTQ students (Davis & Reilly, 1999; Mathison, 1998) and to include LGBT issues in school curricula for moral and democratic reasons (Bickmore, 1999; Petrovic, 1999; Wong & Chng, 1998). This work has also included specific ways to include LGBT themes and to expose the hidden curriculum of heteronormativity in subject content (Letts, 1999; Martino, 1999; Lipkin, 1995).

Including LGBT themes in the curriculum is one way teachers can improve the schooling experience for their LGBT students. As one student pleaded, "Let the [gay people] be mentioned [positively] once in a while. The loneliness can eat a person up" (Kissen, 1993, p. 61). Another student recalls from high school,

> We were doing civil rights stuff. For part of our test we were supposed to write about how you would encourage gay people who are fighting for equal rights to use the lessons of the civil rights movement. I was very happy about that. It took a lot of guts [for the teacher] to do that. (Bass & Kaufman, 1996, p. 213)

The need and desire for inclusion stated here further expose the heinous character of both systematic exclusion and systematic inclusion. Both add to the message to LGBT students that a part of their identity should not and cannot be shared. Getting teachers to implement the recommendations called for by LGBTQ youth and social justice educators will simultaneously require finding ways to overcome the negative attitudes that many teachers hold about LGBT youth and to expose the ways that heteronormative beliefs come into existence, as discursive productions. Drawing from Lipkin (2002) and to a lesser but equally important extent from Straut and Sapon-Shevin (2002), Kluth and Colleary (2002), and GLSEN (2005), we would argue that teachers must be taught to:

1. Understand the significance and language of LGBT issues in education. This will include the experiences of LGBTQ youth and the perceptions of school as described above and demographic facts. It will also include the language to talk about issues including the proper use and definition of terms like queer, lesbian, gay, bisexual, and transgendered.

2. Teach more comprehensively about the human experience through the integration of LGBT subject matter into the core of learning in a variety of disciplines. This requires teachers' attention to information about the invisibility and visibility of LGBT youth in school and society, whether in the curriculum or in school (and other, e.g., military) policies. See also #6.

3. Promote the psychological and physical health and intellectual development of all students. This will include the development of sexual identity, which teachers must be able to address not as a factual matter or as a no-

tion of fixed identity but from multiple perspectives. This will also include the development of skills in guiding respectful discussions of difficult topics.

4. Reduce bigotry, self-hatred, and violence by increasing tolerance for sexuality differences. Teachers must understand the need to disrupt homophobic and other hurtful behaviors, acts, and misinformation and they must be provided guidance and opportunities to develop the skills to do so. No name-calling is the starting point, curricular inclusion the never-ending goal.

5. Aid communication between LGBT youth and their families and schools. Advocating a gay-straight alliance is one way to do this. This may also provide LGBTQ youth a way to integrate with straight peers and feel a greater connection to their school.

6. Facilitate the integration of LGBT families into the school community. This, as with #1, will require understanding the gay community to some degree and appropriate ways to interact. Using gender-neutral language when sending forms home to parents, for example, demonstrates such understanding. Similarly, nondiscrimination policies or diversity statements that include "sexual orientation" and programming around diversity themes that includes LGBT people promotes integration.

7. Nurture the well-being and acceptance of faculty, staff, administrators, and students of all sexual orientations. This requires recognizing differences, not being "color-blind." But it also requires the interrogation of labels. Thus, on the one hand, school personnel must create a climate in which students and others can proudly claim their difference. On the other hand, they must have the skill to be able to challenge, denormalize, and de-essentialize the very labels that people claim.

8. Collaborate with the greater community in achieving these ends. This is, perhaps, the heart of the poststructural because without a greater community, without like-thinking colleagues and friends, the discursive scaffolding necessary to support the construction of an antihomophobic education cannot be achieved and the project will ultimately collapse.

The Challenge to Teacher Knowledge Research

So what can teacher knowledge research contribute to efforts to accomplish these goals? The challenge to understanding why teachers might resist such teaching lies in the discursive aspects of homophobia. Homophobic attitudes often operate at the level of taken-for-granted assumptions in teachers' lives. These assumptions are produced and supported by a complex network of social and linguistic conventions that, following Foucault and others, we will refer to as heteronormative discourses. These heteronormative discourses present serious challenges to the field of teacher knowledge research.

On the one hand, teacher knowledge research undertakes to honor teachers' practical understanding of the work of teaching. This means proceeding on the assumption that teachers, based on their first-hand experience of the classroom, may know something that university-based scholars do not know. On the other hand, one of the most serious obstacles to preparing teachers to better serve LGBTQ students is that they are unaware of the way heteronormative discourses shape their taken-for-granted assumptions about student behavior and feelings. These assumptions influence both their practice *and* their understanding of their practice. This goes back to the earlier claim that "not noticing" and "turning a blind eye to" heteronormative practices and beliefs share the same discursive source.

Given this condition, the possibility must be considered that teacher knowledge research may be incapable of addressing all but the most superficial aspects of homophobia in school. With its focus on the reflections of individual teachers as a source of knowledge, it would seem to put an analysis of the taken-for-granted cultural discourses that shape individual reflection out of reach. Such a conclusion seems premature and, based on the authors' experiences, false. It would amount to saying that teachers themselves have nothing to add to the conversation about how to resist and transform heteronormativity in our schools. For teacher knowledge researchers, this conversation must engage both teachers who are more and who are less resistant. It must involve teachers who already see heteronormativity as a problem and teachers yet to be "queered." While both groups can inform teacher knowledge researchers' understandings in a variety of interrelated ways, we can see that the former group, in already thinking about ways to overcome heteronormativity in schools, will more readily be able to discuss the obstacles to doing so. We can see, similarly, that more resistant teachers have something to tell researchers about the nature and depth of heteronormative subjectivities, hopefully leading to ways to reveal and disrupt those subjectivities toward the promotion of social justice (cf. Petrovic & Rosiek, 2003).

LGBTQ-positive teaching stances no doubt frequently owe some or all of their existence to encounters with emancipatory discourses outside the classroom. However, the practical details of how to support LGBTQ students and families *in the classroom* will be worked out by practitioners. If resisting homophobia in K–12 settings is to move beyond an abstract political and/or moral commitment, then it will be necessary to respect, document, and share what teachers know about this work (in the case of those who are already advocates) as well as how they reconcile their own heteronormative subjectivities with their commitment to providing all students school atmospheres that are conducive to learning (in the case of more resistant teachers).

In other words, enlisting the teacher knowledge research movement in this effort will require finding a way to acknowledge teachers' internalization of homophobic cultural norms while still respecting their ability to think about such matters. It will require developing an approach to teacher knowledge research that moves beyond reflection on individual teaching decisions to reflexive analysis of the cultural discourses that produce taken-for-granted ways of thinking about sexuality and schooling. The first step toward this goal will be finding a conceptual vocabulary that can support such an analysis.

Poststructuralism and Teacher Knowledge Research

One of the most obvious places to look for such a vocabulary is contemporary poststructuralist theory. Structuralist and poststructuralist social theory have provided some of the most influential analyses of sexual identity issues produced in the last half century (Butler, 1993, 1999; Sedgwick, 1990; Foucault, 1978). Part of what has enabled this new analysis of sexual identity has been a profound critique of traditional western notions of selfhood, rationality, and progress. Poststructuralist thinkers have problematized the Cartesian notion of an "individual mind" that is antecedent to culture. They replace this with the concept of a historicized "subject" that is produced by cultural discourses.

Discourse here refers to the systems of symbols, signs, and meanings through which the world or a particular topic is understood by members of a social group. For the poststructuralist, individuals are neither "free" nor "oppressed" by a cultural system. Instead, individual subjects are produced by social discourses that are in turn constituted by binary oppositions like free/oppressed, sane/insane, straight/gay, able/disabled, rational/irrational. According to this theory, these binary oppositions have valences, such that one category is privileged as "normal" and the other as "deviant." Paradoxically, the privileged categories in these oppositions are rendered invisible to the discourse community when it is normalized, while the marginalized or deviant category is rendered visible, but is malignantly ignored. This process of normalization obscures the culturally constructed nature of subject identities to those operating within the discourse community. In other words, cultural discourses are the antecedent phenomena and individual minds are consequences of those discourses, despite the fact that it appears otherwise to individuals themselves.

According to this view, the individual mind ceases to be viable either as a unit of analysis for social theory or as an agent of social change. Instead cultural discourses become the salient unit of analysis and social change is seen as a more distributed phenomena. Applied to teaching, this view implies that professional and cultural discourses shape not only the tools teachers have for describing their experiences, but also the way they have those experiences. Cultural discourses provide both the means by which teachers think of difference in gender, race, ethnicity, class, disability, and sexuality in the class as well as their own identities, pleasures, and revulsions within these discursive formations.

Here we can begin to see both the value and the challenge a poststructuralist approach to sexual identity issues poses to teacher knowledge research. On the one hand, it provides a sophisticated conceptual vocabulary for analyzing the culturally constructed nature of sexual identity categories and the effects of the constructions on student and teacher experience. On the other hand, these theories direct attention away from the individual teacher as an agent of social change and resistance to homophobic oppression. To better explore this tension between cultural conditioning and teacher agency, we need to examine the ideas of the theorist who has written most profoundly about agency within a poststructuralist framework—Judith Butler.

Judith Butler and Teacher Knowledge Research

A complete review of Judith Butler's work is beyond the scope of this chapter. What is salient to the discussion at hand is the way she formulates a conception of resistance to discursive aspects of oppression. Butler reminds that although poststructuralism posits individual subjects as the effects of cultural discourses, the theory does *not* subscribe to a discursive determinism for those subjects. Discourses, in a poststructuralist framework, are never closed systems. They are always open, dependent for their existence on the continuing (re)iteration of their elements by the subjects they produce. Drawing on the work of Austin and Derrida, Butler refers to this dependence on iteration as "performativity." Our performances—of everything from the norms of professionalism to sexual identities—constitute discourses which in turn produce us as subjects that see the performances as necessary, inevitable, and/or desirable.

Using the construct of gender as her primary point of departure, Butler argues that "gender proves to be performative—that is, constituting the identity it is purported to be" (1999, p. 25). Butler goes on to claim, "That the gendered body is performative suggests that it has no ontological status apart from the various acts which constitute its reality" (p. 136). This implies that acts engaged in by the subject (e.g., claiming an essentialized sexual or gender identity, dressing a particular way, or making certain life choices) continually reconstitute the discourses that enable and delimit gender identities.

There are two aspects of Butler's theory of gender performativity that have direct implications for teacher knowledge research on how to resist homophobia in the classroom. The first of these is her conception of transformative agency that operates from within discursive systems: parodic representation. The second is her assertion that knowledge claims about sexual identities are themselves performances that can extend or disrupt heteronormative discourses.

Parodic Representation

Since individuals can only think through discourses they have at their disposal, one of Butler's projects has been to locate a source of agency for subjects working against the grain of a cultural discourse while operating *within* that discourse. The approach she offers is *parodic representation*. Parody uses the terms of a discourse to undermine the naturalized authority of that discourse.

She famously offers the example of dressing in drag. Gender norms can be denaturalized by performances that present gender signifiers in different and unexpected ways.

This opens whole new vistas of inquiry for teacher knowledge researchers. Butler's notion of parodic representation remains abstract and will require considerable elaboration if it is to be of practical use to teachers. What are the discourses about sexuality at work in particular classrooms and communities? How might teachers appropriate elements of these discourses in parodic ways? Are there developmental issues that need to be considered regarding students' age and their ability to interpret irony and parody? How far can teachers go in challenging heteronormative discourses in K–12 classrooms?

The concern might be raised here that the goal of making parody "practical" is code language for making it less political, less transgressive, less transformative. Although the word "practical" is occasionally used that way, this should not distract from the fact that there will be a practical aspect to any transgressive teaching. Further, the assumption should not be made that teachers are incapable of understanding the merits of a Butleresque imperative to denaturalize status quo gender and sexual identities. In a recent edition of the journal *Rethinking Schools*, a principal tells about a student who let her know he planned to cross-dress at school. Fearing for the student's well-being, but unwilling to prohibit the act, she called a faculty meeting to discuss how to both protect the student from bigoted assault and proactively support his freedom. Four male teachers came to school the next day in drag. Sharing insights not just about the fact of doing this, but also how to make the most of such gestures as pedagogical moments, is something teacher knowledge research can and should be doing.

Knowledge as Performance

Building on the work of Michel Foucault (1978) and Eve Sedgwick (1990), Butler (1993, 1999), describes how certain conceptions of knowledge and rationality are tied up in performances of gender and sexuality. In modern heteronormative discourses, sexual identity is presumed to be something we can *know* about a person. As Eve Sedgwick (1990) makes clear, the concept of "the closet" implies there is something potentially hidden about people's sexual identity that can be "revealed."

This assumption of knowability requires the designation of evidence. Such evidence is taken as a sign of a sexual essence (e.g., heterosexuality or homosexuality). In other words, it is the need to know sexual identity that projects the ontological existence of sexual identity, not the reality of an essence that inspires our knowledge. This need to know another's sexual essence is a product of the need to regulate increasingly complex modern societies (Foucault, 1978). Therefore, the evidentiary signs of sexual identity get their meaning, not from some privileged connection to an underlying reality of human sexuality, but from their embeddedness in wider cultural discourses that value certain forms of sexual behavior over others. Persons within these discourse communities become concerned to perform (or avoid performing) certain signs of sexual identity because these performances have real consequences for their lives. In this way broad social discourses enter into an individual's subjective experience and shape their subjectivity.

It is in this tie between the performative nature of sexual identity and regimes of knowledge that important implications for teacher knowledge research can be found. It suggests that if teacher knowledge researchers are to inquire into ways to support LGBTQ students, then they need to think carefully about the conception of knowledge underlying their inquiry. Looking for practical ways to support closeted "gay" and "lesbian" students will not suffice, because the very idea of "closet" already presumes too much. It presumes the child's sexual identity falls neatly into the hetero/homosexual binary, but is hidden (perhaps even to the student).

Butler's theory helps us to see how well-meaning teachers, in their efforts to protect students that may "be homosexual" from harassment and assault, might unwittingly reinscribe narrow sexual identity categories, thus doing violence to students' subjectivities without being aware of it. Teacher knowledge research would, thus, need to explore the ways teachers could become aware of the discourses that shape their own taken-for-granted understanding about sexuality and track the consequences of those understandings for their students' well-being. Put another way, teacher knowledge research would need to become reflexive.

To summarize then, Butler's work points to two avenues of inquiry for teacher knowledge researchers concerned to address homophobic oppression in schools. First, she offers that teachers can denaturalize cultural discourses that narrowly prescribe and proscribe sexual identities through the practice of parodic representation. Exactly how such prescriptions can be revealed, how they play out, and how they can be denaturalized in classrooms need to be empirically explored by practicing teachers and, of course, teacher knowledge researchers. Second, her theories suggest that teacher knowledge researchers need to be careful about the discourses that shape their understanding of what can be known about human sexuality. This means that teacher knowledge research would need to look not just at the effects of teaching practices on student subjectivities, but also at the discourses that produce teachers' own subjectivities and epistemologies.

Limits of Poststructuralism

Recognizing the value of Judith Butler's philosophy for conceptualizing a teaching practice that promotes social justice is by no means an original insight. Applebaum (2004), for example, defends "its usefulness as a foundation for social justice pedagogy" (p. 60) when discussing approaches to antiracist pedagogy. Our question, however, is not the general usefulness of Judith Butler's theories, and poststructuralism in general, for educators. It is the usefulness of these theories for the practice of teacher knowledge research.

Although Butler, and by extension poststructuralist theory generally, adds valuable tools to our understanding of the relation between knowledge, teaching, and sexual identity, we offer that some supplementation to these theories is needed for the purposes of teacher knowledge research. Respect for irony and parody as legitimate and valuable tools in a teacher's performative repertoire is a salutary contribution in that it provides new directions for teacher knowledge research. However, it presumes a preexisting stance of resistance to heteronormativity. What is missing is a conception of how a teacher's lived experience can become a source of constructive insight about resisting heteronormativity in the first place. Poststructuralism offers little support for the idea that teachers' lived experience, especially resistant teachers and those deeply interpellated into homophobic discourse, can reveal anything to help with this project. It is here that the gap between the poststructural and the practical opens.

Building a Bridge with Dewey's Tools of Transaction

To bridge the gap between the poststructural and the practical, we turn to John Dewey. Dewey strongly defended the idea that experience is a primary font of knowledge insofar as one applies intelligence to it. He wrote,

> The serious matter is that philosophies have denied that common experience is capable of developing from within itself methods which will secure direction for itself and will create inherent standards of judgment and value. No one knows how many of the evils of and deficiencies that are pointed to as reasons for flight from experience are themselves due to the disregard of experience shown by those peculiarly reflective. To waste of time and energy, to disillusionment with life that attends every deviation from concrete experience must be added the tragic failure to realize the value that intelligent search could reveal among the things of ordinary experience. I cannot calculate how much of current cynicism, indifference, and pessimism is due to these causes and the deflection of intelligence they have brought about. (Dewey, 1973, p. 277)

Although he did not address issues of gender or sexual identity explicitly in his writings, Dewey provides a much needed supplement to Butlerian poststructuralism (Petrovic, 2005) since he presents a theory of culturally produced subjectivity that can support a more robust conception of teacher education practice that intervenes in heteronormative discourses (Petrovic and Rosiek, 2003). There are many similarities between the work of Butler and Dewey. Where Butler talks about "discourse," Dewey talks about habits of thought, feeling, and action. In many ways, the performative acts described by Butler that constitute discourses through continual repetition, which in turn constitute the subjects responsible for the performances, resemble Dewey's notion of habits that are the products of cultural experience and in turn constitute that cultural experience (Sullivan, 2001). It is here that it can be said that Butlerian and Deweyan conceptions of thought mirror each other to a great degree. For Dewey, "mind is a cultural phenomenon rather than an individual one, and experience is a collective possession of language using beings rather than something like a private movie show in individual heads" (Ryan, 1995).

In addition to his arguably poststructural notion of habits, Dewey's conceptualization of experience further illuminates the antifoundationalism, what Dewey calls the fallacy of intellectualism, that makes his work the most logical bridge between the poststructural and the practical. This conceptualization marks an explicit eschewal of reductive empiricism in favor of reflective inquiry steeped in memory, history, affect, and emotion (i.e., those things of life that give our habits meaning in its most pregnant sense).

Habits and Experience

Dewey views habit as "an acquired predisposition to ways or modes of response, not to particular acts except as, under special conditions, these express a way of behaving" (1922, p. 42). Habits for Dewey are socially acquired. It is within the subject's particular context that habits are formed and begin to shape the subject. Like Butler's cultural discourses, they shape who we are and how we feel; indeed, they constitute the reality of the self. Further, like Butler's rejection of a subject that preexists discourses, Dewey is careful to stress that these habits "project themselves" in order to dispel the "myth" that it is "a mind or consciousness or soul in general which performs these operations" (1922, p. 176). For Dewey, habits project themselves prior to reflection. "Habit incorporates, enacts or overrides objects, but it doesn't know them" (Dewey, 1922, p. 177).

Here it is necessary to consider how Dewey (1925) thinks about "experience." To start with an illustration, consider the following discussion of experience:

> Consequently, I would rather take the behavior of the dog of Odysseus upon his master's return as an example of the sort of thing experience is for the philosopher....A physiologist may for his special purpose reduce Othello's perception of a handkerchief to simple elements of color under certain conditions of light and shapes seen under certain angular conditions of vision. But the actual experience was charged with history and prophecy; full of love, jealousy and villainy, fulfilling past human relationships and moving fatally to tragic destiny. (Dewey, 1925, pp. 34–35)

The experience of seeing a handkerchief is completely different given the viewer's subjective position. It is important to understand the extent to which experience is for Dewey mediated, formed, and reformed through habits, previous lived experience.

To take another example that further illustrates Dewey's theory of experience as well as illuminates the fallacy of intellectualism, consider two different ways of experiencing water. The chemist pours water into a beaker "knowing" that it is two parts hydrogen and one part oxygen. But, certainly, the swimmer diving into a lake on a hot summer's day will "experience" water quite differently. Even more specifically, a competitive swimmer diving into a pool will "experience" water yet another way. The difference among these are the cultural resources (derived, for example, from lived experiences, local associations, professional discourses, etc.) that turn some event into an experience.

In discussing this formulation of experience, Boisvert (1998) explains that reviving the Deweyan sense of the word requires understanding it as an adjective, not a noun. While passive receptivity dominates the latter connotation, the former is much more Deweyan in its suggestion of active involvement, practice, study, and reflection. A novice can experience a chess game. An experienced chess player experiences the same game quite differently, seeing before her a map showing several moves in advance. It is possible, however, that someone habituated to, say, checkers could make a move in chess that, in its utter novelty, befuddles the master. This requires reflection.

Reflexivity and Transactional Realism

Despite his poststructuralesque formulation of "habit," Dewey did not conceive of the experience of individuals to be as thoroughly and totally constituted by social context as poststructuralist theories sometimes imply they are. Although the subject is certainly shaped by socially acquired habits and often led mechanically by them, by virtue of being embodied, these habits are prone to disruption in a wide variety of ways. While she does not speak in terms of disruption of habits per se, Kate Evans' notion of "negotiation" recalls Dewey. We must negotiate our identities as they are impacted by our lived experiences and directed by larger sociocultural forces (i.e., discourses). "Because individual circumstances continually change—and because sociohistorical contexts are vast and varied—our identities are involved in movements, shifts, and surprises. Some of these movements are more conscious than others..." (Evans, 2002, p. 4).

Dewey referred to these "surprises" that raise habits to the conscious attention of the subject as "hitches." In those moments, reflection, even upon one's most deeply socialized habits, can occur. Such reflection is provoked when there is "a hitch in its workings [which] occasions emotion and provokes thought" (Dewey, 1922, p. 178). These "hitches" can be defined as "incompatible factors within the empirical situation....Then opposed responses are provoked which cannot be taken simultaneously in overt action" (Dewey, 1916, p. 326). The subject is then forced to reflect on the tension that such hitches create and devise a way to cope with it. This coping requires the modification of both the subject and object of study. In this transaction the object acquires new meaning for the subject and anytime a subject reconstructs the object of her inquiry she is also changed. For she now "knows" in an altered way, and this new knowing must be made consistent with the other habits that constitute the self.

Such hitches do not, of course, guarantee new understandings that promote more inclusive communities. Consider the problem of insularity put forward by Evans:

> Because dominant identities are read as natural or neutral, those in dominant groups are less likely to be put in situations in which they must engage in the emotional work of positioning themselves in relationship to norms, or others' expectations. Such emotional work for those in privileged groups tends to occur not so much when their own identities are directly challenged or questioned, but when they are in interaction with someone perceived to be an other. (2000, p. 34)

The ability to avoid the emotional work Evans refers to illustrates one problem with passively waiting for "hitches" to occur. Additionally, one can also imagine that even when such face-to-face interactions happen, they could back-fire. An interaction between a Christian conservative and a leather gay is just as likely to harden the heterosexist subject position and habits as it is to promote a transaction leading toward a deeper understanding of social justice.

Here we can see how Dewey's philosophy provides a conceptual bridge between teacher knowledge research's valorization of individual experience as a source of knowledge and poststructuralism's call for a more profound reflexive inquiry into the cultural foundations of that experience. Lived experience is the ontological ground of all knowledge, according to Dewey, and from it we abstract changing conceptions of self and an external environment in transaction. It's not just a thing we know about, such as a student's sexuality, but the historicized habits of thought that create sexuality as an object of inquiry. The latter habits, as much or more than the former topics, are the focus of inquiry in a Deweyan framework. Dewey described the possibility and challenge of this conception of inquiry into our experience:

Selective emphasis, choice, is inevitable whenever reflection occurs. This is not an evil. Deception comes only when the presence and operation of choice is concealed, disguised, and denied. Empirical method finds and points to the operation of choice as it does to any other event. Thus it protects us from conversion of eventual functions into antecedent existence: a conversion that may be said to be *the* philosophic fallacy, whether it be performed on behalf of mathematical subsistences, esthetic essences, the purely physical order of the nature, or God.... (1925, pp. 5–6)

...or, we might add, human sexuality.

The point to be made here, from a Deweyan perspective, is that reflection on some issue external to ourselves alone is an impoverished conception of inquiry. Interrogation of our habits of reflection is also required if the inquiry is to genuinely have the power to transform one's subjective position and practices.

Queering Through an Unqueer Dewey

It needs to be acknowledged that, although we are appropriating Dewey's philosophy to address issues of heteronormativity in teaching practice and teacher education research, Dewey himself never wrote about sexuality issues. More globally, he did not write centrally about the social ills of racism, sexism, or poverty during his career.

So, although in the above arrangement of our argument, we deploy Dewey as a tonic for certain shortcomings we find in poststructuralist theory, at least as regards its relevance to the project of teacher knowledge research, the need for the reciprocal supplementation also exists. Contemporary theorists in the poststructuralist tradition such as Foucault, Butler, Sedgewick, and others have much more vigorously addressed issues of homophobic oppression and heteronormative terror in their work. Our project has not been one of substitution, but of supplementation and synthesis. As Cornel West observes

...it takes us right to the center of the dialogue between various post-modern theorists, who would want to put forth a social constructivist thesis and pragmatists, who themselves claim to endorse social constructivism, but do not render in their own writing a consciousness of the degree to which they are deploying terms which are themselves constructs.

Now see, I would opt for the latter. That is to say that I would opt for the pragmatist who does in fact affirm social constructs from culture to culture, civilization to civilization…we can accentuate the constructed character of individual deed and whathaveyou. Once we have done that, I am not sure we have done as much as some postmodern theorists think we have done. That is the beginning, it seems to me. (1993, pp. 51–52)

Thus, we offer that the combination of contemporary poststructuralist queer theory, as exemplified in the work of Judith Butler, and Dewey's "transactional realism," can provide a promising framework for teacher educators seeking to disrupt heteronormative discourse. By recognizing the relationship between the social construction of knowledge, the professional norms of teaching, and sexual identity, we can see the need for a more critical teaching practice. By framing heteronormativity in terms of habits broadly conceived, we are able to look for ways of bringing different habits of belief and feeling into conflict with heteronormative habits. Such conflicts may provide opportunities in which teacher educators can encourage students to genuinely reconstruct their "knowledge" of issues of sexuality in ways that support more inclusive teaching practices.

This requires a critical integration of the conceptualizations of knowing provided by Butler and Dewey. Knowing for Butler is performative. Generally this knowing is reproductive; the ways that people know are discursively inscribed and, thus, serve to recall and reinscribe those discourses. Knowing becomes transformative under special circumstances characterized by the parodic exploitation of latent contradictions that exist in the discourses in which we all live; parody helps people to recognize the contingency of their ways of knowing. Knowing, for Dewey, is also often a habituated and passive affair. Within even the most ordinary experience, however, lies the possibility for transformation, because our habituated ways of knowing can never account for all that we undergo. Conducting substantive inquiry involves making the most of these excesses.

So what is the integration? On the one hand, teacher knowledge research is a professional discourse, one which is frequently in danger of becoming naturalized (indeed some of its advocates seek exactly that—the reification of the teacher as a "reflective practitioner"). Butler's philosophy suggests that the rhetorical construction of the teacher as "inquirer," "knower," and "reflective professional" needs constant parodic representation to avoid this naturalization. The ironic distance such parody provides would be one way to enable the more reflexive kind of inquiry into lived experience that Dewey called for, one that includes the topic *and* the terms of the inquiry within the frame of the inquiry. The Deweyan approach to this research would depart, perhaps, from a Butlerian approach in sanctioning tentative commitments to the products of that inquiry for the sake of further experience that can inspire further inquiry.

Queering Teacher Knowledge Research and the Great Escape

Beyond a brief introduction to the field of teacher knowledge research, we began this chapter with a review of what teachers need to know about the experiences of LGBTQ youth in schools as well as some of the practical knowledge that teachers must gain around issues of nonheterosexuality. This idea of practical knowledge is, for us, a key issue, the central epistemic space, if you will, in the field of teacher knowledge research.

The centrality of practical knowledge is worth reviewing again at some length here. To review in a slightly different way to the introduction, we can identify, borrowing from Rosiek and Atkinson (2005), four basic approaches to research on teacher knowledge: the scholarship of teaching, action research and teacher research, narrative inquiry, and cultural critical teacher research. The scholarship of teaching is a public, peer-reviewed body of case study research that documents and analyzes teachers' wisdom of practice. The action research/teacher research approach involves the teacher conducting the inquiry on her teaching with the intent to improve her practice. The questions and concerns that drive the inquiry are chosen by the teacher and are shaped by the cultural discourses she has internalized. Narrative inquiry seeks to document the way teachers understand and communicate their experiences through stories. In this approach, teachers ultimately retell or reconceptualize their experiences and teaching practices as they have been filtered through various genres of teacher narratives of practice. Finally, cultural critical teacher research focuses on issues of educational and social inequity and seeks to provide teachers with counterhegemonic discourses that will lead to knowledge and practices that will challenge the status quo.

Rosiek and Atkinson conclude that each of these models "is persuasive in their [sic] implicit and/or explicit critique of the other models." They go on to point out that advocates for a scholarship of teaching, for example, assume that a check is needed on the biases and provincial excesses of individual teacher reflection. They offer that critical peer review processes, like those used by university scholars, can provide this check. Conversely, action research and teacher research advocates critique the potentially distorting influence of peer review processes. Such reviews, it is feared, would impose the priorities of university research on teachers' inquiries, thereby silencing many concerns and insights arising from teaching practice. Similarly, advocates of narrative inquiry are concerned that public discourses in the form of "sacred stories" and "cover stories," can marginalize the "secret stories" grounded in teachers' personal classroom experience. Scholars taking a cultural critical approach to teacher education find the other three models to be insufficiently critical of the way ideology and cultural discourses influence conceptions of teachers' practice. (2005, p. 429)

Clearly, practical knowledge and experience are central concerns in this debate. The challenge to teacher knowledge research lies in understanding and revealing the influence of heteronormativity on the ways that teachers engage their practical knowledge. As we pointed out, if the valorization of the practical knowledge that comes from teachers' classroom and other experiences is too simplistic or does not recognize the potentially technocratic nature of practical knowledge (driven by the increasing bureaucratization of schools), it risks precluding challenges to teachers' homophobia and the extent to which their practical knowledge is situated within and constructed by heteronormative discursive practices.

In order to queer teacher knowledge research, we argued that teacher knowledge researchers must have the conceptual vocabulary that supports queered research and analysis. Here, we rehearsed the poststructural view that many of the social injustices that plague schools and society (sexism, classism, heterosexism, racism, ableism, etc.) are discursively produced, and that these discursive productions are often invisible to those who are influenced by them. This is especially true of heterosexism. As Martin and Van Gunten (2002) point out, "many potential teachers remain unaware of their positionality as racially privileged, class dominant, and heterosexually oriented as advantaged because of gender" (p. 46). From this we argued that teachers must be presented with opportunities to recognize and critically analyze their own positions in those constructions and how their positions affect the ways in which they respond to students. We assume that the purpose of such analysis is not to produce a new, unified, antihomophobic consciousness. Rather the purpose is to destabilize, to queer, all naturalized notions of sexual identity. The work of teacher knowledge research in this should be (1) to explore the ways that teachers make sense of their subjectivities and (2) to seek understanding of the ways in which teachers think about and become (or not) reflexive vis-à-vis nonheterosexuality. Further, we pointed to specific areas of inquiry that postructuralism raises for teacher knowledge researchers.

Nevertheless, the invaluable conceptual tools provided by post-structuralism are insufficient, especially as regards reflexivity. Here, a theory of experience (the source of *practical* knowledge) is required to supplement poststructuralism. At first blush, a queer marriage between Dewey and Butler might seem a stretch. Thus, we took some time to demonstrate how Dewey, as Butler, provides a theory of culturally produced subjectivity. We high-lighted the close conceptual relatedness of Dewey's notion of habit to Butler's notion of discourse. Within this, we argued that Dewey provides a theory of experience, a necessary tool for the work of teacher knowledge research that values teachers' experiences—the ontological ground of their "knowledge" of nonheterosexuality, their teaching practices, and, hopefully, their transforma-tion to "queer" teachers.

The question, of course, is one of means. What are the conditions under which such transformation can be accomplished? It is not enough for teacher educators to turn out teachers with a critical conception of heteronormativity; they must also be able to envision ways, both small and large, to act on that critical consciousness. This consideration brings the conversation back to is-sues that can only be called practical, a word that must be rescued from its technocratic usages to be applied for its transformative potential. In other words, a more reflexive, as opposed to reflective, conception of teaching prac-tice is needed. By extension then, a focus on the reflexive, drawing on the conceptual tools we have presented, must be present in teacher knowledge research.

The field of teacher knowledge research must step up to lead in the quest to understand the discursive construction and deconstruction of heteronorma-tive subjectivities as well as to helping uncover the limits and potential of teacher practices. However, contemporary constructions of teacher knowl-edge research vis-à-vis LGBT issues are wanting. In order to adequately ad-dress the needs of LGBTQ students, a conception of teacher knowledge is required that addresses the way heteronormative attitudes among teachers interact with teachers' professional, moral, and religious identity; the way these identities enable and constrain teaching practice; and the way teachers negotiate these dynamics.

Works Cited

Applebaum, B. (2004). Social justice education, moral agency, and the subject of resistance. *Educational Theory*, 54(1), 59–72.

Ball, D. L. (1996). Teacher learning and the mathematics reforms: What we think we know and what we need to learn. *Phi Delta Kappan*, 77(7), 500–508.

Bass, E., & Kaufman, K. (1996). *Free your mind: The book for gay, lesbian, and bisexual youth—and their allies*. New York: HarperPerennial.

Bickmore, K. (1999). Why discuss sexuality in elementary school? In W. Letts & J. Sears (Eds.), *Queering elementary education* (pp. 15–25). New York: Rowman & Littlefield Publishers, Inc.

Boisvert, R. (1998). *John Dewey: Rethinking our time*. Albany: State University of New York Press.

Butler, J. (1993). *Bodies that matter: On the discursive limits of sex*. New York: Routledge.

Butler, J. (1999). *Gender trouble: Feminism and the subversion of identity*. New York: Routledge.

The Center for Population Options (1992). Lesbian, gay and bisexual youth: At risk and underserved [fact sheet]. Washington, D.C.: Author.

Chandler, K. (1995). *Passages of pride: Lesbian and gay youth come of age*. New York: Random House, Inc.

Chasnoff, D., & Cohen, H. (Producers) (1996). *It's elementary: Talking about gay issues in schools* [film]. San Francisco: Women's Educational Media.

Clandinin, D. J., & Connelly, M. F. (1996). Teachers' professional knowledge landscapes: Teacher stories. *Educational Researcher*, 25(3), 24–31.

Clandinin, D. J., & Connelly, M. F. (2000). *Narrative inquiry*. San Francisco: Jossey-Bass.

Cochran-Smith, M., & Lytle, S. (1993). *Inside outside: Teacher research and knowledge*. New York: Teachers College Press.

Cochran-Smith, M., & Lytle, S. L. (1999). Relationships of knowledge and practice: Teacher learning in communities. *Review of Research in Education*, 24, 249–305.

Davis, P. (Producer), & Reilly, R. (Director). (1999). *Out! Making schools safe for gay teens* [Film]. Verona, WI: Attainment Company.

Dewey, J. (1916). *Essays in experimental logic*. Chicago: University of Chicago.

Dewey, J. (1922). *Human nature and conduct*. New York: Henry Holt and Company.

Dewey, J. (1925). *Experience and nature*. Chicago: Open Court Publishing Company.

Dewey, J. (1973). *The philosophy of John Dewey* (John J. McDermott, Ed.). Chicago: The University of Chicago Press.

Due, L. (1995). *Joining the tribe: Growing up gay & lesbian in the '90's*. New York: 1ˢᵗ Anchor Books.

Elze, D. (1992). It has nothing to do with me. In W. J. Blumenfeld (Ed.), *Homophobia: How we all pay the price* (pp. 95–113). Boston: Beacon Press.

Elze, D. (2003). Gay, lesbian, and bisexual youths' perceptions of their high school environments and comfort in school. *Children and Schools,* 25(4), 225–239.

Evans, K. (2002). *Negotiating the self: Identity, sexuality, and emotion in learning to teach.* New York: RoutledgeFalmer.

Foucault, M. (1978). *The history of sexuality* (R. Hurley, Trans). New York: Pantheon Books.

Friend, R. (1993). Choices, not closets: Heterosexism and homophobia in schools. In L. Weis & M. Fine (Eds.), *Beyond silenced voices* (pp. 209–235). New York: State University of New York Press.

Gay, Lesbian, Straight Educators Network (2005). *The 2005 national school climate survey.* Retrieved on June 19, 2006, from http://www.glsen.org/binary-data/GLSEN_ATTACHMENTS/file/582-2.pdf

Grossman, P. (1990). *The making of a teacher: Teacher knowledge and teacher education.* New York: Teachers College Press.

Herr, K. (1997). Learning lessons from school: Homophobia, heterosexism and the construction of failure. *Journal of Gay and Lesbian Social Services,* 7(4), 51–64.

Kissen, R. M. (1993). Listening to gay and lesbian teenagers, *Teaching Education,* 5(2), 57–68.

Kluth, P., & Colleary, K. (2002). Talking about inclusion like it's for everyone: Sexual diversity and the inclusive schooling movement. In R. Kissen (Ed.), *Getting ready for Benjamin: Preparing teachers for sexual diversity in the classroom* (pp. 105–118). Lanham, MD: Rowman & Littlefield.

Leinhardt, G. (1990). Capturing craft knowledge in teaching. *Educational Researcher,* 19(2), 18–25.

Letts, W. (1999). How to make "boys" and "girls" in the classroom: The heteronormative nature of elementary-school science. In W. Letts & J. Sears (Eds.), *Queering elementary education* (pp. 97–110). New York: Rowman & Littlefield Publishers, Inc.

Lipkin, A. (1995). The case for a gay and lesbian curriculum. In G. Unks (Ed.), *The gay teen* (pp. 31–52). New York: Routledge.

Lipkin, A. (2002). The challenge of gay topics in teacher education: Politics, content, and pedagogy. In R. Kissen (Ed.), *Getting ready for Benjamin: Preparing teachers for sexual diversity in the classroom* (pp. 13–27). Lanham, MD: Rowman & Littlefield.

Martin, R. J., & Van Gunten, D. M. (2002). Reflected identities: Applying positionality and multicultural social reconstructionism in teacher education. *Journal of Teacher Education*, 53(1), 44–54.

Martino, W. (1999). It's okay to be gay: Interrupting straight thinking in the English classroom. In W. Letts & J. Sears (Eds.), *Queering elementary education* (pp. 137–150). New York: Rowman & Littlefield Publishers, Inc.

Mathison C. (1998). The invisible minority: Preparing teachers to meet the needs of gay and lesbian youth. *Journal of Teacher Education,* 49(2), 151–155.

Mudrey-Camino, R. (2002). The educational isolation of sexual minority youth. Paper presented at the meeting of the Mid-Western Education Research Association, Columbus, Ohio.

Noffke, S. (1992). The work and workplace of teachers in action research. *Teaching and Teacher Education,* 8(1), 15–29.

Noffke, S. (1997). Professional, personal, and political dimensions of action research. *Review of Research and Education*, 22, 305–343.

O'Conor, A. (1994). Who gets called queer in school?: Lesbian, gay, and bisexual teenagers, homophobia and high school. *The High School Journal*, 77(1 & 2), 7–12.

Petrovic, J. E. (1999). Moral democratic education and homosexuality: Censoring morality. *Journal of Moral Education*, 28(2), 201–209.

Petrovic, J. E. (2000). Caring without justice: How we deaden the spirits of gay and lesbian children in schools. *The International Journal of Children's Spirituality*, 5(1), 49–59.

Petrovic, J. E. (2005). Reading Butler with Dewey (and vice versa?). *Philosophy of Education Yearbook* (2005), 108–111.

Petrovic, J. E., & Ballard, R. (2005). Unstraightening the ideal girl: Lesbians, high school, and spaces to be. In P. Bettis & N. Adams (Eds.), *Geographies of girlhood: Identity in between.* (pp. 195–209). Mahwah, NJ: Lawrence Erlbaum Associates.

Petrovic, J. E., & Rosiek, J. (2003). Disrupting the heteronormative subjectivities of Christian pre-service teachers: A Deweyan prolegomenon. *Equity and Excellence in Education,* 36(2), 161–169.

Remafedi, G. (1994). *Death by denial: Studies of gay and lesbian suicide.* Boston: Alyson Publications.

Rosiek, J., & Atkinson, B. (2005). Bridging the divide: The need for a pragmatic semiotics of teacher knowledge research. *Educational Theory*, 55(1), 421–442.

Ryan, A. (1995). *John Dewey and the high tide of American liberalism*. New York: W.W. Norton.

Sears, J. T. (1991). Educators, homosexuality, and homosexual students: Are personal feelings related to professional beliefs. *Journal of Homosexuality*, 22(3–4), 29–80.

Sedgwick, E. K. (1990). *Epistemology of the closet*. Berkeley: University of California Press.

Shulman, L. (1987). Knowledge and teaching: Foundations of the new reform. *Harvard Education Review*, 57, 1–22.

Shulman, L. (2000). From Minsk to Pinsk: Why a scholarship of teaching and learning? *The Journal of Scholarship of Teaching and Learning*, 1(1), 48–52.

Shulman, L. (2004). *The wisdom of practice: Essays on teaching, learning, and learning to teach*. San Francisco: Jossey-Bass.

Straut, D., & Sapon-Shevin, M. (2002). But no one in the class is gay: Countering invisibility and creating allies in teacher education programs. In R. Kissen (Ed.), *Getting ready for Benjamin: Preparing teachers for sexual diversity in the classroom* (pp. 29–41). Lanham, MD: Rowman & Littlefield.

Sullivan, S. (2001). *Living in and through skins: Transactional bodies, pragmatism, and feminism*. Bloomington: Indiana University Press.

Uribe, V., & Harbeck, M. (1992). Addressing the needs of lesbian, gay, and bisexual youth: The origins of PROJECT 10 and school-based intervention. In M. Harbeck (Ed.), *Coming out of the classroom closet* (pp. 9–28). New York: The Haworth Press, Inc.

West, C. (1993). *Beyond Eurocentrism and multiculturalism, Volume One: Prophetic thought in postmodern times*. Monroe, ME: Common Courage Press

Wong, F., & Chng, C. L. (1998). Gay, lesbian, and bisexual children: Implications for early childhood development professionals. *Early Child Development and Care*, 147, 71–82.

CHAPTER NINE

Snuff Curricula of Vulgar Scientism Meet the Queer Curriculum

Karen Anijar
Angelika Foerst

Butterflies in Our Midst

Butterflies surround Leigh's school. They dance around a garden she began making ten years ago. Karen is delighted. She doesn't see that many butterflies anymore. Some of Leigh's students take Karen on an extended tour of their special garden. Inside her classroom (decorated with perfect pinks, purples, and turquoises deliberately designed to resemble a tropical paradise), Leigh prepares students for the County Youth Fair's Oratory Contest. The children are emoting all over the place, and Leigh is trying to make them exaggerate their expressions. The bell rang and the children left for lunch.

During the lunch break, Leigh, Karen, and six or seven teachers are sitting around Leigh's large round worktable. Everyone is talking about how much they hate George and Jeb. They hate them because they are both "assholes," and "they have ruined public education." Nilda, a teacher in the room, brought up Ron Paige's "teacher-as-terrorist" comment. "What a prick!" said one of the teachers wearing an apple-laden jumper. Someone else brought up Condoleeza Rice, commenting, "Bet she is doing George." Then, Nilda brought up Bush's comment on Donald Rumsfeld at the White House Correspondents' Dinner:

Do you know what Rummy's favorite TV show is? Queer Eye for the Straight Guy. My Cabinet could take some pointers from watching that show. In fact, I'm going to have the Fab Five do a make-over on Ashcroft. (http://www.townhall.com/news/politics/200403/POL20040325b.shtml)

Nilda giggled a little; apparently, the press corps laughed, but Leigh was incensed. "Why would the Fab Five want to make-over someone who would prefer to see them dead?"

Just then, the children came back into class and continued practicing their oratories. Leigh wanted more expression, and was gesticulating all over the room.

Karen knew there was something going on in the room that is decidedly queer. But, going back to basics, how did Leigh become so sensitive to issues surrounding LGBTI subjectivities? Leigh is straight. Leigh is a Christian. Her faith guides her involvement in human rights issues. She said Jesus would never discriminate against any form of love, because she believes all love is beautiful and perfect. Leigh really doesn't like politics: although she is passionate "about teacher and children's issues and gay rights." Leigh knew the topic of conversation (queering the curriculum) in advance: her first reaction was to twist up her face, raise an eyebrow, and say: "You need to get your priorities in order. I mean it; you need to prioritize! The stuff going on from the top down, from the federal government, to the state board, to the district is frightening…It should scare you too! So, while you are fucking around…. I mean fiddling around with queering, Rome is burning!"

A Methodological Interlude

The United States has changed dramatically since the 2000 election; it is barely recognizable. As the world teeters on the edge of a Bushoid predispensational millennialist nightmare, sound-byte sloganeering designed to deliberately mislead us all abounds. Cynical debased views of the public are pervasive: we are all intellectually assaulted. Assailed with disinformation and absurd conflations, we race toward Armageddon. The Mark Foley story is one such example. Foley is a pedophile, and Foley is gay. The two are not one in the same. But, the way the story is presented rearticulates the subject and transpositions language in an Orwellian fashion. It is hard to write research and connect the dots in such a highly oppressive environment. In this chapter we use an autobiographical form of narrative construction intertextualized with informal interviews with family, close friends (something Karen has referred to in the past as "kitchen table methodology"), as well as more formal structured interviews conducted by Angelika. We also utilize what Karen loosely terms as "net narratives" emanating from a variety of sources in the public domain (which include blogs, bulletin board postings, and Web pages). In addition, the popular media (newsletters, newspapers, magazines, commercials, and television) act as a text. We begin by looking at Leigh's classroom, which is an exercise in performance pedagogy. Given that she continues to labor under codified restrictions of No Child Left Behind (NCLB), we find it necessary to then connect our ethnographic observations to the larger public political pedagogy.

Performance Pedagogy—Watching Leigh Teach

Leigh disrupts anything that ostensibly seems "normal," relegating it to the world of the absurd, and anything that seems peculiar becomes part of the mundane. She strongly feels we need to believe in the tooth fairy and Santa Claus. She played Pee-Wee Herman long before he was even on television, picking out words, to elicit a particular physical response from students. In her magical universe, a cabinet becomes something animated, standards become suggestions, and frenetic activity and fun (yes, fun) remain central to her practice.

When Karen questioned Leigh a second time about conscious activities surrounding "queering her classroom," she looked at Karen quizzically, rolled her eyes, and said, "Now who's essentializing? Teaching cannot be reduced to methodology." She laughed, knowing she had thrown one of Karen's own phrases back in her face. Karen probed, wanting something more specific: "What do you mean?"

> Everything is so macro! So meta! So reduced to best this; or a test, or a policy directive: we are not dealing with what is significant: the individual child. How the child feels, how social issues and policies affect him. Yes, all these methodological and policy directives might look good on paper, but do we forget we are working with human beings? It exists in the relationships between people. I can't describe it. But, don't you think by calling it something we already place limitations on how we can and do relate to one another? So, now are you telling me we are going to have a queer method? Isn't that weird?

"No," Karen responded. "Did I say a queer method? I think I said how do you queer your classroom?" She replied:

I told you once you name it, and reduce it to the queer method, and that sounds pretty queer, as in you are really stupid, you no longer get it. It is gone! Besides, I told you before I am far more worried about NCLB! You can't queer anything if you have that hanging over your head! Get it? Oh my god, I know what I am trying to say: it is in the disposition. Who is teaching? And, how they feel about the children they teach.

Karen rephrased the question: "But, is that queering your classroom?" She answered: "I don't know what you would call it. But, if you have to call it something then doesn't it become set in stone? Doesn't it become normalized? And by your definition then it cannot be queer."

Hijacked Science

On February 18, 2004, a group of over sixty scientists including eleven Nobel Laureates and 10 National Medal of Science winners released a statement calling for the end of government abuses of "science." Dr. Kurt Gottfried, emeritus professor of physics at Cornell University and Chairman of the Union of Concerned Scientists, stated:

> Whether the issue is lead paint, clean air or climate change, this behavior has serious consequences for all Americans. [The Bush Administration's] distortion of scientific knowledge for partisan political ends must cease. (http://www.ucsusa.org/news/press_release.cfm?newsID=381)

The potential impact of (what we label as) "snuff curriculums of vulgar scientism" (embedded in both stealth and explicit moves) toward George Bush's theocratic utopia mandates everyBODY's attention. At this juncture the damage is so extensive, it matters little that Bush won reelection in 2004: "The Bush Administration has so violated and corrupted the institutional culture of government agencies charged with scientific research that it could take a generation for them to recover their integrity..." (http://www.the-nation.com/doc.mhtml?i=20040308&s=kennedy).

Robert Kennedy Jr. wrote in *The Nation*, explaining his own experiences with

> Torquemada's successors: ...Today, flat-earthers within the Bush Administration—aided by right-wing allies who have produced assorted hired guns and conservative

think tanks to further their goals—are engaged in a campaign to suppress science that is arguably unmatched in the Western world since the Inquisition. Sometimes, rather than suppress good science, they simply order up their own. Meanwhile, the Bush White House is purging, censoring and blacklisting scientists and engineers whose work threatens the profits of the Administration's corporate paymasters or challenges their ideological underpinnings. (http://www.thenation.com/doc. mhtml?i=20040308&s=kennedy)

What Roy Cohn, Mary Cheney, and the Judenrat Taught US

Chastity Bono, who disagreed with her father Sonny's position on gay issues when he served in Congress, says she learned from her own experience that politics is so much a game of power and position that public positions and private beliefs are bound to be at odds. "I was very naive in my thinking," she says. "I still kind of believed in this idea of politicians caring about people and voting based on a belief system of their own as opposed to a bunch of people who are really trying to keep their jobs. Because their jobs are powerful, these are people with large egos, are really concerned with power and career, and that completely takes over anything else" (Wildman, 2000; http:// www.advocate.com/html/stories/820/820_cvr_cheney.asp).

Xavier (not his real name) is a professor. He is a friend of Karen's. Sometimes they fight over research methods, particularly because he profits from the Bush Administration's focus on experimental design. Mostly they fight over his ability to prove the "truth." He intends to prove the genetic basis for behavior and ability. Yet, as a gay man, Xavier's position raises ethical questions. The consequences of his actions may inform his future and the future of anyone who is not white, Christian, and straight.

We don't remember the McCarthy hearings, we weren't born, but we do remember their impact. Roy Cohn was Joseph McCarthy's chief council. Cohn and McCarthy subpoenaed gay men in the arts: threatening "to out them" if they did not produce a list of "suspected Communists." For McCarthy and Cohn the terms communist and homosexual were interchangeable (as the proceedings of the HUAC demonstrate). While Cohn lay dying of AIDS, he still refused to state he was gay (despite a very public extravagant lifestyle in the 1970s replete with an entourage of handsome boy- toy cum assistants).

When we think of Cohn (also a Jew, who was NO Angel in America), we also think of the Judenröte. The Judenrat (Judenröte is the plural term) was a council comprised of Jews appointed by the Nazis to enforce Gestapo rule within the Jewish community. They were responsible for organizing the orderly deportation to the death camps and for maintaining records about Jews in the ghettos. How could any Jew do such a thing? How could a gay man engage in research methods that would (ultimately possibly) annihilate LGBTI people? Although most of the Judenröte themselves were eventually arrested, hanged, or sent to labor camps, some had to live with the consequences of their actions dying slowly, and perhaps painfully, much like Roy Cohn.

Mary Cheney is the daughter of the Vice-(P)resident, otherwise known as the puppet-master. How can Mary support an administration whose policies are directly targeted against her? While discussing all of this one evening (with Angelika), Karen received an e-mail:

----- Original Message -----
From:_____
To: <Anijar@asu.edu>
Sent: Friday, January 09, 2004 2:58 PM
Subject: paper presented at 2002 AERA conference

Dear Professor Anijar,

I work with a consulting firm, _____ Associates, that is working on the Department of Education's What Works Clearinghouse (WWC) project. The aim of the WWC project is to build a national clearinghouse on "what works" in education. Specifically, we believe your paper "The Columbine Curriculum" may be of use for the delinquency prevention area. I would like to know how I could get a copy of this paper.

Thank you very much for your help.
Sincerely,

We wondered what Mary would do. Where is the line in the sand? "Scientists, like the rest of us, can be greedy, sloppy, egotistical, biased and politically motivated" (http://www.genomenewsnetwork.org/articles/02_03/chimp_rev. shtml). Karen replied to the e-mail with anger. In this Brave New World of high-stakes testing, evidence-based education, best practices, and other attendant essentialisms, Karen just could not channel Mary Cheney.

Dancing with the Hydra

We live in difficult times, in times of monstrous chimeras and evil dreams and criminal follies. —Joseph Conrad, *Under Western Eyes*

Our concern (to rephrase one of Leigh's comments) is that while we dance to the rhythms of the carnival of a celebratory, albeit stereotypical queerness, our eyes are diverted away from two different revolutions, ostensibly going off in different directions arriving back at the monstrous canon: A canon we will call the bio-techno-religious which increasingly informs every phase of our existence.

The twenty-first century has been named "the biotech century," heralding the converging and ever-more powerful genetic and digital revolutions" (Freder, 2003; e.g., Rifkin, 1999; c.f. Nelkin & Lindee, 1995). Lauded as a dramatic change in epistemology, ontology, and axiology, biotechnology plays a central role in all fields of knowledge. With the emergence of fields such as genomics, bioethics, and infonautics, we not only see new forms of life and "new forms of biological thought" (Keller, 2000, p. 132), but the "centrality of biological thought" in the economic, technological, and ethical engines that drive corporate and intellectual culture. Bio-techno-religious triumphalism constitutes the core of government policies and public and private research initiatives. With science and technology posing increasingly complex ethical conundrums, "bioethicists have set themselves up, almost like Napoleon crowning himself emperor, as the arbiters of what is moral and ethical."

Indeed,

> bioethicists are finding...that policymakers and the public view them as "secular priests." Their pronouncements carry serious weight and often an assumption of impartiality. They're quoted almost daily in the media, testify before Congress, and advise the President. (Boyce, 2001: http://www.usnews.com/usnews/issue/010730/usnews/bioethics.htm)

The "profession,"

> has no formal education or licensing requirements. A "bioethicist"...anyone who cares to hang out a shingle. (Boyce, 2001: http://www.usnews.com/usnews/issue/ 010730/usnews/bioethics.htm)

According to William Saletan,

> the chief tool plucked from the toolbox is proceduralism. The public can be distracted…by elaborate protocols….The slickest way to make yourself look ethical is to narrow the definition of ethics so that it won't interfere with what you want to do. But that won't make you ethical. It'll just make you an ethicist. (2001, p. A-1)

And business is booming. Corporations (particularly drug, gen-tech corporations, public-private partnerships, etc.) pay a high price for bioethicists to determine what is good, right, and just. However, the dominant bioethical articulation of universalist ethics is abstracted from social and power formations as if they did not exist (see Anijar, 2003, p. 29). The presumption/ assumption of universality intermingles with particular notions of reason, and rationality, negating multiplicity (and more often than not, conflating multiplicity with relativity). For example, Dr. Robert Baker (2003) in the *American Journal of Bioethics* (responding to an article about "whiteness") wrote:

> No evidence is adduced showing that African-Americans, Asian-Americans or Native Americans are "other" in the sense that they do not value individualism, autonomy, rights, veracity, beneficence, justice, anti-paternalism or the other values, concepts, and cognitive frameworks attributed to mainstream American bioethics. For, insofar as the values, concepts, and cognitive characteristics of African-American, Asian-American and Native-American are not "other," insofar as they are shared with mainstream American bioethics, there is no problem of difference to be addressed. Hence there is no need to resolve this problem by problematizing the presumed "whiteness" of American bioethics. Ethnic, class and racial discourses will only serve to balkanize bioethics. The resulting babble would not only marginalize minorities, alienating bioethicists from each other, it would also alienate mainstream bioethics from mainstream America. (p. 11)

African American scholars (for example) have articulated (to no avail):

> Bioethics fail African-Americans because bioethicists believe, first, that people behave in ways that can so far be predicted a priori that empirical evidence about their behavior is superfluous and, second, that people think and act rationalistically, seeking always to maximize and exercise autonomy….However, the reality is very different. People act in ways that are more consistent with the values they hold, rather than following any particular bioethical principles. (Randall, 2003, http://academic.udayton.edu/health/05bioethics/)

Erasing and effacing anything or anyone falling outside the normal standard deviation of the bell curve of human existence is a paradoxical condition of "privilege in a society that declares all men are created equal" (Olsen, 2002, p. 409). So, in 1993, when Dean Hamer of the National Institute of Health announced the discovery of the gay gene, science fiction became an Orwellian (possible) reality:

> A DNA sample can be acquired in the first moments of life. This sample could then be immediately analyzed on a DNA chip. The results could inform the parents what "traits" are embedded in their child's genetic code. Decision trees regarding that child's development could then be built to help him or her live a happier, healthier life. That's a wonderful promise and an extraordinary opportunity. But it is also terrifying....Imagine for a moment that the parents learn that the fetus will grow up to be homosexual and that, for whatever reason, the parents decide that homosexuality is not what they want for their child. (Ellis, 1999, http://www.bostonglobe.com)

Advocates of the Human Genome Diversity Project persistently highlight the "scientific" (a.k.a. impartial) basis of their endeavor. Nevertheless, critics cited (to whomever was listening) "a plethora of cultural, legal, and scientific problems with the project, including dangers associated with racism, gene patenting, exploitation, the lack of protection for indigenous peoples, and the imposition of Western notions of informed consent (Harry,1995, http://www.uni-frankfurt.de/~ecstein/gen/iatp/ipr-info7.html; Lock, 1993). Religious symbolism suffuses all discussions surrounding policies. The genetic basis for homosexuality was framed by comparing the genetic codes of heterosexual and homosexual men (methodologically spurious at best). Although it might seem that the theological perspectives of the Christian right are incommensurate with genetic science, two points of convergence form the unexamined nexus of the cultural construction of the *gay gene*. First, the word "homosexual" as an identity (who you are) is a modern invention entering into the Western vernacular in the 19th century. Second, the binary of homo-heterosexuality was a codification of biblical (Christian, Jewish, and Islamic) interpretations (surrounding definitions) of appropriate sexual contact. The alliance of strange bedfellows (for example, Israelis and the Christian right on Right wing Israeli policy or the Green Party and Right-to-Life groups on genetically enhanced food) is very odd (you could almost say "queer" if these "bedfellows" were not so perverse), and the intersection of imperialist science and capitalism with the religious right often feels inescapable.

The impact of the bio-techno-religious conflation of nature and nurture and science in schools can be illustrated by the Montgomery County, Maryland's school board decision to ban discrimination against

> homosexuals....Teachers can forget about inviting a gay man or lesbian to their classes to talk about homosexuality....The same prohibition goes for any attempt to put on prominent display school library books such as "When Someone You Know Is Gay," "Hearing Us Out: Voices From the Gay Community," or "No Big Deal." ..."That would be proselytizing," Superintendent Paul L. Vance said (Beyers, 1996, Metro Section available at http://www.eecs.berkeley.edu/~richter)

In other areas of the country parent advocacy groups, loosely termed political associations, and Web sites abound focusing on *the homosexual agenda* in schools (such as that found at http://www.forthechildren.com):

> Tolerance of diversity is a noble ideal, but diversity should not extend to promotion of a life-shortening behavior such as the practice of homosexuality. The methods being used to promote diversity...encourage students to experiment with a lifestyle known to have serious health consequences.

David, one of the teachers we interviewed for this chapter, told us:

> A fellow educator was irate that I would encourage her students to participate in National Day of Silence—an event in April where students do not speak all day in memory of all GLBTI students who have been silenced by hate and violence. She felt my club had nothing to do on campus and we *promoted homosexuality,* and before the club existed homophobia was not an issue on a *unified* (vilified, more like it) campus like ours.

What is important is how the argument "against homosexuality" is constructed from both cultural and medical models. No matter which way you turn, GLBTQI people are trapped in the crossfire between the market, the backlash against multiculturalism, the privatization of education, and the age-old debate between nature versus nurture.

Pink Badges of Pride or Prejudice?

After all these years of thinking I was just a white male heterosexual Protestant Republican, I realized I was wrong. I'm really a lesbian trapped inside a man's body. Naturally, I was concerned that when I revealed this to my girlfriend (now my wife), she would be alarmed. I even thought it might end our relationship....When I told her about my condition, she came back with this stunning revelation: She's really a gay man trapped inside a woman's body....If the university tries to fire me for my conservative views, I will reveal my Lesbian In a Man's Body Orientation (LIMBO). ...I will argue that my conservative views are caused by my gender identity confusion. If they happen to be oblivious to the status of LIMBOs, I will just go ahead and get a sex change along with my wife (I hope cosmetic surgeons offer "two for one" specials). Certainly, they will decide to keep me if I actually become trans-gendered. And if I don't feel like being a woman anymore, I will simply change back to being a man. Hopefully, trans-trans-gendered persons will have the respect they deserve by the time I have my second surgery....I hope that I haven't used any politically incorrect terminology in explaining my dilemma. If I find out that I have, I will enroll in the new "Queer Theory" course (no, I am not making this up) being offered next semester in the Sociology Department. And maybe the new course in "Queer Theory" will help me answer some other questions. For example, when did it become politically correct to use the term "queer"? And why do we need "queer theories" if sexual orientation is genetically determined? Finally, does anyone in the class want to be seen as an individual?—Dave (an educator)

David explains,

As a straight queer teacher, I was sat down by a professor and warned that my allegiance to queers everywhere would make everyone think I was one of them. My political and cultural views are enigmatic, sometimes, even to me, and I do not care if people think I am gay. And, in part, I must digress here because I feel like I am almost patronizing LGBTQ people everywhere because I have it so easy being a straight white male. I can never know my queer friends and queer students. I can never be like them. Why would I want to? I've been gay bashed (can I say gay bashed if I am not gay?) once. I clammed up and was relieved that another, neutral colleague was present at this confrontation.

David's words paralleled a conversation (below) posted to a student list-serv surrounding the use of the word "queer":

John: I have encountered several folks who identify as straight, and also as queer. They say that they are solely attracted to people of "the opposite sex."

Mary: What does it mean to be queer if it doesn't mean some sort of disadvantage, some sort of oppression? Straight people can be as kinky as they want, and maybe they would take some shit for that from their conservative friends, but they still have rights that I don't have. It DOES feel like co-opting identity.

John: Do you consider "queer" to be a badge only for oppression and the shit we get. I'd rather it be a label for how proud we are!

John should be proud, but he also should be cautious. As a recent debate between bioethicists and the deaf community demonstrates, pride, community, culture, identity, and oppression may be moot points. Deaf people have been forced to justify the existence of their culture. Bioethicists Thomas Balkany, Annelle V. Hodges, and Kenneth W. Goodman insist that deaf leaders and scholars "mislead people purposefully" (2000, p. 83) in order to retain their professional hegemony over the deaf community. Balkany, Hodges, and Goodman maintain deafness is not a culture, nor a community but a disability (2000, p. 87). Since, (they write) cochlear implants can "cure" the deaf, why would anyone choose deafness? They answer their own (seemingly rhetorical) question highlighting "the prevalence of psychological disorders" among deaf people (p. 87). So, if the deaf (or deaf) community is maligned for resisting medicalized regimes of normalcy, what about GLBTQI people? On one hand there is the cultural model (which means homosexuality can be cured) and on the other hand there is the biological model (which also ultimately means homosexuality can be cured). Adding to the "interventionist" transformations occurring in academia are the return "to the old universalisms of truth" (Mills, 2004, http://reviews.media-culture.org.au/index.php). Cultural theorists (for example, Terry Eagleton and Bruno Latour) have called for an end to theory and a return to scientifically premised philosophy, while former (neo)progressives, a.k.a. Stanley Fish, tell academics to depoliticize our classrooms. The journal *Qualitative Inquiry* devoted the entire February 2004 issue to "methodological fundamentalism," meaning:

> [the] return to a much criticized and largely discredited form of research. This fundamentalist research involves large, randomized sample, experimental design studies created (or, more appropriately, re-created) on the clinical model....The reiteration of experimentalism as the "gold standard" of educational and clinical research can be seen, as St. Pierre points out, as a..."backlash," similar to (and as virulent as) the backlash against the women's movement outlined by Susan Faludi more than a dec-

ade ago. Just as the growing strength of the women's movement, with its concomitant issues of equality of opportunity and pay in the workplace, brought on a resurgence of political, social, and religious counter-reaction, so too have the inroads of critical theory, postmodernism, poststructuralism, feminist theory, race and ethnic studies theories, queer theory, and other late-20th century critiques of modernism and experimental research brought on their own reactionary and rearguard actions. One such reaction has been the federal No Child Left Behind Act of 2001 and its statement of what constitutes sound research (primarily experimental design studies) partnered with and legitimated by the NRC report (Feuer et al., 2002). The return of high modernism, the backlash against diverse forms of research, and recent direct governmental actions (such as the NRC report) that would create a science for the "common good" (Foucault, 1991, pp. 94–95) are awakening (some) scholars to the dangers in these present day reconstructions of…"dangerous discourses." (Lincoln & Canella, 2004, pp. 7–8)

Suffice to say the United States shows no signs of relenting in its long slow march toward theocratic hypercapitalist fascism; it is metaphorically much like an inescapable vice slowly tightening equally on all sides suffocating opposition or possibilities for opposition.

Queer Unto Others As You Would Have Them Queer Unto You

Back in the classroom, Angelika (who teaches 7th and 8th grade) decided to ask several colleagues whether they felt they queered their curricula, be it on a performance level (practice) or a content level (theory). She gave no explanations or definitions surrounding the meaning of "queering" or "curriculum."

> Robin: I don't know what you mean…do you mean "what do I think about gay people?"

> Stephanne: What?

> Shannon: No, I don't feel that I "queer" my curriculum. I'm also not sure why that has become a term—don't all sorts of human beings put on shows?

Although Shannon was well aware of the performance aspect of queering curriculum, her universalist position surrounding "all human beings" remains operative. The unit of measure (a universalist Kantian-Hegelian "common" unit) takes on meaning only in direct relation to its own emptiness. What is common (to paraphrase Lacan) is really particular.

Meanwhile, a student named Emily, a self-proclaimed pan-sexual, shared her research project idea (for someone else's class) with Angelika. Emily wanted to stand in front of the class and present a paper on homosexuality. Armed with the teacher's name, Angelika took it upon herself to write a series of questions in a letter to Robin (the name of Emily's teacher). The initial letter precipitated an extended discussion.

> Q: When Alexa informed you that she wished to research homosexuality what was your initial response?

> A: My initial response was, "Leave it to Alexa to pick a controversial subject!" Then my next thought was, "how bold of you to 'out' yourself in 8th grade."

> Q: Did you have any reservations?

> A: I had no reservations whatsoever. If she had wanted to do a report about how she discovered her sexual preference, blah, blah, blah that would not have been OK. I wanted them to do a RESEARCH paper, not a persuasive paper.

> Q: Does this worry you? For example, do you fear parent phone calls?

> A: No, this doesn't worry me at all just like it doesn't worry me that another student is doing his report on Christianity. They are just reporting the facts. It's like the old saying, "you can teach, you can't preach." The "uncomfortable" questions will be answered by her. If she's bold enough to pick the subject that she did (and knowingly pick it when there will be a presentation to be given on it next quarter) then she should be bold enough to accept any consequences/commentaries that arise. If any kids ask me questions about her, I will direct them to her to answer them. I don't fear parent phone calls for two reasons: (1) I'm a big girl and (2) She is in an honors class, which is very mature and they can handle it. Also, if I get questions from outside my class about her, I will direct them to ask her themselves. There shouldn't be anything to hide. It's not like she's talking about Satan worship and how we should put spells on people.

Robin added:

> If she should come under attack (although I don't think this would happen) I would protect her. I would protect any child that's being discriminated against in any way.

The very next day Angelika received a note from Robin: "I need to talk to you personally. What time can I call you?" A frantic call at the beginning of the lunch hour followed. Robin asked: "would I get into trouble for this?" Ultimately, Robin decided to have Alexa report her findings on homosexuality privately. Was there really just cause for Robin's alarm? Was Robin merely taking the easy way out of what could have been an uncomfortable situation? Or, was it just another way to put it all back into the closet?

Angelika continued to interview teachers (April–July 2004). What was apparent looking over the narratives collected (from teachers who voluntarily stated they queered their classrooms) was that queer remained situated within static paradigmatics, within prescribed disciplinary locations. The responses appeared formulaic; for example, the association of the arts with queerness. Robert (a teacher) began the interview by stating: "I'm in the arts, so unusual people of all kinds are more the norm," the specifics of how he queered his classroom, and of queerness in and of itself was diffused and diffracted—much like a prism, a (rainbow) light-ray of obfuscation (refracting and reflecting while misdirecting). Robert's "trompe loeil" normalcy was antithetical to anything queer. "It is just normal for people in the arts to be queer, and to queer their classrooms," he said. If it is normal in the arts then how can it be queer? "Would it be normal in any other class or subject?" "Sure," he said (almost jokingly), "in girls phys-ed." Robert's statements paralleled those of many of the teachers interviewed. Queer had a place, but *only* in certain disciplines. Lisette (another teacher) elaborated "why" she was able to "queer" her classroom: "the arts are always open to all sorts of people, even those who might be seen as unusual by most standards." We were told time and time again that the arts remain a "safe-haven" for queer teachers. "You know," Danny said,

> like Matt Bear, everyone knows he is gay. But, he is the Arts Director and it is okay for him to be gay; it is kind of expected. You could say it is the "gay" position within the school administration. Even the very religious people in the school district office say Matt Bear is a bit eccentric, but that is a code word....He is OUR eccentric, we would never say he is gay. It is all pretense, even though everyone is well aware of what is going on. He may be valued as our "eccentric" but the arts are never given the same funding as science. They don't hold a central place (or any place) in a curriculum increasingly defined by high-stakes testing, privatization, and the bottom line of corporate interests.

Frankly, it really doesn't matter if the arts are queer or queered because the arts don't matter. Come to think of it the Humanities don't matter, and we no longer teach Civics, so Social Studies doesn't matter (although bioethics is now being taught in high schools). What is apparent, however, is the naturalized manner in which the arts still remain a surrogate for gay men, and how the arts are consigned to the margins.

Reginald felt he had "few reservations about addressing the 'gay or queer issues.' I would only make sure my response is *appropriate* to my audience, 7th graders." Manfred said he,

> doesn't have problems addressing any issue properly and politically correctly. But, I try not to discuss anything at great length that is *too controversial*. Equality and free-dom of choice are important to me, but I have to be aware that GLBQT issues are not a *comfortable topic*, just as abortion isn't a comfortable topic (everyone will have their *opinion*).

People are not topics, or issues: let alone controversial issues. Lanie focused "an entire quarter's unit on the subject of equality and fair treatment for ALL people. I feel this is a positive way to approach practicing empathy and accep-tance." Gwenyth had no reservations whatsoever in "talking about gay or les-bian people/issues in the classroom when they come up in my classes." However, she is quick to add, "I do not ever initiate the topic." Maria de-clared, "I don't personally have reservations in talking about gay, lesbian, bi-sexual, and transgendered (GLBT) people (or whatever those letters are this week) and the issues surrounding them. If the subject doesn't come up in class, it's not something I would bring up to my students. Just as I wouldn't bring up other issues like alcoholism, child abuse." Maria's positioning of queerness (much like Reginald's and Manfred's) within a chain of pathologies clearly is just one more articulation using medicine as the institution for social control serving to "maintain the status quo and re-inscribe already known situations and identities as fixed, immutable, locked into normalized concep-tions of what and who are possible" (Walcott, 1998, p. 368). The teacher nar-ratives unfortunately reflect far too many expressions we have heard on the streets, in classrooms, and the Internet. The medicalized pathological model in which:

Homosexuality is unnatural and unhealthy (gays have higher incidences of diseases and shorter lifespans) due to their CHOSEN BEHAVIOR. Therefore, it is akin to cigarette smoking or drug/alcohol abuse. If Phillip Morris were to sponsor class-room assemblies talking about cigarette smokers and their lifestyle (and how others should be tolerant of it), there would be an uproar—anonymous post

Medicalization categorizes people as "sick" or "dysfunctional," obscuring the moral basis of the judgment. Nevertheless, "psychological assessments are al-ways highly normative....Normative judgments are not merely descriptive, they are also prescriptive. They not only describe "the good, the true, and the beautiful," they also provide prescriptions and proscriptions that signify how we are to think and behave in every aspect of our lives" (Hartman & Laird, 1998, p. 272).

No Child Left Behind...No Queers Anywhere to Be Seen

I know I have been teasing you a lot lately. And, I am sorry. I know you are trying to write a chapter, and maybe I have not been that helpful. You just have to under-stand, things are different now than when you taught in the schools. I...Young teachers don't care about anything but test scores, and not getting in trouble.

Conservatives have co-opted our school board. People play to sound bytes: they use words like pluralism and egalitarianism or compassionate conservatism, but, in real-ity, they are waging a war....You know the axiom "NCLB leaves everyone behind." I am not into some sort of touchy-feely tolerance thing—you know that. All I am trying to do is hold it all together and teach, which is becoming increasingly difficult. And, then you ask me how I queer my classroom? I hope and pray that I will have a classroom in ten years given the war in Iraq and war on Terror. But, with everything going on with Bush and the rest of them...I hope I have queers in my classroom to teach in ten years.—Leigh

No Child Left Behind (U.S. Congress, 2001) mandated that federal research funds be used only to support "scientifically based research." Scientific research is understood and defined as "rigorous, systematic and objective procedures to obtain valid knowledge...evaluated using experimental or quasi-experimental designs" (Slavin, 2002, p. 15). "One of the hallmarks of the technocratic mod-ernist state, according to Canadian philosopher Ian Hacking, is an avalanche of numbers. It is through counting, census, assessment...and the generation of numbers that public policy is made and legitimacy established" (Luke & Luke

2001, p. 9). Everything is enumerated, including aesthetics, subjectivity, knowledge, and human beings, becoming materials for the explosive exponential growth of business. In the managerial state, society becomes one long uninterrupted moment of production as business disguises "its hegemony and interest in exploitation...pass[ing] off its conquest...as being in the general interest" (Dyer-Witherford, 1999, p. 51).

The Bush Administration's truth and facts are in fact designed to advance their larger ideological agenda. An agenda that includes removing evidence of global warming in Environmental Protection Agency reports, banning the use of generic drugs (since it would cut into the profits of large pharmaceutical corporations), removing information posted on the Department of Health and Human Services Web sites (concerning condom effectiveness) and purging databases from other governmental agencies such as the National Cancer Institute (it was found abortion did not increase the risk of breast cancer).

An "objective reality" derived from "empirical evidence" (which is why abstinence-only education has proven to be more effective than condoms in the spread of sexually transmitted diseases) and why creationism is a "hard science" and evolution is merely a theory.

The National Human Research Protections Advisory Committee has been dismantled (the committee was unfriendly to industry). Members of the Centers for Disease Control (CDC) Advisory Committee on Childhood Lead Poisoning Prevention have been systematically replaced with "individuals who are affiliated or openly sympathetic with the views of the lead industry" (Madsen, 2004, http://blog.mmadsen.org/2004/02/the_attack_on_s.html). The Administration's appointments to the Presidential Council on bioethics (after removing members who did not agree with the President's agenda) include Benjamin Carson who moonlights from his position at John Hopkins as a motivational speaker. He lectures on how "we live in a nation where we can't talk about God in public" (Madsen, 2004, http://blog.mmadsen.org/ 2004/02/ the_attack_on_s.html).

And, Diana Schaub, who stated in an academic venue that embryos are used as "the evil of the willful destruction of innocent human life" (Madsen, 2004, http://blog.mmadsen.org/2004/02/ the_attack_on_s.html).

And, Peter Lawler, chairman of Government at Berry College in Georgia (an undergraduate Christian college) who has stated "If a country is bad enough to embargo, it is bad enough to conquer," and "Darwin is kinda corny, and Machiavelli is a Sinatra kind of guy" (Madsen, 2004, http:// blog. mmadsen.org/2004/02/the_attack_on_s.html).

And,

> the Administration reportedly wants W. David Hager MD, appointed chair of FDA's important Reproductive Health Drugs Advisory Committee. Dr. Hager not only recommends that women read biblical scripture to treat their gynecological conditions, but he reportedly doesn't prescribe contraceptives to unmarried women and wants the FDA to ban the abortion pill RU-486. (Pizzo, 2004, http://www. alternet.com)

The Administration attempted to appoint Jerry Thacker to the Advisory Council on HIV and AIDS. The same Jerry Thacker who called AIDS a "gay plague" and homosexuality a "death-style" (Weiss, 2003, http://www.truth-out.org).

We *ALL* have to *fight* the snuff curricula of vulgar scientism (that reduces bodies to commodities of various value to be bought and sold for and by the marketplace). We have to *fight* forms of biotechnology that fornicate with the religious right and hyperintensified capitalism.

We have to *fight* forms of infonautics (the study of databases) that would invade our right to privacy; we have to *fight* genomics that would act in the service of genocide. In our estimation, Leigh's fears are not unfounded; her points (we think) are well-taken: *we should think about queering the classroom, but first we have to insure that there are queers in our future!*

Works Cited

Anijar, K. (2003). Into the heart of whiteness. *American Journal of Bioethics*, 3(2), 29–31

Baker, R. (2003). Balkanizing bioethics. *American Journal of Bioethics*, 3(2), 13–14.

Beyers, Dan (1996). NO GAY BIAS, NO 'PROSELYTIZING,' NO END TO MONTGOM-ERY DEBATE: Despite school board vote, homosexuality still an issue. *Washington Post*, *Metro Section*, April 1, 1996. Available at http://www.eecs.berkeley.edu/~richter

Boyce, N. (2001). And now, ethics for sale? Bioethicists and big bucks. http://www.usnews.com/usnews/issue/010730/usnews/bioethics.htm. *U.S.News* 7/30/01.

Bragg, L. (2000). From, http://www.dsq-sds.org. [*Disability Studies Quarterly*, 20(4).]

Bush, G. (2004). Transcript of remarks by President Bush at the Radio and Television Cor-respondents Association Dinner in Washington on March 24, 2004, provided by the White House Press Office: http://www.townhall.com/news/politics/200403/POL-20040325b.shtml

Dyer-Witherford, N. (1999). *Cyber-Marx: Cycles and circuits of struggle in high-technology capital-ism*. Urbana and Chicago: University of Illinois Press.

Ellis, J. (1999). New politics of abortion. http://www.bostonglobe.com

Freder, K. (2003). The biotech mode of (re)production. http://home.uchicago.edu/~ksfreder/ biotech.doc.

Harry, D. (1995). Patenting of life and its implications for Indigenous Peoples. http://www.uni-frankfurt.de/~ecstein/gen/iatp/ipr-info7.html

Hartman, A., & Laird, J. (1998). Moral and ethical issues in working with lesbians and gay men. *Families in Society*, 79(3), 263–276.

Keller, E.F. (2000). *The century of the gene*. Cambridge, MA: Harvard University Press.

Kennedy, R. F. Jr. (2004). The junk science of George Bush. http://www.thenation.com/doc.mhtml?i=20040308&s=kennedy posted 2.19/2004

Lincoln, Y., & Canella, G. (2004). Dangerous discourses: Methodological conservatism and governmental regimes of truth. *Qualitative Inquiry*, 10(1), 5–14.

Lock, M. (1993). *Encounters with aging: Mythologies of menopause in Japan and North America*. Berkeley: University of California Press.

Lockhart, T. (2000). *Moral uncertainty and its consequences*. New York: Oxford University Press.

Luke, A., & Luke, C. (2001). Calculating the teacher. *Teaching Education*, 12(1), 1–15.

Madsen, M. (2004). The attack on science continues, part 2: Extended phenotype: Exploring the confluence of society, politics, law, and evolution. http://blog.mmadsen.org/2004/02/the_attack_on_s.html

Mills, C. (2004). Theory is passé, but philosophy is back in style. Posted Media Culture Reviews, posted July, 13, 2004, http://reviews.media-culture.org.au/index.php

Nelkin, D., & Lindee, S. (1995). *The DNA mystique: The gene as a cultural icon*. New York: W.H. Freeman.

Olsen, J. (2002). Whiteness and the participation inclusion dilemma. *Political Theory*, 30(3), 384–409.

Pizzo, S. (2004). The Christian Taliban independent media institute alternet. Posted March 28, 2004.

Randall, V. (2003). Bioethics and race. http://academic.udayton.edu/health/05bioethics/

Saletan, W. (2001). The ethicist's new clothes. *New York Times*, August 2, 2001 (Late Edition), A1; (also at) http://www.ccwv.net/EssayDisplay, asp? recordID=276

Slavin, R. E. (2002). Evidence-based education policies: Transforming educational practice and research. *Educational Researcher*, 31(7), 15–21.

Union of Concerned Scientists (February 18, 2004). Preeminent scientists protest Bush Administration's misuse of science: Nobel Laureates, National Medal of Science Recipients, and other leading researchers call for end to scientific abuses. http://www.ucsusa.org/news/press_release.cfm?newsID=381

Walcott, R. (1998). Queer texts and performativity: Zora, rap, and community. In William F. Pinar (Ed.), *Queer Theory in Education*. Mahwah, NJ: Lawrence Erlbaum Associates.

Weiss, R. (2003). Bush misuses science: Report says Democrats say data are distorted to boost conservative policies. *Washington Post*, Friday, 8 August 2003, http://www.truthout.org

Wildman, S. (2000). Hiding in plain sight. Mary Cheney may be silent, but her presence speaks volumes about the relationship between family and sexual identity. *The Advocate*, September 12, 2000, http://www.advocate.com/html/stories/820/820_cvr_cheney.asp

CHAPTER TEN

Giving an Account of Queer: Why Straight Teachers Can Become Queerly Intelligible

David V. Ruffolo

The intelligibility of subjects in society is dependent on how the subject is constituted as a social being and the ways in which the subject provides an account of itself. The circulation of norms in society re/produce binary positions that maintain un/privileged relations through the interactions of "identities"—binary conceptions of the "I" that further privilege the majoritized and further subordinate the minoritized.[1] This chapter engages a radical politic of the self through a discussion of queer ideologies informed by queer theory. Queer theory's theoretical shift from *identities* to *identifications* highlights the negotiations of differences, rather than similarities, among subjects.[2] The appreciation of differences vis-à-vis identificatory practices are embedded in unstable and unfixed realms of *queer*—a radical positioning that is committed to disturbing, disrupting, and decentering normative[3] discourse that excludes in its attempts to include.[4] I challenge the notion of "straight"[5] teachers by theoretically exploring the processes that make subjects intelligible[6]—how the straight teacher became "straight." *Queering* straight teachers is a reconceptualization of what (heterosexual) identity looks like using queer ideologies to reconstitute the "straight" self as an implicated subjectivity of circulating norms. Consequently, I radically reconsider how straight teachers are negotiated in social spaces; that is, I discuss how straight teachers can become queerly intelligible by introducing a radical process to explore how straight teachers can give an account of queer.[7] Therefore, the questions *what are straight teachers* and *who are straight teachers* can be theoretically radicalized by asking *why are straight teachers*.

Straight teachers can become *queerly intelligible* by *giving an account of queer*—an account that articulates how the "I" is implicated in circulating norms that constitute an un/intelligible subject.[8] If, according to Foucault and Althusser, the subject (straight teachers) is brought into being through subjectivation—discursive and ideological modes of producing the subject, respectively—and if, according to Butler, the subject is asked to give an account of itself, *how can straight teachers become queerly intelligible if queer ideologies disrupt straight practices and straight practices resist queer ideologies* and *how can straight teachers give an account of queer if "straightness" emphasizes the fixed subject and "queerness" focuses on the mobile and fluid subject?* This chapter critically examines how subjects (straight teachers) are in/formed in society and radically explores the possibility of straight teachers becoming queerly intelligible by exposing how they can give an account of queer. It works to expose what Butler terms the "matrix of intelligibility"[9]: the circulation of norms that constitute fully intelligible subjects that maintain a strong cohesion among coherent identities (sex, sexuality, gender, etc.) so as to produce a fully knowable subject (e.g., man, white, heterosexual, masculine, etc.). Consequently, the following questions emerge throughout the chapter in order to challenge this matrix: (1) what does heterosexuality look like through a queer lens? (2) what does it mean to queer straight teachers? (3) what does it mean for straight teachers to become queerly intelligible? (4) how can straight teachers give an account of queer?

Queering the *Straight* "I"

The radical politic of queer theory[10] provides a critical framework for exploring how straight teachers can become queerly intelligible and how they can give an account of queer.[11] Queer theory's emphasis on difference creates an important shift from *identities*—fixed and stable articulations of the collective "I"—to *identifications*—mobile and fluid negotiations among momentary subjects—in order to disturb binary ideologies that exclude in their attempts to include. Binary "identities" are problematic for they maintain "us" and "them" ideologies that produce subordinated positions: Sedgwick (1990), for example, argues that binary oppositions—in her discussion, heterosexuality/ homosexuality—are complex relations, where "first, term B is not symmetrical with but subordinated to term A...[and] second, the ontologically valorized term A actually depends for its meaning on the simultaneous subsumption and exclusion of term B" (pp. 9–10).[12] In other words, conceptualizing the self using binary identities (i.e., male/female; masculine/feminine; able/disabled; straight/gay, etc.) supports hierarchical, patriarchal, and heteronormative[13] ideologies that place subjects in fixed collective categories that exclude minoritized others in order to maintain its privileged status as a majoritized binary. The radical politic of queer disturbs, disrupts, and decenters binary identities embedded in normative discourses so as to appreciate mobile and fluid identifications among subjects with no fixed "identity" position. The notion of "queer" in queer theory, therefore, is not an articulation of a stable identity (noun), but instead is a radically strategic process that troubles all things "normal" (verb).[14] Queer theory can provide a critical lens to explore the intersections of the *politics of identity* and the normative practices of *identity politics*.[15] The radical politic of queer and queer theory provides an analytical lens that can create spaces to appreciate the unfixed, unstable, mobile, and fluid identifications of subjects—a necessity for projects that envision difference as a foundation for equity.[16] The radical process of queering straight teachers does not attempt to replace a "straight" identity with a "queer" identity (identity politics), but instead works to trouble how and why "straight" "identities" become intelligible (politics of identity)—exposing how straight teachers can become queerly intelligible by giving an account of queer.[17]

Although queer (theory) invites a radical process to disturb normative practices and binary ideologies, it is somewhat unclear as to *how* queer can be embodied as a radical tool.[18] More particularly, how straight teachers can become queerly intelligible by giving an account of queer. The embodiment[19] of queer (a queer politic) does not necessarily displace or embrace queer as a verb or a noun. The embodiment of queer, however, can be a descriptive position committed to radical (queer) processes. *Queer* can therefore be considered the intersection of queer as a verb and queer as an adjective: giving an account of queer highlights the radical process of reconsidering identity politics (verb) so as to describe and articulate the self as an ongoing negotiation working through the politics of identity (adjective). Accordingly, *the queering of straight teachers* reconsiders "straight" identities (identity politics) in order to expose the "straight" self as an implicated subject of circulating norms (politics of identity)—becoming queerly intelligible.

Consequently, I explore how straight teachers can give an account of queer in a society that produces normative subjects through the processes of subjection (Foucault) and interpellation (Althusser). Answering the questions *how can straight teachers become queerly intelligible* and *how can straight teachers give an account of queer* can begin with an exploration of how ("straight") subjects are formed and informed in society—the subjectivation of subjects—thus asking *why is the straight teacher*. The works of Foucault, Althusser, and Butler are primarily used to expose the processes of subjectivation. Therefore, Butler's question "How are we formed within social life, and at what cost?"[20] is placed at the core of this *queering* so as to present how straight teachers can become queerly intelligible through giving an account of queer—a disruptive account stressing the radical politics of implication.

Foucault, Subjection, and the *Ab / Normal* Subject

The process of exploring how straight teachers can give an account of queer— a temporary account of a momentary subjective positioning that reworks exclusionary normative discourses—includes an examination of how ("straight") subjects come into being: *assujettissement* (subjectivation). In *The Psychic Life of Power*, Butler (1997) explores Foucault's notion of subjection as a necessary articulation of how (social) subjects are constituted through discourses of power. Butler describes subjection as follows:

> Subjection is, literally, the *making* of a subject, the principle of regulation according to which a subject is formulated or produced. Such subjection is a kind of power that not only unilaterally *acts on* a given individual as a form of domination, but also *activates* or forms the subject. (p. 84)

In other words, subjects simultaneously reproduce the same discourses that constitute their intelligibility: in order to be an intelligible subject, a subject must reproduce normative discourses; as a result, normative discourses can not exist without their reproduction. The discourses of power that circulate in society *form* and *inform* the subject through a gaze of objective power. The circulation of power, therefore, not only acts as a disciplinary agent that conditions subjects—for example, the production of "straight" and "gay" teachers—but also acts as a necessary tool for the engagement of agency among subjects—how "straight" and "gay" teachers negotiate their identities in social spaces. The disciplinary practices that in/form subjects—for example, hierarchical observations, normalizing judgments, and examinations explored in *Discipline and Punish* (Foucault, 1977)—administer power over the subject as well as create and maintain a continuous state of dependency on these disciplinary practices. The notion of subjection, therefore, produces dependent subjects that are intelligible through the reproduction of normalized discourses: discourses that are produced through disciplinary powers that constitute the "normal" subject. The straight teacher exists only through the reproduction of normalized practices that constitute a "straight" teacher. In other words, the straight teacher becomes intelligible by reproducing the "straight" norms that are discursively policed by disciplinary powers. The key concern with practices of subjection is its necessary ability to create and reproduce unequal subject positions in order to maintain intelligible subjects; for example, the obedient and disobedient prisoner (Foucault). This can also be noted if the examination of straight teachers (normal) is placed next to an examination of gay teachers (abnormal).[21] The production of norms in disciplinary power and the reproduction of norms through subjection attempt to maintain coherent subjects that are socially responsible to and in society: the coherent straight teacher is one who is able to successfully reproduce the identity norms of straight.[22] Furthermore, the failure to reproduce such norms results in the minoritization and subordination of subjects: the binary of the "normal" subject is the "abnormal" subject. As Butler states:

> The subject is compelled to repeat the norms by which it is produced, but that repetition establishes a domain of risk, for if one fails to reinstate the norm 'in the right way,' one comes subject to further sanction, one feels the prevailing conditions of existence threatened. (1997, pp. 28–29)

The production of "normal" subjects as a *re*production of normative discourses embedded in practices of disciplinary power presents the body as a negotiable commodity that is discursively produced through power. In concurrence with Butler, power, in the form of subjection, is something that "precedes the subject, effecting and subordinating the subject from the outside" (p. 13). However, in considering the subject as an integral component of the production of power and normative discourses—the concept of subjection—the subject, then, maintains a sense of agency through its re/production of power and normative discourses. Therefore, although the subject is the site for the "reiteration"[23] of disciplinary power, it is through this reiteration that the subject can engage agency: straight teachers can trouble inequitable practices that support heteronormativity through the process of reiteration—or lack of reiteration.

The notion of subjection is one account of how subjects are produced as un/intelligible: one account of how straight teachers are constituted as intelligible subjects. Foucault's emphasis on disciplinary power and the reproduction of circulating norms can provide a framework for working toward the possibility of straight teachers becoming queerly intelligible. Consequently, understanding the process of subjection—how subjects are constituted as intelligible subjects—can create spaces to disturb the reproduction of normative practices. Straight teachers can give an account of queer through understanding how they are constituted as intelligible subjects that reproduce normative ideologies that privilege some and subordinate others. Giving an account of queer is therefore a theoretical and epistemological exploration of how straight teachers can radically reconceptualize their intelligibility so as to disrupt normative discourses that reproduce binary conceptions of the self.

Althusser, Interpellation, and the *Grammatical* Subject

Becoming queerly intelligible by giving an account of queer cannot rely solely on Foucault's notion of subjection, since Foucauldian subjects work within the discursive confinements of normative discourses that reproduce their un/intelligibility. In addition to exposing how subjects are constituted through power (subjection), it is also critical to recognize how subjects are "hailed" into being through ideology—Althusser's notion of interpellation. It is through this recognition—how subjects are constituted through subjection *and* interpellation—that straight teachers can begin to become queerly intelligible and therefore give an account of a disruptive radical politic—of queer.

In "Ideology and Ideological State Apparatus," Althusser (2001) suggests that "*all ideology hails or interpellates concrete individuals as concrete subjects*"

(p. 117). In Althusser's infamous allegory of an individual becoming a subject through the process of being hailed by a police officer, it becomes clear that "ideology 'acts' or 'functions' in such a way that it 'recruits' subjects among the individuals...or 'transforms' the individual into subjects" (p. 118).[24] The hailing of an individual by the police officer constitutes the subject in a particular ideology: "By this mere one-hundred-and-eighty-degree physical conversion, he becomes a *subject*" (p. 118). The process of transforming an individual into a subject—Althusser's interpellation—requires two critical elements of subject-constitution: (1) the subject who hails the individual has prior knowledge as to where and who the hail should be directed; and (2) the individual who is being hailed has prior knowledge to recognize the hail. Althusser's notion of interpellation highlights the critical element of *naming* in the process of subject constitution. The straight teacher is similarly hailed into being through interpellation: the labeling of a teacher as "straight" ideologically transforms the teacher into a "straight" teacher. When a student calls on teacher *X* with the title *Mrs.*, the student who hails the teacher has prior knowledge that assumes the proper title and the teacher who is being hailed has prior knowledge to recognize the hail of the student. Both the hailer (student) and the hailed (teacher) constitute what it means to be a *Mrs.* In doing so, the titles *Ms.*, *Miss*, and *Mr.* are also ideologically reproduced: *Mrs.* is intelligible because it is not *Ms.*, *Miss*, and *Mr.* Therefore, in addition to appreciating how subjects are constituted through subjection, it is also important to explore how naming vis-à-vis interpellation also re/produces normative ideologies. In this case, the student reproduces normative ideologies through the process of hailing the teacher with a particular title and the teacher reproduces normative ideologies by recognizing and associating oneself with the title.

Althusser's notion of interpellation is embedded in *speech acts*.[25] The process of hailing an individual into subjecthood requires an articulation on behalf of the hailer. I agree with Butler's following claim in *Excitable Speech* (1997): Althusser's interpellation suggests that "the speech act that brings the subject into linguistic existence precedes the subject in question" (p. 24).[26] The speech that is articulated by the hailer—a speech that exists prior to its articulation[27]—is recognized by the subject, and through this recognition, the subject assumes the hailing in order to exist as an intelligible "I" in that particular interaction. *Mrs. X* enters (linguistic) subjecthood by assuming the hailing of the student—the subject becomes an intelligible "I." Speech acts, then, are forms of *performativity*, where there is no origin of articulation—speech is renegotiated the moment it interacts with the subject (p. 40).[28] Along with being subjected to power discourses, the body is also defined through language vis-à-vis the performatives of speech acts. In addition to demonstrating how language can be a form of violence (i.e., hate speech) as it constitutes minoritized subjects,[29] Butler also suggests that *censorship* is always an integral part of the production of subjects through interpellation:

> Censorship is a productive form of power: it is not merely privative, but formative as well. I propose that censorship seeks to produce subjects according to explicit and implicit norms, and that the production of the subject has everything to do with the regulation of speech. The subject's production takes place not only through the regulation of that subject's speech, but through the regulation of the social domain of speakable discourse. (1997, p. 133)

The censorship, as articulated by Butler, re/produces norms through the interpellation of individuals into subjecthood. The implicit and explicit norms that are produced and reproduced through hailing maintain normative discourses that are negotiated through bodies—discourses that create and support the "normal" (grammatical)[30] subject. The straight teacher, therefore, maintains its intelligibility as a "normal" subject through the numerous ideological interpellations that reproduce "straight" norms. The process of exposing how subjects are constituted through interpellation raises a critical concern when working toward the possibility of straight teachers giving an account of queer: as Butler states, the site of critical disruption is not which speech acts are and are not censored, "but how a certain operation of censorship determines who will be a subject depending on whether the speech of such a candidate for subjecthood obeys norms governing what is speakable and what is not" (p. 133). In other words, *who* becomes a straight teacher and *why*. The re/production of (implicit and explicit) norms in the speech acts of interpellation (Althusser), similar to the re/production of discursive norms in the process of subjection (Foucault), re/produce a binary relation of "normal" and "abnormal" subjects—majoritized and minoritized subjects. The hailing of individuals into subjecthood through speech acts and the constitution of subjects through disciplinary power are both critical sites of subjectivation. Foucault and Althusser's exploration of subjectivation provide an understanding of how subjects are normalized in the reproduction of discourses vis-à-vis disciplinary practices and speech acts that circulate "norms." The recognition of how subjects are ab/normalized through subjectivation is of great importance for the ability of straight teachers to become queerly intelligible for it provides a process for straight teachers to (temporarily) commit themselves to in order to disrupt the normative processes that constitute their "straight" intelligibility.

Butler, Accounts, and the *Ethical* Subject

The re/production of norms in the modes of subjectivation offered by Foucault and Althusser offer different lenses for understanding how "individuals" enter subjecthood—how "individuals" become "straight" teachers. In *Giving an Account of Oneself*, Butler (2005) explores the "social and linguistic conditions" that provide subjects with an ethical sense of self—an "I" that accounts for itself only through the relational and temporary associations with the other. The ethical conditions offered in *Giving an Account of Oneself*, in conjunction with Foucault and Althusser's modes of subjectivation, expose how subjects are called into being—a call that, in agreement with Butler, requires the subject to give an account of itself. The incorporation of Butler's moral philosophy is critical for straight teachers to become queerly intelligible in a normative society that re/produces binary relations through various modes of subjectivation. It is through an exploration of Butler's account of the "I" that straight teachers can begin to consider how to give an account of queer—an account that will always be temporal and relational.

Giving an Account of Oneself places the "I" at the core of subjecthood. The "I," however, is not an autonomous position that is and/or can be viewed outside of subjectivation. On the contrary, the "I" is a site of relation and negotiation; the "I" is never stable and therefore can never be fully definable. The circulation of norms, as suggested above, are re/produced as performatives—norms change the moment the subject engages it. Consequently, the "I" is continuously re/produced through its encounters with norms and at the same time, norms are re/produced through their encounters with the "I" (2005, p. 7). Therefore, when the "I" gives an account of itself "it will find that this self is already implicated in a social temporality that exceeds its own capacities for narration" (p. 8). Similar to how subjects are the objective lens of disciplinary

power (Foucault) and interpellation (Althusser), the "I" is also a malleable positioning that is re/produced when it gives an account of itself. Butler's conception of the relationship between the self and the other is similar to the
interactions among subjects and disciplinary power and speech acts, where
these processes are all modes of subjectivation that constitute the subject's
intelligibility as a social being.

The circulation of norms, as discussed by Foucault, Althusser, and Butler,
is a foundational ingredient in subjectivation. Consequently, the subject is
formed through the circulation of norms that make an intelligible subject. As
Butler states, "[t]here is no making of oneself (*poiesis*) outside of a mode of subjectivation (*assujettissement*) and, hence, no self-making outside of the norms
that orchestrate the possible forms that a subject may take" (p. 17). The "set of
codes, prescriptions, or norms" that circulate in subjectivation maintain cohesive identities through the reproduction of fixed and stable signifiers. As a result, the straight teacher is not a displaced and independent self that
constitutes "straight" norms, but is instead constituted by continuously
re/negotiated norms: "straight identities" become intelligible through the
re/production of circulating norms. According to Butler, norms are necessary
relations that provide spaces for subjects to engage with each other, where
they "work not only to direct...conduct but to condition the possible emergence of an encounter between [the self] and the other" (p. 25). Therefore,
since the "I" negotiates and re/produces norms through the self in relation to
the other, the "I" then becomes a site where norms are articulated—the "I" is
the agent of norms (p. 26). The "straight" "I" of a teacher is the site where
norms are articulated—the "straight" "I" is an agent. Therefore, the "I" is not a
representation of norms but is its articulation. Accounts of the "normal" self,
then, are not *true* accounts of an essential "I." There is no essential "straightness" to straight teachers outside of the circulating norms that constitute the
"straight" "I." Instead, the seemingly fixed and stable "I" is a negotiation of
norms that are temporarily produced as performatives. Therefore, what is
considered the "normal" "I" is also an articulation of mobile and fluid representations. Accounting for the self, then, is not an individual articulation. On
the contrary, accounts of the self are always socially negotiated. According to
Butler,

> An account of oneself is always given to another, whether conjured or existing, and this other establishes the scene of address as a more primary ethical relation than a reflexive effort to give an account of oneself. Moreover, the very terms by which we give an account, by which we make ourselves intelligible to ourselves and to others, are not of our making. They are social in character, and they establish social norms, a domain of unfreedom and substitutability within which our 'singular' stories are told. (p. 21)

Accounts of the self, then, are not articulations of essential truths of the "I," for truths are always constructed through the circulating norms in subjectivation that are articulated through accounts of the "I." This is not to suggest that there is no *truth* to the self per se. It suggests that the *truths* of the self are socially negotiated as unstable signifiers of norms—norms that are never fully attainable.

Giving an account of oneself is an articulation of circulating norms that are re/produced through the various modes of subjectivation. In addition, accounts are always an address of truth to the other. Butler claims that an account of oneself is always an account of *dispossession*:

> No account takes place outside the structure of address, even if the addressee remains implicit and unnamed, anonymous and unspecified. The address establishes the account as an account, and so the account is completed only on the occasion when it is effectively exported and expropriated from the domain of what is my own. It is only in dispossession that I can and do give any account of myself. (2005, pp. 36–37)

The relationship between the self and the explicit or implicit other is one that negotiates and re/produces the norms that make a subject intelligible. *Mrs. X* becomes intelligible through the relationship with *student X* as seen through the reproduction of norms vis-à-vis the use of a particular title. Accounts of the "I," therefore, are never true "narrative" accounts that are unique to the self.[31] In contrast, accounts of the self are re/articulations of performatives (norms) that have no specific essence to a particular subject: "The narrative authority of the 'I' must give way to the perspective and temporality of a set of norms that contest the singularity of my story" (p. 37). The act of *Mrs. X* writing "Mrs. X" on a blackboard is not an articulation of *Mrs. X*'s essential "I," but is a re/articulation of norms that constitute *Mrs. X*. Therefore, accounts of experience are always articulations of a *truth* of the self in relation to the other while being oriented through norms. As such, there are no *origins* of narrative accounts—only emergences of subjective negotiations.[32] Consequently, accounts of a coherent self as a fixed identity is problematic and arguably idealistic (if not impossible), for the intelligibility of the self is never stable considering how the "I" comes into being through subjectivation: the intelligibility of a "straight" teacher as a completely coherent and fixed subject is an idealistic impossibility. The result of accounting for the self as a coherent identity is what Butler calls an *ethical violence*.[33] The violence of (supposedly) coherent identities, as articulated through accounts of the "normal" self, results in the need for straight teachers to become queerly intelligible—to give an account of queer. In order to explore how straight teachers can give an account of queer—an account that is brought into being through subjectivation and negotiated through norms—the "straight" "I" can be reworked as an implicated social articulation of temporary norms that can expose the *ethical violence* of coherent accounts of the self.

Exposing the *Techniques / Technologies* of the Temporary "I"

A radical disruption of the coherent/normal self can create social spaces that are equitable: spaces that can appreciate the discontinuity, mobility, and instability of subjective identifications embedded in notions of difference. In addition to exposing how subjectivation produces norms that are reproduced through negotiations with the other and articulated as accounts of the "I," it is necessary to demonstrate how the self can be considered a technique/technology.[34]

In "Subjectivity and Truth," Foucault (1994) asks what it means to "know one self" (p. 88). An appreciation of the techniques/technologies[35] of the self can provide a critical lens to explore the social practices that govern bodies. Techniques/technologies of the self express the relationship between the embodiments of subjects in society and the discursive practices that regulate the body as an intelligible "I." The techniques/technologies that produce intelligible subjects place the body at the core of subjectivation, where, according to Foucault, the body is not meant to "be discovered but to be constituted, to be constituted through the force of truth" (1993, p. 203). The placement of bodies at the center of subjectivation vis-à-vis the techniques/technologies of the self create new spaces to reconsider the "I." Exposing the politics of the body, as articulated through the *procedures* and *reflections* of techniques/technologies of the self, respectively, stimulate a realization that the self is never a stable being that can be fully articulated, nor discussed outside of the realms of subjectivation and normative discourses. Therefore, giving an account of the self is not an articulation of identity politics. It is an exposition of the politics of identity seen through the techniques/technologies of the self—a self that is the objective lens of subjectivation. As Foucault states:

> Maybe the problem of the self is not to discover what it is in its positivity, maybe the problem is not to discover a positive self or the positive foundation of the self. Maybe our problem is not to discover that the self is nothing else than the historical correlation of the technology built in our history. Maybe the problem is to change those technologies. And in this case, one of the main political problems would be nowadays, in the strict sense of the word, the politics of ourselves. (pp. 222–223)

The *procedures/reflections* of techniques/technologies of the self, respectively, can encourage subjects to disrupt the normative practices that constitute social bodies. An understanding of how bodies become social subjects is vital for straight teachers to give an account of queer, where, as Foucault states, "the target nowadays is not to discover what we are, but to refuse what we are" (1994, p. 336). Giving an account of queer is not a reproduction of existing technologies/techniques of the self. Giving an account of queer is not an absorption of a preexisting "queer identity." On the contrary, it is a radical reworking of how techniques/technologies of the self negotiate and articulate norms through the *procedures/reflections* of the self as an unstable, unfixed, and somewhat unrecognizable subject.

Giving an Account of Queer

Judith Butler's question "How are we formed within social life, and at what cost?" has been the primary focus of this chapter. The intersection of Foucault's *disciplinary power*, Althusser's *interpellation*, and Butler's *accounts* provide a unique lens into how subjects are constituted: all three modes of subjectivation are critical to understanding how subjects (straight teachers) are produced, hailed, and accounted for in social spaces. It has been articulated that the subjectivation of subjects—the processes in which subjects are produced—are negotiated through discursive norms that are articulated from the self and through the other as performatives, where the "I" is asked to give an account in order for it to be intelligible. The norms that circulate through subjects, however, are re/produced as *coherent* "identities" that are fixed and stable articulations of binary associations. If *queer* is a radical politic that disturbs stable identities so as to appreciate a multiplicity of differences among subjects vis-à-vis mobile and fluid identifications, how can straight teachers become queerly intelligible in normative discourses that resist a radical politic? How can queer become intelligible in normative discourses of (straight) "identity," where stable and fixed identities are produced and maintained through exclusionary norms? How can queer become a radical politic that commits itself to normative discourses so as to disrupt normative ideologies? *How can straight teachers give an account of queer?*

The radical politic of queer can interrogate normative ideologies that reproduce norms through its strategic and temporary positioning as an implicated norm in the practices that prohibit its radical existence. The accounts articulated by straight teachers are therefore not accounts of an essential, fixed, or stable "I." Giving an account of queer is a radical temporary articulation that can expose how the "straight" "I" is implicated in the reproduction of circulating norms. Giving an account of queer as a temporary and implicated norm is not a positioning that strives to become a stable signifier of normative discourses. On the contrary, since norms are re/produced through the interactions of subjects, it is through giving an account of queer that queer can become a *momentary* norm that can rework the discourses that exclude its being as a positioning outside of binary conceptions. Consequently, straight teachers do not become intelligibly queer, but become queerly intelligible.[36] Although the politic of queer and the queering of politics resist all forms of normalization, giving an account of queer as an implicated and temporary norm is everything but a stable and fixed account: straight teachers do not assume a queer "identity"—if a *queer identity* is even desirable or possible.[37] On the contrary, giving an account of queer as an implicated norm is radically strategic through its momentary commitments to the negotiations of norms so as to disrupt the modes of subjectivation that re/produce intelligible subjects in society. *Mrs. X* can therefore give an account of queer by exposing how the "*Mrs.*" is an implicated (identity) norm that constitutes the "*X*" as an intelligible subject. Consequently, straight teachers can become queerly intelligible by becoming radical subjects that re/negotiate new "norms" that are unstable, unfixed, and indefinable.

The radical process of straight teachers giving an account of queer can destabilize the practices/ideologies that re/produce norms as cohesive intelligibilities that maintain "normal" subjects—the "straightness" of straight teachers, for example. The examination of subjectivation creates opportunities to recognize that there are no *straight* teachers per se. Instead, there are teachers who negotiate "straight" norms that translate into seemingly fixed and stable "straight" identities through the ongoing re/production of circulating norms vis-à-vis accounts of the self. Straight teachers can become queerly intelligible through momentary commitments to the processes of subjectivation as a radically political norm of disruption. As such, the re/production of queer as a norm is not a binary to nonqueer—the queerly intelligible straight teacher is not a binary to a straight teacher—but is a binary to the ideology of binaries as a temporary norm that can disrupt how subjects are implicated in exclusionary discourses. In other words, the queerly intelligible straight teacher is a binary to the ideology of (identity) binaries. Giving an account of queer recognizes that the "I" is never fully achievable for it is always partially constituted as a performative that is *re*constituted the moment it interacts with norms: becoming queerly intelligible is a radical process that is continuously being re/negotiated, where the "I" can never be fully constituted or knowable. The "narrative" accounts of the straight "I" are always unique to the subject and at the same time can never be unique to the subject: giving an account of "straight" is always a socially re/produced account. Giving an account of queer, however, is an account of implication: it is an articulation of what the "I" is not and what the "I" can never be—not what the "I" is and what the "I" can be. Radical agency as the articulation of implicated norms—what Butler considers the "I"—is then the intersecting disruptions of the multiple modes of subjectivation. If straight teachers are to become queerly intelligible, it is critical to resist normalization into binary ideologies while temporarily committing and reworking normative processes: giving an account of queer involves momentary commitments that insert queer ideologies into the crevices of normative discourses so as to rework a "new" (queer) disruptive norm that can be reproduced as a mobile and fluid identification—an identification that can never be fully knowable or completely coherent.

The radical process of straight teachers becoming queerly intelligible by giving an account of queer coincides with queer theory's critical shift from identity to identification. Giving an account of queer is a disruptive practice that temporarily commits itself to circulating norms so as to expose how the "I" is implicated in normative ideologies that subordinate the minoritized and privilege the majoritized. Becoming queerly intelligible can rework the modes of subjectivation that maintain binary conceptions of the self—fixed and stable identities that remain unbalanced and unequal in order to exist. The modes of subjectivation offered in this chapter—that of Foucault, Althusser, and Butler—provide snapshots into some of the interpretations of how subjects, primarily straight teachers, are constituted as intelligible. Giving an account of queer can be a strategic positioning that engages radical projects that resist exclusionary normative discourses. The radical reworking of ("identity") norms vis-à-vis giving an account of queer can create new discursive spaces to stimulate *queer intelligibilities*—intelligibilities that can radically expose the body in a third space outside of binary ideologies.

Notes

1. I share an understanding of the "I" with Jean Bobby Noble's articulations in *Sons of the Movement* (2006): "articulating one's self as a subject (engendered, racialized, sexed, nationed, classed, etc.) is the process through which we learn to identify our 'I' relative to bodies, power grids, as well as culturally available categories like pronouns, and then attempt to become that configuration" (p. 23).

2. The relationships among identities, identifications, and disidentifications are fully explored in the following texts: Butler, 1990; Fuss, 1995; Munoz, 1999.

3. My use of the word *normative* reflects the production of "norms" in the processes of subjection (Foucault) and interpellation (Althusser).

4. This is primarily noted in binary ideologies where one term excludes its binary other to uphold its privileged status: X is X because X is not Y. For example, heterosexuality is heterosexuality because it is not homosexuality.

5. My use of quotations here and throughout this chapter suggests a *queering* of the term straight. This paper uses queer ideologies to trouble fixed and stable identities (i.e., straight) to work toward exploring the self as a mobile and fluid negotiation embedded in difference and implication.

6. My use of the word *intelligible* throughout this chapter refers to the ways in which subjects negotiate themselves in the social: how subjects are capable (or incapable) of negotiating their subjective positions so as to successfully (or unsuccessfully) navigate their sense of self among social subjects.

7. The use of the phrase "give an account" (and its variations throughout the chapter) is a reflection of Butler's articulations in *Giving an Account of Oneself* (2005).

8. Becoming *queerly intelligible* is a radical process where straight teachers can reconsider how their "I" is constituted: troubling and exposing how the privileged status of the "straight" "I" is a result of circulating norms. Therefore, becoming *queerly intelligible* focuses on how all subjects are implicated in norms that privilege the majoritized and subordinate the minoritized.

9. See 1990, pp. 22–33.

10. Suggested readings that inform queer theory: Butler, 1990; Foucault, 1978; Jagose, 1996; Morland & Willox, 2005; Pinar, 1998; Sedgwick, 1990; Sullivan, 2003; Warner, 1993; Wilchins, 2004.

11. Butler defines the account as "an act—situated within a larger practice of acts—that one performs for, to, even *on* an other, an allocutory deed, an acting for, and in the face of, the other and sometimes by virtue of the language provided by the other" (2005, p. 130).

12. Sedgwick's use of term *A* and term *B* can replace any binary (identity) categorization.

13. See Warner, 1993.

14. Therefore, in considering *queer* as a verb (i.e., a radical process), it is critical that queer not be an articulation of an umbrella term for minoritized sexualities.

15. Dennis Carlson also explores the politics of identity through the lens of "gay and queer identity politics" in his essay "Who Am I? Gay Identity and a Democratic Politics of the Self" (1998).

16. See, for example, Britzman, 1995, 2000; Bryson & de Castell, 1997; de Castell & Bryson, 1998; Luhmann, 1998; Morris, 1998.

17. There is therefore a critical difference between replacing "straight" with "queer" and giving an account *of* queer: whereas replacing "straight" with "queer" works within the realm of identities (identity politics), giving an account of queer focuses on how the "I" is implicated in identity norms (politics of identity). This critical shift is discussed throughout the chapter.

18. See, for example, Kirsch, 2000.

19. My use of the word *embodiment* coincides with the notion that bodies and culture are dialogically produced. Therefore, there is no clear and distinct differentiation between bodies and culture, as they are produced dialogically. The embodiment of queer is a radical dialogical process of engaging queer ideologies through bodies and culture. A discussion of the dialogical can be found in the works of Bakhtin (1981, 1984).

20. Butler poses this question at the conclusion of her text *Giving and Account of Oneself* (2005, p. 136).

21. This is clearly not to suggest that gay is abnormal (if there is or can ever be a definition of ab/normal). It highlights, however, how binary ideologies and therefore terminologies always have subordinated and privileged positions: one term cannot exist without the other.

22. The adverb used here (*successfully*) clearly has no definitive measurement. However, for the purposes of this chapter, the *successful* straight teacher will be one who is not considered a gay teacher. Although this dichotomy is oversimplified, the oversimplification strategically exemplifies the inequitable associations of identity politics.

23. According to Butler, agency can be found through disrupting the reiteration of power: "Power is never merely a condition external or prior to the subject, nor can it be exclusively identified with the subject. If conditions of power are to persist, they must be reiterated; the subject is precisely the site of such reiteration, a repetition that is never merely mechanical" (p. 16).

24. See pp. 115–120.

25. My references throughout this section to *speech acts* are taken from Butler's *Excitable Speech* (1997).

26. On the contrary, in *Giving an Account of Oneself*, Butler suggests that speech and subject emerge at the same time.

27. "The one who speaks is not the originator of such speech, for that subject is produced in language through a prior performative exercise of speech: interpellation" (p. 39).

28. For a thorough discussion of performativity, see Butler (1990, 1993).

29. "The utterances of hate speech are part of the continuous and uninterrupted process to which we are subjects, an on-going subjection (*assujettissement*) that is the very operation of interpellation, that continually repeated action of discourse by which subjects are formed in subjugation" (p. 27).

30. My use of the word *grammatical* echoes Butler's articulation that "the subject exists only as a grammatical fiction" prior to its interpellation as a subject (p. 135).

31. For example, accounts based on one's experience are not *true* articulations of an experience that is unique or owned by a particular subject. On the contrary, "narrative" accounts, as Butler suggests, can only be understood as temporary and relational.

32. For a discussion of *origins* and *emergences*, see Foucault, 1998.

33. "Suspending the demand for self-identity or, more particularly, for complete coherence seems to me to counter a certain ethical violence, which demands that we manifest and maintain self-identity at all times and require that others do the same. For subjects who invariably live within a temporal horizon, this is a difficult, if not impossible, norm to satisfy" (p. 42).

34. A thorough exploration of techniques/technologies of the self can be found in Foucault's "Technologies of the Self" (1994a) and "Subjectivity and Truth" (1994b). Although Foucault compares *techniques* and *technologies* in these pieces, for the purposes of this chapter, I will use them both—techniques/technologies—as he does in "About the Beginning of the Hermeneutics of the Self" (1993).

35. Although I am not explicitly differentiating *techniques* from *technologies* of the self in this chapter, it is appropriate to note how Foucault discusses them: Techniques of the self are "the procedures...suggested or prescribed to individuals in order to determine their identity, maintain it, or transform it in terms of a certain number of ends, through relations of self-mastery or self-knowledge" (p. 88); technologies of the self are the "reflection[s] on modes of living, on choices of existence, on the way to regulate one's behavior, to attach oneself to ends and means" (p. 89).

36. In other words, straight teachers do not assume a new *identity* position, for *queer* is nego-tiated in a third space outside of binaries.

37. I am suggesting here that a *queer "identity"* is an idealistic impossibility as queer ideologies resist fixed and stable notions of the self-identities. In some respects, a *queer* "identity" is an oxymoron.

Works Cited

Althusser, L. (2001). *Lenin and philosophy and other essays.* New York: Monthly Review Press.

Bakhtin, M. M. (1981). *The dialogic imagination: Four essays by M.M. Bakhtin.* M. Holquist (Ed.), C. Emerson & M. Holquist (Trans.). Austin, TX: University of Texas Press.

Bakhtin, M. M. (1984). *Rabelais and his world.* Helene Iswolsky (Trans.). Foreword by Krystyna Pomorska. Bloomington, IN: Indiana University Press.

Britzman, D. P. (1995). Is there a queer pedagogy? Or, stop readings straight. *Educational Theory*, 45(2), 151–165.

Britzman, D. P. (2000). Precocious education. In S. Talburt & S. R. Steinberg (Eds.), *Thinking queer: Sexuality, culture, and education* (pp. 33–60). New York: Peter Lang.

Bryson, M., & de Castell, S. (1997). Queer pedagogy? Praxis makes im/perfect. In S. de Castell & M. Bryson (Eds.), *Radical in<ter>ventions: Identity, politics, and difference/s in educational praxis* (pp. 269–293). Albany: State University of New York.

Butler, J. (1990). *Gender trouble.* New York: Routledge.

Butler, J. (1993). *Bodies that matter: On the discursive limits of "sex."* New York: Routledge.

Butler, J. (1997). *Excitable speech: A politics of the performative.* New York: Routledge.

Butler, J. (1997). *The psychic life of power: Theories in subjection.* Stanford, CA: Stanford University Press.

Butler, J. (2005). *Giving an account of oneself.* New York: Fordham University Press.

Carlson, D. (1998). Who am I? Gay identity and a democratic politics of the self. In W. F. Pinar (Ed.), *Queer theory in education* (pp. 107–119). Mahwah, NJ: Lawrence Erlbaum Associates.

de Castell, S., & Bryson, M. (1998). From the ridiculous to the sublime: On finding oneself in educational research. In W. F. Pinar (Ed.), *Queer theory in education* (pp. 245–250). Mahwah, NJ: Lawrence Erlbaum Associates.

Foucault, M. (1977). *Discipline and punish: The birth of the prison.* New York: Random House.

Foucault, M. (1978). *The history of sexuality: An introduction (Vol. 1).* New York: Random House.

Foucault, M. (1993). About the beginning of the hermeneutics of the self. *Political Theory*, 21(2), 198–227.

Foucault, M. (1994). The subject and power. In J. Faubion (Ed.), *Michel Foucault: Power* (pp. 326–348). New York: The New Press.

Foucault, M. (1994a). Technologies of the self. In J. Faubion (Ed.), *Michel Foucault: Ethics, subjectivity and truth* (pp. 223–251). New York: The New Press.

Foucault, M. (1994b). Subjectivity and truth. In J. Faubion (Ed.), *Michel Foucault: Ethics, subjectivity and truth* (pp. 87–92). New York: The New Press.

Foucault, M. (1998). Nietzsche, genealogy, history. In J. D. Faubion (Ed.), *Michel Foucault: Aesthetics, method, and epistemology* (pp. 369–391). New York: The New Press.

Fuss, D. (1995). *Identification papers*. New York: Routledge.

Jagose, A. (1996). *Queer theory: An introduction*. New York: New York University Press.

Kirsch, M. H. (2000). *Queer theory and social change*. New York: Routledge.

Luhmann, S. (1998). Queering/querying pedagogy? Or, pedagogy is a pretty queer thing. In W. F. Pinar (Ed.), *Queer theory in education* (pp. 141–155). Mahwah, NJ: Lawrence Erlbaum Associates.

Morland, I., & Willox, A. (2005). Introduction. In *Queer theory* (pp. 1–5). New York: Palgrave.

Morris, M. (1998). Unresting the curriculum: Queer projects, queer imaginings. In W. F. Pinar (Ed.), *Queer theory in education* (pp. 275–286). Mahwah, NJ: Lawrence Erlbaum Associates.

Munoz, J. E. (1999). *Disidentifications: Queers of color and the performance of politics*. Minneapolis: University of Minnesota Press.

Noble, J. B. (2006). *Sons of the movement: FtMs risking incoherence on a post-queer cultural landscape*. Toronto: Women's Press.

Pinar, W. F. (1998). Introduction. In W. F. Pinar (Ed.), *Queer theory in education* (pp. 1–47). Mahwah, NJ: Lawrence Erlbaum Associates.

Sedgwick, E. K. (1990). *Epistemology of the closet*. Berkeley: University of California Press.

Sullivan, N. (2003). *A critical introduction to queer theory*. New York: New York University Press.

Warner, M. (1993). Introduction. In M. Warner (Ed.), *Fear of a queer planet: Queer politics and social theory* (pp. vii–xxxi). Minneapolis: University of Minnesota Press.

Wilchins, R. (2004). *Queer theory, gender theory*. Los Angeles, CA: Alyson.

CHAPTER ELEVEN

Queer Theory and the Discourse on Queer(ing) Heterosexuality: Pedagogical Considerations

Nelson M. Rodriguez

> The challenge in this sort of debate is to use humor to try to show that in some ways these people are ridiculous but not to the point where people forget that it's very serious. I mean ridiculous people can unfortunately do serious harm.
> Representative Barney Frank—from *Let's Get Frank*

The above epigraph is from a recent film by Bart Everly (2006), *Let's Get Frank*, a documentary that chronicles Representative Barney Frank's personal life and political career, especially during the Clinton impeachment hearings. In this section of the documentary, Frank appears on the *Charles Grodin Show*, with then Representative Bob Barr, to discuss and debate the topic of removing government officials from office for sexual impropriety. Frank and Barr were, of course, discussing this topic on national television in light of being embroiled in, albeit on opposite sides of, the debate within the House of Representatives to recommend that Clinton be impeached from the Office of the Presidency. The conversation takes a funny turn after Frank speaks about his own sexual scandal and misrepresentation of his sexual orientation back in the late 1980s. Indeed, after that conversation, Charles Grodin turns to Bob Barr and asks: "Have you ever misrepresented your sex life?" To which Barr responds: "No; I'm not gay, and I've never maintained that I'm gay." Grodin then follows up with: "Would you consider becoming gay?" And Frank quickly interjects with: "No; we'd vote against that. We had a meeting and rejected his application." It is at this point in the documentary that Frank comments on this exchange between himself, Barr, and Grodin, with: "The challenge in this sort of debate is to use humor to try to show that in some ways these people are ridiculous but not to the point where people forget that it's very serious. I mean ridiculous people can unfortunately do serious harm." Commenting here in part on the Clinton impeachment hearings, Frank suggests that the hearings, and the sexual panic which they triggered, were no less absurd than the "ridiculous people" who feverishly committed themselves to impeaching a highly popular, sitting President for lying about receiving oral sex from a White House intern. Regarding the politics of sexuality on a broader level, however, Frank's comment is significant in two ways. First, through his use of humor, Frank insightfully intimates that conservative sexual politics often function by *constructing* crises around sex and sexuality. And second, although people who instigate and politically and morally try to capitalize on such crises might indeed be "ridiculous," they nevertheless, as Frank smartly reminds us, "can unfortunately do serious harm."

I begin with Frank's humor, wit, and thoughtful commentary about the harmful effects that can flow from the irrational and hyperbolic politics of right-wing sexual moralizing in order to carve out a general distinction between two classes of straight people, and the "serious harm" from each, that we gay, lesbian, bisexual, transgender, queer (GLBTQ) folks face. On the one hand, there are heterosexuals who would no doubt do us physical and psychological harm; or, put another way, there are gays of all stripes worldwide who face on a daily basis a range of forms of "heterosexual terrorism"—for example, the little boy who relentlessly is called "fag" and bullied on the playground for not complying with the scripts of hegemonic heterosexual masculinity; or the teen who is made homeless by homophobic, cruel, and holier-than-thou parents for having the courage to come out and live openly as lesbian, gay, bisexual or transgendered; and the barbaric public execution by hanging of two young gay men in Iran in front of a screaming hateful mob. In each of these examples, the outcome of the harm that is done at the hands of some heterosexuals is a literal and/or symbolic expelling of the gay "Other" for not adhering to the dictates of what Adrienne Rich (2003) back in 1980 aptly termed "compulsory heterosexuality." On the other hand, there are many straights who do not react violently to our presence, nor do they go out of their way necessarily to cause us harm. No, these straights often do not act in any mean-spirited way, yet their actions still so often maintain heterosexual hegemony and its harmful effects—for example, the in-law who "forgets" to ask for a picture of you and your partner to place on the mantle alongside all the other pictures of heterosexually paired couples in your family; or the ways in which one's heterosexual colleagues don't ever quite know what to make of that "queer theory stuff"—or described a bit differently by drawing on the humorous insight of gay Asian comedian Alec Mapa (http://www.logoonline. com/shows/dyn/wisecrack/series.jhtml): "I'm like that condensed can of milk in your mother's pantry: everybody knows what I am, nobody knows what I'm there for"; and lastly, the way in which the New Jersey State Legislature granted us civil unions—for which I am thankful—but in the process has contributed to the further solidification of the antidemocratic ideology of "separate but equal."

Significantly, what links these two classes of straights, in my mind, is a lack of *critical* engagement with (hegemonic) heterosexuality. I do not mean to suggest, however, that straight folk never think about their heterosexuality. In fact, it could be argued that many heterosexuals today are experiencing "'status anxiety'—the panic experienced by those 'who fear a loss of status, either due to competition from other groups or general social and economic changes'" (Becker, 2006, p. 29). Legal scholar J.M. Balkin (1997) insightfully comments on the paradox that marks the rise of status anxiety with the decline of social hierarchies: "The paradox of status is that intense social conflict between status groups emerges not at the height of a system of social stratification but during its decline. The more clear-cut and well-defined that status hierarchies are, the less overt are the kinds of discontent and strife one may see" (p. 2327). Similarly, in his superb publication *Gay TV and Straight America*, Ron Becker (2006) explains that the rise in what might be called "straight status anxiety" is in part the result of shifts in attitude and sensibility in the culture regarding the "uncertainty" of meaning attached to the-at-one-time clearly demarcated categories of homosexuality and heterosexuality, and this ambiguity of meaning has given rise to what Becker calls "straight panic":

> What is the difference between (male) homosexual panic and straight panic? If male homosexual panic held sway in a culture unsure about the ontology of sexuality but utterly convinced of homosexuality's depravity, then straight panic arises in a culture not only uncertain about the ontology of sexual identity but also uncertain about heterosexuality's moral authority. More simply put, male homosexual panic

describes what happens when heterosexual men, insecure about the boundary between gay and straight, confront the threatening specter of a socially prohibited homosexuality. Straight panic describes what happens when heterosexual men and
women, still insecure about the boundary between gay and straight, confront an increasingly accepted homosexuality. (p. 23)

The notion of straight panic challenges naive assessments that heterosexuals do
not "see" their heterosexuality, especially in the wake of the politics of gay cultural visibility over the last several decades. From this perspective, straight
panic has been the inevitable upshot of a "broader social anxiety experienced
by a once naïve mainstream confronting the politics of social identity and difference" (Becker, 2006, pp. 24–25) throughout much of the 1990s and up to
the present day. The mixed, and oftentimes illogical and irrational, not to
mention contradictory, reactions to gay marriage by straight America are arguably the quintessential illustration in the contemporary moment of straight
panic.

Yet "feeling one's heterosexuality" in the form of straight panic does not
engender a critical sensibility toward it, nor does it lead one necessarily to an
intellectual space for cultivating a "queer critique of sexual normativity"
(Schlichter, 2004, p. 545). To cultivate such a critique one must first take a
"queer(ing) detour through theory." From this perspective, my primary purpose here is to contribute to the discourse on queer(ing) heterosexuality and
identity by intersecting that discourse with pedagogical theorizing that might
inform the meaning and practice of both queering heterosexuality and straight
(teacher) identity. In addition, I situate my work as an ongoing and, therefore,
of necessity, incomplete search for critical theoretical vocabularies that might
be politically and pedagogically efficacious in de- and reconstructing heterosexuality and identity with the aim of unsettling the hegemony of heterosexuality and the sociocultural system that installs it as a form of dominance. With
these two purposes in mind, this chapter is divided into three sections.

I begin by situating queer theory within a broader constellation of intellectual movements—most notably poststructuralism and postmodernism—that
significantly shaped its theoretical and political trajectories and made possible
its emergence. In particular, I focus on several key intellectuals from the mid
to late 20th century whose work played a pivotal role in "denaturalizing the
subject," a key notion in contemporary critical thought in the humanities and

social sciences. With this broader context in place, I examine one of queer theory's central tenets: the denaturalization of the *sexual* subject. This central tenet, I argue, is important for the project of queering heterosexuality and straight (teacher) identity, because it provides the theoretical conditions both for de- and reconstructing heterosexuality—that is, for constructing a language of critique and possibility for what it might mean, on the one hand, to critically interrogate straightness and, on the other hand, to queer it.

In the second section I take up Calvin Thomas' (2000), "Straight with a Twist: Queer Theory and the Subject of Heterosexuality," a seminal essay representative of the discourse on queering heterosexuality. I also examine an important critical response to his work by Annette Schlichter (2004) titled "Queer at Last?: Straight Intellectuals and the Desire for Transgression." I situate Thomas' work as the outcome of a theoretical struggle to de- and reconstruct heterosexuality and identity. From this perspective, I argue that his work represents an excellent example of what I call "the pedagogical search for theory"—briefly defined here as a critical performative practice that creates the pedagogical conditions (either for oneself or for others) whereby the straight self, in encountering and engaging with discourses that subject heterosexuality to a queer critique is, in the process, reconstituted (i.e., queered) by the very discourses of that critique—and the straight self is queerly reconstituted *antagonistically* to hegemonic heterosexuality. As Thomas eloquently puts it:

> …if there is any political value in straight queer aspiration, in straight disloyalty to straight identity, it may be only this: to assist in working the weakness in the heterosexual norm, to inhabit the practice of heterosexuality's rearticulation and inhibit its hegemonic dominance. If heterosexual norms are, as Butler puts it, "continually haunted by their own inefficacy," then perhaps the work of the straight theorist with queer aspirations is somehow to be that inefficacious ghost in the house of heteronormativity. (p. 31)

How Thomas discursively queers the straight subject—that is, theoretically produces the figure of a "straight with a twist" to be "that inefficacious ghost in the house of heteronormativity," coupled with a critical analysis of the strengths and weaknesses of his "theoretical performance" —will constitute the primary focus of this second section.

I conclude by briefly turning to the later work of French historian and philosopher Michel Foucault, examining his notion of "care of the self" as a "theoretical tool" useful for the project of queering heterosexuality and straight (teacher) identity. Although I do not develop an extensive analysis of his concept of care of the self, I find it important to highlight for two reasons. First, the project of queering straight (teacher) identity can be framed as the ongoing and nonteleological practice of "critical care" of the straight self, a queer criticality cultivated within the constraints of "heterosexual subjection" arising out of a society and culture heteronormatively structured. In his publication *Insult and the Making of the Gay Self*, Didier Eribon (2004), one of France's foremost public intellectuals, illuminates well the relationship between identity formation and the process of subjection: "A 'subject' is always produced in and through 'subordination' to an order, to rules, norms, laws, and so on. This is true for all 'subjects.' To be a 'subject' and to be subordinated to a system of constraints are one and the same thing" (p. 5). "Queer critical care," then, is the practice by which the straight self begins to understand and respond to the complex processes of heterosexual subjection and the ontological and epistemological limitations such subjection creates for living an ethical and more free life, both in relation to itself and in its relations with the GLBTQ "Other." Second, I highlight Foucault's discourse on care of the self in order to make the following point: the practice of the pedagogical search for theory need not limit its "search" to discourses that constitute themselves, or are constituted by others, as "queer." In other words, there are many discourses that do not upfront frame themselves as a queer theory yet might still be highly useful for the intellectual labor of imagining the range of possibilities for what it might mean in theory and/or in practice to queer heterosexuality and/or straight (teacher) identity. Foucault's care of the self is, in my mind, an example of one such discourse. But before examining that discourse, I first turn to a number of other "nonqueer" discourses, that is to say, a cluster of critical theories on subjectivity that are not positioned as queer theories yet "can be seen as [significantly] shaping the theoretical porridge that has generated Queer Theory" (Beasley, 2005, p. 165).

The Broader Intellectual Context for Queer Theory

Queer theory, as a critical theoretical methodology, did not emerge in isolation; instead, it arises out of a broader constellation of discourses that collectively fall under the rubric intellectual movements known as postmodernism and poststructuralism. Insofar as "identity" is concerned, these movements have profoundly destabilized (at least in theory) the notion of a "unified self." From this perspective, queer theory, as Katherine Watson (2005) succinctly puts it, "follows a general trend of interrogating the historical and cultural positioning of the unified 'self' (a self endowed with a coherent identity including gendered identity), characteristic of the Western constitution of the subject" (p. 68). To put it slightly differently: the subject in poststructuralism is the product or outcome of discourse and therefore has no essence or irreducible nature, thus rendering identity in terms described as nonessentialist, nonhomogeneous, unstable, and fluid. This central tenet of poststructuralist thought has resonated across many disciplines in the humanities and social sciences. As Annamarie Jagose (1996) notes,

> as an intellectual model, queer has not been produced solely by lesbian and gay politics and theory, but rather informed by historically specific knowledges which constitute late twentieth-century thought. Similar shifts can be seen in both feminist and postcolonial theory and practice, when, for example, Denise Riley problematises feminism's insistence on "women" as a unified, stable and coherent category, and Henry Louis Gates denaturalizes "race." Such conceptual shifts have had great impact within lesbian and gay scholarship and activism and are the historical context for any analysis of queer. (p. 77)

Offering a similar account of the broader intellectual context for queer theory, Chris Beasley (2005), in her publication *Gender & Sexuality: Critical Theories, Critical Thinkers*, situates the rise of queer theory within the "post-modern turn in sexuality studies" (p. 162). From this perspective, Beasley notes that queer theory is understood as a specific kind of sexuality studies approach, one that not only deconstructs coherent identity but "necessarily also involves deconstructing mutually reinforcing neat divisions of identity binaries such as men/women and heterosexual/homosexual. This Queer trajectory has much in common with similar and sometimes strongly interconnected Postmodern turns in Gender Studies and Race/Ethnicity/Imperialism Studies" (p. 162). In short, one way to describe the impact of poststructuralist and postmodern theorizing on identity is to say that these intellectual movements have "queered" identity; or, as Donald E. Hall (2003) puts it in his publication *Queer Theories*, these academic movements have provided the critical ground for a "'queer' manipulation of identity or identities" (p. 4).

More specifically, this broader intellectual context in which queer theory emerged was significantly impacted by several key theorists in the second half of the 20th century, including Louis Althusser, Sigmund Freud, Jacques Lacan, Ferdinand de Saussure, and, perhaps most importantly, by the work of Michel Foucault. While there was certainly (fierce) disagreement among these theorists on the meanings and processes of the formation of the subject—that is, on what the subject is and where it comes from—collectively, "their work made possible certain advances in social theory and the human sciences which, in the words of Stuart Hall, have affected 'the final de-centering of the Cartesian subject'" (Jagose, 1996, p. 78). With what Jagose calls a "Marxist structuralist approach to subjectivity" (p. 78), Althusser reworked Marx's notion of historical constraints on individuals which impact their actions. Specifically Althusser argued that individuals do not preexist as free subjects, but instead are "interpellated," that is, brought forth as subjects by ideology "through a compelling mixture of recognition and identification" (Jagose, 1996, p. 78). What is significant in Althusser's work in the way of theoretically undermining notions of the self as rational, coherent, and self-determining is that he argued "one's identity is already constituted by ideology itself rather than simply by resistance to it" (Jagose, 1996, p. 78). In Freud's work, of course, the notion of subjectivity as stable and coherent is seriously thrown into question by his theorization of the unconscious: "In establishing the formative influence of important mental and psychic processes of which an individual is unaware, the theory of the unconscious has radical implications for the common-sense assumption that the subject is both whole and self-knowing" (Jagose, 1996, p. 79). Significantly revising the work of Freud, Lacan argued for an understanding of self-formation as the result of the complex interplay between internalization/acculturation and the acquisition of language/encounter with "the symbolic order." As Hall (2003) lucidly and succinctly explains: "Lacan argued that an individual's 'self' is formed through the internalization of larger social constructs and hierarchies of value in the process of acquiring language. The child thus becomes acculturated through her or his encounter with the 'Symbolic'—which comprises language, images, and other means by which society communicates and replicates" (pp. 61–62). Also important in making a substantial theoretical contribution to the complex relationship between language and subject formation, Swiss linguist Ferdinand de Saussure argued that language does not simply describe an already existing reality; instead, language actually constructs social reality. Indeed, "language is not some second-order system whose function is simply to describe what is already there. Rather, language constitutes and makes significant that which it seems only to describe" (Jagose, 1996, p. 79). If language creates rather than simply describes our realities, then this insight upsets the notion of a subject who exists prior to language or the system of signification. From this perspective, language, for Saussure, does not so much describe an "authentic self," nor is it the means by which the subject expresses "privately owned" thoughts and emotions. Instead, the "interiority of the self" is itself constituted by language, leading me to ask this question: Within the critical project of denaturalizing the subject is the self constituted "all the way down"? For the French historian, Michel Foucault, the answer seems to be "yes."

On a general level, the work of Michel Foucault has been focused on "the formation of the subject," that is, on how human beings are socially constructed by power relations. From this perspective, Foucault (1982) explains what has been the focus of much of his academic inquiry:

> I would like to say, first of all, what has been the goal of my work during the last twenty years. It has not been to analyze the phenomenon of power, nor to elaborate the foundations of such an analysis. My objective, instead, has been to create a history of the different modes by which, in our culture, human beings are made subjects…[thus], it is not power, but the subject, which is the general theme of my research. (pp. 208–209)

Foucault's sustained interest in how subjects "only come into existence through the complex interplay between power and language" (Mansfield, 2000, p. 58) has significantly contributed to the debunking of the notion of the autonomous subject—that is to say, of an individual that exits prior to (in a self-contained and complete form), as opposed to being the effect of, networks of power. Foucault (1980) explains this distinction in the following way:

> The individual is not to be conceived as a sort of elementary nucleus, a primitive atom, a multiple and inert material on which power comes to fasten or against which it happens to strike, and in so doing subdues or crushes individuals. In fact, it is already one of the prime effects of power that certain bodies, certain gestures, certain discourses, certain desires, come to be identified and constituted as individuals. The individual, that is, is not the vis a vis of power; it is, I believe one of its prime effects. The individual is an effect of power, and at the same time, or precisely to the extent to which it is that effect, it is the element of its articulation. The individual which power has constituted is at the same time its vehicle. (p. 98)

Modern subjectivity, then, for Foucault is not a naturally occurring entity waiting to be fashioned by this or that discourse; rather, it is actually "contrived by the double work of power and knowledge to maximize the operation of both" (Mansfield, 2000, p. 59). And this understanding of where the subject comes from is connected to Foucault's substantial reworking of the concept of power. In short, for him, power is not something that only oppresses or negates; instead, power *produces*:

> In defining the effects of power by repression, one accepts a purely juridical conception of that power; one identifies power with a law that says no; it has above all the force of an interdict. Now, I believe that this is a wholly negative, narrow, and skeletal conception of power which has been curiously shared. If power was never anything but repressive, if it never did anything but say no, do you really believe that we should manage to obey it? What gives power its hold, what makes it accepted, is quite simply the fact that it does not weigh like a force which says no, but that it runs through, and it produces things, it induces pleasure, it forms knowledge, it produces discourse; it must be considered as a productive network which runs through the entire social body much more than as a negative instance whose function is repression. (Foucault, 1979, p. 36)

The substantial retheorizing of the concept of power and the conceptual impact this had on his model of identity formation has positioned Foucault's work as highly influential in the development of queer theory. This is in part because a chunk of Foucault's (1978) most popular work—namely, his publication of *The History of Sexuality, Volume 1: An Introduction*—aimed at "denaturalizing dominant understandings of sexual identity...[by] emphasizing that sexuality is not an essentially personal attribute but an available cultural category—and that it is the effect of power rather than simply its object" (Jagose, 1996, p. 79). What makes Foucault's work on sexual identity a "denaturalizing project," then, is that he cogently argued sexual identities have *histories*—indeed, they are the historical products of power/knowledge. The epistemological consequence of this insight, especially for subsequent queer scholarship and activism, is twofold: On the one hand, if sexual identity is the effect of power, then the notion of a naturally occurring sexual self (hetero or homo) is seriously thrown into doubt. For marginalized sexual identities—like homosexuality—this means that such identities "are not merely victims of power—a natural form of self repressed by power—but produced by power" (Beasley, 2005, p. 165), which leads to the second point: If indeed sexual identities are historical products, then they play a major role in the organization of a (hierarchical) society. The ontological opening for Foucault of such a dual understanding is that "we can construct a fictional or hypothetical selfhood outside of, or in pure hostility to, the conventions modern life seeks to normalize" (Mansfield, 2000, p. 63). Foucault's later work on the "aesthetics of existence" takes up this ethical care of the self, to which I return in the last section of this essay as a way to begin outlining its possibilities for the project of queering heterosexuality and straight (teacher) identity.

Queer Theory and Its Uses: The Work of Judith Butler

Within the context of these broader intellectual movements, the impact of the poststructuralist theorization of identity as provisional has been significant in shifting (or at the very least enlarging) the approach taken to the study and teaching of nonheterosexual identities and same-sex sexual practices. To be sure, informed by poststructuralist thought, queer theory emerged in the early 1990s in the academy as a way to seriously problematize the theoretical and political limitations of, and the unexamined yet implied inherent stability in, nonheterosexual categories of identification, such as gay and lesbian, and with the use of exclusionary academic phrases like "gay and lesbian studies." As Jagose (1996) explains:

> Queer is a product of specific cultural and theoretical pressures which increasingly structured debates (both within and outside the academy) about questions of gay and lesbian identity. Perhaps most significant in this regard has been the problematising by post-structuralism of gay liberationist and lesbian feminist understandings of identity and the operations of power. This prompts David Herkt to argue that "the Gay identity is observably a philosophically conservative construct, based upon premises that no longer have any persuasive academic relationship to contemporary theories

of identity or gender." The delegitimation of liberal, liberationist, ethnic, and even separatist notions of identity generated the cultural space necessary for the emergence of the term "queer"; its non-specificity guarantees it against recent criticisms made of the exclusionist tendencies of "lesbian" and "gay" as identity categories. (p. 76)

While indeed queer theory's "nonspecificity" or antiessentialist approach "marks a suspension of identity as fixed, coherent, and natural" (Jagose, 1996, p. 98), queer theory has nevertheless been productively critiqued for arguably reifying that which it aims to undermine: unitary and binary models of identity. In particular, its predominant focus on "all matters sexual" has meant that queer theory has been marked by "defining absences," including a lack of engagement with gender as an important site for queer theorizing. In addition, its almost exclusive focus on "nonnormative" sexual identities and practices has created an analytic gap in productively incorporating questions of heterosexuality and identity within the context of queer theorizing and critique. As Beasley (2005) explains:

> While Queer Theory remains a positioning that questions identity affiliations, critics of its selections and exclusions have noted its tendency to refuse a location in relation to gender identity while shoring up a sexual identity positioning. Queer Theory's positioning may be further specified. It is almost invariably associated with the non-heterosexual. For this reason, Queer Theory's analysis of heterosexuality and the extent to which heterosexuality is included within Queer thinking is the subject of continuing debate. Some Queer writers suggest that the point about Queer thinking is precisely that it is not attached to any identities and hence, heterosexuality, as much as any identity, can be queered. By contrast, most other writers on this question simply assume Queer's links with sexualities other than the heterosexual, or suggest that the inclusion of the heterosexual in a Queer agenda amounts to "gatecrashing" by already privileged heterosexuals and politically accomplishes nothing. A more critical assessment of the association between Queer and the non-heterosexual regards Queer as replete with its own insider/outsider politics, noting its inclination to fix heterosexuality as opposed to its supposedly subversive agenda. Once again there appears to be a tension between Queer's aim of resisting identity and its unresolved legitimation of particular identities. (pp. 169–170)

Judith Butler has insightfully examined the complex intersection between gender and (hetero)sexuality within the context of a queer critique—and hence can be utilized as a model of sorts for incorporating questions of gender and heterosexuality within queer theorizing. As Beasley (2005) points out: "Her analysis of gender and sexual identity as non-natural, as 'performative,' as artifice, and her view of gender as central to 'heteronormativity' (hetero-sexuality as compulsory norm and non-heterosexuality as deviant) provides connecting links between Feminism (which focuses upon gender) and Sexual-ity Studies (which focuses upon the heteronorm)" (p. 109). In one of her well-known essays, "Critically Queer," Butler (1993a) suggests that queer's mobil-ity leaves open the possibility for including the matter of heterosexuality and identity within queer politics and theory: "the term 'queer' itself has been pre-cisely the discursive rallying point for…lesbians and gay men and…for bi-sexuals and straights for whom the term expresses an affiliation with anti-homophobic politics….That [queer has] become such a discursive site whose uses are not fully constrained in advance ought to be safeguarded…" (p. 230). In addition to providing a useful example of a queer theory that "includes het-erosexuality," Butler's work offers two important conceptual tools—namely, her strategy of "identity displacement" and her model of gender performativ-ity—that might prove useful for the project of queering heterosexuality and straight (teacher) identity.

Drawing from the broader constellation of discourse on the denaturaliza-tion of the subject, and in particular from the work of Foucault, Butler's 1990 publication, *Gender Trouble: Feminism and the Subversion of Identity*, has proved pivotal both for informing the theoretical contours of queer theory and for generating a critical vocabulary linked to its emergence. Butler's general strat-egy is one of "identity displacement," that is, a refusal of identity and identity politics as a basis for feminist (and queer) politics. As Beasley (2005) notes: "[For Butler] 'queer' politics authorises, has as its 'identity,' a refusal of set identity. It resists calculation and revels in unpredictability" (p. 108). Butler's critical project, then, can be framed as a theoretical attempt to show how forms of resistance that draw on supposedly natural and stable identity catego-ries actually reify the very forms of dominance such forms of resistance try to counter. From this perspective, Butler takes on feminism's use of the category woman as a basis from which to launch a politics and argues that such a unify-ing category actually reproduces gender and sexual norms, rather than sub-verts them, "because a politics invoking 'women' (gender identity) conceals the politically constructed non-natural, mutable character of gender" (Beasley,

2005, p. 107). This leads Butler to advocate a strategy of gender and sexual identity displacement and to propose a politics that emphasizes,

> "sexual crossing," [that is,] mixing up multiple or at least more than one identity pathway, and by doing so refusing the set identities laid out for us.... [in this way, Butler highlights] terms like Feminism, gender or women [not] to represent a stable subject—that is, an identifiable group or group concerns—[but instead] to demonstrate *how* socially constituted processes (power relations) generate forms of supposedly natural belonging and what they silence. (Beasley, 2005, pp. 107–109)

In considering Butler's strategy of identity displacement, coupled with a politics of sexual crossing, or what Butler specifically calls "pastiche"—"that is, an imitation which involves a medley of identity forms and hence mocks any notion of an inner truth or original core self" (Beasley, 2005, p. 107)—how might these two elements of her approach to "queering (gender) identity" be useful in generating questions that might inform the theory and/or practice of queering heterosexuality and/or straight (teacher) identity? For instance, can the critical practice of queering heterosexuality be seen as a way to "displace" hegemonic heterosexuality and identity? If so, what multitude of specific discourses might be deployed to "do the theoretical job" of displacement? What would heterosexuality and identity look like during and after such a relentless theoretical assault; what, in other words, would characterize their queerness?

In *Gender Trouble*, Butler (1990) introduces another critical vocabulary that, in my view, could prove highly useful in further theoretically informing the work of queering heterosexuality and/or straight (teacher) identity; that is, her theory of gender performativity. For Butler gender is the outcome or product of never-ending "citation and reiteration" of normative categories under constraint; this means that gender "is not something one *is*, it is something one *does*, an act, or more precisely, a sequence of acts, a verb rather than a noun, a 'doing' rather than a 'being'" (Salih, 2002, p. 62). The illusion of coherent and natural gender identity arises out of these endless acts, always "performed" "within a highly rigid and regulatory frame" (Butler, 1990, p. 33). This leads Butler to argue that the notion of a subject who expresses authentically his or her gender identity is a fiction. Instead, in Butler's critical frame, the interiorized self is *naturalized* (i.e., gendered) from the outside; thus, Butler (1990) arrives at this formulation: "There is no gender identity behind the expressions of gender; that identity is performatively constituted by the very 'expressions' that are said to be its results" (p. 25). What is additionally significant about Butler's theory of gender performativity is that it examines how gender and heterosexuality imbricate to create the notion of stability and necessity in certain normative gender and sexual performances and configurations. In this way, "heterosexuality is naturalized by the performative repetition of normative gender identities" (Jagose, 1996, p. 85). Butler's theory of performativity, then, denaturalizes gender as much as it does heterosexuality, making it as much a gender as a queer critique.

One way Butler's work has been taken up in relation to the theoretical and everyday operations of performativity is that many readers have literalized it as performance; that is, have overemphasized her concept of performativity *as performative subversion* rather than performativity *as the precondition of the subject*. I make this distinction here because, while self-reflexive subversion of hegemonic straightness and straight identity matters, what might be more important, especially for the project of queering heterosexuality and/or straight (teacher) identity, is a curriculum that engages teachers and students in a critical ongoing understanding of the complex and contradictory ways the (hegemonic) straight subject *comes into being by way of performativity*. While Butler's model of performativity does indeed include, as part of its theory, subversive performances, it also, and perhaps much more importantly, "explains those everyday productions of gender and sexual identity which seem most to evade explanation. For gender is performative, not because it is something that the subject deliberately and playfully assumes, but because, through reiteration, it consolidates the subject" (Jagose, 1996, p. 86). Several years after *Gender Trouble*, Butler (1993b) published *Bodies that Matter: On the Discursive Limits of "Sex"* in part as a way to reemphasize this distinction:

> Performativity cannot be understood outside of a process of iterability, a regularized and constrained repetition of norms. And this repetition is not performed by a subject; this repetition is what enables and constitutes the temporal condition for the subject. This iterability implies that "performance" is not a singular "act" or event, but a ritualized production, a ritual repeated under and through constraint, under and through the force of prohibition and taboo, with the threat of ostracism and even death controlling and compelling the shape of the production, but not, I will insist, determining it fully in advance. (p. 95)

Butler's stress on performativity as compulsory performance might best be illustrated in one of her most often-cited phrases from *Gender Trouble*: "Gender is the repeated stylization of the body, a set of repeated acts within a highly rigid regulatory frame that congeal over time to produce the appearance of substance, of a natural sort of being" (p. 33). While indeed Butler's *Gender Trouble* and theory of performativity are first and foremost situated within the context and concerns of feminism, one of *Gender Trouble*'s "most influential achievements," notes Jagose (1996), "is to specify how gender operates as a regulatory construct that privileges heterosexuality and, furthermore, how the deconstruction of normative models of gender legitimates lesbian and gay subject-positions" (p. 83). I would add that, within the context of a project of queering heterosexuality and/or straight (teacher) identity, Butler's theory of performativity as a compulsory "act" provides a theoretical framework by which the straight (teacher) subject might critically examine the complexity of the following question: In what ways are heterosexuality and heterosexual identity "consolidated" as normative within culture and society and, more specifically, within the everyday practices in, and institutional structures of, educational contexts? It strikes me that it is in this sense that performativity becomes a highly useful concept for queering the straight (teacher) self by way of a curriculum that deconstructs "the thousands of ways" the straight self is performatively constituted to, borrowing from Butler, "appear like a substance, like a natural sort of being." Denaturalizing the straight subject in this way creates a pathway for adding another layer to a queer(ing) critical curriculum: one in which the straight subject "falls out of love" with its imposed heteronormative subjectivity by reconstituting itself in the process of engaging in a queer(ing) critique of (hegemonic) heterosexuality. It is to this complex process of queer-hetero subject (de)formation to which I now turn.

The Pedagogical Search for Theory

> For whatever the level of "our" straight aspirations toward or negotiations with queer theory may be, it needs, I think, to be accounted for, to be theorized. (Calvin Thomas, 2000, p. 22)

In this section, I critically examine Calvin Thomas' (2000) essay, "Straight with a Twist: Queer Theory and the Subject of Heterosexuality," a seminal work that represents the discourse on queer heterosexuality. In addition, I think through an excellent response to his essay by Annette Schlichter (2004) titled, "Queer at Last?: Straight Intellectuals and the Desire for Transgression," a response that is "less invested in searching for the true queer straight than in exploring the emergence of the figure and its role in an antinormative knowledge project" (p. 545). Thomas' work is a highly visible exemplar of how some heterosexual scholars "have begun to interrogate critically the heterosexual subject 'after' queer theory" (Schlichter, 2004, p. 544). From this perspective, it is significant to take up his work in trying to understand what meanings, politics, potential problems and possibilities are being generated by the discursive production of the queer heterosexual by straight intellectuals who hope their critical praxis dismantles their own (hetero)normative positionality. "When heterosexuality becomes the object of a possible de- and reconstruction," notes Schlichter (2004), "the question of the relationship of heterosexual subjects to critically queer activities also becomes relevant" (p. 548). Stated a bit differently in the form of a question, a critical sympathizer of Thomas' work (as I am and I think Schlichter is too) might ask: What is at stake—epistemologically, ontologically, and politically—when a critical politics arising out of a privileged status seeks to identify with a "minority" position? With this question in mind, reading Thomas' work, and Schlichter's response to it, I raise several questions throughout this section about how the "debate" between Thomas and Schlichter might be "good to think with" for critically exploring the problems and possibilities of "the paradoxical figure of the queer straight" (Schlichter, 2004, p. 545) as well as for considering how a critical assessment of this paradoxical figure might inform the theoretical and political complexities involved in the project of queering heterosexuality and/or straight (teacher) identity.

Thomas' (2000) "Straight with a Twist" can be framed, within the context of the transformative efficacy of the intersection between pedagogy and critical theory, as an example of what I refer to as "the pedagogical search for theory" as a constitutive element of queer critical practice—that is, the practice of encountering and engaging with (queer) theory and being seriously open to the possibilities this practice enables for a radical de- and reconstruction of the straight self and, on an institutional level, what this could mean for dismantling heteronormativity. Thomas begins his essay by engaging in what might very well be one of the most important aspects of queer critical practice: the asking of *(critical) theoretically informed* questions about (hegemonic) heterosexuality and queerness; in addition, he asks those questions in such a way that they articulate (i.e., bring together) in an ongoing, problematized, and unresolved manner, the complexities and potential productive possibilities of the intersections between the categories of queerness and heterosexuality:

> To what extent could an otherwise "straight" subject elaborate a queer criticism? If, as Lauren Berlant and Michael Warner suggest, membership in "queer publics" is "more a matter of aspiration than it is the expression of an identity or a history," what accounts for, or disallows, the decidedly ambiguous labor of straight queer aspiration? What problems and possibilities are opened up by questions of straight engagement with or participation in queer theory (or as Berlant and Warner prefer to call it, "queer commentary")? Of what, if anything, might "otherwise straight" "critical queerness" consist? What exactly would it, or should it, if anything, perform? Other than voyeurism, appropriation, theoretical trendiness, or the desire to be a "good," responsible heterosexual critic, what might the draw of queer theory for straights be? What can antihomophobic straights do to help "make the world queerer than ever"? (pp. 11–12)

In my view, each of Thomas' questions suggests the paradoxical, yet productively open-ended, up-till-now-to-be-explored aspect of the intersection between queerness and straightness. It's this problematic yet potentially efficacious paradox—i.e., efficacious for possibly undoing "the sociocultural system, which inscribes a heterosexual identity as a hegemonic position" (Schlichter, 2004, p. 546)—between the "union" of queerness with straightness, and specifically how this paradoxical coming together generates important questions about the meaning and practice of queer(ing) heterosexuality and straight (teacher) identity, that I wish to explore for the remainder of this section.

What is striking, at first glance, about Thomas' questions is that they are able to be posed or even understood as a paradox. In other words, there is a "prior" epistemological unraveling regarding "the subject" which has made possible the emergence of the paradoxical figure of the queer straight in the first place. As I discussed earlier in this essay, the poststructuralist critique of a humanist framework of identity—that is, of a stable, naturally occurring subject—has brought forth numerous theoretical trajectories which have cogently destabilized identity—and this has engendered much debate about the "nature of the subject," including the heterosexual subject. Annette Schlichter (2004) eloquently sums it up this way: "I find the debate important for critical theories beyond the immediate context of queer scholarship because the paradoxical figure of the queer straight sheds light on the difficult and complex conditions—and the necessary contradictions—of conceptualizing the subject of a political and cultural critique in the current postmodern moment" (p. 545). Within the context of the rise of the paradoxical figure of the queer straight, the irony of the denaturalization of the subject is that it provides the "grounding" for, say, straight intellectuals "with queer aspirations," like Calvin Thomas, to be able to make heterosexual claims to queerness. As Schlichter (2004) highlights:

> It is the critique of stable identity positions that creates spaces for a critical rereading of heterosexuality and for the participation of heterosexual critics in a discourse of the marginalized. This destabilization of identities has a double effect for an understanding of straightness and the role of straight critics within a radical critique of sexuality. It creates theoretical conditions for the participation of straight critics and simultaneously requires a complicated negotiation of their subject positions. (p. 545)

Schlichter (2004) outlines three theoretical moments that have significantly contributed to the rethinking of the subject of heterosexuality which, in turn, have enabled the rise of the figure of the "queer-straight." First, she notes that queer theory has argued for an analytical distinction between the "cultural system that produces and regulates sexual identities" from "heterosexuality as the hegemonic position arising from this system" (p. 546). This system to which Schlichter refers is what Judith Butler (1990) has termed the *heterosexual matrix*—"that grid of cultural intelligibility through which bodies, genders, and desires are naturalized" (p. 151). If heterosexuality is "installed" as the hegemonic position arising out of the heterosexual matrix, then the political significance of arguing for a distinction between the sociocultural system that produces identity from the identities themselves is that it "implies the possibility of a heterosexual's disidentification with the normative apparatus, which might in turn allow for a critical analysis of his or her compliance with the dominant structure" (Schlichter, 2004, p. 546). The second important theoretical moment identified by Schlichter is connected to Judith Butler's theory of gender performativity. In short, if gender norms amount to a regulated system of performances, then this implies that a constant repetition of those norms is required to keep them going; that is, to keep them "in play." For Butler, such constant repetition makes gender highly unstable and therefore susceptible to "rearticulation." As Mansfield (2000) explains: "Each of us, in some small or trivial way, sometimes fails to repeat perfectly. This failure to repeat is not only more evidence of the artificiality of the gender system, but it also shows that there is inevitably—even accidentally—a continuous, even unplanned resistance to the norms of gender" (p. 77). In a similar way, if heterosexuality is a repeated regulated set of behaviors, then it, too, is unstable and incoherent, and it is this very aspect of it—its instability—that becomes the condition for its possible rearticulation. In discussing how heterosexuality must constantly prove to itself its own ontological condition, its "realness," and arguably to a degree to which gender and racial identities do not, Calvin Thomas (2000) notes the following:

> Despite postmodern theory's destabilizations of such "biological" matters as sexual difference or skin pigmentation as self-evident empirical indices of gendered or racialized identity, the dominant culture itself blithely continues to behave as if such matters could be taken "for granted" as compelling or reassuring evidence of identity-formation. But the dominant culture is more suspicious, more self-suspicious— and hence more self-policing—when it comes to "proving" heterosexuality. For it is possible, after all, to "fake" the "realest" possible "evidence" of heterosexuality: man or woman, one can participate in heterosexual marriage and even help produce a brood of spawn and still "turn out" to have been "living a lie," to have been "really" gay or lesbian all along. Precisely because there is no final "proof" of heterosexuality, heterosexuality must constantly set about trying to prove itself, assert itself, insist on itself. Indeed, as Butler argues, heterosexuality as hegemonic institution is finally nothing more than its own repetitive self-insistence, nothing other than "a constant and repeated effort to imitate its own idealizations".... Heteronormativity, then, has something—itself—to prove but has no other proof of itself than its own repeated efforts at self-demonstration. (p. 28)

It is this constant repetition, then, that creates an opening for the emergence of "failed imitations." And while "Butler regards such reiterations with a difference as the results of unconscious failures rather than conscious violations of the norm, she offers a [theoretical] vantage point from which to think about a 'reworking' of heterosexuality" (Schlichter, 2004, p. 546). Indeed, what a "failed" heterosexual identity (and "performance") looks like—that is, what ongoing meanings and practices would constitute (i.e., queer) it, would be attached to it—and how such an identity contributes to an anti(hetero) normative project is what underlies the theoretical and political task of the discourse on queer(ing) heterosexuality. Finally, drawing on Michael Warner's (1993) well-known definition of queer (theory), where he states that "'queer' gets a critical edge by defining itself against the normal rather than the heterosexual" (p. xxvi), Schlichter (2004) identifies the third theoretical moment as the separation of critically queer practice from specific (sexual) identities, thus "open[ing] the queer project to the participation of heterosexual critics" (p. 546). Both from a theoretical and political perspective, then, the significance of the rise of the paradoxical figure of the queer straight, coupled with the different theoretical moments which have ushered in its emergence, is that it *does*, however "productively problematic," create a major opening for straight participation in queer critical practice. Paying attention to the discourses that constitute this figure can help illuminate how efficacious the overall discourse on queer(ing) heterosexuality is in contributing to "the growing authority of the critical tendencies that aim at unsettling the hegemony of heterosexuality" (Schlichter, 2004, p. 544).

Drawing on Eve Kosofsky Sedgwick's hypothesis "of the force of 'queer' as a perverse performative of experimental self-perception and filiation,'" (Schlichter, 2004, p. 548), two textual variations of the perverse performative outlining the contours of the paradoxical figure of the queer straight within the discourse on queer heterosexuality are identified by Schlichter. These are the "testimonial form" and the "theoretical performance" (Schlichter, 2004, p. 548). Testimonial texts describe the process of becoming "queerly heterosexual." Arising out of a range of different "border crossing" experiences by straights into queer spaces, which includes a range of "transformative encounters" with the GLBTQ "Other," these texts describe the experiential process leading to a straight subject's identification as a "queer straight." An example of such an experience might be a straight student who, after encountering a queer (theory) course that challenges the notion of stability in gender and sexual categories, no longer is able to identify as "singularly straight." From this perspective, these "various forms of affiliation with queer communities serve as an entrance into a critical discourse and offer an opportunity to reconfigure straight identity" (Schlichter, 2004, p. 549).

Within the context of queer theory, one important function of these testimonial texts is that they productively queer the discourse of queer theory itself. That is, they provide experiential accounts that "trouble" the overdetermined straight-queer dichotomy that continues to dominate much queer writing today. As Schlichter (2004) explains:

> Contradicting the intention to destabilize the "subject of heterosexuality," the queer/straight binary underwrites the notion of heterosexuality as an essentialized, monolithic identity position. This understanding of heterosexuality is not necessarily to be seen as a willful production; rather, it is a kind of default version of heterosexuality that results from a lack of investigation into the practices and experiences of straightness. While the focus on the relationship between heteronormativity and lesbian and gay identities has been immensely productive for a radical critique of sexuality, it has also meant that little attention has been paid to an interrogation of the "subject of heterosexuality." (p. 549)

Although these testimonial forms provide one way by which to "open up" queer theory to its "own blindspots, lapses, inconsistencies, and nervous avoidances" (Hall, 2003, p. 8), Schlichter does identify two related problems with these testimonial writings. On the one hand, they *assume* a queer straight identity. That is, many of these narratives assume that a queer-straight identity has been constituted by way of the experiences of border crossing. On the other hand, and related, this assumption implies that a queer heterosexual is a teleological identity, one that is "reached," as opposed to one that represents an *ongoing* site of struggle of critical self-(de)formation situated within relations of power. For Schlichter (2004), then, the figure of the queer straight that emerges from the testimonial narratives is one whose personal horizons are indeed expanded by experiences of queer affiliations; however, "the self-representations as queer simultaneously function as closures of the narratives of becoming" (p. 550). Shifting to an analysis of texts that do not assume the existence of a queer-straight identity but instead struggle to *theorize* its meanings and practices, Schlichter (2004) identifies within the general discourse on queer(ing) heterosexuality a second set of perverse performatives she calls "theoretical performances" (p. 548). These theoretical writings function to produce a queer-straight position in the process of critically interrogating the subject of heterosexuality. Or more simply stated, theoretical perverse performatives "begin to *theorize* a critically queer position of a straight subject"

(Schlichter, 2004, p. 551). Calvin Thomas' (2000) "Straight with a Twist" is an example of such writing, and Schlichter (2004) productively analyzes his text as an exemplar of a "perspective on diverse critical technologies of the perverse performative" (p. 549).

Thomas' (2000) "Straight with a Twist" functions in two specific ways as a perverse performative. The first is in terms of his own identity formation. His theoretical performance, that is to say, his critical engagement with, and reconfiguration of, the subject of heterosexuality by way of a queer critique—what I'm specifically characterizing as the practice of the pedagogical search for theory—simultaneously positions *himself* as a "queer subject." In other words, his intellectual performance produces "the figure of the author as straight 'with a twist'" (Schlichter, 2004, p. 552). In addition, his pedagogical search for theory engenders the paradoxical figure of the queer straight in the form of a "twisted straight" or "straightness with a twist." For Thomas (2000) this specifically means a straight subject who is twisted or queered by "the recognition and acknowledgement that straightness, like all identity formation, is an effect of constitutive exclusion and thus never ceases to depend on the excluded, the *part maudit*, the abjected itself—the recognition and acknowledgement that all along one has needed 'the queer' that one really is(n't) to be 'the straight' that (no) one (ever) really is" (p. 30). Thomas (2000) further elaborates by noting:

> For if…compulsory heterosexuality "secures its self-identity and shores up its ontological boundaries by protecting itself from what it sees as the continual predatory encroachment of its contaminated other," then radical heterosexuality or self conscious straightness—which is to say, other-conscious straightness, straightness that recognizes and somehow acknowledges its dependence on the queerness in which it does(n't) participate—would not protect but rather open itself to the possibility of its own structural dependence on its constitutively excluded other. It would, in other words, own up to the exclusions by which it proceeds… For if heteronormativity (or institutional heterosexuality) is nothing more than the effort to live up to its own relentlessly reiterated ideals, "a constant and repeated effort to imitate its own idealizations," then self(-as-other)-conscious straightness—straightness, that is, with a twist—is not and can never exactly be the "ideal" (institutional, compulsory) way for heterosexuality to reiterate or imitate itself. Straightness with a twist would, rather, work to mitigate, or militate against, those institutional, compulsory ideals, those compulsory performances. (pp. 30–31)

Thomas' theoretical production of an "other-conscious straightness," that is, of a straight subject who becomes "twisted" (i.e., queered) by an understanding of, and openness to, its dependence on the constitutive exclusion of the queer outside for its own (hetero)self-constitution raises two questions that, I think, might be useful for informing a queer(ing) curriculum structured around the practice of the pedagogical search for theory: What constellation of critical vocabularies might be continuously sought in order to explore with (straight) teachers and students the complexity and contradictions of heterosexuality's "dependence" on queerness for it's own constructed (in)coherence? And how might such a queer(ing) curriculum contribute to the general discourse on queer(ing) heterosexuality by proliferating images of the paradoxical figure of the queer straight? These questions, among many other possible ones, suggest the value of articulating Thomas' theoretical figure of the twisted straight to a queer(ing) curriculum, both as a way to think through the complexities of the project of queering the straight (teacher) self and to contribute to a broader discourse on a radical politics of sexual and gender justice.

As much as Thomas' "straightness with a twist discourse" contributes to the discursive project of queering heterosexuality and/or straight (teacher) identity, a critique of the shortcomings of his theoretical perverse performative also proves highly valuable for reflecting on the direction of such a project. Returning to Schlichter (2004), she argues that Thomas' theoretical performance ends up being more about *claiming* a critical queer subjectivity than about subverting hegemonic heterosexuality and identity. "The displacement of critical energy from the denaturalization of a straight hegemonic identity to self-representation as queer," notes Schlichter (2004), "is one of the most conspicuous aspects of the various representations of queer heterosexuality" (p. 553). This is a significant critique, for the "slippage from the queering of heterosexuality to heterosexual claims to queerness" (Schlichter, 2004, p. 554) can potentially overshadow the importance of a "substantive" queer critique—which is to say, a critique that is invested in deconstructing the processes by which heterosexuality and identity are institutionalized as hegemonic. Schlichter (2004) explains the problematic this way:

> Intending to perform their particularity as twisted straights through disloyalty to heternormativity, queer straights can do so only from the position of heterosexuality inscribed as universal. This condition of possibility of self-queering enunciations is

never deconstructed, for the formation of "the heterosexual subject" through a heteronormative apparatus always disappears behind the concerns for straight transgressions. (p. 555)

Within the context of constructing a queer(ing) curriculum informed by the critical practice of the pedagogical search for theory, how might the "slippage" Schlichter importantly highlights and critiques be avoided? The approach she proposes is "to twist the perspective once more and turn (back) to the subject of heterosexuality as an object of knowledge" (Schlichter, 2004, p. 557). In particular she recommends a critical examination of the various ways in which the reproduction of the institutionalization of heterosexuality functions as "an apparatus of normalization" (Schlichter, 2004, p. 557). In the next and final section I briefly consider her suggestion of analyzing the complex processes of "heterosexual subjection" as a vehicle (i.e., an "apparatus") of (hetero)normalization while proposing the anti(hetero)normative practice of "queer critical care" as a counterpractice to heterosexual subjection and, more generally, to hegemonic heterosexuality.

By Way of Conclusion: Heterosexual Subjection and Foucault's Care of the Self

When Schlichter proposes turning back to "the subject of heterosexuality as an object of knowledge," she is thinking of "the subject" here in two ways: the heterosexual subject itself and the subject (i.e., topic) of heterosexuality as an institution. As she notes: "While feminist and queer scholars have broken the ground in constituting heterosexuality as an object of knowledge, there remains a wide range of work to be done to arrive at a more nuanced understanding of the construction of heterosexuality as an institution and an identity position" (Schlichter, 2004, p. 557). Critically examining heterosexuality as identity and institution, and how the two imbricate in complex ways, Schlichter (2004) aims "to interrogate and contest heteronormative productions of heterosexuality" (p. 557). One suggestion she proposes is to engage in a critique of "the subject of heterosexuality" by critically taking up and challenging processes of "heterosexual subjection" as contributing to "heteronormative productions of heterosexuality." Drawing on Butler's definition of subjection as "'the [paradoxical] process of becoming subordinated by power as well as becoming a subject,'" Schlichter (2004) defines heterosexual subjection "as an overdetermined process of 'becoming straight' under the conditions of heteronormativity" (p. 559). Constructing a curriculum that explores with (straight) students and teachers the "overdetermined process of becoming straight" as a counterhegemonic act to heterosexual subjection would initiate, I propose (and hope), the ongoing subversive practice of "queer critical care (of the straight self)" and could significantly contribute to the general discourse on the meaning and practice of queer(ing) heterosexuality within the context and concerns of sexual/social justice. But what do I mean by "care" within the notion of queer critical care? To answer this question, I conclude by drawing from (i.e., briefly outlining) Foucault's concept of "care of the self" as one possible critical framework for informing the theory and practice of queer critical care.

In his later work, and during the last years of his life, Foucault shifted from an interest in politics to a concern with ethics. In *Saint Foucault: Towards a Gay Hagiography*, David Halperin (1995) characterizes Foucault's intellectual shift as a movement "from [the study of] an analytics of power to an interest in the relation of the self to itself" (p. 68). In particular, Foucault inquired into ancient ethics which, according to Halperin (1995), "concerned itself less with the forbidden than with the voluntary" (p. 68). Foucault's inquiry led him to discover transformative practices or "technologies of the self" by which some members of the Greek upper classes—mostly elite males—carved out for themselves a moral and ethical life. Foucault referred to these practices and to the ethics they engendered as "an aesthetics (or stylistics) of existence" or the "arts of existence." Halperin (1995) describes what Foucault meant by this phrase as "an ethical practice that consisted in freely imposing on the form of one's life a distinctive shape and individual style, and thereby transforming oneself in accordance with one's own conception of beauty or value" (pp. 69–70). Specifically in his research on the ancient Stoics and other late antique philosophers, Foucault provides a specific example of these arts of existence in his writings on what he called "*la culture de soi*: 'the culture and cultivation of the self'" (Halperin, 1995, p. 70). He takes up the notion of "care of the self" in his essay "The Cultivation of the Self" in his publication *The Care of the Self: The History of Sexuality, Volume 3* (Foucault, 1988).

For Foucault, care of the self is not about self-attachment or self-fascination, nor is it a process of "self-discovery," that is, a search for one's "true self." As I mentioned earlier in this essay, Foucault adamantly rejected the notion of a naturally occurring self, and in his later work he maintained that position. In this way, then, Foucault's concept of care of the self is not, as Halperin (1995) highlights, "an ancient forerunner of New Age mysticism...[nor is it to be equated with] the modern, normalizing, pop-psychological ethic of 'self-realization'" (p. 74). In addition, "the self" in Foucault's care of the self is not an identity or a substance per se. In fact, according to Halperin (1995) the self here is a highly *impersonal self*—that is to say, a self who cares for itself "by becoming other than what one is" (p. 76). From this perspective, Foucault's meticulous historical investigations can be understood as attempts to demonstrate how we have come to believe in the "truth" of certain subjectivities in order that we might try to escape such imposed forms of subjectivity. As Mansfield (2000) states: "since there is no authentic or natural [heterosexual] self that we can simply recover and liberate, subjects should be geared towards a dynamic self-creation, an experimental expansion of the possibilities of subjectivity in open defiance of the modes of being that are being laid down for us constantly in every moment of our day-to-day lives" (p. 63). Taken in this context, it's not surprising Foucault would make the following comment regarding the underlying drive for much of his intellectual work: "'One writes...in order to become other than what one is'" (Halperin, 1995, p. 76). Thus, what care of the self *isn't*, coupled with its impersonal element, are important considerations when pedagogically taking up the practice of queer critical care as a counterpractice to heterosexual subjection. Indeed, a curriculum that aims to queer the straight (teacher) self by critically deconstructing heterosexual subjection as "an over-determined process of becoming straight" would want to be leery of suggesting that an "authentic straight self" might be possible to recuperate—that is, one that can be located outside of the processes of heterosexual subjection. Such a search would not only prove futile but also would impede the importance of cultivating an impersonal self as the ongoing practice, in this case, of struggling to become other than the straight subject of heterosexual subjection.

As a practice among the late antique philosophers, what then constituted care of the self as Foucault understood and described it, and what contemporary practices of self-fashioning did Foucault identity as resonating with the ancient cultivation of the self? In many ways, the ancient practice of care of the self can be compared with a kind of "training routine" characterized as Halperin (1995) notes, as,

> a strenuous activity, a practical exercise, a constant, demanding, laborious exertion. …Far from being a mere vehicle of aesthetic recreation or personal self-absorption, the ancient cultivation of the self consisted in a set of elaborate and rigorous practices designed to produce a heightened scrutiny of oneself, a constant monitoring of one's behaviour and dispositions, a holistic and therapeutic regimen of mind and body…. "Taking care of oneself [was] not a rest cure." (p. 70)

The intensification of the relationship of the self to itself also brought forth "'an intensification of social relations'" (Halperin, 1995, p. 70); in this way, the ancient practice of care of the self can be understood as a *social practice* as well, specifically in that: "It led one to seek help and guidance from others, and it was undertaken together with others in philosophical communities, aristocratic households, and other institutional settings" (Halperin, 1995, p. 70). This social aspect of care of the self suggests that, within the context of a critical analysis of heterosexual subjection by the straight self as a form of queer critical care, the straight self would want to seek out the voices and perspectives of the GLBTQ "Other." How this might play out in the social space of the classroom would be highly useful to theorize.

Foucault referred to all of this arduous and ongoing activity of self-cultivation as "'ascesis'…or ethical work" (Halperin, 1995, p. 76). In his essay "The Ethics of the Concern for Self as a Practice of Freedom," Foucault (1997) explained and defined *ascesis* as follows: "It is what one could call an ascetic practice, taking asceticism in a very general sense—in other words, not in the sense of a morality of renunciation, but as an exercise of the self on the self by which one attempts to develop and transform oneself, and to attain a certain mode of being" (p. 282). In terms of specific practices of transforming oneself as ethical work in contemporary times, Foucault identified homosexuality and philosophy as technologies of self-transformation "and therefore as modern versions of 'ascesis'" (Halperin, 1995, p. 77). I find that my own use of the word "theory" in this essay, and in particular as I've introduced it within the notion of "the pedagogical search for theory," to be very similar to how Foucault understands and deploys philosophy as a technology of self-transformation. Halperin (1995) states that for Foucault,

> "philosophy was a spiritual exercise, an exercise of oneself in which one submitted oneself to modifications and tests, underwent changes, in order to learn to think differently."...[Foucault asked famously] "What is philosophy today...if it does not consist *not* in legitimating what one already knows but in undertaking to know how and to what extent it might be possible to think differently?"...Foucault remark[ed] that the living substance of philosophy consists in a transformative experiment or test that one performs on oneself by playing games of truth: philosophy, in that sense, is still for Foucault "what it was in times past, namely, an ascesis, an exercise of the self...in the activity of thought." (p. 77)

As a technology of self-transformation, one used in the service of continually becoming other than the straight self one is under the terms of hegemonic heterosexuality, it's my hope that the pedagogical search for theory as a constitutive element of the practice of queer critical care provokes a sustained criticality, a disposition, as Foucault would say, of "permanent criticism" *as a form of care* among straight (teacher) subjects in facilitating understanding of the following queer argument: that "the normative regimes [heterosexuals] inhabit and embody are ideological fictions rather than natural inevitabilities, performatives rather than constatives" (Thomas, 2000, p. 13). And isn't it ironic that the straight self should need to care for itself in a culture and society drenched in heteronormativity? Now that's queer.

Works Cited

Balkin, J. M. (1997). The constitution of status. *Yale Law Journal*, 106(8), 2313–2374.

Beasley, C. (2005). *Gender & sexuality: Critical theories, critical thinkers*. London: SAGE Publications.

Becker, R. (2006). *Gay TV and straight America*. New Brunswick, NJ: Rutgers University Press.

Butler, J. (1993a). Critically queer. *GLQ*, 1, 17–32.

Butler, J. (1993b). *Bodies that matter: On the discursive limits of "sex."* New York: Routledge.

Butler, J. (1990). *Gender trouble: Feminism and the subversion of identity*. New York: Routledge.

Eribon, D. (2004). *Insult and the making of the gay self*. Durham: Duke University Press.

Everly, B. (Producer/Director). (2006). *Let's get Frank* [Documentary]. United States: First Run Features.

Foucault, M. (1997). The ethics of the concern for self as a practice of freedom. In Paul Rabinow (Ed.), *Michel Foucault: Ethics, subjectivity and truth* (pp. 281–302). New York: The New Press.

Foucault, M. (1988). *The care of the self: The history of sexuality, Volume 3*. [Trans. Robert Hurley]. New York: Vintage.

Foucault, M. (1982). The subject and power. In Hubert L. Dreyfus & Paul Rabinow (Eds.), *Michel Foucault: Beyond structuralism and hermeneutics* (pp. 208–226). Chicago: The University of Chicago Press.

Foucault, M. (1980). *Power/Knowledge*. [Ed. Colin Gordon]. New York: Pantheon Books.

Foucault, M. (1979). Truth and power: Interview with Alessandro Fontano and Pasquale Pasquino. In *Michel Foucault: Power, truth and strategy* (pp. 29–48). [Trans. Paul Patton & Meaghan Morris]. Sydney: Feral Publications.

Foucault, M. (1978). *The history of sexuality: An introduction (Vol. 1)*. New York: Random House.

Hall, D. E. (2003). *Queer theories*. New York: Palgrave Macmillan.

Halperin, D. (1995). *Saint Foucault: Towards a gay hagiography*. New York: Oxford University Press.

Jagose, A. (1996). *Queer theory*. New York: New York University Press.

Mansfield, N. (2000). *Subjectivity: Theories of the self from Freud to Haraway*. New York: New York University Press.

Mapa, A. (n.d.). Retrieved December 20, 2006, from http://www.logoonline.com/shows/dyn/wisecrack/series.jhtml

Rich, A. (2003). Compulsory heterosexuality and lesbian existence (1980). *Journal of Women's History*, 15(3), 11–48.

Salih, S. (2002). *Judith Butler*. New York: Routledge.

Schlichter, A. (2004). Queer at last?: Straight intellectuals and the desire for transgression. *GLQ*, 10(4), 543–564.

Thomas, C. (2000). Straight with a twist: Queer theory and the subject of heterosexuality. In C. Thomas (Ed.), *Straight with a twist: Queer theory and the subject of heterosexuality* (pp. 11–44). Urbana and Chicago: University of Illinois Press.

Warner, M. (1993). *Fear of a queer planet: Queer politics and social theory*. Minneapolis: University of Minnesota Press.

Watson, K. (2005). Queer theory. *Group Analysis*, 38(1), 67–81.

CONTRIBUTORS

Karen Anijar is an Associate Professor of Curriculum and Cultural Studies at Arizona State University. Her most recent book is *Culture and the Condom* (Peter Lang, 2005), co-edited with Thuy Dao-Jensen.

Yin-Kun Chang holds a Ph.D. in Curriculum and Instruction from the University of Wisconsin-Madison (2005) where he focused on queer theory, cultural studies, and critical pedagogy. Working with Professor Michael W. Apple, his dissertation is titled *No More Gods and Monsters: Remapping Queer Cultures in Educational and Cultural Fields*. He is currently an Assistant Research Fellow (2005–2006) at the Research Center of Curriculum and Instruction at Tamkang University (Taiwan). His research interests include: critical pedagogy, sociology of education, curriculum studies, cultural studies, and queer/gender studies.

Angelika Foerst is a doctoral student in curriculum studies at Arizona State University whose dissertation is on *Xena the Warrior Princess* as lesbian curriculum.

Valerie Harwood is a Senior Lecturer in the Faculty of Education, University of Wollongong, New South Wales, Australia. She has recently published a book in 2006, *Diagnosing 'Disorderly' Children*, which critically examines the growing phenomenon of the diagnosis of behavior disorders in children and young people. Valerie's research focuses on youth, and she is currently working on a research project titled "The New Outsiders," which investigates the effects of emerging cultures of behavior disorder on disadvantaged youth in marginalized communities.

Jane L. Lehr (Department of Education & Professional Studies, King's College, London) is a Post-Doctoral Research Associate at the Center for Informal Learning and Schools, a National Science Foundation Center for Teaching and

Learning, at King's College London, UC Santa Cruz, and the Exploratorium (ESI-0119787). She recieved her M.S. (2002) and Ph.D. (2006) in Science & Technology Studies at Virginia Tech. Her research analyzes the intersection of science education and nonscientist citizenship from a feminist and equity-oriented perspective. She is the 2003 recipient of an Outstanding Graduate Student Award at Virginia Tech in recognition of her commitment to social justice work as a teacher, researcher, and community organizer and teaches courses in Women's Studies, Science and Technology Studies, and the Social Foundations of Education. Address: Department of Education & Professional Studies, King's College, London, Franklin Wilkins Building, 150 Stamford Street, London SE1 9NH; telephone: +44 207 848 3780; fax: +44 207 848 3182; email: jane.lehr@kcl.ac.uk

Cris Mayo is an Associate Professor in the Department of Educational Policy Studies and in the Gender and Women's Studies Program at the University of Illinois at Urbana-Champaign. Her publications in the areas of gender and philosophy of education include *Disputing the Subject of Sex: Sexuality and Public School Controversies* (Rowman and Littlefield, 2004), as well as articles in *Educational Theory*, *Philosophy of Education*, and *Philosophical Studies in Education*.

Elizabeth J. Meyer is a Ph.D. candidate at McGill University investigating how teachers understand and respond to gendered harassment in secondary schools. She completed her M.A. at the University of Colorado, Boulder where her thesis title was "Equal Educational Opportunity and Sexual Minority Youth." She taught French and coached ice hockey and softball in New Hampshire and was selected for a Fulbright Teaching Exchange Grant to teach in France in 2001. She was also awarded a McGill Major Fellowship in 2005 and 2006.

Jane Mitchell is a Senior Lecturer in the Faculty of Education at Monash University. Her research interests focus on teacher education curriculum, policy, and practice.

John Petrovic is Associate Professor in the Social and Cultural Foundations of Education at The University of Alabama and teaches in the areas of philosophy of education, multicultural education, and language policy. His current research focuses on applying critical and poststructural lenses to education policy especially as concerns language minority students and nonheterosexual students. His recent publications include "Unstraightening the Ideal Girl: Lesbians, High School, and Spaces to Be," "Disrupting the Heteronormative Subjectivities of Christian Pre-Service Teachers: A Deweyan Prolegomenon," and "The Conservative Restoration and Neoliberal Defenses of Bilingual Education."

William F. Pinar teaches curriculum theory at the University of British Columbia, where he holds a Canada Research Chair and directs the Centre for the Study of the Internationalization of Curriculum Studies. He is the author, most recently, of *The Synoptic Text Today and Other Essays: Curriculum Development after the Reconceptualization* (Peter Lang, 2006).

Mary Louise Rasmussen is a Senior Lecturer in the Faculty of Education, Monash University, Australia. In 2004, she co-edited (with Rofes and Talburt) *Youth and Sexualities: Pleasure, Subversion and Insubordination* and in 2006 authored a monograph *Becoming Subjects: Sexualities and Secondary Schooling*. She is currently researching epistemological foundations of sex education curriculum in Australia, and the relationship between space, pedagogy and school architecture.

Nelson M. Rodriguez is Assistant Professor of Cultural Foundations of Education and Women's and Gender Studies at The College of New Jersey. He received his Ph.D. in Critical Theory and Cultural Studies in Education from The Pennsylvania State University. He is co-editor of *Dismantling White Privilege: Pedagogy, Politics, and Whiteness* (Peter Lang, 2000) and *White Reign: Deploying Whiteness in America*, winner of The Critics' Choice Award. He is currently working on a new book, titled: *Queer Masculinities: A Critical Reader in Education*.

Jerry Rosiek is an Associate Professor of Education at the University of Oregon, where he teaches qualitative research methods and the cultural foundations of education. He has a B.S. in Physics and a B.A. in Philosophy from Texas A&M University and a Ph.D. in Education from Stanford University. His articles have appeared in leading journals such as *Harvard Educational Review, Educa-*

tional Researcher, *The Journal of Teacher Education*, *Curriculum Theory* and *Educational Theory*. His current research focuses on the nature and content of teachers' practical knowledge, specifically the knowledge that enables teachers to teach across cultural differences and in unjust institutional circumstances.

David V. Ruffolo is a doctoral candidate in the Department of Theory and Policy Studies in Education with the Higher Education Group at the Ontario Institute for Studies in Education of the University of Toronto. His work radically theorizes bodies, subjectivities, and democracies. His dissertation reconsiders the conceptualization of bodies in poststructuralism through an exploration of *becoming postqueer*. He has recently received an award from the Canadian Society for the Studies of Higher Education for his work titled "Queering the 'I' in Academic Discourse" (2006).

Reta Ugena Whitlock, Assistant Professor of Adolescent Education at Kennesaw State University near Atlanta, Georgia, received her Ph.D. in Curriculum & Instruction from Louisiana State University in Baton Rouge. She has published several articles in professional journals and made presentations at professional conferences. Her research interests include curriculum studies of place and queer fundamentalism. Her first book, *This Corner of Canaan: Curriculum Studies of Place and the Reconstruction of the South*, has recently been published (Peter Lang, 2007).

INDEX

Index

OMPLICATED

A BOOK SERIES OF CURRICULUM STUDIES

This series employs research completed in various disciplines to construct textbooks that will enable public school teachers to reoccupy a vacated public domain—not simply as "consumers" of knowledge, but as active participants in a "complicated conversation" that they themselves will lead. In drawing promiscuously but critically from various academic disciplines and from popular culture, this series will attempt to create a conceptual montage for the teacher who understands that positionality as aspiring to reconstruct a "public" space. *Complicated Conversation* works to resuscitate the progressive project—an educational project in which self-realization and democratization are inevitably intertwined; its task as the new century begins is nothing less than the intellectual formation of a public sphere in education.

The series editor is:

Dr. William F. Pinar
Department of Curriculum Studies
2125 Main Mall
Faculty of Education
University of British Columbia
Vancouver, British Columbia V6T 1Z4
CANADA

To order other books in this series, please contact our Customer Service Department:

(800) 770-LANG (within the U.S.)
(212) 647-7706 (outside the U.S.)
(212) 647-7707 FAX

Or browse online by series:

www.peterlang.com